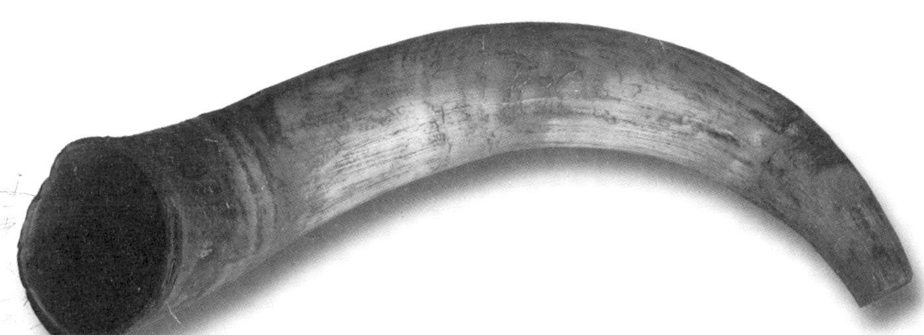

A LIFE OF CONQUEST

STUDIES IN JOSHUA

PAUL W. DOWNEY

Greenville, South Carolina

Library of Congress Cataloging-in-Publication Data

Downey, Paul W., 1957-
A life of conquest : studies in Joshua / Paul W. Downey.
p. cm.
Summary: "This is a devotional commentary on the book of Joshua"—Provided by publisher.
Includes bibliographical references.
ISBN 1-59166-619-8 (pbk. : alk. paper)
1. Bible. O.T. Joshua—Devotional literature. I. Title.
BS1295.54.D69 2006
222'.207—dc22
2005032293

Cover Photo Credits: Artville's Weathered Backgrounds (Jim Ward Morris), Medioimages Landscapes

A Life of Conquest: Studies in Joshua

Design by Holley VanDenBerg
Composition by Melissa Matos

Greenville, South Carolina 29614

Printed in the United States of America

ISBN 1-59166-619-8

15 14 13 12 11 10 9 8 7 6 5 4 3 2 1

To my wife, Sherry

Next to Christ,

my most beloved companion and friend

Without your faithful support and encouragement

this project would never have been completed

TABLE OF CONTENTS

Introduction

Like most folks who grew up attending Sunday school and church, I was introduced to Old Testament heroes at an early age. I heard stories about the crossing of Jordan and the collapse of the walls of Jericho that stirred my youthful heart with wonder. But my first intimate contact with this great book came shortly before my twenty-first birthday.

I had just started my final semester in Bible college, working toward a bachelor's degree in music education, when I was assigned the task of teaching the book of Joshua to an eighth-grade Bible class as part of my student teaching responsibilities. I was to use nothing but the Bible for my text. So I started reading. I had a good idea what the book contained but was a little surprised to realize that about half of Joshua deals with the details of the distribution of the land of Canaan among the tribes of Israel. One of the few things about which I was confident as I prepared to teach that class was that most eighth graders couldn't care less that "'Achzib' is modern ez-Zib, about nine miles north of Acco."[1] So I confined most of my energies and spent most of my time in the chapters that describe conquering the land rather than those that describe dividing the land.

To be perfectly honest, I don't find the minutiae of the geography of Palestine in the late-fifteenth/early-fourteenth century BC particularly compelling myself. In this book, I'll deal with a few of those facts I think are interesting or significant. But if you're looking for discussion of geographic details, I'm afraid you'll be disappointed with this volume. Information like "*Silchim*, called *Sharuchen* in chap. xix. 6 and *Shaaraim* in 1 Chron. iv. 31, may possibly have been preserved in Tell *Sheriah*, almost half-way between Gaza and Beersheba"[2] is readily available in books such as the ones I've cited, for those who are interested.

Seminary professors will understandably prefer more scholarly works than mine. But this book was never intended to be a graduate-school textbook. I want to provide the Christian public with a devotional commentary to enhance their understanding of Scripture, to encourage their faith, and to edify their walk with the Lord. I want it to contain enough information to be useful

[1] Donald H. Madvig, "Joshua," *The Expositor's Bible Commentary* (Grand Rapids: Zondervan, 1992), p. 345. Comment on Joshua 19:29.

[2] C. F. Keil and F. Delitzsch, *Joshua, Judges, Ruth* (Grand Rapids: Eerdmans Publishing Co., 1968 reprint), p. 163.

to the pastor and teacher while remaining accessible to any believer. I leave it to you to decide whether I've succeeded.

I can't say for sure how much I accomplished in the lives of my eighth-grade students years ago, but God did a work in my heart. By the end of the semester, I had developed a lifelong love for teaching the Word, particularly the Old Testament narratives. I had set out to teach music, which I did for several years. But the Lord eventually took me into the pastorate and through three seminary degree programs.

Through the years it has been my joy to occasionally return to Joshua as a teaching text. The stories are exciting, and the lessons are rich. Joshua is a leader worthy of admiration and emulation. But even though it bears his name, Joshua isn't really about *Joshua* as much as it's about God and His dealings with His people. *Its primary message is that for the Christian to enjoy the blessing of God in his life, he must be obedient to the instructions of God.*

In some ways, Joshua records a real-life application of the parallel truths of God's sovereignty and man's responsibility. There is repeated tension between God's absolute promise (i.e., "I have given"—Josh. 6:2) and His conditional command (i.e., "ye shall"—Josh. 6:3). God promises the believer many things, and those promises are guaranteed in Christ, on the basis of His finished work on the cross and His conquest of death in the Resurrection. But God expects the believer, the regenerated new creation in Christ, to obey. "Dependent diligence is God's plan for you to anticipate a warm welcome home."[3]

The eternal life that is ours in Christ does not depend on our earning it or keeping it—it is all a gift of God's grace. But the obedient believer can anticipate the reward of hearing his Savior say, "Well done, good and faithful servant" (Matt. 25:21, 23). Just as Israel had to depend on God and then walk obediently into the Jordan River, or depend on God and march repeatedly around the city of Jericho, believers today are to depend on Christ and diligently live for Him.

To the praise of the glory of Christ,

Paul W. Downey

---

[3] Sam Harbin, "Sanctification: God's Work or Mine?" a sermon delivered at the National Leadership Conference, Calvary Baptist Ministries, Lansdale, PA, February 27, 2003.

1
Getting Started

Who wouldn't want to be victorious? I've never heard the fans at a ball game chanting, "We're number TWO!" Everyone wants to be "number ONE!" But what does it take to be a winner? How does a person live victoriously?

As you study through the book of Joshua, you'll learn several lessons that are illustrated by a variety of characters and events. But all of these lessons reinforce a single theme: *spiritual victory comes through obedient faith*. That is, the believer who wants to defeat the enemies of his soul—the world, the flesh, and the Devil—must *believe* God's promises and *obey* God's instructions.

Before we actually begin the study of Joshua, I want to spend a little time examining the background of the book and its title character. Those readers who want to jump right in to see what Joshua has to say will be tempted to skip to chapter three of this book, but I wouldn't recommend it. Have you ever had to assemble a playground swing set that came in a box with printed instructions? I have. It wasn't pleasant. Sure, it's important to follow the directions, but even that isn't the first step to "victorious assembling." I've learned from experience that I save myself a lot of time and frustration if I start by sorting and identifying all the pieces. It can be tedious, but it's not nearly as stressful as getting to step fourteen to find that I need bolt "G" and discovering that I used it by mistake when I should have used bolt "D" in step six.

Try to think of these first two chapters as prep time in which we lay out the pieces in their proper order so that we can begin assembling the structure of Joshua without false starts or misunderstanding. Bypassing such background study in your haste to begin has at least two weaknesses. First, you may overlook significant features of Joshua's book that can be seen only when compared with other parts of Scripture or in the light of historical or language background information. Second, such haste may actually lead to false conclusions when you fail to consider important information only available elsewhere. Becoming familiar with the context and background of a book is the first step toward understanding the book itself.

What Is the Bible?

The Bible is actually a collection of sixty-six distinct books. Those books have much in common. Although they were written by men, all of the books of the Bible were authored by God Himself—communicated through the inspiration of the Holy Spirit Who guided the writers so that they accurately wrote the very words of God (2 Tim. 3:16; 2 Pet. 1:21). Since all sixty-six books[4] have a common source, they also have the same overriding theme: God's communicating to humanity His plan of redemption.

It is important to remember that the books of the Bible were originally written in three different languages. The primary language of the Old Testament was Hebrew, but much of the book of Daniel and other isolated passages were written in Aramaic (sometimes called Syriac or Chaldean). The New Testament was written in Greek, but there are Aramaic words and phrases in the New Testament too. Only students who are proficient in these ancient languages have the freedom to study the Scriptures directly or "unfiltered." Everyone else is restricted to reading from a translation. And since God intentionally scrambled human languages at Babel (Gen. 11), no translation is capable of transmitting perfectly every shade of meaning expressed by the original language.[5] That is why the diligent student of Scripture should consult more than one translation.

---

[4] For a detailed description of how and why the Canon of Scripture includes the sixty-six books of the Bible and no others, see "Canonization and Apocrypha," in *From the Mind of God to the Mind of Man: A Layman's Guide to How We Got Our Bible*, J. B. Williams, ed. (Greenville, SC: Ambassador-Emerald International, 1999), pp. 31–64.

[5] Bible translator Hantz Bernard has written an important essay on the theory, theology, and process of Bible translation called "The Autograph Though Dead Yet Speaketh," in *God's Word in Our Hands* (Greenville, SC: Ambassador-Emerald Int., 2003), pp. 279–333. While confident that the Bible can be accurately translated and retain its character as the Word of God, he says, "There cannot really be such thing as a word-for-word translation. It is linguistically impossible. Philo's idea that a translation can be 'identical' to the original text or the present day calls of some Christians for word-for-word translations would require that

Further, the individual books demonstrate a wide range of differences. They are written in a variety of literary forms—some are poetry, some are prose, some contain both. They vary in literary style—there are books of law giving regulations for civil and religious life, books of wisdom literature with practical instructions for living, books that are primarily prophetic with pronouncements of blessing or judgment from God, books that reveal God's work through historical events, books about the life and ministry of Jesus Christ, and letters that are both theological and practical written to individuals and to groups. The books were written over a period of more than fifteen hundred years, and in many ways each reflects the era in which it was written. The books were penned by over forty different authors, each with his own style, vocabulary, and cultural perspective. Every book addresses its own human circumstances and needs. Among other things, preliminary background studies should identify the biblical and historical context of the book, the author or authors of the book, the original readers of the book, and the occasion and purpose for its writing.

Context of the Book of Joshua

Joshua is the sixth book of the Old Testament, immediately following the five books of Moses. Deuteronomy, the last book of Moses, closes with an account of Moses' death and Joshua's promotion to leadership. Joshua opens with the words "Now after the death of Moses . . ." To understand what's coming, we need to know at least a little bit about what has gone before.

Joshua's Bible

When Joshua talks about the "word of the Lord" or the "book of the law" he means something specific. His references to Scripture don't include the prophecy of Isaiah, the instructions of Paul, or the Gospel of John. What does he mean? The Scripture that Joshua would have known begins with the book of Genesis. Genesis covers a period of over two thousand years—essentially, the first third of human history. It provides accounts of the creation of the heavens and earth, the fall of man into sin, God's judgment of mankind with the Flood, the establishment of a new order through Noah and his family, the establishment of the nations by scattering mankind from Babel, and God's calling Abraham and his offspring to be the people of God. Doctrinally, Genesis

---

the languages be de-mixed. If that could be done, there would then be only one language in existence and no need for, nor avenue for, translation" (p. 308).

emphasizes God's sovereign right to control creation and direct the affairs of men as He sees fit.

The book of Job is also likely to have been a part of Joshua's "Bible." Because it is written entirely in Hebrew poetry, Job's place in the Bible has traditionally been with the other poetic books.[6] It's impossible to say for sure who wrote Job, but conservative scholars agree that it was written at a very early date. The events recorded in Job occurred no later than the events in the last half of Genesis and probably happened before the call of Abraham.[7] The doctrinal theme of Job is that God is the sovereign ruler of the universe, including spirit beings, nature, and men.

Genesis is followed by Exodus, which serves as the historical sequel to the account of the life of Joseph found at the end of Genesis. Exodus is actually the first volume of the history of Israel's deliverance from Egypt. It covers events spanning a period of about two years, taking Israel from Egypt to Sinai, where the Law is given to Moses and the tabernacle is constructed. Exodus also includes much of the civil law along with some description of how it was given and how it was received. The doctrinal theme of Exodus is God's redemption of the people He chose to call to Himself in Genesis, emphasizing God's power and authority over history, nature, and humanity.

Leviticus, with Numbers 1–10, covers a period of less than two months. The book is named for the tribe of Levi since the bulk of its content deals with regulations governing Israel's worship rituals and the establishment of Levi's tribe as the priests of Israel, specifically through the family of Aaron. Doctrinally, Leviticus teaches that God's chosen people were redeemed to fellowship with God and worship Him, emphasizing the need for personal holiness.

---

[6] Psalms, Proverbs, Ecclesiastes, and Song of Solomon. Lamentations is the exception, following Jeremiah because he was its author. Other books contain poetry but are not predominantly poetic. It is important for the Bible student to remember that the books of the Bible are arranged by category, not chronology.

[7] There are several indications that Job lived in the period between the Flood and the life of Moses, and probably just a few generations following Babel. First, the Levitical priesthood must not have yet been established since Job acted as priest for his family. Second, Job's wealth was measured in terms consistent with the patriarchal period and the money used was like that of Jacob's day. Third, Job's longevity was similar to that of the patriarchs. Fourth, Job's death was described in terms similar to the descriptions of Abraham's and Isaac's. Fifth, in all the discussion of Job's suffering and the accusations of his friends, there is no mention of the Law. There are two additional, and somewhat more speculative, points to consider. In Job, God describes leviathan and behemoth, creatures with which Job was familiar, that almost certainly became extinct shortly after the Flood. Further, Job uses more references to ice, snow, and frost than the rest of Scripture combined, which may imply a much cooler climate in the Middle East than existed at the time of the patriarchs. If so, that might place Job's life close to the brief "ice age" that many creation scientists believe occurred immediately after the Flood.

The history recorded in Numbers, especially chapters 11–36, continues the narrative begun in Exodus. It spans the thirty-eight years between Israel's move from Sinai and their entrance into Canaan. The Hebrew title for the book is *bemidhbar*, meaning "in the wilderness," which is really a better description of the book's contents than given by the more familiar title. It can be thought of as "The Exodus, Volume 2," but was called "Numbers" in the Septuagint[8] because it begins with the census of Israel taken at Sinai (chap. 1), includes a census of the Levites eligible for service (chap. 4), and provides statistics from a third census taken just before Israel entered Canaan (chap. 26). The central theological message of Numbers is God's continued longsuffering with His chosen people in spite of their repeated failure to obey.

The books of Moses conclude with Deuteronomy, which means "second law." The book gets its title from the Septuagint's mistranslation of Deuteronomy 17:18, where the phrase "a copy of the law" was rendered "this second law." This book provides the historical bridge between Israel's wandering in the wilderness of Sinai and their entrance into the land God had promised to give them. It covers a brief time, and it is written in the form of a sermon or series of sermons. They comprise Moses' parting message to the people of God, reminding them of the Law God had given them and the covenant He had made with them. He repeats the promised blessings if Israel will obey and the promised judgment that will come if they forsake their God. Moses makes a passionate appeal to Israel to recognize God's grace in His dealings with them and to respond in love and loyalty. The doctrinal theme of Deuteronomy is that God will graciously provide for His people, but He expects wholehearted obedience. This was the message Joshua heard almost immediately before the opening of the book that bears his name.

Joshua's Book

Joshua continues the record of how God revealed Himself to mankind through history. It provides our only account of Israel's carrying out Moses' charge to go in and possess the Promised Land. Moses tells us how God set Israel free from slavery, but Joshua tells us how Israel changed from being a group of nomadic tribes to becoming established as a nation in the land God had promised their forefathers. *Doctrinally, Joshua provides a picture of sanctification—victory and growth in the Christian life by trusting God and obeying His Word.* In Joshua, entering Canaan meant *accepting and fulfilling the responsibilities of living as God's people.* God had given them the land, but they

---

[8] The Septuagint is the Greek translation of the Hebrew Scriptures that was produced during the second century BC. It was the Old Testament commonly in use in Jesus' day. At least 80 percent of the New Testament quotations from the Old Testament are from the Septuagint rather than the traditional Hebrew.

must possess the territory by conquering the enemies of God that were living there at the time.

Have you ever sung "I Am Bound for the Promised Land"?

> On Jordan's stormy banks I stand,
> And cast a wishful eye
> To Canaan's fair and happy land,
> Where my possessions lie.
>
> All o'er those wide extended plains
> Shines one eternal day;
> There God the Son forever reigns,
> And scatters night away.
>
> When shall I reach that happy place,
> And be forever blest?
> When shall I see my Father's face,
> And in His bosom rest?
>
> I am bound for the Promised Land,
> I am bound for the Promised Land;
> O, who will come and go with me?
> I am bound for the Promised Land.
>
> —Samuel Stennett

While this song expresses the believer's expectation of blessing in heaven, it has missed the point of the Promised Land. Israel's crossing Jordan into the land of promise is *not* a picture of a believer's death and entrance into heaven, despite the fact that this and many other traditional hymns say otherwise. Life in Canaan involved several challenges that represent obstacles believers face in their personal lives today. But when the believer dies and enters heaven's glories, there are no walled cities to conquer or giants to slay.

Entering the Promised Land illustrates in some ways an unbeliever's salvation or a disobedient believer's restoration and revival, while *conquering* the Promised Land pictures the believer's growth in Christ. Of course, the best Old Testament picture of salvation is found in the Passover. Those who believed God were spared because an innocent lamb was slaughtered and its blood was applied to the lintel and doorposts of the house in which they resided. Remember that the events of the Exodus illustrate redemption from slavery to freedom accomplished through a blood sacrifice.

To get the whole picture of what God saved us *from*—bondage to sin—through what He saves us *to*—freedom to live in obedience—we have to compress events from the Passover through the crossing of Jordan. Otherwise we might get the idea that salvation is a process—that a person comes to initial faith and is redeemed but must later come to another crisis point or make another decision or experience a second work of grace that will lead to submission to the Lord and obedience to His Word. While wandering in the wilderness in fear and disobedience may characterize the lives of many believers, it is not normative Christian living.

During the period of wilderness wandering, Joshua and Caleb illustrate what believers are *supposed to be*. The rest of their generation provides an illustration of what many believers *are*: fearful, wavering, disobedient, presumptuous, provocative, and eventually dead. Paul calls that kind of Christian "carnal" (1 Cor. 3:1–4) and indicates that a believer's persistent disobedience can lead to death (1 Cor. 11:28–32). Unbelieving and/or disobedient Israelites died in the wilderness. The generation that believed and obeyed the promise of God would mark the end of wandering in sinful rebellion by entering and taking the land of promise. The theme of Joshua to keep in view is that *they were unable to enter the land and conquer the people on their own, but they were responsible to enter and fight at God's command.*

Overview of the Book of Joshua

Joshua's Purpose

Joshua as an author has been described as a "theocratic historian." That's a technical way of saying that in his writing of history Joshua's main concern was to show how God was working through historical events. A *theocracy* is a government in which the leaders answer directly to God. There has been only one such government in history: ancient Israel under Moses, Joshua, the judges, David, and Solomon. I've omitted Saul intentionally because he acted more as a monarchial despot—a king who answered to no one but himself—than as a theocratic king.

Joshua doesn't really provide an autobiography of a leader. He was recording those events that had special spiritual significance for his generation and for generations to follow. Recognizing Joshua's purpose in writing helps explain why certain details were included and others were left out. Great military campaigns lasting years are summarized in a few verses while isolated events may take a chapter or more to describe. Joshua wasn't keeping a journal of his personal exploits; he was telling the story of God's work in and through His people.

Joshua's Theme

The key to Joshua is found in the opening verses, Joshua 1:1–9, which contain God's instructions to Joshua. As far as Joshua knows at the outset, this is all God is going to tell him. These verses also include God's promise of blessing if Joshua obeys. The rest of the book tells how Joshua obeyed God and how God kept His promises. The first twelve chapters describe the conquest of Canaan, which took about seven years (Josh. 14:10; cf. Deut. 2:14). Chapters 13–21 describe the distribution of the land, including geographic markers that set the boundaries of the portions given to each group. Chapter 22 recounts the return of the tribes of Reuben and Gad and half the tribe of Manasseh to the east side of the Jordan to receive the inheritance Moses had promised them. After a gap of several years during which Israel actually settled the land given to each tribe, the book closes with Joshua's final instructions in chapters 23 and 24.

As I said at the start of this chapter, Joshua has a single recurring theme. Joshua repeatedly insists that Israel's conquest of the land of Canaan wasn't due to Israel's strength or courage. They were victorious because God gave them the land and fought for them. But taking possession of the land also required their obedience.

The groundwork for this message was laid with the two censuses recorded in Numbers. When Israel first arrived at the edge of Canaan, they decided that they weren't strong enough to take the land from such powerful enemies. At that time the total number of fighting men in Israel was 603,550 (Num. 1:45–46). A generation later, when God again brought Israel to the edge of Canaan, their army numbered only 601,730 (Num. 26:51–53). They weren't any stronger than they had been forty years earlier. Besides that, when Israel first approached Canaan, God brought them in from the south. From that direction, they would have had easy and direct access to the land. When the children of that fearful generation returned nearly forty years later, God brought them in from the east. From that direction, they were faced with the enormous obstacle of the flooded Jordan River.[9] To make matters worse, Israel was now facing an enemy that had forty years advance notice of their coming. The cities would be more heavily fortified and the armies better equipped

[9] The fact that Israel could have entered Canaan without crossing the Jordan had they done so when they first came to its borders argues for the crossing of Jordan to be more a picture of revival than of redemption. However, most of Israel refused to enter Canaan at that time, tried to do it after the fact and were defeated, and then died in the wilderness leaving a new generation to enter the land later. This, besides several spiritually significant aspects of the crossing that will be discussed as we go, supports the idea of seeing the crossing of Jordan as a picture of salvation. In much the way that our salvation today is on the basis of the sacrifice of Christ two thousand years in the past, the new generation of Israel could enter Canaan only because of the nation's redemption from Egypt forty years earlier. Each individual would have to believe God's promise.

than would have been the case had they entered the land when they first got there under Moses. By the time Joshua and the nation under his command finally entered Canaan, both strategic and psychological advantage had been sacrificed by the former generation's faithlessness. It was abundantly clear that victory would be God's alone.

Defense of the Book of Joshua

Some commentators express negative feelings about the events recorded in Joshua. Others seem to speak with some embarrassment as the events are described. Donald H. Madvig says, "The single greatest problem in the Book of Joshua is the extermination of the Canaanites."[10] This confusion comes from a casual reading of the book or a study of it without considering its historical and biblical contexts. Israel's behavior is sometimes compared with the barbarism of the Mongols under Genghis Khan or the Huns under Attila. It is said that Israel swept into Canaan, brutalized the peaceful Canaanites, and stole their land. One religious leader has gone so far as to describe "the God of the Old Testament" as a "dirty bully."

Granted, the absolute slaughter of the Canaanites commanded by God and carried out by Israel was ruthless. But was it cruel and barbaric, as it is sometimes described? There are three important truths that you will have to keep in mind, or you too may begin to criticize God's instructions.

First, *God's judgment is just*. The Canaanites were an accursed people (Gen. 9:25). The judgment being meted out in Joshua was pronounced centuries earlier. The Canaanites were also a wicked people. In Leviticus 18 God warns Israel that they must not commit several specific sins, including incest, homosexuality, bestiality, and human sacrifice. He concludes the list by saying, "For all these abominations have the men of the land done, which were before you, and the land is defiled" (Lev. 18:27). Under Joshua, God was using Israel as a rod of justice in the same way that He later used Assyria against Israel when Israel persisted in idolatry and shame. By using Israel to destroy the Canaanites, rather than using disease or natural disaster, God made it impossible for Israel to later rationalize God's help by putting it down to natural causes. God also drove home to Israel's consciousness just how much He detests sin, particularly idolatry. As you will see in your study of the book, such judgment was executed against some of Israel's people as well—when Achan sinned, Israel

[10] Madvig, p. 246.

destroyed him and his whole household (Josh. 7:24–26). The ruthlessness was not motivated *ethnically* but *ethically*. They were not destroying Canaanites because they were Canaanites. They were destroying the enemies of God.

Second, *God's patience is great*. God had promised the land to Abraham and then repeated and confirmed the promise to Abraham's heirs, Isaac and Jacob (Gen. 15, 26, 28). God had provided witnesses in the land for at least three generations of Abraham's family, and Melchizedek's presence is noted during Abraham's time in Canaan. With the destruction of Sodom and Gomorrah, God provided a graphic warning to the people of the land, revealing how He would deal with wickedness. As we've seen from Leviticus, the Canaanites of Joshua's day were at least as debased as the inhabitants of those cities had been. During Jacob's day, God sent further notice of His displeasure by afflicting the land with such a severe famine that Jacob and his family had to leave the area to survive. God still granted four more centuries of grace while Israel multiplied in Egypt and the Canaanites continued their descent into godlessness. Even when God brought His people out of Egypt, He permitted forty-years notice to a rising generation of Canaanites who were well aware of the coming judgment. All but the family of Rahab of Jericho and the inhabitants of Gibeon responded to these warnings with fierce opposition.

Finally, *God's authority is absolute*. God has the right to judge sin wherever and whenever He chooses. In the events recorded by Joshua we see God exercising His sovereign right to rule as King over all the earth. We also see God demonstrating His righteousness. The Canaanites had forfeited their land by their sin. Israel would keep it only by their obedience (Josh. 1:8; cf. Lev. 18:28). Israel will always be God's chosen people, and God will keep all His promises to that nation. God gave them the land of Canaan forever, but any given generation could temporarily forfeit their right of occupation by their disobedience, particularly idolatry.

Spiritual Significance of the Book of Joshua

There are many spiritual truths to be learned from this book. Specific lessons will be seen and developed as you study the text of the book itself. There are two general emphases that you'll see illustrated and reinforced. Joshua makes it clear that *God hates sin, even in the life of the believer*. Much of modern "evangelism" tries to get people to simply make a verbal profession of faith in response to a message that "God loves you." Such a message often ignores or even denies the need for repentance and rejection of sin.

> The extermination of the Canaanites is but one of the many evidences in the Bible, as well as in real life, that evil is real and that the Devil exists. Evil does not flee at the snap of one's fingers. The struggle with sin and the Devil took the Son of God to the cross. There was no easy victory even for him. Only by his suffering and death has he overcome evil once and for all. Those who will not be separated from their sin by repentance will be destroyed with their sin, as Jesus said, "If you do not believe that I am the one I claim to be, you will indeed die in your sins" (John 8:24). God's severity in his treatment of sin and of sinners is but the obverse side of his grace and love. Sin and evil destroy the people he loves and prevent the full establishment of his glorious kingdom.[11]

Modern evangelists claim that "coming to Christ" will solve all of a person's problems. They minimize or gloss over the battle to be fought and the race to be run in the Christian life.

Joshua also demonstrates that *defeat in the Christian life doesn't have to be the norm*. There's nothing in Scripture indicating that the genuine believer should expect frequent and inevitable defeat. Yes, the sin nature is still present. No, the believer isn't capable of sinless perfection while still living in his natural flesh. Even the best of us may be wounded or may stumble in the heat of the conflict, but we don't have to be *overcome*. Joshua shows us how to successfully overcome sin and encourages us to enter present victory in the power of Christ.

---

[11] Madvig, p. 247.

2
Who Was Joshua?

In the United States most people who hold government offices have been elected to their positions by the voting public. Exactly how some of these characters get elected is anybody's guess. When an officeholder proves to be spectacularly incompetent or corrupt, have you ever noticed how hard it is to find anybody who admits to having voted for him or her?

As important as it is, the process of narrowing the field of candidates before the election has problems. The procedure starts months (*many* months) in advance as different individuals announce their intention to run for office. In the weeks that follow these announcements we're inundated by an avalanche of information about the candidates. We hear what they have to say about themselves—usually presenting themselves as having sterling character and impressive records. We also hear what they have to say about their opponents—invariably presenting a less complimentary picture. Then we hear and read media analysts' opinions about all these descriptions—and media opinions vary according to the ideology of the individual, network, or publication.

You and I, as conscientious voters, are faced with the daunting task of sifting all of this information for the truth. We're confronted by a field of candidates who all claim to be either the best qualified, the most experienced, or the most trustworthy individual for the office. Many of these candidates are people we've never heard of and about whom we know nothing. The first thing we have to do is learn enough about each one to determine if there is any evidence to support their claims. Then we have to weigh the evidence to do our best to make an informed decision. That's a lot of work. It's the price we pay for living in a democratic republic.

Ancient Israel didn't choose their leaders this way. They were living in a *the*-ocracy (government by God), not a *dem*ocracy (government by the people). When Moses died and Israel needed a new leader, they didn't have candidates, campaigns, primary elections, or hanging chads. Joshua didn't announce his candidacy and make lots of empty promises to woo voters. He wasn't subjected to media investigation of his qualifications. God simply told Israel that Joshua would be their next leader.

But Joshua's rise to prominence in Israel didn't happen overnight. He didn't simply burst onto the scene in Joshua 1 the way Elijah does in 1 Kings 17. By the time Joshua was appointed to lead Israel, he'd been an important figure in Israel's history for forty years—at least since Israel left Egypt. The books of Moses provide occasional glimpses into Joshua's life, revealing elements of his character and experience before he shows up as Israel's new leader.

Joshua's First Forty Years

The Bible doesn't tell us very much about Joshua's first forty years, and what it does say is indirect. When Joshua is introduced shortly after Israel leaves Egypt, he is already forty years old. But there is at least one thing we know about any Israelite who was forty years old when he left Egypt: he had spent his first forty years as a slave.

Exodus says that the treatment of the Hebrew slaves was especially harsh in the years leading up to God's delivering them from Egypt, so it is safe to assume that Joshua's first forty years were less than pleasant. He had to work hard in a harsh environment. Forty years before he was born, Pharaoh had implemented a policy of infanticide, ordering the murder of all Hebrew baby boys. Exodus 2 tells the story of how God providentially saved Moses from that decree. That policy was probably temporary, or there wouldn't have been any Israelites for Moses to lead eighty years later. But given Pharaoh's fear of the numerical growth of the Hebrew people, Joshua's very existence would have been considered a threat to Egyptian stability. Joshua's birth occurred about the time Moses killed the Egyptian taskmaster for beating an Israelite slave (Exod. 2:11–15). To avoid prosecution, Moses left Egypt and spent forty years in "the backside of the desert" (Exod. 3:1) tending sheep.

We know that Joshua was born and grew to manhood in a condition of servitude and political suppression. In such a setting, he learned obedience and submission to a hard master. In the years to come he would find obeying and serving God much more gratifying and rewarding than serving his Egyptian masters had been.

As for Joshua's family background, Numbers 13:8 says that his father's name was Nun, and he was from the tribe of Ephraim. That makes Joshua a direct descendant of Joseph, who was Ephraim's father. Such a heritage probably gave Joshua some status among his people, since Ephraim was the privileged son (Gen. 48:14) of Joseph, and Joseph's years as grand vizier (sort of a prime minister) of Egypt made him the only member of Jacob's clan to have risen to international prominence before Moses became the foster son of the princess.

First Chronicles 7:27 adds another bit of information that is important. Joshua wasn't just the son of Nun—he was the *firstborn* son of Nun. Ancient tradition practiced something called *primogeniture*—the right of inheritance passing to the firstborn son. In God's dealings with men in the Old Testament that tradition is often overruled in favor of a younger son.[12] The significance of Joshua's being firstborn wasn't in his position as heir but in the fact that the *Passover* would have special meaning for Joshua. The tenth plague, the one that finally convinced Pharaoh to let Israel go, was *the death of the firstborn*. Put yourself in his place. On the night that God killed all the firstborn of Egypt, Joshua stood in his father's home as the firstborn son who would have died had it not been for the blood placed over the door as proof of their faith in God's deliverance (Exod. 12:1–30). Moses, as the second son of Amram, would not have felt the deliverance of God as keenly as Joshua would have. Joshua would never forget the night the firstborn of Egypt fell and he was spared. The lesson of faith and obedience would leave an indelible mark on his character.

---

[12] God did not work through the firstborn son of Adam (Cain), but through Abel and later Seth. The Hebrews descended from Shem, the second son of Noah. Abraham was at least second, and probably third, of the sons of Terah. Isaac was Abraham's second son, although the first by Sarah. Jacob was the younger twin of Esau, making him second-born to Isaac. Judah, from whom Christ would come, was fourth-born to Jacob. David was the seventh son of Jesse. In fact, it is impossible to prove from the genealogies in Scripture that even one member of the line of Christ from Adam until David was a "firstborn son." Other examples include Ephraim's being favored over his elder brother, Manasseh, and Moses' selection for leadership over his older brother Aaron (although Aaron was given primacy in worship).

Joshua's Next Forty Years

Joshua's First Appearance

Joshua spent the next forty years of his life as understudy to Moses. That was his job when he is first mentioned in the Bible in Exodus 17:8–14.

> Then came Amalek, and fought with Israel in Rephidim. And Moses said unto **Joshua**, Choose us out men, and go out, fight with Amalek: to morrow I will stand on the top of the hill with the rod of God in mine hand. So **Joshua** did as Moses had said to him, and fought with Amalek: and Moses, Aaron, and Hur went up to the top of the hill. And it came to pass, when Moses held up his hand, that Israel prevailed: and when he let down his hand, Amalek prevailed. But Moses' hands were heavy; and they took a stone, and put it under him, and he sat thereon; and Aaron and Hur stayed up his hands, the one on the one side, and the other on the other side; and his hands were steady until the going down of the sun. And **Joshua** discomfited Amalek and his people with the edge of the sword. And the Lord said unto Moses, Write this for a memorial in a book, and rehearse it in the ears of **Joshua**: for I will utterly put out the remembrance of Amalek from under heaven.

Joshua is introduced as a warrior. Moses obviously considered him capable of leadership. He entrusted Joshua even with the selection of the men who would fight the enemy. This battle was fought on two fronts. The physical enemy was confronted in the valley by the army under Joshua's command. But Moses, with the help of Aaron and Hur, interceded with God from the mountain. As long as Moses' hands were lifted toward heaven, indicating Israel's submission to and dependence upon God, the army in the valley prevailed. When his hands slumped toward the earth, the enemy prevailed.

Ultimately, Israel won this battle, defeating the Amalekites. Joshua and all Israel clearly understood that the victory was accomplished by God, not the strength of the army. Joshua's military action in the valley was *necessary*, but it was not *sufficient* in itself to defeat the enemy. It is significant that God chose to record this event as our first glimpse of Joshua—*he is introduced as an obedient servant of God who knew firsthand the importance of relying on God for victory*. This event is a vivid example of the kind of warfare Joshua would be involved in for the rest of his life. It also illustrates the spiritual warfare in which every believer is engaged.

The spiritual lesson for Joshua, as well as for you today, is that *victory is always possible but always depends on both faith in God and obedience to His commands.* Like Moses on the mountain, Christ's intercession with the Father on your behalf guarantees victory (Heb. 7:25). Like Joshua in the valley, your victory over the forces that oppose you will also depend on faithful obedience (Rom. 6:16–18). In your study of Joshua, you will see a repeated emphasis on the fact that God accomplishes His will *according to* His sovereign power and that He does so *through the means of* His obedient people. Exactly how God's sovereignty works with man's responsibility is difficult to understand or explain, but we can't help recognizing that both are necessary.

I think it is also important that at the end of the battle God commanded Moses to record the event and "rehearse it in the ears of Joshua." From the moment Joshua appears in Scripture, it is evident that he will be important to the future of Israel. Further, the key to Joshua's future success will be for him to remember what was written and to follow instructions. Forty years later, God's charge in the opening verses of Joshua will remind him of this event:

> This book of the law shall not depart out of thy mouth; but thou shalt meditate therein day and night, that thou mayest observe to do according to all that is written therein: for then thou shalt make thy way prosperous, and then thou shalt have good success. Have not I commanded thee? Be strong and of a good courage; be not afraid, neither be thou dismayed: for the Lord thy God is with thee whithersoever thou goest (Josh. 1:8–9).

Joshua's Second Appearance

The second time Joshua is mentioned is in Exodus 24:13.

> And Moses rose up, and his minister **Joshua**: and Moses went up into the mount of God.

The context of this passage actually continues through nearly ten full chapters, ending in Exodus 33:11. In this section of Exodus you can read about the time Moses spent on Mount Sinai as God gave him the stone tablets and instructions for building and worshiping in the tabernacle. Joshua is shown to be Moses' faithful assistant, who accompanied him up the mountain. Joshua sat there for forty days, in the middle of such violent thunder and lightning that the Israelites at the base of the mountain were terrified, while Moses communed with God. The text indicates that Moses fasted during his time with God without saying the same about Joshua, so we don't know for sure if Joshua also fasted. We do know that Joshua went with Moses to a place where Aaron never went.

Aaron, who would become high priest of Israel, stayed at the base of the mountain. When Moses and Joshua came down from Mount Sinai, they found the camp of Israel involved in idolatry, worshiping a golden calf that

Aaron had made. Maybe because Joshua was forty years younger than Moses, it was Joshua who first commented on the noise of idolatrous revelry in the camp below (Exod. 32:17). Joshua was with Moses when Moses broke the stone tablets engraved by the hand of God. Joshua stood by him when he judged Israel by overseeing the execution of three thousand of the rebels. Evidently, Joshua went with Moses when he returned to the tent of meeting to beg God to spare Israel (Exod. 32:31–35). When Moses left the tent of meeting at God's command, "his servant Joshua, the son of Nun, . . . departed not out of the tabernacle" (Exod. 33:11)—Joshua stayed behind and kept praying. While the Levites came to Moses' aid (Exod. 32:26–29), representing a turning point in the history of that tribe, *Joshua seems to have been the only man of all Israel who could and would pray with Moses at this time of national crisis.*

Joshua's Third Appearance

Joshua next appears in Numbers 11:24–29.

> And Moses went out, and told the people the words of the Lord, and gathered the seventy men of the elders of the people, and set them round about the tabernacle. And the Lord came down in a cloud, and spake unto him, and took of the spirit that was upon him, and gave it unto the seventy elders: and it came to pass, that, when the spirit rested upon them, they prophesied, and did not cease. But there remained two of the men in the camp, the name of the one was Eldad, and the name of the other Medad: and the spirit rested upon them; and they were of them that were written, but went not out unto the tabernacle: and they prophesied in the camp. And there ran a young man, and told Moses, and said, Eldad and Medad do prophesy in the camp. And **Joshua** the son of Nun, the servant of Moses, one of his young men, answered and said, My lord Moses, forbid them. And Moses said unto him, Enviest thou for my sake? would God that all the Lord's people were prophets, and that the Lord would put his spirit upon them!

Moses had called for a group of leaders identified as the seventy elders of Israel to assemble at the tabernacle to receive a blessing from God. Two of them, Eldad and Medad, had disobeyed Moses' command and stayed at their own tents. When God's blessing was bestowed on the assembled elders, they began "to prophesy." But so did Eldad and Medad. When a messenger told Moses that those two were also prophesying, Joshua immediately suggested that Moses should order them to stop. Joshua believed that they were disqualified from service as prophets because they had disregarded Moses' instructions. His zeal for defending Moses was admirable, but it was misdirected. Moses rebuffed Joshua gently, reminding him that God can do whatever He wants—Moses' reputation or honor wasn't the issue. In this event *Joshua demonstrated loyalty but also learned humility*. This would be another important lesson for him in his rise to national prominence.

Joshua's Fourth Appearance

Not much later, Joshua shows up for the fourth time when he is named as the representative of the tribe of Ephraim who would be going into Canaan as a spy.

> Of the tribe of Ephraim, **Oshea** the son of Nun. And Moses called **Oshea** the son of Nun **Jehoshua**. (Num. 13:8, 16*b*)

The variation in spelling and the indication of a name change is a little confusing. Apparently, the name given to Joshua by his parents was actually Oshea, which means "salvation."[13] But here we are told that Moses modified his name, changing it to "Jehoshua"—abbreviated to "Yeshua" ("Joshua")—meaning "Jehovah [Yahweh] is salvation," or "by whom the Lord will save." Name changes are not unusual in the Bible, particularly in connection with a significant event in the life of the individual. We've already seen evidence that Joshua is being groomed for leadership, but the significance of his name change in this context is the clearest indication yet that Joshua will be the leader of all Israel when Moses is gone.

This event is probably the best known of all Joshua's exploits prior to his taking responsibility for the whole nation. Israel had been gone from Egypt for about two years, most of that time spent camped at the base of Mount Sinai learning the Law and constructing the tabernacle. Now God has brought them to the southern edge of the Promised Land, and Moses is preparing the people to enter the land. But before they go in, God tells Moses to send men into the region "that they may search the land of Canaan, which I give unto the children of Israel" (Num. 13:2). The responsibility to spy out the land fell to the leaders of each of the twelve tribes. Numbers 13:4–15 gives the names of all twelve spies, but because of the outcome of the story, most of us remember only two of the names: Caleb, from the tribe of Judah, and Joshua, from the tribe of Ephraim.

The task assigned to the twelve men is spelled out in Numbers 13:17–20.

> And Moses sent them to spy out the land of Canaan, and said unto them, Get you up this way southward, and go up into the mountain: and see the land,

[13] This is an example of a characteristic of the Bible text that occurs frequently. People and places are often called by the name that would be familiar to the writer's audience from the beginning of a narrative, even though that name may not have been given until later in the narrative. For instance, when Abram first moved through the land God would promise to give him, he camped at a place "on the east of Bethel" (Gen. 12:8), which is the first time the place called Bethel is mentioned. It was not until Jacob camped at this place and had his dream of a ladder from earth to heaven that Jacob named the place "Bethel," or "the house of God." Prior to that time the place had been known as Luz (Gen. 28:19). About 150 years had passed in the narrative between the time that Bethel was first mentioned and the time the place was actually named "Bethel."

> what it is; and the people that dwelleth therein, whether they be strong or weak, few or many; and what the land is that they dwell in, whether it be good or bad; and what cities they be that they dwell in, whether in tents, or in strong holds; and what the land is, whether it be fat or lean, whether there be wood therein, or not. And be ye of good courage, and bring of the fruit of the land.

The men were told to scatter throughout Canaan, gathering information on the lay of the land, the strength and number of the people, the nature of their fortifications and defenses, and the quality of the land's produce. They finished this dangerous assignment over the course of the next forty days. Then they brought their report to Moses and the people of Israel. This story is sometimes told as if ten of the spies lied about their findings and only Joshua and Caleb told the truth. That's not what happened. The twelve spies brought one report—all twelve told the same story. They said the land truly "floweth with milk and honey," but "the people be strong" and "the cities are walled, and very great" (Num. 13:26–29).

Apparently there was an audible reaction from the assembled people of Israel when they heard the report because Caleb immediately had to quiet the crowd before speaking (Num. 13:30). After the unified message of the twelve spies had been announced, Caleb offered his personal commentary: "Let us go up at once and possess it; for we are well able to overcome it" (13:30). It's here that the first disagreement among the spies is seen. The point of contention was not what they had seen in the land, but how they *interpreted* what they had seen. They didn't disagree about what Canaan was like; they disagreed about what to do about it.

Caleb's recommendation that they proceed into the land to possess it was met with instant opposition. Ten of the spies began to complain that the enemy was strong and that the land was demanding. Both objections were true. No one disputed the size or strength of the enemy. Nor did anyone dispute that settling into an agrarian lifestyle, providing for themselves by cultivating crops and tending animals, would be more demanding than gathering manna every morning.

Why, then, is this report characterized as "evil"? The report was "evil" in that it focused on the difficulties rather than on the promise of God. Ten spies looked at the enemy and the land and concluded, "We can't do it; we'll have to work too hard." Only Caleb and Joshua (Num. 14:6–9) opposed this view. They didn't contradict any of the facts that had been presented. The difference was in their focus. Rather than emphasizing the hardness of the land and the strength of the enemy, they saw the goodness of the land and the strength of God.

I can't help but notice the similarities between what happened among the Israelites on the edge of the Promised Land and what happens in many church business meetings. Often one or more church members will find some reason to object to any new strategy or plan—we can't afford it; we don't need it; we've never done it that way before; it will be too much work. Every church seems to have its own handful of "sanctified obstructionists" who act as if it is their responsibility to make sure the church never ventures beyond a traditional comfort zone that they get to define. That's not to say that every harebrained scheme leadership proposes must be rubber-stamped by a gullible or intimidated congregation. Church leaders are capable of recommending actions that are far from being biblical and God-honoring. But when a local church has prayed and planned and formulated a strategy for the future of their ministry based on the application and implementation of the Word of God, standing in the way can be a dangerous posture.

The same is true on an individual level. Have you ever hesitated to step out and take possession of the territory God has given you? Nobody likes to face opposition, and we've all made excuses for failing to invest the energy necessary to succeed. But spiritual growth takes purposeful effort. Spiritual growth demands change. Change can be uncomfortable and may seem dangerous. Change takes hard work. But *God has ordered you to grow in Christ and to conquer sin in your life.* Failing to grow because it's too hard or too frightening is inexcusable. You have to take your eyes off the problems you face and focus on the promises of God. Instead of flinching from the obstacles, you must cling to the Savior.

The assembly of Israel had heard the report of the spies and was faced with conflicting recommendations. The majority opinion urged retreat while the minority opinion argued for confidence. Joshua and Caleb were the only ones who offered encouragement to proceed to do what God had told them to do.

> And Joshua the son of Nun, and Caleb the son of Jephunneh, which were of them that searched the land, rent their clothes: and they spake unto all the company of the children of Israel, saying, The land, which we passed through to search it, is an exceeding good land. If the Lord delight in us, then he will bring us into this land, and give it us; a land which floweth with milk and honey. Only rebel not ye against the Lord, neither fear ye the people of the land; for they are bread for us: their defense is departed from them, and the Lord is with us: fear them not (Num. 14:6–9).

The people of Israel responded to the two proposals by demanding that Moses accept the majority opinion. They were fearful of the enemy and faithless toward God. If nothing else, this incident disproves the popular American adage "The majority is always right." The truth is the majority is usually wrong.

Even in democratically run congregational-style churches, the majority isn't always right. Unless the majority of the people are Spirit-led, submissive servants of God, their choices aren't likely to be consistent with the will of God.

At this point in their history, this particular generation of the congregation of Israel proved to be more interested in doing what they thought would provide them with safety and security than in obeying God's command. Overruling the desperate pleas of Joshua and Caleb, Israel decided to retreat from the land of promise. When they said they had rather die in the wilderness than be killed by the Canaanites, God told them He would grant their request. That generation would die in the wilderness, but not immediately. God would lead them from place to place in the wilderness, never entering Canaan, until the adults had died off. Then He would give the land they had turned their backs on to their children. Thirty-eight years later, when that promise had been fulfilled and it was time for Joshua to assume leadership of Israel, God would charge Joshua in language that sounds a lot like the words Joshua and Caleb had spoken to the people on that day. The similarity is surely intentional:

> Be strong and of a good courage; be not afraid, neither be thou dismayed: for the Lord thy God is with thee whithersoever thou goest (Josh. 1:9).

Israel had chosen the easy way—the way of fear and distrust. They evaluated the situation according to human standards, giving no regard to the power of God. Believers today are prone to have exactly the same response to difficulties. When confronted by "giants" or "fortified cities," you may see no human solution to the problems you face. You may be tempted to give in to fear, despairing of any help. Like Israel, many decide it is easier to wander in the wilderness than to progress to victory.

Joshua's Subsequent Appearances

The preceding paragraphs discussed the first four contexts in which Joshua is mentioned in Scripture, which have revealed important aspects of his character and his faith. If you continue through the books of Moses, you'll find seven additional references to Joshua. The next three are found in the continuing record of Israel's sojourn in the wilderness. In Numbers 27:18–22, Moses describes a ceremony in which Joshua was formally ordained to be Moses' successor. In Numbers 32:11–12 Joshua and Caleb are named as the only members of the generation that refused to enter Canaan who would survive the wilderness wandering and enter the land. When Moses gives instructions about dividing the land when Israel finally enters Canaan, he names Joshua and Eleazar the priest (son of Aaron) as the two men who would have the authority to distribute the land among the tribes (Num. 34:17).

The last four times Joshua is mentioned before the beginning of his book are all found in Deuteronomy. First, in Deuteronomy 1:38 Moses clearly identifies Joshua as the man who "shall cause Israel to inherit" Canaan. Second, in Deuteronomy 3:21 Moses encourages Joshua and Israel by reminding them of what God had done to enemies in the past and by promising that God would do the same as Israel faced new enemies in the Promised Land. Third, Moses calls Joshua to stand before him in a public assembly and "in the sight of all Israel" charges him to be a courageous leader.

> And Moses called unto Joshua, and said unto him in the sight of all Israel, Be strong and of a good courage: for thou must go with this people unto the land which the Lord hath sworn unto their fathers to give them; and thou shalt cause them to inherit it. And the Lord, he it is that doth go before thee; he will be with thee, he will not fail thee, neither forsake thee: fear not, neither be dismayed (Deut. 31:7–8).

Finally, following Moses' death, we're specifically told in Deuteronomy 34:9 of the people's acceptance of Joshua as their new leader.

Joshua's Character

Joshua had been prepared by God to lead Israel, and Israel had been prepared to follow Joshua as their leader. Joshua's forty years in slavery had prepared him to serve God by helping Moses. Joshua's forty years as Moses' assistant forged a man of great character and faith. There are at least four important lessons that Joshua learned that will prove to be vital to his success in the years to come.

Joshua has learned that *difficulties can be either occasions for defeat and failure or opportunities for victory and growth*. He has seen firsthand the consequences of fearing man more than fearing God. Much of a Christian's struggle today is due to allowing difficulties to distract us from following God.

Joshua has demonstrated the confidence that *God's promises are worth more than popular support*. He knows that standing with God is sufficient, even if no one else stands with him. Churches today are caving in to the pressure to conform their message to that which is politically correct or socially expedient. Believers are surrendering the unique and exclusive message of the gospel to a philosophy of relativism, tolerance, and ambiguity. The message has gone from being "Thus saith the Lord," to being "This is what I believe," or even worse, "This is what I *feel*." Many are so worried about offending people that they're willing to risk offending God. Joshua has learned the folly of such attitudes.

Joshua has learned that *size does not determine significance*. Yes, the enemy is large. Yes, they have walled cities. Yes, they have well-equipped armies. But Joshua has God. It seems to me that many evangelical Christians have adopted fearful and faithless Israel's mindset. In our desire to be popular, we tailor our ministries to the felt needs of the unbelieving community. We make the same mistake when we evaluate churches on the basis of the size of their congregation or evaluate preachers, teachers, or authors on the size of their audiences. "Big" does not necessarily mean "right," and "small" does not necessarily mean "wrong." It is possible to assemble a large audience without honoring God. It is also possible for God to be honored by the faithful service of a handful. *Joshua was never intimidated by the size or strength of his opponent or discouraged by the small number or limited resources of the faithful.* He was willing to obey and let God do what He would.

Finally, we see that Joshua had learned to *trust God in every circumstance*. It is easy to give in to fear when facing opposition from unbelievers, but Joshua trusted God in the battle with Amalek. Our faith may waver when God seems distant or His presence seems threatening, but Joshua trusted God in the thunderstorm on Mount Sinai and when Moses confronted rebellious Israel. We tend to disobey when God's commands seem difficult and His promises seem unattainable, but Joshua trusted God when facing the task of taking Canaan from its mighty inhabitants even though he was opposed by virtually the entire congregation of Israel. Even Christian leaders, or especially Christian leaders, may become fearful or self-serving in the exercise of their ministries. But Joshua trusted God when he assumed the mantle of leadership with the responsibility of taking Israel into a place Moses had been unable to take them. He avoided the twin dangers of being overwhelmed by the potential demands or being puffed up with a sense of celebrity. As we move into our study of the book of Joshua, we'll find that *whether following, leading, resting, or fighting, Joshua was always trusting.*

3
Joshua's Commission

Joshua 1:1–9

Most Americans spend the bulk of the first eighteen years of their lives getting a basic education. Many high school graduates go on to college for another four years. Some jobs require college graduates to stay in school for three or four additional years finishing advanced degrees. A person may spend seven or eight years after high school getting a law degree only to get a job with a firm that expects him to spend a few years more as an associate before becoming a partner. Another may spend a similar number of years in medical training and then face years of residency before being licensed to practice medicine. Part of the reason so few people become highly trained professionals is the time it takes to complete the training. Not many are willing to spend thirty years preparing for their vocations.

We're an impatient bunch. Do you honk the horn at the driver in front of you who hesitates when the light turns green? When the shopper in front of you in the grocery checkout pulls out a folder full of coupons, do you sigh in exasperation because you know it'll take several minutes to process the discounts? We want microwave meals and drive-through banking. We want immediate fixes for our problems and instant gratification of our desires. Like the one who prayed, "Lord, make me a patient person, and do it soon," we want spiritual victory and we want it *now*.

Imagine how Joshua must have felt. He didn't spend twenty years in school and four or five as an intern. He spent *forty* years in the classroom of Egypt and *forty more* years as an intern in the wilderness. Finally, after *eighty years* of preparation, it was time for Joshua to assume leadership of the people of

Israel. And you thought reading two chapters of background material was tedious!

In the opening verses of Joshua we find God's charge to the new leader. This is, in a sense, Joshua's "Great Commission" because this is where God defines Joshua's responsibilities. God reveals two distinct but interrelated characteristics that Joshua must display and exercise in order to successfully please God: *faith* and *faithfulness*. God wants Joshua to *trust* Him completely and to *obey* Him fully.

Call to Faith

Unbelievers often scoff at Christians for what they think of as "blind faith." They believe that the Christian faith is just wishful thinking with no real basis for confidence, and they think that believers are either delusional or simply gullible. Even professing Christians have occasionally tried to make a distinction between reality and faith, defending their faith with comments like Soren Kierkegaard's famous statement, "I believe it because it is absurd."

But Christianity isn't a "leap into the dark." God provides us with evidence for everything He calls on us to believe. Early in the morning on the first day of the week following Christ's crucifixion, some of the women went to the tomb where Christ's body had been placed because they wanted to complete the burial preparations that had been cut short by the Passover holy day. When they arrived, they did *not* find a sealed tomb with a messenger telling them, "He is not here; take my word for it." No, the angelic messenger challenged them to look at the evidence that Jesus was really risen. He actually said,

> He is not here: for he is risen, as he said. **Come, see the place where the Lord lay**. And go quickly, and tell his disciples that he is risen from the dead; and, behold, he goeth before you into Galilee; **there shall ye see him** (Matt. 28:6–7).

When the apostle Paul defends the doctrine of the Resurrection in 1 Corinthians 15, he confirms his testimony by listing eyewitnesses who saw the risen Lord. We aren't asked to believe in the truth of the resurrection of Jesus Christ contrary to the evidence but on the basis of the evidence.

That's why we had to take the time to consider the background information on Joshua. That study proves that by the time God called on Joshua to believe that He would enable him to lead Israel in the conquest of Canaan, Joshua had plenty of evidence of God's trustworthiness. In fact, that's implied in the very first word of the text.

A Continuing Message

> Now after the death of Moses the servant of the Lord (1:1*a*).

Joshua starts his book in a way that would have made my high-school English teacher cringe. The first word of the Hebrew text is *waw*, usually translated "and." The word *and* belongs to the category of words known as *conjunctions* because they serve to connect words or ideas. Since English grammar rules expect the word *and* to be used only when connecting two or more words, phrases, or clauses, starting a sentence with *and* is generally discouraged, which explains why the King James translators chose in this instance to render *waw* as an adverb of time—"Now"—rather than as a coordinating conjunction—"And." They gave us a legitimate translation that communicates the same basic idea but makes the wording fit the way we expect English to be written.

The grammar rules for Hebrew are different from the rules for English. In Hebrew *waw* serves the same purpose as the English *and*, but the Hebrew language permits the word to start a sentence. *Waw* is used to show consecutive thought or action. One of the reasons I do not believe that Genesis 1 permits either a "day-age theory" or a "gap theory" of Creation is the use of this word. After the first verse ("In the beginning God created the heaven and the earth") every verse except verse 27, which is subordinated to verse 26, begins with the word *waw* (*and*). This indicates a continual chain of uninterrupted events.

Hebrew even permits *waw* to start a book. But why start a book with "And"? Exodus starts with *waw* to connect it with Genesis. Leviticus and Numbers continue the series, both also starting with *waw*. Deuteronomy does not start with *waw* because, instead of continuing the account of Israel's history, it reviews what had happened in the wilderness. Joshua picks up the continuing narrative of Israel's history, so he starts his book with *waw*. By doing so, Joshua connects his book with a message begun earlier, tying it to the books of Moses as the continuing revelation of God. This one word indicates that the call to faith at the start of Joshua is based on the evidence of God's work in and for His people that is provided in the books of Moses.[14]

---

[14] The progression doesn't stop with Joshua. The pattern continues through the history of Israel up to and including the book of Ezra. Judges, Ruth, 1 Samuel, 2 Samuel, 1 Kings, 2 Kings, and Ezra all begin with *waw*. The two books of Chronicles do not, because they (like Deuteronomy) cover a period of history already addressed in earlier books (1–2 Samuel and 1–2 Kings). So the first four books of the Bible provide a continuing history of God's work

A New Leader

> Now after the death of Moses the servant of the Lord it came to pass, that the Lord spake unto Joshua the son of Nun, Moses' minister, saying, Moses my servant is dead; now therefore arise, go over this Jordan, thou, and all this people, unto the land which I do give to them, even to the children of Israel (Josh. 1:1–2).

Moses is dead. That somber message is driven home in the first two verses of Joshua. The book picks up the narrative "after the death of Moses the servant of the Lord." Then God's first words to Joshua are "Moses my servant is dead." What a gloomy, even terrifying, start! Moses, who had been used of God to deliver Israel from bondage, was dead. Moses, who had been used of God to make a way through the Red Sea, was dead. Moses, who had for forty years represented Israel before God and represented God before Israel, was *dead*. Just as Israel was on the verge of reaching the objective set before them by Moses, their valiant leader was dead. They must have thought that surely they needed Moses now more than ever.

But God's plan for Israel was progressing. The emphasis on Moses' death and the accompanying emphasis on Joshua's being a new leader for Israel proves that *God's program is never hindered by the death of His servants.* God, Who is the giver of life and the controller of death, is never frustrated or confused when one of His servants dies. Matthew Henry, an eighteenth-century Bible commentator, said, "God will change hands to show that whatever instrument he uses, he is not tied to any."[15] That is, God will accomplish His purposes and meet our needs as He sees fit. Occasionally God will replace a deceased leader with a younger man who had been the former leader's assistant as in the case of Moses/Joshua (or Elijah/Elisha). At other times when a leader dies, God meets the needs of His people through other means. But in virtually every case, God's people move through some sort of transition.

One of the most difficult tasks God may give a man is to take over leadership of a group of people who have been following the same respected leader for many years. On the one hand, that can be frustrating to the new leader who wants to emulate the man he follows. The new leader must remember that he is called to follow Christ, not the former leader. On the other hand, differences between the new leader and the old will also be frustrating to the people the new man tries to lead. How often has a new pastor been faced with the constant refrain, "Pastor (old leader) never did it that way," or "always did it this way!" No new leader replicates the old in every way. If God had needed

---

among His people *outside* the land of promise. The next eight books (omitting Chronicles) describe God's continuing work among His people *in* the land of promise.

[15] Matthew Henry, *Commentary on the Whole Bible*, vol. 2 (Peabody, MA: Hendrickson Publishers, 1991 reprint), p. 2.

leadership identical to that provided by the former leader, He could have left the former leader in place. *God's purposes for His people are not static.* He doesn't lead us in perpetual circles. He expects us to progress in our Christian lives. That will require constant growth. Growth involves facing new challenges. New challenges often require new leadership.

It is possible for an old and respected leader to have made mistakes. It is also possible for a new leader to make mistakes. The simple fact of differences between the leaders does not prove that one or the other is wrong. It may well be that the old leader accomplished the work God intended him to do and it's now time for a new leader to build upon what the old leader accomplished. Moses had led Israel from Egypt. Joshua would lead them into Canaan. Israel under Joshua would face new challenges, beginning with crossing the Jordan River. Israel under Moses had been prepared for the challenges they were about to face. Joshua had been promoted in God's time and by God's command.

An Old Promise

Immediately after God tells Joshua to lead Israel across Jordan, He restates the promise He had made to Israel's forebears. God promised the land of Canaan to Abram in Genesis 15:7–21. He confirmed the promise to Jacob in Genesis 28:13–14. He now tells Joshua, "I do give to them" this land (v. 2), and He amplifies the promise by giving some geographic boundaries.

> Every place that the sole of your foot shall tread upon, that have I given unto you, as I said unto Moses. From the wilderness and this Lebanon even unto the great river, the river Euphrates, all the land of the Hittites, and unto the great sea toward the going down of the sun, shall be your coast (Josh. 1:3–4).

The land God promised Israel extended to the borders of Egypt. The Promised Land included "all the land of the Hittites." Earliest archeological evidence places the Hittite homeland in Anatolia, the territory known today as Turkey.[16] However, the Bible indicates that Abraham had dealings with Hittites in Canaan (Gen. 23:10) centuries before Israel came back under Joshua's leadership. It is possible that God referred to the land of Canaan as "all the land of the Hittites" despite the fact that there were few if any Hittites found there at the time of Israel's conquest. It is also possible that the extent of the land promised Israel was greater than we think.

The Promised Land extended at least to the Euphrates, now in Iraq, and included all the eastern Mediterranean coast of Palestine. It is possible to interpret Israel's movements during this period as a conquest of more territory un-

[16] Harry A. Hoffner Jr., "Hittites," *Peoples of the Old Testament World*, Hoerth, Mattingly, Yamauchi, eds. (Grand Rapids: Baker Books, 1994), p. 128.

der Joshua than they would control at any other time in their history, including under Solomon or following the Six-Day War. Even so, they conquered only a fraction of what God promised them. The promise of all that land has yet to be fulfilled, but it will be completely realized when Christ establishes His millennial kingdom on earth (if not before).

In these opening verses of Joshua we find the theme for the entire book. God would tell Joshua and Israel to do things they were unable to do; then He would enable them to do those things. God insists that He has *given* Israel this land. From the outset, God expected Israel to realize that *they did not deserve the promise*. He also wants them to know that *they cannot earn the victory*. Without God's promise, without God fighting for them, without God taking them every step of the way, the land would remain in enemy hands.

God also wanted them to understand that the land must be *won* by obedience. *Their participation was required*, and *their responsibility was enforced*. Getting Israel from Egypt to Canaan was God's responsibility—a picture of salvation. Conquering the land was theirs with God's help—a picture of sanctification. What did Israel have to do? They had to cross Jordan, capture cities, fight battles, conquer Canaanites, establish their law, and settle and cultivate the land. That's a tall order. God had promised victory, but His strength would be applied on their behalf only as they yielded to His authority and followed His orders. They would come into the land the same way the Christian grows in Christ—"little by little" (Exod. 23:29–30; cf. Deut. 9:3).

An individual's salvation *from* sin *to* new life in Christ is an instantaneous event, based on Christ's blood sacrifice, accomplished through the regeneration of the Holy Spirit, and applied through personal faith. The events in Israel's history that provide this picture are spread out over a generation. The Passover in Egypt depicts and foreshadows Christ's sacrifice as Israel was *delivered from* slavery. The crossing of Jordan as Israel enters Canaan represents that Israel was *delivered to* new life. The conquest of Canaan parallels the Christian life as the believer grows in Christ.

The conquest of the Promised Land doesn't show us what eternity will be like, as if crossing Jordan pictured entering heaven. It provides a pattern for our present sanctification. Our own *salvation* is initiated and accomplished by God (see Ps. 115:1; Eph. 2:8–10; Titus 3:5–6). Our *sanctification* is a concursive work—a sort of teamwork in which God must sanctify us (Exod. 31:13; Lev. 20:8; 21:8) and we must sanctify ourselves (Lev. 11:44; 20:7).

Some people have the mistaken notion that God never commands us to do something we can't do. The fact is that God *constantly* tells us to do things we can't do (e.g., "Go and sin no more" [John 5:14; 8:11]; "Be ye holy" [Lev.

20:7; 1 Pet. 1:15, 16]). We are not even capable of responding to the gospel in faith unless the Father draws us (John 6:44) and it is given to us by the Father (John 6:65). But we are commanded to "believe on the Lord Jesus Christ" to be saved (Acts 16:31; cf. John 3:16). Similarly, we can't conquer our own flesh and stand against the temptations of the world and the attacks of Satan (Rom. 3:10–23; 7:14–24), but we're commanded to do so (Rom. 6:1–18).

If you're hoping I'll be able to explain the mechanics of how all this works, I'm afraid you'll be disappointed. But we must not deny either of the poles of the paradox simply because we don't know exactly how it works. The apostle Paul insists that you must "work out your own salvation with fear and trembling" (Phil. 2:12), but he immediately adds that "it is God which worketh in you both to will and to do of his good pleasure" (Phil. 2:13). *God promises victory, but He demands that we engage the enemy in lifelong battle.*

A New Promise

> There shall not any man be able to stand before thee all the days of thy life: as I was with Moses, so I will be with thee: I will not fail thee, nor forsake thee (Josh. 1:5).

After reminding Joshua of the old promise to give Israel the land, God encourages Joshua with a new promise especially for him. He wants Joshua to know that His help for Joshua personally and for Israel collectively will be available and operating throughout Joshua's life. Enemies would fall before him. In fact, no enemy would be able to withstand his approach. But it is understood in the command that Joshua must confront the enemies. God didn't say there would be no enemies to face. Rather, the enemies Joshua would surely encounter would be overcome by God through Joshua's obedience. As you will see, Israel's victory over Jericho would be due only to God's intervention. But Jericho wouldn't fall if Israel stayed in the camp. God would cause the enemies to fall, but Israel would have to attack.

Again, we see a parallel for our own sanctification. God's help is not simply theoretical. It is always available for us. He has promised, "I will never leave thee, nor forsake thee" (Heb. 13:5*b*). On the basis of that promise, "we may boldly say, The Lord is my helper, and I will not fear what man shall do unto me" (Heb. 13:6). This promise isn't an excuse to disengage the enemy as if there were no battles to fight. The promise motivates us to act because we know that victory doesn't depend on us alone.

A general rule of thumb to keep in mind is that *promises do not preempt precepts*. That is, a promise of God never nullifies a command to obey. For instance, biblical teaching on divine election (John 10:24–29; 15:16; Eph.

1:4; 2 Thess. 2:13–14; etc.) in no way sets aside God's command to "preach the gospel to every creature" in order to win the lost (Matt. 28:18–20; Mark 16:15; Luke 24:47–48; etc.) Similarly, promises of the eternal security of the believer (Rom. 8:35–39; Phil. 1:6; Heb. 13:5–6; etc.) in no way set aside God's command to personal holiness (John 14:15; 1 John 1:6–10; 3:4–10; etc.) The promises of God must never be used as excuses for laziness (lethargy) or unconcern (apathy).

Command to Faithfulness (1:6–9)

In laying out the theme of Joshua in the introductory verses, the text moves from the promises God wants Joshua to believe to commands God intends Joshua to obey.

Exhortation to Strength and Courage

> Be strong and of a good courage: for unto this people shalt thou divide for an inheritance the land, which I sware unto their fathers to give them. Only be thou strong and very courageous, that thou mayest observe to do according to all the law, which Moses my servant commanded thee: turn not from it to the right hand or to the left, that thou mayest prosper whithersoever thou goest (Josh. 1:6–7).

Have you ever wondered why God had to tell Joshua not to be afraid? After all, God had just promised victory over all enemies and occupation of the land. What did Joshua have to fear? For starters, there was the Jordan River God had told him he had to cross (1:2). Then there were the inhabitants of the land that would have to be dispossessed. Joshua had been in the land and knew its strengths. The Canaanites were many and strong. Their cities were fortified. Their armies were formidable, equipped with chariots. The Israelites under Joshua's command were fewer than their enemy. They had no fortified base of operations. Their strength was relatively untested. Their supply was uncertain. They had no supply center, and no protection or provision beyond what they could capture. They would be hampered by the presence of and their concern for their families and possessions. Conquest wouldn't be easy. There was plenty for Joshua to fear.

Joshua would be afraid only if he developed an earthly perspective. If he focused on the obstacles and the dangers, he could be overwhelmed. That's what had happened to the generation before him. They'd seen the difficulties and were afraid to take the land. God is reminding Joshua of Joshua's own words to Israel (Num. 14:9) and Moses' words to Joshua (Deut. 31:7–8). The blessing of victory over their enemies and conquest of the land would be obtained only by complete obedience. Joshua wasn't given the authority to be selective, choosing which commands of God to obey and which to ignore. The person who chooses which instructions to obey is acting out of a desire to please himself, not God.

Expectation to Rely on God's Word

> This book of the law shall not depart out of thy mouth; but thou shalt meditate therein day and night, that thou mayest observe to do according to all that is written therein: for then thou shalt make thy way prosperous, and then thou shalt have good success. Have not I commanded thee? Be strong and of a good courage; be not afraid, neither be thou dismayed: for the Lord thy God is with thee whithersoever thou goest (Josh. 1:8–9).

This passage may constitute the first time in history that a military leader is told to be guided by a book. In some ways, the book Joshua has to follow had been prepared specifically for him. God had told Moses to record certain things in a book and "rehearse [them] in the ears of Joshua" (Exod. 17:14). It would now be up to Joshua to fulfill part of what had been promised in the book. God's instruction for Joshua to rely on the book of the Law would communicate two vital truths to the mind of Joshua.

For all Joshua's importance to the people and to God's plan, God lets Joshua know that *the book is more important than Joshua*. Fulfillment of God's purposes depends much more upon His Word than upon the human instruments He uses. The implication is that no man is indispensable to God's work. If God could take Israel into Canaan without Moses, He could do it without Joshua too. It is God's Word that is indispensable. Leaders of God's people today would do well to remember this. No ministry "belongs" to the man or men God has put in positions of leadership. The work of the Lord must never be built upon personalities but upon God's Word. Similarly, believers must remember that we are called not to follow men but to follow God's Word. Blind allegiance to personalities is tantamount to idolatry. Only God deserves our absolute devotion, and only His Word is our authoritative guide.

God has told Joshua that this book is not simply good advice or wise counsel. It is the Law. Joshua was not to consider the contents of the book suggestions for living but as *mandates*. Disregarding the book would not be simply foolish; it would be rebellion. Because Christ Jesus came to fulfill the Law (Matt. 5:17–18), believers today do not have the same relationship to the Law that characterized Old Testament Israel. That does not mean that believers are free to live as we please. The Bible contains numerous commands that we ignore to our peril. That is Paul's point in Romans 6:15–18.

> What then? shall we sin, because we are not under the law, but under grace? God forbid. Know ye not, that to whom ye yield yourselves servants to obey, his servants ye are to whom ye obey; whether of sin unto death, or of obedience unto righteousness? But God be thanked, that ye were the servants of sin, but ye have obeyed from the heart that form of doctrine which was delivered you. Being then made free from sin, ye became the servants of righteousness.

The Law shows us our need of a Savior, but no one has ever become a Christian by keeping the Law. On the other hand, no believer ever becomes Christlike without obedience to God's Word.

Joshua was commanded to rely upon the book of the Law. God said it "**shall** not depart out of thy mouth; but thou **shalt** meditate therein day and night" (1:8). Studying the Word of God was not an optional activity or an occasional luxury for Joshua. It was a daily mandate, morning and evening. When God told Joshua he must "meditate" on God's Word, what did He mean? I'm afraid that the image of meditation that may come to mind is that of a person practicing yoga, sitting in the lotus position in a trancelike state. Our thinking has been corrupted by the influence of Eastern mysticism.

Madvig says, "The word translated 'meditate' (*hagah*) literally means 'mutter.' When one continually mutters God's Word to himself, he is constantly thinking about it."[17] Meditating on God's Word involves careful reflection on what God has said and application of His Word to our lives. Ask yourself, "How does this truth impact my attitudes, my thinking, and my actions?" "What must I change to conform to God's Word?" "How can I implement these truths in my life today?" This will take more time and effort than simply reading a few verses in your "devotions." To meditate on God's Word, you'll have to devote time to really understanding what the Bible says and consciously applying it to your life.

Joshua was going to be busy. He may have had as many as two million people for whom he was responsible. He was going to have to get them over the river and take them into enemy territory that would not be surrendered without a fight. His time wouldn't be his own. Yet God said that he *must* make time for careful meditation on God's Word or he would *surely* fail. Meditation was for the purpose of equipping Joshua "to do according to all that is written therein." Careful study was necessary for Joshua to learn obedience.

---

[17] Madvig, p. 257.

How often do you allow yourself to be distracted from your study of God's Word because you are too busy? We all need to realize that when we are too busy to study God's Word and to carefully consider its implications for our lives, we are acting in the flesh. Our hearts have been deceived about where our treasure lies. The truth is, we all have the same amount of time each day. We make time for those things most important to us. The real problem is rarely lack of opportunity to read and reflect on God's Word. Rather, it is a lack of love for God and His Word.

While meditation on the Word of God would be foundational for Joshua's obedience, courage would also be necessary. In the verses we've been considering, God issues three separate calls to Joshua to be courageous. The first call comes in verse 6: "Be strong and of a good courage: for unto this people shalt thou divide for an inheritance the land." In this case, the call to courage is *in view of the task before him*. The job was enormous and would profoundly impact the future of the nation. To divide the land they must conquer its inhabitants. Once the peoples were conquered, how would Joshua decide who should live where and what borders would mark the limits of their territories? He was facing a task fraught with potential difficulty and disputation. No wonder God had to call Joshua to be courageous in the face of such an undertaking!

The second call to courage comes in verse 7: "Only be thou strong and very courageous, that thou mayest observe to do according to all the law." This call is *in view of Joshua's responsibility to obey* the book he was to follow. He would be held accountable for his obedience. No one else could obey for him. When we consider that God tells us that perfect obedience is impossible in our own strength, we again see the need for courage in the face of such responsibility. Even today, God says the leaders of His people must be "blameless" (1 Tim. 3:2; Titus 1:6). It's a frightening thing to realize that God expects this of us and that we're incapable of measuring up.

That is why God issued the third call to courage in Joshua 1:9—"Have not I commanded thee? Be strong and of a good courage; be not afraid, neither be thou dismayed: for the Lord thy God is with thee whithersoever thou goest." This final call to courage is *in view of his Commander's enablement*. The question, "Have not I commanded thee?" isn't a reminder of an order given earlier. God is not saying, "Look, Joshua, I told you before that you shouldn't be afraid." He is saying, "*Joshua, you have nothing to fear because I am your Commander*." God had always been Joshua's Commander. Joshua was being given enormous responsibilities, but God would continue to be his Commander as He had always been. While the first two calls to courage were to serve as encouragement for service, this third call was to encourage Joshua to inner peace. Joshua need not fear that he was being sent on alone and unprotected. His Commander would never leave him. His Commander would never forsake him.

Believers today have the same promise from God. Hebrews 13:5–6 quotes Joshua 1:5 and alludes to Joshua 1:9 when it says, "For he hath said, I will never leave thee, nor forsake thee. So that we may boldly say, The Lord is my helper, and I will not fear what man shall do unto me." Hebrews 13:8 adds, "Jesus Christ the same yesterday, and to day, and for ever." The One Who commanded Joshua to obey, and then promised to enable him, is the same One Who is your Commander today, and gives you the ability to serve Him. You can say with the apostle Paul, "I can do all things through Christ which strengtheneth me" (Phil. 4:13).

4
The Response of Faith

Joshua 1:10–18

Do you ever find your responsibilities so distasteful that you have a hard time making yourself do what you know you should? I do. I hate confrontation. I can't think of anything about pastoral ministry that I find more difficult to do than to rebuke someone who is in the wrong. I know it's important. I know they need it. But I don't like to do it. When I have to do something I don't want to do, it's easy to find (or invent) excuses to put it off. I guess a part of me hopes that if I ignore a problem long enough it'll go away, despite the fact that experience teaches that delay is likely to make the situation worse.

Other jobs can be difficult to begin. Even for something as seemingly mundane as writing this chapter, I find myself having a hard time mustering the motivation to start. Writing doesn't come easily for me. Once I get started, I can generally keep going. The hard part is getting started. The first paragraph of every chapter looms like a walled city or a flooded river that must be overcome before I can generate the momentum to see it through to the end.

Immediate Obedience

One reason I admire Joshua is that I see in him none of my native tendency to hesitate or procrastinate. He makes no excuses and tolerates no delay. God gave Joshua a responsibility, saying, "Arise, go over this Jordan, thou, and all this people, unto the land which I do give to them." God started the command with the word *now*. Joshua's response to God's command was immediate, even bold. There was no hesitation. He simply obeyed.

> Then Joshua commanded the officers of the people (Josh. 1:10).

Delay Is Disobedience

The word translated *then* is often rendered *therefore*. It indicates continuous action based on what has gone before. God had told Joshua to get moving. He had told Joshua He would be with him. So Joshua started. He knew that delay is disobedience.

We know it is hypocritical to say we're willing to obey and then to delay, but we still hesitate and procrastinate. We're slow to break off that relationship that is a bad influence or to give up that habit that is a bad testimony or to share the gospel with the person who we fear will reject it. I suppose in some ways our American spirit of independence encourages us to think we're entitled to an explanation for every instruction. Then if we don't like the explanation we're given, we act as though we're free to disregard whatever we were told. Such a skeptical attitude may be good and healthy when applied to the influence of the world around us, but it is disobedience when applied to the Word of God. When God tells us to do something, we'd better do it.

We also have to recognize the dangers of rashness or impulsiveness. *Rash* behavior generally involves an element of extreme risk. *Impulsive* behavior is based on sudden, emotional decisions. Let me give an example. Pastor Jones (not his real name) returned from a spring Bible conference several years ago and announced to his congregation that they were going to start a Christian school that summer. He said it was "the Lord's will" for their church to launch a day school ministry right away. When some folks asked more questions, they became convinced that their pastor had no real Bible authority for his plans. Pastor Jones could provide no biblical support for insisting that they start a Christian school at all, much less that it be done immediately. I happen to believe that there is plenty of biblical justification for a church having a Christian school ministry. But it is difficult to prove that God commands it of any *particular* church, and it is impossible to prove that He expects it of *every* church. What had happened was that several churches that had schools were featured at the conference Pastor Jones attended. Their pastors talked about how they thought every church should have a school. Pastor Jones came home emotionally energized (*impulsive*) to immediately launch a school ministry that would require huge financial commitments (*rash*). It may well be that the Lord really did want Pastor Jones to start a school, but diving in with no preparation or planning threatened the stability of the church itself. If you don't have a clear biblical mandate for what you plan to do, decisions should be made only after careful deliberation and much prayer.

There are situations in which God's instructions are perfectly clear. When God says, "Thou shalt," or "Thou shalt not," there is really no excuse for misunderstanding. Other times, when His instructions are not quite so clear, you have to act on the basis of biblical principles. In general, when you know God's will, you must act and leave the consequences to Him. When God's will isn't clearly expressed, you have to evaluate the situation and make a decision based on the evidence. Then, when you act on that decision, you need to be prepared to take personal responsibility for the outcome.[18]

Chain-of-Command Is Important

The wording of verse 10 indicates that Joshua also understood that a chain of command is important. God had commanded Joshua. Joshua commanded the officers. The officers commanded the host of Israel. Joshua allowed the officers to do their jobs, and the people learned to obey delegated authority. It is not unusual in churches today to find people who have a problem with authority. When your independent spirit gets the better of you, you can begin to think that you answer to no one. True, each believer is a member of a "royal priesthood" (1 Pet. 2:9) and has personal access to God (Heb. 4:16). But that is no excuse for disorganized, free-wheeling self-assertiveness. God has established a hierarchy of responsibility within His church. Titus was instructed to "exhort and rebuke with all authority" (Titus 2:15). I know exhorting or

---

[18] Perhaps it would be appropriate at this point to suggest a series of steps I've found helpful for making decisions that will honor God.

1) Define exactly what decision you must make.
2) Think of as many solutions or choices as possible, keeping in mind that your final decision will be no better than the best alternative listed or a combination of alternatives listed.
3) Carefully and prayerfully evaluate each alternative in your list. Seek counsel where appropriate. As you pray for wisdom, consider
   a) Scriptural instructions
   b) Financial considerations
   c) Time limitations
   d) Family obligations
   e) Possible ramifications
   f) Other factors, such as personal abilities, interests, and preferences
4) Make your decision. If you've followed the first three steps, it should be a wise one.
5) Activate the decision and take responsibility for the outcome.

A special note to keep in mind: Timing is important. Avoid making important decisions when you are emotionally upset, fatigued, ill, hungry, or extremely excited. In such situations it is difficult to think objectively. Emotional decisions are generally not good ones. If you must make an important decision under pressure, make it as objectively as possible and pray for wisdom.

rebuking is no fun—not when you have to do it, and not when you have to receive it. If Titus was to give what amounts to disciplinary instruction with "all authority," then there must be people who were expected to respond with all submission. You'll find the parallel instructions to subordinates in Hebrews 13:17, where believers are told to "obey them that have the rule over you and submit yourselves."

A word of caution to pastors is in order, particularly in churches like mine that follow a congregational form of government and are independent of denominational oversight. Too many men in such pastorates seem to think they stand in relation to their congregations as a Joshua (or a David) to Israel. Pastoral authority in the church has a closer parallel to that of the officers of Israel than to that of Joshua. Joshua's relationship to Israel was like Christ's is to the church. Pastors answer to Christ, the Head of the church, in a manner similar to how the officers answered to Joshua. Pastoral authority over the ministry and direction of the church has its place, but it is a delegated authority, strictly limited by recognition of both the priesthood of the individual believers and the pastor's accountability to God for obedience to Christ, the Head of the church.

Preparation for Action

In responding to the command of God to take the people across Jordan, what orders did Joshua issue? He told the officers of the people to

> Pass through the host, and command the people, saying, Prepare you victuals; for within three days ye shall pass over this Jordan, to go in to possess the land, which the Lord your God giveth you to possess it (Josh. 1:11).

Joshua had no idea *how* Israel would cross Jordan. He vividly remembered that during Israel's escape from Egypt God had led the refugees into what looked like a trap. Their only way of escape was to cross the Red Sea, and there was no way across—until God made a way. Israel faced a similar challenge at this time, confronted as they were by the flooded Jordan River. God could have brought them to Canaan from the south and avoided the river, but He hadn't. God had told Joshua they must cross the river, not march around it. Joshua didn't know how God planned to get them across, but he knew they couldn't do it without God's help. That meant that on Israel's part, *faith* would be required. The river presented the first major challenge to their faith.

If I'd been in charge when it came time to move, I imagine that I might have told the people to get busy building boats or rafts. But not Joshua. Instead of telling the people to prepare some way to cross the river, he told them to prepare *food.* Joshua didn't know what Israel would need to cross the river, so he didn't risk wasting resources on busywork making things they might not need. He did know, however, that the Israelites would need strength for whatever challenges they might face. He knew that if they prepared food in advance, they might have the time necessary to invest in other projects as God would direct.

The significance for believers today is too important to miss. We, too, must be well fed to be equipped for our spiritual warfare. Have you ever found yourself unprepared for Satan's attacks? In some instances, it may be that you wasted preparation time frivolously. You need to feed your spirit every day on the Word of God in order to have the necessary strength to face the unexpected challenges you will surely encounter. Where did Israel get these "victuals" they were to prepare? The primary food source Israel had enjoyed for years was the manna that God provided for them daily. From what do we prepare our spiritual "victuals"? We feed on the milk and meat God has provided in His Word (1 Pet. 2:2; Heb. 5:12–13). Once again we see the teamwork of God and man in our spiritual walk. God furnishes the "victuals," but we must prepare them (see Ezra 7:10). Great feats of spiritual strength—such as Israel's exercising the faith to walk through the river, your confidence in your security in Christ despite hard circumstances (Rom. 8:18–39), or your ability to live through the death of a loved one (1 Thess. 4:13–18)—require spiritual nourishment only God can provide.

This has enormous implications for the pastor's teaching ministry. It is possible for a congregation to be very *busy* and still not be adequately *prepared.* All too often we pastors focus energies and resources on the wrong things. Programs and activities are impressive because they are visible—they show up in monthly calendars and annual reports and they make good advertising copy. Spiritual nutrition and growth is harder to see and describe. So we preachers are inclined to spend our time and effort building and running programs (preparing boats and rafts) instead of providing the spiritual instruction necessary for every believer's walk with Christ (preparing "victuals"). *The primary ministry of the pulpit is to help the congregation be properly fed for the spiritual battles they will encounter in their lives.* This truth is reflected in Paul's words to Timothy—"Let the elders that rule well be counted worthy of double honor, *especially they who labor in the word and doctrine*" (1 Tim. 5:17; cf. Acts 20:28).

Special Instructions for Three Tribes

Once the general order had been given to the people of Israel to prepare food in anticipation of crossing the Jordan River, Joshua issued special instructions for the tribes of Reuben, Gad, and half the tribe of Manasseh.

> And to the Reubenites, and to the Gadites, and to half the tribe of Manasseh, spake Joshua, saying, Remember the word which Moses the servant of the Lord commanded you, saying, The Lord your God hath given you rest, and hath given you this land. Your wives, your little ones, and your cattle, shall remain in the land which Moses gave you on this side Jordan; but ye shall pass before your brethren armed, all the mighty men of valour, and help them; until the Lord have given your brethren rest, as he hath given you, and they also have possessed the land which the Lord your God giveth them: then ye shall return unto the land of your possession, and enjoy it, which Moses the Lord's servant gave you on this side Jordan toward the sunrising (Josh. 1:12–15).

Moses' Promise

Moses had promised these three tribes that they could have the land on the east shore of the Jordan River (Num. 32:20–28). Joshua knew the books of Moses well enough to be prepared to take the initiative in addressing this promise. He made it clear that he would be bound by Moses' word, but he would also enforce Moses' condition. Before the people of Reuben, Gad, and Manasseh could begin to settle that land, the men of the tribes must first help the other tribes subdue the land on the west side of Jordan. They would be allowed to leave their families on the east of Jordan, but they could return to them only when all of the tribes could enjoy "rest" in the land.

The idea of *rest* communicates "secure borders that eliminate all danger of attack from without."[19] In this context the "rest" is relative. They would be at rest because there would be no more wandering in a land not their own. Even after the territory had been occupied and the enemy had been driven out, defeated, or subdued, constant vigilance and hard work would still be necessary for the land to remain safe and productive. This is an important parallel to your life in Christ. The forgiveness of sins that you enjoy in Christ and your participation with Him in victory over sin and death provide a measure of "rest" for you now—you have peace with God and the promise of heaven. But you still live in the flesh, caught up in the middle of a sin-cursed world. You

[19] Madvig, p. 246.

have to stay alert and work hard to be spiritually productive. God is working in you; you must work with Him (Phil. 2:12–13).

The Tribes' Responsibility

After restating the promise of Moses, Joshua reminded Reuben, Gad, and Manasseh that they were obligated to fight with and for their brethren. Joshua didn't beg them to keep their word as a personal favor to him. He didn't appeal to them on behalf of their brethren. He didn't even remind them of their promise to Moses. He reminded them of what God required of them.

We often try to obey, or get others to obey, on the basis of a wrong motive. Some people will agree to participate in a particular ministry or project as a personal favor to the pastor, but that is the wrong motive. Some people can be convinced to act on behalf of others in need, but that, too, is the wrong motive. *We should obey because God tells us to obey.*

For instance, some people have responded to the widespread immorality in our society by calling for "abstinence education" for teens. Teaching young people to abstain from sexual activity before they are married is both biblical and vital. But most of the instruction given on the need for sexual abstinence encourages young people to forgo sexual activity until they "are ready" on the basis of their own self-worth. That is, they are being encouraged to maintain their virginity either on the basis of *pride* ("you are worth waiting for") or on the basis of *fear* ("you could get a disease"). Such an approach is doomed to failure. People who wait on the basis of pride will eventually engage in sexual activity when they decide it suits them. They have been told their primary concern is pleasing themselves. People who wait on the basis of fear will eventually engage in sexual activity when they have some form of "protection" and believe it is "safe." Surely we ought to teach young people to maintain sexual purity. But the only proper motivation for sexual purity is that *God demands it*. Any reason for sexual purity that does not invoke the command of God has no real authority and is ultimately based on how a person feels.

Similarly, I believe we have spent far too much time and energy trying to convince people to share the gospel with the lost by developing a "burden for souls"—emphasizing the needs of others as our motivation. Frankly, whether or not you should witness for Christ has little to do with the plight of the lost. You are to do so because *God commands it*. If you serve the Lord for any other reason, it becomes easy to make excuses when you don't feel like doing what you're told. Your feeling that you do not have "a burden" or "a gift" for evangelism is no excuse for disobedience. For that matter, the primary motive for a sinner to repent is *not* to find personal peace and happiness but because *God commands it* (Acts 17:30).

Your obedience must not be determined by how you *feel*—you should obey whether or not you feel like it. Joshua knew this. That is why he commanded Reuben, Gad, and Manasseh to obey on the basis of God's command. Joshua reminded these three tribes of their obligation to obey the command of God given through Moses. Only after making that clear did Joshua bring other motivators into the message to reinforce the instructions. The inheritance of these tribes was already secured. God had been good to them. Their wives and children would be permitted to live in safety on the east side of Jordan while the men went to war. They should obey God out of *gratitude* for His goodness. But the land they would inherit had been conquered under Moses with the assistance of all the tribes. The men of Reuben, Gad, and Manasseh owed it to their relatives in the other tribes to help the rest of Israel secure their land. They should obey out of *love* for their brethren. Not only were they not permitted to rest, they were required to *lead*—"ye shall pass *before your brethren* armed" (Josh. 1:14).

Response of the Three Tribes

Reuben, Gad, and Manasseh responded to the command of Joshua with faith and encouragement.

> And they answered Joshua, saying, All that thou commandest us we will do, and whithersoever thou sendest us, we will go. According as we hearkened unto Moses in all things, so will we hearken unto thee: only the Lord thy God be with thee, as he was with Moses. Whosoever he be that doth rebel against thy commandment, and will not hearken unto thy words in all that thou commandest him, he shall be put to death: only be strong and of a good courage (Josh. 1:16–18).

Their promise to Joshua exceeded the promise they had made to Moses. They had given their word to Moses that they would cross into the land to fight. They specifically promised Joshua to go "whithersoever thou sendest us." They also volunteered to act as Joshua's personal army to enforce his will, promising to execute any individual who disobeyed any of his commands. Such an enthusiastic response to his leadership had to have been an encouragement to Joshua. These tribes even concluded their promise by offering their own words of encouragement: "only be strong and of a good courage."

A teacher's greatest gratification comes from seeing enthusiastic obedience and receiving encouragement from his pupils. This is true in any setting:

grade school, algebra class, music lessons, basketball practice, employee training, and so forth. It is also true at church. There is nothing more gratifying to a pastor than to see his congregation respond positively to the teaching of the Word of God. When individuals take to heart the instruction from God's Word and show evidence of growth in Christ, the faithful pastor feels as if his time and energy have been well spent. That is what John meant when he wrote, "I have no greater joy than to hear that my children walk in truth" (3 John 4). Conversely, little will discourage a pastor more than to see people routinely disregard the teaching of the Word. One of the most effective ways to drive your pastor to despair is to listen to all his messages, shake his hand and thank him for his good sermons, and never change.

This section of Joshua teaches us that every believer has a dual responsibility in relation to those in authority. This is true in civil (governmental) authority, filial (parent/child) authority, or temporal (employer/teacher) authority, but I'm mainly talking about ecclesiastical (church) authority. First, you must do nothing to hinder those in authority from fulfilling the work of the Lord (passive assistance.) Second, you must do everything you can to make their tasks easier (active assistance.) Instead of standing in the way of the work of the Lord by either your unconcern or your outright opposition, you must "put [your] hand to the plow" (Luke 9:62) and "pass before your brethren armed" (Josh. 1:14).

5
Joshua's First Move

Joshua 2:1–7

Many of us can remember quite vividly the opening days of the conflict known as Operation Iraqi Freedom. As the television provided constant updates on the progress of the US-led coalition forces, I watched with special attention. One of the men from my church was in command of an armored division on the ground in Iraq, and my wife's brother was a reservist deployed to the region within weeks of the initial engagement. I was fascinated to see that the operational tactics of that effort were conducted on the basis of information gathered by electronic surveillance, particularly spy satellites and robotic spy planes. The precision targeting of military installations and even particular tanks and trucks was truly amazing to see. Do you think that Joshua might have liked to have had access to such technology?

Sending Out the Two Spies

Joshua would find during Israel's war with the Canaanites that he would enjoy the assistance of God in a more immediate way than the coalition forces had reason to expect in our conflict in Iraq. But like any military leader, he had command responsibilities. Before launching any attack, he wanted some current information on the enemy's situation. He could not download signals from orbiting cameras. He had to rely on what the military today calls HUMINT ("HUMan INTelligence"). People actually had to enter enemy territory and infiltrate their society in hopes of escaping with information that would be useful to Joshua in making command decisions. These were Joshua's Special Forces.

> And Joshua the son of Nun sent out of Shittim two men to spy secretly, saying, Go view the land, even Jericho (Josh. 2:1*a*).

Joshua's decision to send spies into Jericho is sometimes criticized as an act of unbelief. Those critics are assuming that Joshua put these men at risk just to gather information he probably didn't need since God had promised to give Israel the land. It is important to remember, however, that God had given Joshua the responsibility to conquer the land without telling him *how* to do it or *when* and *in what measure* he could expect God's assistance.

Further, God told Joshua to study "this book of the law" and to do what it said (Josh. 1:8). Moses had sent twelve spies into the land thirty-eight years before (Num. 13). Joshua himself had been one of the twelve. Those spies had been sent at God's command (Num. 13:1–2). The activity and report of the spies had been recorded in the book Joshua had been commanded to follow. When Joshua ordered spies to enter Jericho, he was *following a precedent*. Joshua had every reason to believe that sending spies into Canaan was justifiable. He even had reason to believe that *failure* to send spies into Canaan could be interpreted as *disobedience* to God's command to obey the instructions he found in the books of Moses.

We also need to realize that in sending spies into Canaan, Joshua was *performing his duty*. God expected him to prepare an appropriate strategy for taking the city of Jericho—a significant city Israel would encounter immediately after crossing the Jordan at the point to which God had led them. To do this, Joshua would have to seek out Jericho's strengths and weaknesses. I know that you know how they eventually conquered the city because you have the advantage of reading ahead, but Joshua was living the events in the narrative. God's plan for taking Jericho was still a secret unrevealed even to Joshua.

The principle at work here is that *faith does not preclude duty*. The Lord Jesus taught His disciples to pray for daily provision (Matt. 6:11; Luke 11:3). That's faith. But Paul rebukes any who "provide not for his own, and especially for those of his own house." That's duty. Paul adds that one who neglects to provide for his own has "denied the faith, and is worse than an infidel" (1 Tim. 5:8). That is, if you fail to perform your duty, you may as well have denied your faith. The instruction in Proverbs 3:5 to "trust in the Lord" doesn't permit you to be negligent or careless of your responsibilities. As Oliver Cromwell advised his troops, "Trust in God and keep your powder dry."

Entering Jericho

Having been commissioned by Joshua, the two spies set out to gather information on the city of Jericho.

> And they went, and came into a harlot's house, named Rahab, and lodged there. And it was told the king of Jericho, saying, Behold, there came men in hither to night of the children of Israel to search out the country. And the king of Jericho sent unto Rahab, saying, Bring forth the men that are come to thee, which are entered into thine house: for they be come to search out all the country (Josh. 2:1*b*–3).

One of the characteristics of the narrative of Joshua is his frustrating tendency to understatement. Joshua doesn't give nearly as much information as I'd like to have about many of the events he records. An adventure novelist would have given much more detailed descriptions of the movement of the spies. Dozens of questions remain unanswered. How did the men manage to cross the Jordan River? What covert tactics did they use to cross the open space between the river and the city? What kind of cover story did they use to enter the city? Did they disguise themselves as Canaanites, or merchants, or travelers? How did they plan to gather information? How did they expect to exit the city and return to Joshua with their report? Did they have an emergency response team ready to rescue them if they should be captured? My curiosity remains unsatisfied. All we are told is that "they went."

Lodging with Rahab

The first detail we're given is that they entered "a harlot's house, named Rahab, and lodged there." Different commentators have tried to make Rahab's occupation more palatable than this reading implies. Some have suggested that Rahab was really an innkeeper because the men found lodging there. But there is no getting around the meaning of the Hebrew word *zanah*—"to commit illicit sexual intercourse." As much as we might wish to protect Rahab's honor, the biblical text repeatedly refers to her by a word correctly rendered by the KJV as "harlot" and by the NIV as "prostitute."

While her house may have served as an inn, it was known to be a brothel, and Rahab was a prostitute. Rahab's occupation may have been respectable in the pagan culture of Canaan and may even have been honorable as a part of the practice of their religion. But Joshua does not flinch from describing her with a word carrying the strongest negative connotations to the Hebrew reader. In fact, the Bible seems almost to emphasize it. Of the eight times Rahab is mentioned in Scripture, she is described as "the harlot" five times (Josh. 2:1; 6:17, 25; Heb. 11:31; and James 2:25).[20]

Why would the spies seek refuge in such a disreputable place? I can think of at least two practical reasons. Staying at a brothel would provide an inconspicuous cover for the spies. Strangers going in and out at all hours would not look suspicious. Besides, it is quite possible that the inhabitants of Jericho would know enough about the character of the Israelites camped across the river to know that engaging in prostitution was forbidden by Hebrew law. If so, they would not expect to find Israelite spies there. Second, such a place would be a clearinghouse of information. Much like the hotel/saloon of the American Wild West, it would be an ideal location to gauge the mood of the community by simply listening to the unguarded conversations of locals and travelers alike.

There is a more important reason for the spies to have been in Rahab's house that isn't revealed until the story unfolds. The spies' contact with Rahab was a divine appointment. *God directed the spies to Rahab's home because God intended to save Rahab.* Why did God plan to rescue this harlot? Certainly not because she was the most honorable person in Jericho. Both her reputation and her behavior in this instance indicate that she was not personally righteous. Some argue that it is because God foresaw her faith, as infantile as it would prove to be. That is a possible interpretation, but it isn't clearly indicated in the text. The truth is that God spared Rahab for the same reason he saved me—*He delights to show grace to the undeserving.* I'll say more about this as the story develops. The point here is that God directed the spies to seek refuge in an unexpected place and to receive help from an unlikely person because God had plans for Rahab.

Hiding from the King

The camp of Israel, estimated to be about two million strong, would have been impossible to hide. Their exploits, intentions, and location were known by the Canaanites. Surely the Canaanites wouldn't ignore them. They'd have the camp under constant surveillance, making it very difficult for even two men to slip out of camp and enter Jericho unobserved. A generation earlier twelve spies had managed to enter Canaan and travel throughout the land for forty days, returning with specific information about the land and its inhabitants without ever having been detected. For all their attempts at secrecy implied by the designation "spies," Joshua tells us that the two Israelites who entered

---

[20] Rahab is mentioned without the epithet "harlot" in Joshua 2:3 and 6:23 and in Matthew 1:5, where her name is spelled "Rachab" in the KJV. Uses of the name "Rahab" in Psalms 87:4, 89:10, and Isaiah 51:9 are generally interpreted to be figurative references to Egypt.

Jericho were immediately forced into hiding. Apparently, they were spotted entering the city, were identified as Israelites, and were followed to Rahab's house. They'd been discovered and their mission compromised on their first day out! Such failure must have been demoralizing as they wondered, "Why would God have allowed this?" and "How will God get us out of this?"

The actions of the king of Jericho were predictable and parallel Satan's activity today. Rahab confessed to the spies that "your terror is fallen upon us" (Josh. 2:9). Such fear motivated the king to be alert to any threat. Likewise, Satan dreads God's pronouncement of his sure defeat. In desperation, he tries to thwart God's intentions and disrupt God's program by doing everything he can to trap individual servants of God (1 Pet. 5:8). The alertness of the king of Jericho also illustrates the fact that the wicked tend to be much more vigilant in protecting their interests than the righteous are. The world vigorously opposes anything that hints of legislative restriction on their libertine practices (i.e., abortion rights supporters and homosexual activists). They even label personal criticism "violent speech" and "hate crimes." Christians have gradually adopted much of the world's way of thinking. Several studies conducted in the last few years have concluded that there is little or no distinction between the lifestyle and attitudes of professing evangelical Christians and those of their unbelieving neighbors. The church at large has adopted the world's lifestyle because we haven't been vigilant against the subtle influence of the enemy.

The watch posted by the king of Jericho proved to be effective. They spotted the spies, tracked them to their hiding place, and dispatched officials to arrest them. The fact that they failed reminds us that "except the Lord keep the city, the watchman waketh but in vain" (Ps. 127:1). Despite the vigilance of the enemy, God was still in control of the situation.

Receiving Aid

I wonder what thoughts ran through the minds of the spies when they heard the voices of the officers at the door? Their lives were in danger! They had failed their commander! They had accepted a dangerous assignment, and look where it had gotten them! They must prepare to defend themselves! Rahab's actions must have come as a great surprise because *Rahab's help was unexpected.*

> And the woman took the two men, and hid them, and said thus, There came men unto me, but I wist not whence they were: and it came to pass about the

> time of shutting of the gate, when it was dark, that the men went out: whither the men went I wot not: pursue after them quickly; for ye shall overtake them. But she had brought them up to the roof of the house, and hid them with the stalks of flax, which she had laid in order upon the roof. And the men pursued after them the way to Jordan unto the fords: and as soon as they which pursued after them were gone out, they shut the gate (Josh. 2:4–7).

It is possible that Rahab and the two spies had talked enough that she knew their identities, but I don't think it is very likely that they would have revealed their purpose in Jericho voluntarily. There isn't any clear indication in the narrative that Rahab knew who the men were before the king's men came to the door. Either way, she made a quick decision that altered her destiny. Hebrews 11:31 says that Rahab had welcomed them in peace. The spies must have been greatly encouraged. They had not only found an unexpected ally but also had seen evidence of God's direction.

To protect the spies, Rahab hid them[21] under the stalks of flax she had left to dry on the roof. Some have suggested that the presence of the flax indicated a change of profession—Rahab may have been a prostitute at one time, but she was now a merchant. That seems to be at best a stretch since she is never called anything other than a harlot. It is more likely that in Canaan's society even prostitutes ran "legitimate" businesses on the side. It is interesting, however, that it would be flax under which Rahab chose to hide the spies. Flax is the source of linen. The garments worn by the priests of Israel were to be made of fine linen (Exod. 28:5, etc.) because linen garments were symbolic of covering of righteousness. The spies' being hidden from destruction by the flax illustrates the believer's protection from judgment by being covered in the righteousness of Christ.

Rahab helped the spies in defiance of the king of Jericho. She was willing to betray her country for the sake of the spies. While at first glance it may look as though she helped them just to save her skin, you'll see that she accepted grave personal risk for the sake of the two Israelites. One provision of Hammurabi's Code specified, "If felons are banded together in an ale-wife's [prostitute's or innkeeper's] house and she has not haled [them] to the palace, that ale-wife shall be put to death."[22]

It would have seemed far safer to turn the spies over to the king—unless you factor in the power of God.

---

[21] The KJV follows the LXX rather than the Hebrew for this word. The Hebrew uses a singular suffix, "him," while the LXX supplies the plural, "them." Either the translators of the LXX edited the text to fit the context, or they had access to a different Hebrew source.

[22] S. R. Driver and J. C. Miles, *The Babylonian Laws* (Oxford: Clarendon, 1956), 2:45, cited by Madvig, p. 260.

Rahab's defiance of the king is the first indication of her repentance. She was turning her back on her entire life—her city, her livelihood, her people—to identify with the invading army. But more than that, Rahab was cutting ties to her gods and the enemies of the one true God, refusing to join them against God's people. *The sudden and total change of allegiance demonstrated by Rahab is precisely the repentance demanded by Christ Jesus*: "If any man come to me, and hate not his father, and mother, and wife, and children, and brethren, and sisters, yea, and his own life also, he cannot be my disciple" (Luke 14:26).

With that said, it is important to note that *Rahab's lie was unjustifiable*. She told the officers who came to her house that the spies had left when in fact they were hidden on the roof. Some have argued that this incident teaches that lying is acceptable for the protection of life. While that argument may have some merit, it would seem to conflict with the words of Paul in Romans 3:8—"And not rather, (as we be slanderously reported, and as some affirm that we say,) Let us do evil, that good may come? whose damnation is just." Such an interpretation also seems perilously similar to that of the Jesuits who believe that any means are justifiable if the desired end is worthy. If we aren't careful, we'll use this event to argue for situational ethics—defining "good" and "evil" relatively on the basis of circumstances. Rahab may have been ignorant of God's law, and her heathen background may mitigate her responsibility. But her ignorance does not excuse her. A lie is still a lie.

Furthermore, *Rahab's lie was unnecessary*. Assuming that Rahab had to lie to protect the spies leaves God out of our thinking. Had she remained silent, or even revealed their presence, couldn't God have protected them? On a later occasion, God enabled one man to kill six hundred enemy soldiers with an ox goad (Judg. 3:31). Later yet, another man killed a thousand enemy soldiers with only an animal bone for a weapon (Judg. 15:15). I have no doubt that God could have done something similar in this case. But Rahab's lie demonstrated an immature faith. God honored her faith in His ultimate victory, even though she doubted His ability to protect the spies. The fact that God used her conduct does not vindicate her. A lie is always wrong, even when God uses the lie to bring about that which He intended. God often uses the unrighteous acts of men to accomplish His purposes. Surely we would not suggest that Judah's illicit relationship with Tamar was justified because the son she bore them continued the line to Christ. Neither would we argue that Jacob's sons were justified in selling their brother Joseph into slavery on the ground that "God meant it unto good" (Gen. 50:20). There will be many times in your life that you will not understand why God uses the evil acts of men and women to accomplish His purposes, but you can take comfort in the knowledge that He does so.

Righteous motives never justify wrong actions. Our flesh can cause us to do wrong even when we are trying to do good (Rom. 7:14–21). God has seen fit to record this incident, preserving the lives of the spies by means of Rahab's lie so that we can learn from it. God did not save Rahab because she was good any more than He extends grace to you and me because we deserve it. Isaiah declares, "But we are all as an unclean thing, and all our righteousnesses are as filthy rags; and we all do fade as a leaf; and our iniquities, like the wind, have taken us away." In Romans 3:10–23, Paul reiterates this truth:

> As it is written, There is none righteous, no not one: there is none that understandeth, there is none that seeketh after God. They are all gone out of the way, they are together become unprofitable; there is none that doeth good, no, not one. Their throat is an open sepulchre; with their tongues they have used deceit; the poison of asps is under their lips: whose mouth is full of cursing and bitterness: their feet are swift to shed blood: destruction and misery are in their ways: and the way of peace have they not known: there is no fear of God before their eyes. Now we know that what things soever the law saith, it saith to them who are under the law: that every mouth may be stopped, and all the world may become guilty before God. Therefore by the deeds of the law there shall no flesh be justified in his sight: for by the law is the knowledge of sin. But now the righteousness of God without the law is manifested, being witnessed by the law and the prophets; even the righteousness of God which is by faith of Jesus Christ unto all and upon all them that believe: for there is no difference: for all have sinned, and come short of the glory of God.

We are justified not on the ground of our goodness but in spite of our wickedness. We're justified solely by the grace of God. Paul immediately adds, "Being justified freely by his grace through the redemption that is in Christ Jesus" (Rom. 3:24).

Both the behavior of Rahab and the plight of the spies teach us that we must pray, "Lead us not into temptation, but deliver us from evil" (Matt. 6:13; Luke 11:4). We have to pray earnestly that God will keep us from situations where we're tempted to rationalize evil by our good intentions. We also have to pray diligently for protection from the enemy of our souls, who seeks to destroy us in order to frustrate God's purposes.

> Be sober, be vigilant; because your adversary the devil, as a roaring lion, walketh about, seeking whom he may devour: whom resist steadfast in the faith, knowing that the same afflictions are accomplished in your brethren that are in the world. But the God of all grace, who hath called us unto his eternal glory by Christ Jesus, after that ye have suffered a while, make you perfect, stablish, strengthen, settle you. To him be glory and dominion for ever and ever. Amen (1 Pet. 5:8–11).

6
Rahab's Faith

Joshua 2:8–11

When George W. Bush and Tony Blair presented their case for going to war in Iraq, one of the reasons they gave to justify the war was that we would be liberating an oppressed people. They told us that the Iraqi people would thank us for removing a vicious, repressive regime. In late winter of 2003 as the armies moved through Iraq in the first weeks of the war, reporters and observers frequently asked, "Where is the Iraqi celebration? We see no evidence of rejoicing at our presence." The standard rejoinder was, "They're afraid. Once Saddam is removed, you'll see rejoicing." Our leaders anticipated an initially cautious response—Iraqi citizens wanted the Americans to come, but they wanted to be sure we would be victorious before declaring their support. If we were to fail, Saddam's reprisals would be terrible.

We understand that response. We would have found it remarkably courageous, maybe even foolish, for Iraqi citizens to voluntarily offer our soldiers support, lodging, and provision before the conflict ever started—before we were even committed to entering Iraq. When Israel was camped across the Jordan River, Rahab not only admitted the two Hebrew spies but also hid them and deceived the soldiers of her own king. She actually committed herself to forsake her people and become an Israelite. Rahab's actions took a significant measure of both courage and faith.

Rahab's Perspective

Facing Imminent Destruction

Consider Rahab's situation. She is a woman who is identified as a harlot. She runs a brothel, which apparently serves as an inn, there in the city of Jericho. We will find that her establishment is located on the wall, which becomes important later in the story. The two spies Joshua had sent have come into town looking for a place to hide while they gather information. As we saw in the last chapter, they were discovered on their first day out, which did not bode well for the success of their mission. The king's men have spotted them coming into the city, even identifying the place where they were staying. Jericho's department of "homeland security" was doing its job.

> But she had brought them up to the roof of the house, and hid them with the stalks of flax, which she had laid in order upon the roof. And the men pursued after them the way to Jordan unto the fords: and as soon as they which pursued after them were gone out, they shut the gate. And before they were laid down, she came up unto them upon the roof (Josh. 2:6–8).

When the king's men came to find the spies, Rahab surprised the spies by hiding them. As far as she was concerned, she was facing imminent destruction. Keep in mind that Israel was probably better described as a *camp* than as an *army*. Their military experience was limited and their weapons were simple. They were essentially nomads traveling with their women and children. They were well organized and numerous and would have been an impressive sight, but they weren't well trained or well equipped. They were still separated from the Canaanites by the flooded Jordan River, beyond which Israel's camp was pitched. The river was a formidable obstacle, but the people of Canaan obviously didn't think it was enough. I mean, it wasn't as big as the Red Sea, and they had already heard that story.

Permitted an Unexpected Opportunity

Rahab was convinced that she and her people faced immediate, inevitable destruction. Here she was, like the rest of the inhabitants of Canaan, for all practical purposes in the throes of panic and despair. Suddenly, unexpectedly, into her house come two enemy spies. How would you react in similar circumstances? Rahab had options. She could have seen this as a cause for even greater fear—"The enemy is already among us!" She could have interpreted this as an opportunity to help her people and at least postpone the imminent destruction that would come from Israel—"I have to report this; these men must be captured!" She did neither. She decided that the Israelite spies were the only two people who could offer her any real hope. She recognized that she had been given an incredible opportunity to ask for help.

As we've seen illustrated by events in Iraq, Rahab's reaction wasn't the most likely response from a human perspective. If we look at it from God's point of view, we see His hand at work providentially. God sent these men exactly where He wanted them to go. *God directed these men to Rahab's house because they needed to deal with a woman God intended to save.* God had plans for this woman. Why else would the spies show up *there*? God had brought Israel to this particular place to cross the river so that Jericho would be the first city they would encounter. He sent the spies into *this* city to investigate the situation, and they found their way to *this* particular home when they first arrived. God's providence was directing their steps. The evidence is strong that God was working things out in such a way that "the purpose of God according to election might stand" (Rom. 9:11).

On the other hand, we find from her human perspective that *God brought the spies to her house because she desperately wanted help*. The truth is that not everybody in Jericho was responding the way Rahab did. She seems to be unique. Everybody else was preparing fortifications, readying their defense, and trembling in fear of the coming destruction. But here is the key person in Jericho that God was going to save, and she was interested in being saved. What we see going on here is a real-life illustration of God demonstrating the relationship between the twin truths of election and free will. God was working according to His purposes; Rahab was responding in faith.

This also illustrates something on a much larger scale. In Genesis 12 we have another example of God's sovereign election working with free will: God's calling of Abram.

> Now the Lord had said unto Abram, Get thee out of thy country, and from thy kindred, and from thy father's house, unto a land that I will shew thee: and I will make of thee a great nation, and I will bless thee, and make thy name great; and thou shalt be a blessing: and I will bless them that bless thee, and curse him that curseth [or *despises*—different Hebrew word] thee: and in thee shall all families of the earth be blessed (Gen. 12:1–3).

God was separating Abram (Abraham)[23] from his people, similar to how He was about to separate Rahab from her people. God was going to make of Abraham a great nation, but that wasn't His whole purpose in blessing

[23] The name *Abram* means "great father." Later, God changed his name to *Abraham*, meaning "father of many nations," reflecting subsequent expansions on this promise.

Abraham. His purpose for creating the nation of Israel was that they could in turn be God's tool to minister to all the nations. Israel lost sight of that for several generations, but that didn't change God's purpose. This purpose is ultimately fulfilled in the person of Jesus Christ, but we also see that God intended Israel to perform the role of the mediator between God and the Gentile nations. Even in the end times period called the Tribulation God has promised a band of 144,000 "sealed witnesses"—Israelites who will preach the gospel of Christ to the nations (Rev. 7:3–8). Under their ministry an innumerable multitude from "all nations, and kindreds, and people, and tongues" will be saved during that terrible time (7:9).

Finding Impartial Grace

What we see being played out in the little household of Rahab is a story that illustrates God's gracious calling of the Gentiles. We have seen this in small ways in earlier events. God used Tamar, whose nationality is unidentified, and her illicit relationship with Judah to bring a son named Pharez (Perez), who would continue the line to Christ (Gen. 38:13–29). Some of the Egyptians came with Israel in the Exodus and became part of Israel's national identity. Some have suggested that Caleb, called a "prince in Judah," may have been born an Edomite.[24]

In Rahab we have a representative of the Canaanites, being dealt with mercifully. Why is this especially significant? The Canaanites, and their various tribal groups (Gen. 10:15–18), were a people upon whom God, through Noah, had pronounced a curse (Gen. 9:25–27). Despite the curse, God had given the Canaanites ample opportunity to know the truth. Over five hundred years prior to the events of Joshua 2, God had sent Abraham to live and minister in the region. Melchizedek was ministering there during Abraham's lifetime (Gen. 14:18). The Canaanites also had the testimony of Isaac and Jacob, but they continued to reject God. God pulled Israel out of the region to spend over four hundred years in Egypt, allowing the Canaanites to go their own way. By Joshua's day, Israel and the Canaanites had reached the point in history at which God said, in effect, "OK, the wickedness of the Canaanites

---

[24] Genesis 36:10–11 identifies a man named Kenaz as the grandson of Esau. Esau was also called Edom, and his descendents came to be called Edomites. Caleb is identified in Numbers 32:12 as "the son of Jephunneh the Kenezite," and "Kenezite" means "descendant of Kenaz." In Joshua 15:17 and in Judges 1:13 and 3:9 the name Kenaz is associated with Caleb either as his father or brother—the grammatical construction would permit either. If Kenaz was Caleb's brother, it would represent a tradition of passing on a family name. If those verses mean "father," it is a reference to a progenitor since Numbers 32 says Caleb's immediate father was Jephunneh. References to progenitors are common in the Old Testament. It is possible, but far from certain, that the purpose of this repeated identification of Kenaz as Caleb's forebear is intended to indicate descent from Esau.

is now full; not only is it time for Me to fulfill My promise and give Israel the land, but it is also time for Me to remove My mercy and grace from the Canaanites and destroy them for their continued rejection" (Deut. 9:4–5).

The Canaanite people had been cursed for rejecting God and were condemned to destruction. The Israelites had been forbidden to intermarry with the heathen nations (Lev. 21:14)[25], particularly specific tribes of Canaanites—the Hittites, the Girgashites, the Amorites, the Canaanites, the Perizzites, the Hivites, and the Jebusites, (Deut. 7:1–3)—that included the people from whom Rahab descended (the Amorites). I believe that this passage in Joshua (with Josh. 6:25), as well as other examples in the Old Testament,[26] proves something very important: *The issue of intermarriage was never the "race" of the spouse*—it was always *unbelief.*

I realize that last sentence probably raised some eyebrows (and maybe some hackles). I don't intend to make this study in Joshua a treatise in support of interracial marriage, but I do want to briefly explain what I believe the Bible teaches on this subject.

When Solomon took "strange wives" (1 Kings 11:7), aside from the obvious sin of polygamy, God took him to task not for "interracial"[27] marriage but

[25] This verse also forbids taking a wife who is not a virgin, especially a harlot (see also Lev. 21:7).

[26] During the time of the judges, a Moabitess named Ruth is converted. With the obvious blessing of God, she marries Boaz from the tribe of Judah and produces a son who is one of David's (and Christ's) forebears. Later, an Ammonitess named Naamah becomes one of Solomon's wives. Despite the fact that she led Solomon into worshiping Milcom (Molech?), and Solomon provoked God's displeasure for his disobedience, she bore a son named Rehoboam, also next in line for both the throne of Israel and the posterity of Christ.

[27] I've used quotation marks around words that imply division of humanity into "races" because I believe such terminology is based on a fundamental misunderstanding of humanity. I'd even suggest that Christians should abandon words like *interracial* because they represent theological error. Many Christians seem unwilling to consider the significance of the fact that God is "color blind." God made Adam, from whom He formed Eve, and every human who has ever lived descended from that couple. Sometime later, God narrowed the gene pool by destroying most of the population and sparing only Noah, his wife, and their three sons and daughters-in-law. All three of Noah's sons became fathers of diverse people groups—there are dark-skinned peoples descended from each one. Granted, the Hamites were predominantly dark skinned, the Shemites were predominantly middle-brown or olive skinned, and the Japhethites were predominantly light skinned, but none were exclusively so.

Skin color has been the identifying mark we've used for a long time to distinguish "races," but such a practice was given an aura of respectability by the theories of Charles Darwin. He gave people a scientific sounding excuse for "racism" by theorizing that different "races" came from different sets of prototypical parents that evolved in different ways and at different rates. Darwin, and others who followed him, suggested that the black "race" developed from a pair of humanoid parents who evolved in central Africa. They called that group Negroid. They said that people with Oriental features descended from a pair of parents who because those women brought their false gods with them and Solomon set up places for them to worship their false gods (11:1–8). Israel's intermarriage with foreigners when they returned to Israel to rebuild Jerusalem and the temple after the Exile was condemned because they were worshiping the false gods of their wives (Ezra 9:10ff.). *In both the Old and New Testaments, intermarriage is always forbidden on religious grounds, never on ethnic grounds* (2 Cor. 6:14–16; cf. Acts 17:26; 10:28; 1 Cor 7:39).

I suspect that we talk so little about racism and preach against it so rarely for two reasons. First, we're afraid of the subject because advocates of the "social gospel" preached against racism. Since we don't want people to think we've abandoned the gospel of salvation from sin through faith in Christ, we are tempted to skirt the issue. Second, talking about racism makes us uncomfortable because bigotry is a universal human tendency. We don't like to think about it or talk about it; our congregations don't want to hear it; so it's easy to leave the subject alone. But the Scriptures are really pretty clear on this. God created only one human, from whom all of the rest of us descended. Every human being is physically related to every other human being. We are all made of the same stuff. Further, we all answer to God the same way. God is no respecter of persons (Acts 10:34). Differences in the shades of our skin are more *noticeable* than differences in the color of our eyes or hair, but they are no more *significant*.

Numerous arguments have been made for keeping the "races" separate. Some of them are based on creative interpretations of Scripture. I've heard Christians claim that being dark skinned was the curse of God, either when He "marked" Cain or when He cursed Canaan, despite the absence of any statement in Scripture that skin color was in any way associated with either circumstance. Some have suggested that God "made some people black" in connection with some event not mentioned in Scripture. This is actually the doctrine of Mormonism since it is expressly taught in their *Book of Mormon: Another Testament of Jesus Christ* (2 Nephi 5:20–23).[28] People who read this

---

emerged in or around Mongolia—hence the name Mongoloid. They believed that fair-skinned people came from parents who evolved in or around the Caucasus Mountains in Eastern Europe, calling them Caucasians. In this way they suggested that mankind is not unified but made up of three similar yet distinct "races." This conflicts with the clear biblical teaching that we are all of one race (Acts 17:26).

Eventually, philosophers like Friedrich Nietzsche and politicians like Adolph Hitler became convinced that the white "race" was more highly developed, more "evolved," than other "races." Such assumptions were used to justify the extermination of Jews and blacks (and others) as simply the intentional, informed, advancing of the species—the "survival of the fittest" being acted out on purpose rather than being left to chance. It makes perfect sense, if that theory were correct. The problem is, the theory is wrong—it is contrary to God's Word.

[28] Second Nephi 5:20–23 says, "Wherefore, the word of the Lord was fulfilled which he spake unto me, saying that: Inasmuch as they will not hearken unto thy words they shall be

into Scripture don't agree on when it happened, but they agree that "blackness" is associated with the disfavor of God.

Others who are more charitable argue that since the division of the nations was God's purpose and separating peoples was His intent, it seems evident that He used skin color to segregate people. This view has some support on the basis of practical evidence—people are grouped geographically, and tend to group themselves socially, on the basis of skin color. The weakness of this view is that there is no *biblical* evidence for skin color being the basis for the separation of people groups. What the Bible actually says is that God used the confounding of *languages*, not appearances, to scatter the nations (Gen. 11:1–9). You could build a stronger biblical case arguing that it is sinful to learn a foreign language or to marry someone who speaks a different native tongue than to argue for division on the basis of differing physical characteristics. But the fact that at Pentecost God intervened to temporarily undo what He had done at Babel would refute that argument for segregation.

Some have also suggested that we should discourage "interracial" marriage on the ground that such mingling of the "races" will assist the Antichrist in implementing his one-world government. One problem with this view is that it would seem that cross-cultural missions and international business should be discouraged or forbidden on the same ground. Granted, the Antichrist will strive to unite the world with one government, one currency, one language, one religion—essentially one culture. While it is possible that one "race" could be a by-product of his efforts, Scripture seems to indicate otherwise. In Matthew 24:7, a prophecy concerning end times generally understood to refer to the period during which the Antichrist will rule, Jesus said that "nation shall rise against nation." The Greek actually reads, "*ethnos* shall rise against *ethnos.*" The strife will be between political entities, because Jesus also said "and kingdom against kingdom," but the "nation . . . against nation" statement indicates that the kingdom of the Antichrist will be characterized by increasing ethnic *division*, not increasing ethnic *unity*. Further, we can't forget that the Antichrist is called *anti*-Christ because he will *try to counterfeit* by human means on earth what God *will produce* in heaven and in the kingdom. A

---

cut off from the presence of the Lord. And behold, they were cut off from his presence. And he had caused the cursing to come upon them, yea, even a sore cursing, because of their iniquity. For behold, they had hardened their hearts against him, that they had become like unto a flint; wherefore, as they were white, and exceedingly fair and delightsome, that **they might not be enticing unto my people the Lord God did cause a skin of blackness to come upon them**. And thus saith the Lord God: I will cause that **they shall be loathsome unto thy people**, save they shall repent of their iniquities. And **cursed shall be the seed of him that mixeth with their seed for they shall be cursed even with the same cursing**. And the Lord spake it, and it was done."

color-blind church seems to be more a reflection of the kingdom of God than the kingdom of Antichrist.

More common in this debate are those who argue for "racial" division in the church on the basis of the social issues involved. Much of our society still recoils from "interracial" relationships—and the reactions come from all sectors and ethnic groups. Many believers contend that these pressures alone make mingling of skin colors in a marriage relationship inappropriate. I agree that such a marriage would almost certainly be difficult, and in many cases inadvisable. But I could not call it *wrong* for any biblical reason. It seems inconsistent for Bible believers to defend our faith and practice *despite* cultural opposition on virtually any other subject, but we remain segregated *because of* "cultural pressure."

The rescue and assimilation of Rahab illustrates that God is more concerned with our *faith* than with our *ethnicity*. In Joshua 2 we see the faith of Rahab, the Canaanite prostitute. In Joshua 6:25 we will see that she marries into the tribe of Judah. Later, in Matthew 1:5, we find that her husband's name was Salmon and that she, too, was in the line of Christ. The sad truth is that the average Christian parents would be far happier to have their children marry unbelievers of the same "race" than to have their children marry fellow believers of a different ethnicity. We can be grateful that neither Salmon of Judah nor his son Boaz (see Ruth 4:21) had that attitude.

Rahab's Confidence

Rahab had been given a remarkable opportunity, and she acted upon it in confident faith.

> And she said unto the men, I know that the Lord hath given you the land, and that your terror is fallen upon us, and that all the inhabitants of the land faint because of you. For we have heard how the Lord dried up the water of the Red sea for you, when ye came out of Egypt; and what ye did unto the two kings of the Amorites, that were on the other side Jordan, Sihon and Og, whom ye utterly destroyed. And as soon as we had heard these things, our hearts did melt, neither did there remain any more courage in any man, because of you: for the Lord your God, he is God in heaven above, and in earth beneath (Josh. 2:9–11).

Most of what Rahab tells the spies simply describes the mood of the people of Jericho. This was actually the information the spies had come to get. But the first statement in the passage above, "I know that the Lord hath given you the land," and the last, "for the Lord your God, he is God in heaven above and in earth beneath," were Rahab's own profession of faith. She did not attribute those statements to anyone else.

Contrast with Israel's Last Generation

Do you see the interesting pair of contrasts in this passage? When Israel left Egypt, they crossed the Red Sea and moved toward Canaan. When they got there, the people of the land were big and had walled cities, but they were absolutely petrified. The Canaanites were convinced that God was going to destroy them. It was Israel who didn't think it would work. The ones who had crossed the Red Sea and had been victorious over Sihon and Og were the ones who doubted the power and promises of God. The Canaanites had no doubts. Rahab's expression of confident belief was in stark contrast with the fearful unbelief of an entire generation of Israelites who died in the wilderness. Here is a prostitute in Canaan who had more faith in God's ability to give Israel the land than Israel had had. Rahab voiced the same statement of faith Joshua and Caleb had expressed. Is it any wonder that God honored that faith?

Contrast with Canaan's Current Generation

Rahab's faith is also in contrast with the attitude of the rest of the Canaanites. They were all terrified of the destruction they believed was sure to come, but they did not respond in *repentance*. Only Rahab said, "The Lord your God, he is God." This is a broad statement and is the first time in the Old Testament that we see a pagan making such a pronouncement—that God is not just Israel's God. That's an incredible statement from someone coming from the polytheistic background in which Rahab was immersed. The Canaanites worshiped many gods and believed the gods were territorial. Rahab declared that she believed the Lord (*Yahweh*, or Jehovah) is the God of both the heaven above and the earth beneath—He is the God of everything.

Rahab responded differently than the rest of the Canaanites did to the same information, the same message. People today do the same thing, don't they? I'm often amazed at the different ways people respond to the same set of facts—particularly the gospel. But God has told us the reason is that people's hearts are naturally hard. People are sinners who don't want to acknowledge the truth. It is only the grace of God and the work of the Holy Spirit in a person's heart that enable him to see the truth and to respond in faith. The key difference between Rahab's response and that of the rest of the Canaanites was the convicting power of the Holy Spirit bringing her to repentance and to faith.

According to Hebrews 11:1, "Faith is the substance of things hoped for, the evidence of things not seen." The writer defines faith by using contradictory terms: the *substance* of things you *don't* have, the *evidence* of things you *can't* see. As Hebrews 11 progresses, the writer further describes our faith in God as the creator of all things, then begins to summarize the faith of several key historic individuals. It's an impressive list. The author starts by mentioning Abel (v. 4), Enoch (v. 5), Noah (v. 7), Abraham (v. 8ff.), Isaac (v. 20), Jacob (v. 21), Joseph (v. 22), and Moses (v. 23ff.). Then he goes until verse 31 before another name is mentioned. And whose name is it? It's Rahab—"By faith the harlot Rahab perished not with them that believed not, when she had received the spies in peace." This is a clear statement that she believed and others didn't.

Do you know what I find remarkable about Rahab's inclusion in Hebrews 11? It's that Joshua *isn't* there. Was Joshua's faith less? No, Joshua was a great man of faith, one of only two people of his generation who was permitted to enter the land of promise because he believed God. He is lifted up in the Scriptures in ways that few are, as a man of tremendous faith and confidence in the Lord. The remarkable thing about Rahab's faith is that she had so little to base it on. All Israel had more evidence on which to base their faith than did Rahab, and many of them had not believed. God is actually going to use Rahab in a way he never used Joshua because she would be included in the line of Christ.

Rahab's Faith

It is important to see that Hebrews 11:31 says that Rahab proved the genuineness of her faith by her actions. She hid the spies. Had she said, "You know, I really think you guys are going to win this war; as a matter of fact, we're all scared to death; but I really can't afford to risk everything to help you," her "faith" would have been useless (Greek *arge*, translated "dead" in James 2:20). Rahab's profession of faith was verified and validated by her actions. God had really changed her heart; she wasn't just making an empty claim. Her protection of the spies proved that God had changed her heart and that she had chosen to be identified with Him and His people.

We each need to personalize this lesson. Genuine conversion is the result of the regenerating power of the Holy Spirit making each of us a new creature. There is an inevitability about the Spirit's work of regeneration. He enables us to believe (John 3:8; Eph. 2:8–9; Phil. 1:29; Titus 3:5–7). He will begin to cause us to choose to do those things that please God (Phil. 2:13; Heb. 13:20–21;

1 John 2:29). We begin to fear God more than we fear our neighbors. We become willing to put our safety at risk for His sake. He makes us willing to do the right thing because God said it's right, even though it may be painful or costly. That is the kind of conversion that demonstrates the faith James talks about and the faith Rahab exercised. Any claim to "faith" that isn't reflected in a changed life, new loyalties, and altered goals is just as useless as it would have been for Rahab to say, "I believe, but I dare not show you any kindness." Real faith works. If it doesn't work, it isn't faith—it's just wishful thinking.

Rahab hid these spies when they had made no promises. She told the king's men that the spies were gone when she had no evidence that she could trust them, even if they would promise help. But she was desperate. She had no place else to turn. She believed their God was good and powerful, and that was enough. She didn't know the timetable, but she was willing to wait. The spies were going to return to camp and report to Joshua. Joshua would bring the people to the river, and they would cross it. Joshua would then circumcise the army, and they would spend time in camp recovering from the surgery. Then they would begin their strategy of marching around the city for a week. Jericho wouldn't fall for at least two weeks, but Rahab demonstrated that she had placed her absolute trust in the sovereign, holy God to Whom she now realized all would answer.

I wonder how Rahab spent that time before Jericho fell. It must have been tense. She had put everything on the line. She risked her family, at least potentially. As the passage progresses, we'll find that the men offered protection to her family as well, but at this point she had no reason for confidence that her family would join her in her faith or share in any protection she might be offered. She knew that there would be at least some members of her family that she would never see again. Rahab also risked her people, her nation. She was giving them up, in effect saying, "My people are finished because of what your God is going to do; I don't want to share their fate—I want to be with your God." Rahab even risked her life. If the king of Jericho were to discover she had helped these men, what do you think he would do? Don't you think he'd execute her? She put her life in the hands of two men she'd never seen before, and might never see again. She had no way to force them to keep any promise they might make. She risked everything and withheld nothing.

Rahab's *faith*, though in some ways meager and relatively uninformed, was *genuine* because its source and object was the one true God (Heb. 12:2). My son's pet is not a dog because it barks—it barks because it's a dog. Likewise, *Rahab's actions did not make her a convert—they proved that she was a new creature.*

I can't help but imagine that in future years Rahab would repeat this story to her children, her grandchildren, maybe even her great-grandchildren. Surely she retold these events repeatedly to her son Boaz when he was young. Can you hear the story?

"I was a wretched sinner, living as a harlot in the land of Jericho. Our people were about to be destroyed by the people of God, when God brought to my door—*my door*, can you believe it?—two men. They were the only two men who could help me. While we were talking, the king's soldiers came to the door. I didn't know what to do. I was terrified! So I quickly hid them on the roof and told the soldiers they were gone. Then I asked them for help. I can't even imagine why I would have done such a thing had God not been working in my heart. *God saved me*—He changed me forever and gave me a new life!"

Don't you think she told that story? It's a story I'd tell. I'd want my children to know what God did for me. If you read through the book of Judges, you'll find periods in which the people trusted God and He blessed them, followed by periods in which they didn't trust God and He punished them. We're told the reason for Israel's departure from God was that parents failed to tell their children and grandchildren what God had done (Judg. 2:10). Generations would grow up who didn't know how God had saved them. The people forgot the stories of faith and of the victories of God, so they didn't care. God help us never to forget what He has done for us!

7

Rahab's Protection

Joshua 2:12–24

In my undergraduate days I attended a Christian college that was in its infancy. The campus was still under development and the college was using some elementary and high school facilities for classroom space. Because the school was young and the student body was small, the administration was still formulating and modifying the regulations that would govern campus life. Many of the rules were based on the administration's taking seriously their responsibility to provide a safe environment for the students under their care. One regulation that was imposed for the students' protection was a rule that forbade any physical contact between members of the opposite sex. Students were warned about the dangers of fleshly temptation and were admonished to scrupulously maintain moral purity. A sliding scale of punishments would be imposed for violations, depending on the nature and seriousness of the infraction.

One day, a group of six or eight young men and women on the way to class came to a place on campus where they had to walk across a railroad track. As they stepped over the rails, one of the girls tripped and fell, scraping her knees badly. The two or three young men in the group just stood there, not sure what to do. As the boys watched, the other girls in the group helped the injured girl to her feet and gathered up her books, and one of them escorted her to the nurse's office for treatment.

By early the next morning, word of the incident had reached the administration's ears. The young men were called in and asked why they had failed to help the girl who was hurt. They explained that to help her up they would have had to touch her, and they didn't want to get in trouble for violating the rule forbidding physical contact. That day, the dean addressed the student body to explain something that young adults should have learned long before—in some circumstances a higher order of law takes precedence over specific rules. He asked the male students, "If a girl were about to be run over by a bus, would you pull her to safety? Or if she were drowning, would you pull her out of the water and perform CPR?" It should be obvious that in such cases, the protection of or care for someone who is in danger or who has been injured is more important than refraining from touching a member of the opposite sex.

In any complex legal system you will find circumstances in which specific regulations come into conflict with general principles. People faced with such conflicts have to rely on a sort of hierarchy of laws. Some rules must be understood to take precedence over others. Some of the laws in the Bible are absolute because they are based on the *holiness* of God. Such laws include prohibitions against worshiping idols, against murder, against adultery, and so on. Other laws in the Bible are based on the *sovereignty* of God—His divine right to make the rules. God sometimes permits exceptions to these regulations in circumstances in which they come into conflict with the absolute standards.

In God's regulations for Israel's worship, one of the rules was that the priests were to prepare loaves of bread for presentation on a table in the tabernacle (Exod. 25:30). This "shewbread" was dedicated to the Lord—to eat it would be sacrilege. But in 1 Samuel 21 we read of an incident in which David and his men were running from King Saul and came to the tabernacle weary and hungry. The only food available was the showbread. The priests gave it to David and his men (replacing it later with fresh loaves). The Lord Jesus defended the priests for feeding David (Matt. 12:3–4), citing this incident in defense of His disciples' plucking grain and eating it on the Sabbath. His point was that protection of life takes precedence over specific regulations—plucking a few handfuls of grain on the Sabbath didn't violate the sanctity of the day any more than using the showbread to feed some hungry men in God's service violated the sanctity of the tabernacle. I happen to believe that Hebrews 10:25—"Not forsaking the assembling of ourselves together"— means that believers ought to gather regularly for corporate worship—that is, we ought to attend church. I also believe that there are some circumstances in which we should *not* go to church—for instance, if our children are sick, we should stay home and take care of them.

In Joshua 2:12–13 Rahab asked the spies who had come to her house to make a covenant with her. Unwittingly, she put the spies in the awkward position of having to decide whether honoring her request would conflict with the instructions they had been given by God through Moses. Moses had said,

> And when the Lord thy God shall deliver them before thee; thou shalt smite them, and utterly destroy them; thou shalt make no covenant with them, nor show mercy unto them (Deut. 7:2).

The spies had to decide on the spot whether promising protection to Rahab and her family conflicted with the general instructions given for the conquest of the land. Would sparing Rahab violate Israel's mandate to destroy the inhabitants of the land?

Rahab's Request

Asking for Mercy

Immediately on the heels of her profession of faith in the God of Israel, Rahab asked the spies to make her a promise.

> Now therefore, I pray you, swear unto me by the Lord, since I have showed you kindness, that ye will also show kindness unto my father's house, and give me a true token: and that ye will save alive my father, and my mother, and my brethren, and my sisters, and all that they have, and deliver our lives from death (Josh. 2:12–13).

Before she even told the spies what she wanted, she invoked the name of Israel's God, *Yahweh* (Jehovah). Rahab correctly assumed that any oath these men would make in the name of *Yahweh* could be trusted—that they would consider themselves honor-bound to keep their word. This is another subtle verification of Rahab's faith. She was willing to take the word of men who would swear "by the Lord."

What was Rahab's request? She could have asked for payment, but she didn't. She could have offered to guide them to a place of safety if they would take her with them when they made their escape, but she didn't. Essentially, she asked them to reciprocate the "kindness" she had shown them. The Hebrew *hesed* (often rendered "love" in the NASB and the NIV, or "lovingkindness" in the KJV) communicates the ideas of loyalty and love. She had been more than "friendly." She had saved their lives at great risk to her own. So she asked them to promise to spare the lives of all in her father's household: her parents, her siblings, and "all that they have" (or "all who belong to them"). She included herself only by implication when she concluded by asking them to "deliver **our** lives from death." She didn't leave with the spies because she had others in Jericho she wanted to rescue.

Receiving a Promise

The spies don't seem to have hesitated. They agreed to what we would call a provisional covenant.

> And the men answered her, Our life for yours, if ye utter not this our business. And it shall be, when the Lord hath given us the land, that we will deal kindly and truly with thee (Josh. 2:14).

The spies promised to protect Rahab and her father's household if they would meet and maintain certain conditions. Rahab and her family ("ye" is plural) must maintain silence concerning the spies and their mission. Essentially, if Rahab would demonstrate the genuineness of her faith under pressure for an indefinite period, they would honor her faith in kind. Rahab's recruiting her family to her faith while keeping any word of the spies' mission from reaching the authorities in Jericho would demonstrate both her loyalty to God and her love for God's people. She would be linking her destiny to Israel's and proving her confidence in God.

The fact that they made this promise provides two insights into the character of the spies and of Israel. First, Joshua's leadership was not tyrannical and his ego was not fragile. These spies were apparently men of some prominence in Israel. Joshua had obviously given them a great deal of discretionary authority in the field. They would have to exercise significant influence over Joshua and the people of Israel to be able to guarantee the safety of anyone in the city of Jericho when it would come under attack. Second, this promise indicated that the Israelites were not the bloodthirsty barbarians their critics have sometimes described. They clearly understood that the command of Deuteronomy 7:2 to destroy the Canaanites without showing them any mercy was to be interpreted in light of the greater mandate against idolatry cited as the general principle on which the specific command was based:

> For they will turn away thy son from following me, that they may serve other gods. . . . For thou art a holy people unto the Lord thy God (Deut. 7:4*a*, 6*a*).

When Rahab voluntarily identified herself with Israel and Israel's God, eagerly pledging to forsake her people and their religion, she was no longer under the ban of judgment. She was eligible for their protection, and even participation in their blessing. That is why the spies were willing to make a conditional covenant—equally binding on both sides. As she did, they would do. If she kept her part of the promise, she would live; but if she reneged on her part of the promise, she would die. Likewise, if the spies failed to keep their word to her, they would pay with their lives. Rahab wasn't converted or saved by her eventual obedience. Hebrews 11:31 indicates that she was saved by faith from the start, demonstrated by having "received the spies in peace." She wasn't saved because of her actions, but *her faith was made visible to observers by her obedience.*

Rahab's Preservation

Acting in Faith

Once the spies had given Rahab their promise of protection, Rahab helped them escape the city.

> Then she let them down by a cord through the window: for her house was upon the town wall, and she dwelt upon the wall. And she said unto them, Get you to the mountain, lest the pursuers meet you; and hide yourselves there three days, until the pursuers be returned: and afterward may ye go your way (Josh. 2:15–16).

We see in this passage that Rahab's house was on the wall. I'll say more about this in chapter 12 when we consider Israel's assault on Jericho. For now I want you to think about two reasons this fact is important. The first will be seen in the manner in which Jericho eventually falls. When the walls of Jericho collapse, how would a house on the wall be left standing and the people inside protected from harm? Only by God's intervention. When God brought down the walls of Jericho, God left Rahab's house standing. God left no doubt about whether the spies had been right to offer Rahab protection. Rahab's destiny hadn't really been in the hands of the spies after all—she'd been protected by God all along.[29]

A second reason having a home located on the wall was important was that its location made the spies' escape easier. They wouldn't have to make their way across town and out the gate. I think it is significant that God used human means, including judgment and ingenuity, to effect their escape. The spies did

[29] Marshall Neal makes the following point: "In Joshua 6:17 and 25 the spies are called messengers, the same word as the name of the last book of the Old Testament, Malachi. Also in James 2:25 when he refers to Rahab he calls the spies messengers. . . . Is it possible that these two men were more than mere spies? Joshua sent them across the Jordan as spies but God, in His providence, sends them to Rahab as messengers to announce the coming destruction of Jericho and to provide a means of deliverance for her" ("Accomplishing God's Will Through Means," *Biblical Viewpoint* [Greenville, SC: Bob Jones University], November 1992, p. 8).

not recklessly say, "OK, God, our safety is Your concern," and march straight back to camp in full view of the enemy. Could God have transported them miraculously back to camp? Of course. God sometimes provided miraculous intervention for people's transport. He parted the waters of the Red Sea for Israel to escape Egypt. He parted the waters of the Jordan for Israel to enter Canaan. The Holy Spirit transported Philip miraculously to a place where he could meet and teach an Ethiopian eunuch God intended to save. God could have used miraculous means to get the spies back to camp, but He didn't. He left it to them to manage their own escape. He expected them to use their own resources wisely to accomplish His purposes, but it was still God Who protected them.

The Scriptures teach that God is sovereign over all things, but God has given us certain responsibilities. If you want to raise a garden, you must prepare the soil, plant the seeds, tend the plants, and harvest the vegetables. When you sit down to dinner to eat the produce of your garden, I hope you thank God for what He has given you. You had to work the garden, but it was God Who made the vegetables.

> For he who has fixed the boundaries of our life, has at the same time entrusted us with the care of it, provided us with the means of preserving it, forewarned us of the dangers to which we are exposed, and supplied cautions and remedies, that we may not be overwhelmed unawares. Now, our duty is clear, namely, since the Lord has committed to us the defense of our life,—to defend it; since he offers assistance,—to use it; since he forewarns us of danger,—not to rush on heedless; since he supplies remedies,—not to neglect them.[30]

Receiving Final Instructions

Before departing, the spies gave Rahab two further instructions.

> And the men said unto her, We will be blameless of this thine oath which thou hast made us swear. Behold, when we come into the land, thou shalt bind this line of scarlet thread in the window which thou didst let us down by: and thou shalt bring thy father, and thy mother, and thy brethren, and all thy father's household, home unto thee. And it shall be, that whosoever shall go out of the doors of thy house into the street, his blood shall be upon his head, and we will be guiltless: and whosoever shall be with thee in the house, his blood shall be on our head, if any hand be upon him. And if thou utter this our business, then we will be quit of thine oath which thou hast made us to swear (Josh. 2:17–20).

---

[30] John Calvin, *Institutes of the Christian Religion*, Henry Beveridge, trans. (1800), Vol. I, Ch. 17, Sct. 4 (Albany, OR: AGES Software *Comprehensive John Calvin Collection*, Version 2.0, 1996, 1997), p. 248.

She had used a scarlet rope to let them down from her window, and the spies told her to keep the rope in the window. It would serve as a sign to them that she was keeping her word, and it would serve as a marker to Israel for the household they were to spare. The fact that the rope was scarlet was reminiscent of the blood that Israel had put on the doorposts of their homes in Egypt on the night of the death of the firstborn. That night the blood identified the homes of the faithful and protected the firstborn of the family inside. It was symbolic of the blood of Christ. It is the application of Christ's blood to our hearts that cleanses us from sin (1 John 1:7) and makes us acceptable to God (Col. 1:20–22).

Rahab and any family members who chose to identify with her and Israel must remain inside her house. In the battle for the city, they could not guarantee their safety unless they stayed in that house. This, too, had spiritual significance, picturing their separation. Being in the house separated Rahab's family *from* the people with whom they had been associated and separated them *to* God and His people. We must not miss the significance of the two sides of this promise. Not only was there the threat of judgment on any *who were not* in the house but there was also the absolute promise of protection for those *who were* in the house. The spies promised that if anyone so much as laid a hand on any of her family who proved their faith by following the terms of the agreement, the spies would pay with their own lives. Similarly, our being in Christ separates us *from* the world with which we used to be identified and sanctifies us (sets us apart) *to* God (Eph. 2:1–6). The only place of safety for Rahab's family in the coming judgment on Jericho was in the house protected by God, and that safety was guaranteed. Just so, the only place of safety for your soul in the coming judgment on humanity is in Christ, but those in Christ are absolutely secure (Rom. 8:33–34).

Keeping Her Word

Rahab must have realized that it would be hard to remain inside her house and listen to the destruction of her city and her people that would occur right outside her door. But when the spies told her what she must do, Rahab made a final statement of her faith, indicating her repudiation of everything that had been her life up until now.

> And she said, According unto your words, so be it. And she sent them away, and they departed: and she bound the scarlet line in the window. And they went, and came unto the mountain, and abode there three days, until the pursuers were returned: and the pursuers sought them throughout all the way, but found them not. So the two men returned, and descended from the mountain, and passed over, and came to Joshua the son of Nun, and told him all things that befell them: and they said unto Joshua, Truly the Lord

> hath delivered into our hands all the land; for even all the inhabitants of the country do faint because of us (Josh. 2:21–24).

Did you notice that the spies took Rahab's advice? She was the one who had suggested they should head into the mountains and stay for three days before making their way back to camp. It could have been a trap. She might have second thoughts after they were gone and turn them in. But the spies were confident enough of Rahab's sincerity and God's sovereignty that they followed her counsel and went to the mountains for three days. After that, they made their escape, which further proved Rahab's intention. She hadn't sold them out. She had kept her word. Is it any wonder that the writer of Hebrews tells us she "perished not with them that believed not" (Heb. 11:31)?

Rahab's Honor

While this is just about the extent of Rahab's story in the Bible, Scripture does tell us a little something of her story after her contact with the spies. As I discussed in the last chapter, and we will see in Joshua 6:25, after the city of Jericho fell, Rahab "[dwelt] in Israel." It isn't until we come to Matthew 1:5 that we find that Rahab didn't just live in Israel in some sort of refugee camp. She married a man named Salmon, who was a leader in the tribe of Judah. She and Salmon had a son named Boaz (Ruth 2:1, etc.), who had a son named Obed, who had a son named Jesse, who had a son named David (Matt. 1:5–6).[31] Rahab becomes one of only four women named in the genealogy of Christ. What a place of honor!

From the divine perspective, this account illustrates that God arranges circumstances providentially to accomplish His will and to produce faith. From the human perspective, we see that God honors faith wherever it is found.

[31] The chronology of the period of the Judges presents a little difficulty. It is generally estimated that the period between the conquest of Canaan and the establishment of the monarchy lasted about 350 years. It is not impossible, but seems unlikely, that these four generations stretched out over the entire time. On the other hand, the events of the book of Judges cannot be easily compressed to the 150 years or so that is thought to be a more likely period spanned by four generations. The answer may be that many of the events of Judges overlapped, and the period may not have been quite as long as is usually thought; or this particular line of descent may have been especially long-lived (Moses lived 120 years) and the sons in the line may have been born in their fathers' old age (David was Jesse's seventh son), or for reasons unrevealed in Scripture there were intervening generations not mentioned in the lineage. Each of these possibilities has its own merits and its own difficulties, the discussion of which goes beyond the scope of our present study.

We also see that genuine faith *works* (James 2:20–26)—that is, genuine faith *produces*. James even used Rahab's actions to prove his point that real faith is seen in the actions it produces. Rahab didn't just give verbal assent to what the spies asked of her. She didn't just say, "I believe you." She tied the scarlet rope in her window, and she did it *immediately*. The spies had told her to tie the rope in the window "when we come into the land" (Josh. 2:18), but Rahab didn't wait until Israel's army showed up at Jericho's gates. She wanted there to be no doubt in the minds of the Israelites that she was committed to this course. This was no half-hearted conversion of convenience, which is really no conversion at all. This was denying herself, taking up her "cross," and following (Matt. 16:24) that proved visibly the reality of the change God had wrought in her heart.

8
Preparing to Cross Jordan

Joshua 3:1–6

When the two spies returned from Jericho, they brought to Joshua an encouraging report: "Truly the Lord hath delivered into our hands all the land; for even all the inhabitants of the country do faint because of us" (Josh. 2:24). In more than one way, the land of Canaan was ripe for the taking. The people of the land were so terrified and demoralized that they were virtually defenseless. The victory that God had promised Israel was within their grasp. There was nothing between Israel and the occupation of the Promised Land . . . except the Jordan River.

I know a young couple who met at Bible college and married shortly after graduation. While students, they both became convinced that the Lord wanted them to serve as missionaries, so they continued their education, focusing on missions training. After they married, they set up housekeeping and got jobs to support themselves while they continued to pray for the Lord to direct them to a particular field of service. Over the course of the next couple of years, as they managed to pay off small college debts, the Lord answered their prayers by pointing them toward a mission board that was recruiting people to go to a particular country. They applied to the board and were accepted as missionary candidates. Because most of their preliminary training had been accomplished in college, they were soon on the way to visit the field. They returned from their brief trip armed with lots of pictures and filled with excitement in anticipation of getting started. The people spoke English where they were going, so they wouldn't need to learn a new language. There was nothing standing between this couple and the work to which the Lord had called them . . . except a little thing called deputation. They still had to gather the necessary funds to get them to the field and to support them in the work. They spent a little over two years visiting churches and presenting their plans before they had finished raising the support they would need to go to the field.

Life is full of obstacles of one kind or another. Like this couple, I imagine Joshua and the people of Israel felt mingled eagerness and dread at the prospect of entering Canaan. At the height of their excitement in anticipation of the fulfillment of God's promise, there were still obstacles to overcome. The first one Joshua had to deal with was the flooded Jordan River. There are lessons for us to learn by how he handled it.

A Major Obstacle

The first thing we see about how Joshua dealt with the Jordan River was that he got an early start.

> And Joshua rose early in the morning; and they removed from Shittim, and came to Jordan, he and all the children of Israel, and lodged there before they passed over (Josh. 3:1).

The fact that Joshua "rose early in the morning" shows that he was diligent in the performance of his duty. There was nothing slothful or indolent about him. He knew that the first item on his agenda for the conquest of Canaan was to get Israel across the Jordan River. He had no clue how to do it, but he knew it had to be done. Further, the fact that Joshua moved the camp of Israel closer to the river shows that he expected God's leading. He didn't wait for God to tell him how to cross the river; he simply anticipated crossing. Having gotten an exciting report about the mental state of the Canaanites, Joshua wasted no time getting started. How different from the way many people deal with problems! Most of us prefer to delay confronting our problems or even to avoid them altogether. Joshua knew there was no going around this obstacle. He immediately started Israel moving toward the challenge.

We aren't told exactly how long Israel had occupied their present camp, but it had probably been at least a few weeks. Remember that they had no permanent homes—everything they owned was in the "camp." Striking camp was not a task undertaken lightly or accomplished easily, particularly if you were moving only a short distance before having to set up camp at another site. Nevertheless, Joshua had Israel evacuate a comfortable camp and move to a new location. It probably took most of a day to break camp and then travel the ten miles from Shittim to the Jordan.

Why did Israel have to stop for three more days with the barrier of the Jordan River in full view? It is one thing to hear about a challenge that must be overcome, but it is quite another to have to stare it in the face. Three days looking at the flooded Jordan River and thinking about the children, livestock, and other property that each person would have to take to the other side proved to Israel their own insufficiency. They were inadequate to the task. How could they conquer Canaan? They couldn't even cross the river! God brought Israel to the end of their own resources before He began to act on their behalf.

This principle is taught repeatedly in the Scriptures. Psalm 107:6 says, "Then they cried unto the Lord in their trouble, and he delivered them out of their distresses." This refrain is repeated almost exactly in verses 13, 19, and 28. In each case, the verse immediately preceding the refrain emphasizes the *inability* of those the Lord redeemed:

> Hungry and thirsty, **their soul fainted in them**. Then they cried unto the Lord in their trouble, and he delivered them out of their distresses (Ps. 107:5–6).
>
> Therefore he brought down their heart with labour; they fell down, and **there was none to help**. Then they cried unto the Lord in their trouble, and he saved them out of their distresses (Ps. 107:12–13).
>
> Their soul abhorreth all manner of meat; and **they draw near unto the gates of death**. Then they cry unto the Lord in their trouble, and he saveth them out of their distresses (Ps. 107:18–19).
>
> **They** reel to and fro, and stagger like a drunken man, and **are at their wit's end**. Then they cry unto the Lord in their trouble, and he bringeth them out of their distresses (Ps. 107:27–28).

A New Way

After three days staring at the impassible Jordan River, Joshua turned Israel's attention from the trouble toward the solution. He told them to look to the ark of the covenant.

> And it came to pass after three days, that the officers went through the host; and they commanded the people, saying, When ye see the ark of the covenant of the Lord your God, and the priests the Levites bearing it, then ye shall remove from your place, and go after it. Yet there shall be a space between

> you and it, about two thousand cubits by measure: come not near unto it, that ye may know the way by which ye must go: for ye have not passed this way heretofore (Josh. 3:2–4).

Israel was about to move into a new region and to follow a path they'd never before walked. But when Joshua told Israel that they hadn't "passed this way" before, he wasn't talking about their move into a *new territory*. He meant they'd be moving by a *different method*. For forty years they'd moved around the wilderness following the fiery cloud with the ark of the covenant in the middle of their ranks. Now a *new order* was required. The ark would go first, and they would follow it.[32]

The Ark Was Significant

The ark is mentioned twenty-one times in Joshua 3 and 4 alone. The reason it was called the ark "of the covenant" is that the stone tablets of the Law were stored inside. God made His covenant with Israel in the Law given at Sinai, so the box (ark) in which the Law was carried became "the ark of the covenant." The Law on the inside of the ark represented the justice of God. However, the ark also had a lid that was called the mercy seat (Exod. 25:17–22). The only reason that Israel, or you and I, can have fellowship with God is that the mercy of God covers the justice of God. In the Septuagint (ancient Greek version of the Old Testament—ca. 150 BC) the Hebrew word *kapporeth*, translated "mercy seat" in Exodus 25, is rendered *hilasterion*. Paul used the same Greek word to refer to Christ in Romans 3:25—

> Whom God hath set forth to be a **propitiation** [*hilasterion*] through faith in his blood, to declare his righteousness for the remission of sins that are past, through the forbearance of God.

As the lid of the ark, the mercy seat, covered Israel's transgressions of the Law given at Sinai, so Christ satisfies the just wrath of God toward our sin and makes fellowship with God possible. Israel had been traveling with the ark for forty years but had merely wandered in the wilderness because of their unwillingness to obey. Now Israel had to follow the ark in obedient faith in order to *leave* the wilderness and move into the Promised Land. Similarly, you and I can move from our lost state in "Egypt" to obediently following Christ only by looking to the Lord and Savior.

---

[32] "The ark was carried in front of the people, not so much to show the road as to make a road by dividing the waters of the Jordan. . . . The Lord, through the medium of the ark, was leading them to Canaan by a way which they had never traversed before, *i.e.* by a miraculous way." Keil and Delitzsch, p. 41.

The Ark Was Symbolic

A second reason for moving the ark to the front of the column of Israel was what it symbolized. Phillip Keller aptly observed, "This was no ordinary taking of territory in the tradition of an army on the attack. This was a mass movement of a people under divine direction."[33] God had promised that Israel would be victorious. He had also told them they must keep the Law. But we know that they were unable to fully obey the Law.

The interrelationship between law and grace can be misunderstood. Today we live in a period often called "the age of grace." Paul's statement that "ye are not under the law, but under grace" (Rom. 6:14) has been interpreted by some to mean that we are no longer obligated to obey God. That is a gross misrepresentation of what Paul meant. In the introductory verses of Romans 6, Paul said,

> What shall we say then? Shall we continue in sin, that grace may abound? God forbid. How shall we, that are dead to sin, live any longer therein? . . . For he that is dead is freed from sin (Rom. 6:1–2, 7).

The *grace* of God doesn't give us the liberty to disregard the *law* of God. Rather, God's grace gives us the desire and ability to obey. Our victory today depends on God's fulfillment of the Law in Christ (Matt. 5:16–19) and His gracious intervention for us in Christ. Putting the ark in front provided an important picture for them and for us. Israel must follow the Law, but God would provide the strength for success.

We have to be careful here. No one is ever saved by obeying the Law of God—if that were the case, the Son of God did not need to become a man and die for our sins. But *Christ* obeyed the Law. God's mercy and grace imputes Christ's perfect righteousness to those who believe on Him. This sets us free from the law of sin and death (Rom. 8:2) and enables us to obey Him by faith (Rom. 9:30–31; cf. 1 John 2:6). We are saved on the basis of Christ's obedience and His blood sacrifice in our place, which God's grace applies to our account through faith. Israel's following the ark into Canaan indicated that they entered the Promised Land led by the Law, which was covered by God's mercy.

The Ark Was Sanctified

A third reason God ordered the ark to the front at this time was to emphasize that it was *sanctified*—it was holy. It wasn't just a little way out in front. It was to lead Israel by a distance of two thousand cubits (about three thousand feet).

[33] W. Phillip Keller, *Joshua: Man of Fearless Faith* (Waco, TX: Word Publishing, 1983), pp. 71–72.

Other than the priests designated to carry it, no one was to approach closer than a little over half a mile. Following at such a distance demonstrated both reverence for God and fear of His immediate presence.

It has become popular for Christians to speak about or to God in such a casual or familiar manner that I'm afraid we're often guilty of irreverence. Does it bother you to hear people refer to God as "the Man upstairs" or "the Big Guy"? It bothers me. I know Hebrews 4:16 says, "Let us therefore come boldly unto the throne of grace," but the verses that precede those words remind us that we can hide nothing from God and that our only hope is the intercession of Jesus Christ, our great High Priest. Because of Christ, we can come "boldly" to God, confident that we will "find grace to help." Yes, God is our Father, and there ought to be a closeness and familiarity between our Father and His children. But we must never come to God irreverently. We must never forget that the place we are encouraged to approach is a *throne*. The God Who occupies that throne is our Creator, the Sovereign Ruler of the universe, the One "with whom we have to do" before Whose eyes "all things are naked and opened" (Heb. 4:13). Further, it is a throne of *grace*—we don't deserve to be there and we couldn't come on our own merit. *The better our grasp of Who God is, the greater our reverence before Him.*

The Ark Was Supreme

The emphasis placed on the ark by putting it so far in front of Israel also illustrated the ark's supremacy—not as a relic, but as it represented God. Israel could enter Canaan only because God entered first. He went before them, taking possession on their behalf.

A Sanctified Congregation

Joshua had one more command for the congregation of Israel before he gave them instructions for crossing the Jordan.

> And Joshua said unto the people, Sanctify yourselves: for to morrow the Lord will do wonders among you (Josh. 3:5).

To be *sanctified* is to be cleaned and set apart.[34] *Sanctification* and *holiness* mean essentially the same thing. Generations of theologians have debated the

[34] The sanctification, or consecration, expected of Israel included bathing, washing their clothes, and abstaining from sexual relations (Exod. 19:14–15).

question "Is sanctification the work of God or the work of man?" One theological perspective emphasizes verses that say sanctification is God's work in us.[35] Another theological view emphasizes verses such as Joshua 3:5 that indicate we are to sanctify ourselves.[36] On the basis of Scripture, we have to conclude that in some sense both of these perspectives are true. How can these seemingly contradictory instructions be reconciled?

Some theologians use the terms *indicative* and *imperative* to distinguish between God's role and man's role in our sanctification. *Indicative* sanctification is that act of God by which He sets His people apart by declaring them to be righteous. God indicates that we are His people, not because we behave righteously but because God imputes Christ's righteousness to us. That is, *God sanctifies us* by treating us as if we were righteous on the basis of Christ's behavior, not our own. *Imperative* sanctification is that act of man personally cleansing himself in order to be able to approach the Holy One. Because of God's command, it is imperative that we obey Him; therefore, *we sanctify ourselves* by doing what God tells us to do. Another way the dual aspects of sanctification are distinguished is by using the terms *positional* sanctification and *practical* sanctification. This distinction says that *God sanctifies us* by giving us our position in Christ and that *we sanctify ourselves* by practical obedience.

Both of these descriptions are helpful. We can be in Christ, sanctified positionally, only by an act of God. We can demonstrate the image of Christ only by acting like Him. But there is an element of duality involved both in being established in Christ and in living like Christ.

Positional Sanctification

First, our positional sanctification in Christ is accomplished by God, but not without our consent. It is true that the natural man is lost in sin (Rom. 3:10), is not seeking God (Rom. 3:11–23), is an enemy of God (Rom. 8:5–8), and is spiritually dead (Eph. 2:1–5). Without the intervention of God we couldn't respond to the gospel (John 6:44, 65; 1 Cor. 2:14; Eph. 2:1). Without the gift of faith we couldn't believe (Eph. 2:8–10; Phil. 1:29; Heb. 12:2). However, no one will ever have his sins forgiven and be redeemed without consciously trusting Christ to save him. We must believe to be saved (John 3:16–18; 5:24; 6:40; Acts 16:31; Eph. 1:13). Our salvation is initiated and accomplished by God, and we can believe only by God's enablement, but we are involved as participants who respond to the work of God in us by expressing faith.

[35] Examples include Numbers 8:17; Jeremiah 1:5; John 10:36; Acts 26:18; Romans 15:16; 1 Corinthians 1:2 and 6:11; Hebrews 2:10–11 and 10:9–10; and Jude 1:1.

[36] Examples include Leviticus 11:44 and 20:7; Numbers 11:18; Joshua 7:13; 1 Samuel 16:5; 1 Chronicles 15:12; 2 Chronicles 35:6; and 2 Timothy 2:21.

Practical Sanctification

The practical aspect of our sanctification, which follows regeneration and conversion, is accomplished by the believer, but not without God's help. Yes, we're commanded to put away all external defilement (1 Cor. 7:1; Eph. 4:24–31; cf. Gen. 35:1–2; 1 Sam. 16:5) and put on Christ. We're also told that we must discipline our hearts and minds into an appropriate attitude for meeting with God (Phil. 2:2–5; 4:8). Numerous passages give believers specific instructions that we're responsible to obey. However, we're not able to obey on our own—external cleansing is important, but it's inadequate. We can obey properly only as God works in us (Rom. 8:1–5; Rom. 12:1–2; Phil. 1:6, 11; 2:13; Heb. 10:22). We're to keep ourselves unspotted by the world (James 1:27), but it is Christ Who sanctifies to Himself a spotless bride (Eph. 5:25–28).

Both of these truths are illustrated by the manner of Israel's entrance into Canaan. God would take them in, but they must cross the river. God would give them the land, but they must fight the enemy.

An Obedient Example

There is one more verse I want to look at before I close this chapter. This is the last verse in the text before God speaks to Joshua again.

> And Joshua spake unto the priests, saying, Take up the ark of the covenant, and pass over before the people. And they took up the ark of the covenant, and went before the people (Josh. 3:6).

At this point in the narrative, Joshua gave instructions to the priests responsible for carrying the ark. He told them they would be crossing ahead of the people, so they picked up the ark and moved to the front of the assembly. They set an example of obedience.

The priests bearing the ark represented the spiritual leadership of Israel. Like the "officers" of Israel mentioned in Joshua 1:10 (discussed in chapter 4 of this book), the role of the priests here has its parallel in a church's pastor. Men in such positions bear an awesome responsibility—and "awesome" doesn't mean "cool"; it means "inspiring reverential fear." That responsibility is twofold. First, when a pastor stands to preach, he must remember that *he is to speak for God*. That is what Peter had in mind when he said, "If any man speak, let him speak as the oracles of God" (1 Pet. 4:11*a*). Recognizing this responsibility should inspire not arrogance but humility. Remembering that we are

God's messengers should help curb our human tendency to sermonize our own opinions. That is why James said, "My brethren, be not many masters [let not many of you become teachers], knowing that we shall receive the greater condemnation [we will incur a stricter judgment]" (James 3:1). It is a fearful thing to realize that you will be held accountable for speaking God's words accurately and clearly to God's people.

But the pastor must also remember that *he is to live like Christ.* Paul told Timothy, "Let no man despise thy youth; but be thou an example of the believers, in word, in conversation, in charity, in spirit, in faith, in purity" (1 Tim. 4:12). God's expectations for men in positions of pastoral leadership are high. Paul starts his list of qualifications for those in positions of oversight by saying that they "must be blameless" (1 Tim. 3:2), following that with more than fifteen more characteristics that should be displayed. As a pastor myself, that's a hard thing for me to admit. It's frightening to realize that people ought to be able to look at their pastor and see a living example of how they should live. But before church members start casting accusations at their imperfect pastors or pastors toss this book aside as unrealistic legalism, bear in mind that every one of the characteristics Paul listed as qualifications for pastoral ministry in 1 Timothy 3:1–7 is found in other contexts as commands to *all believers.* They are just gathered together in one place by Paul to make the point that *pastors are to set an example of obedience that all are to emulate.*

Paul sums up God's expectations for spiritual leaders in the following words to Titus: "In all things showing thyself a pattern of good works: in doctrine showing uncorruptness, gravity, sincerity, sound speech, that cannot be condemned" (Titus 2:7–8*a*). Spiritual leaders must really lead. But God's people are also expected to follow. The people of Israel were to follow the priests as far as they carried the ark, but no farther. In the life of the local church, the pastor is responsible to lead the way in all matters of life, but each believer has the responsibility to follow. Hebrews 13:7 commands believers to "remember them which have the rule over you, who have spoken unto you the word of God: whose faith follow, considering the end [result] of their conversation [conduct]." But each believer is also expected to be just as godly as the leadership.

Peter wrote the following to all of us: "But ye are a chosen generation, a royal priesthood, an holy nation, a peculiar people; that ye should shew forth the praises of him who hath called you out of darkness into his marvellous light" (1 Pet. 2:9). While the pastor should lead the way, each believer must fully submit to God.

9
Crossing Jordan

Joshua 3:7–17

Several years ago my wife and I decided we needed to get more exercise than our teaching jobs provided during the day, so we joined a fitness center. Four days a week we'd go by after school for a workout, and we'd go in for a couple of hours on Saturday, too. The club's owner, Joe, was a serious bodybuilder. He was also the head trainer, and we got to know him well over the course of the two or three years we trained there.

I'd say that Joe and I became friends, but that wouldn't exactly describe our relationship. The man was ruthless. After one or two sessions, I tried to time my workouts so that he wasn't around. It seemed as if he wasn't satisfied, no matter how hard I trained. I was sure he was getting sadistic pleasure out of my pain. After a couple of months, though, I admitted the truth—the problem wasn't that Joe expected too much. The problem was that I wanted to stop too early. I would lift as much as I thought I could handle and do as many repetitions of the exercise as I could before it started to hurt. Then I was ready to move on to something else. If Joe was there, he wouldn't let me get away with that. He'd spot for me and make me do as many reps as I could do. Then he'd make me do two more. If I could do the last two reps without his help, I still wasn't finished. You see, Joe and I had different goals for my workout. I wanted to lose a little weight. Joe wanted me to get in shape. I could lose a little weight without working too hard, but to get in shape I'd have to regularly push beyond what I'd been capable of doing before.

In our study of Joshua, Israel has come to a point where they need to push the limits of their faith. They have a river to cross, and they can't do it on their own. It's going to be like those last two reps of my workout—they've reached their limit and can't go on without help. Israel will need the miraculous intervention of God to cross the Jordan.

The Miracle

Magnification of Joshua

For the first time in several days, Joshua heard from God. The last words the Lord had spoken to Joshua are recorded in Joshua 1:2–9. God told him to study the "book of the law," lead the people across the Jordan, and conquer the land. God promised to be with Joshua wherever he went, but He hadn't promised any further instructions. Apparently, everything Joshua had done since that time was done on his own initiative according to "this book of the law." His faith led him to prepare for a river crossing without God's having revealed His plan. He had moved the people to the verge of the river, still having no idea how they would cross. God's words to him at this time must have come as quite a relief.

> And the Lord said unto Joshua, This day will I begin to magnify thee in the sight of all Israel, that they may know that, as I was with Moses, so I will be with thee (Josh. 3:7).

Before telling him what to do to cross Jordan, the Lord announced His intention to "magnify," or exalt, Joshua immediately. God's exaltation of Joshua was, first of all, a result of Joshua's obedient faith. He believed God and performed his duty. It was also the fulfillment of the promise God had made in Joshua 1:5—"as I was with Moses, so I will be with thee." While Joshua's exaltation would bring him personal recognition, that was never God's primary purpose. Joshua's magnification was for the purpose of leading God's people. It was the opening move in the process of fulfilling the promise of giving Israel the land under Joshua's leadership.

Joshua's magnification foreshadows the magnification of Christ Jesus in several ways. Christ's exaltation was *a result of His obedience*.

> And being found in fashion as a man, he [Christ Jesus] humbled himself, and **became obedient unto death**, even the death of the cross. **Wherefore God also hath highly exalted him**, and given him a name which is above every name (Phil. 2:8–9).

Jesus' exaltation was *something God had promised.* According to the context of the passage above, Christ's exaltation was for the purpose of providing redemption (see Phil. 2:5–13). In another passage, we read that before His creation of the world, God promised that Christ Jesus would redeem those Paul refers to as "God's elect."

> Paul, a servant of God, and an apostle of Jesus Christ, according to the faith of God's elect, and the acknowledging of the truth which is after godliness; in hope of eternal life, **which God**, that cannot lie, **promised before the world began** (Titus 1:1–2).

Since Titus 1:2 is often cited to prove the veracity of God—He cannot lie—it is easy to miss the significance of the rest of the verse. Because God cannot lie, we know He keeps His promises. Paul is confident that he possesses eternal life because God promised it. But to whom did God make the promise? Not to Paul, who was not around "before the world began." The promise had to be made to Christ since it was made before anything or anyone had been created. So Christ's exaltation in His redemption of sinful men was something God had promised to do before He began to create.

A third parallel between Joshua's magnification and Christ's exaltation is seen in the circumstances of the situation. Joshua would be magnified when Israel passed through the Jordan River, and Jesus' ministry began when He was baptized in the waters of the Jordan. Jesus' baptism occurred about the same geographic point at which Israel crossed the river. John preached in the wilderness of Judea and baptized Jesus in the Jordan (see Matt. 3:1–13). That would have put him in the general vicinity of Jericho, certainly within the range of the riverbed that dried up for Joshua. I'll mention other ways Israel's crossing the Jordan pictures Christ's work of redemption as the narrative unfolds.

There is, however, an important point of contrast between God's exaltation of Joshua and His exaltation of Christ. Israel did not respond to Joshua the same way they responded to Jesus. We'll see in Joshua 4:15 that Israel believed Joshua and obeyed his instructions. But when Jesus was presented as their Messiah, Israel didn't believe Him and disobeyed His instructions (John 1:11). Throughout their history, Israel focused on rituals and missed their significance. That is the point being made in Hebrews 9:19–10:10. The Old Testament rituals were given to illustrate something better. Christ's sacrifice for sins perfected, or completed, the rituals, making them no longer necessary. Tragically, Israel accepted the type but rejected the antitype. Their fixation on the illustration distracted them from the reality.

Instructions for the Priests

After announcing His intention to magnify Joshua, God gave him some instructions for the priests.

> And thou shalt command the priests that bear the ark of the covenant, saying, When ye are come to the brink of the water of Jordan, ye shall stand still in Jordan (Josh. 3:8).

The first fact I notice in this verse is that Joshua is expected to exercise high authority. He is not to *ask* the priests to do something nor is he to *suggest* to the priests that they do this. He is to *command* the priests, and they are expected to obey without question. Likewise, Christ is our Commander and expects our unquestioning obedience.

The second fact I see here is that Joshua is expected to exercise great faith. Read the verse again. Do the instructions make sense to you? They don't make sense to me—not in any practical way. The instructions were clear, but they seemed absurd. There is little question about *what* they were to do, but there is no hint as to *why* they should do it. Even if you can "come to the brink of the water of Jordan" and "stand still in Jordan," how does that help get Israel across the river? If I'm one of the priests carrying the ark, I'm not crazy about these instructions. The prospect of standing still in a flooded river is less than attractive.

One of the lessons God wants us to learn through His method of dealing with the Jordan is that you and I shouldn't flinch from the floodwaters of life. Sometimes we face situations that threaten to overwhelm us, but God doesn't permit us to retreat, nor does He encourage us to find a way around those obstacles that seem impassible. "He asks us to believe quietly that: It is He who brought us here. It is He who will keep and preserve us here. It is He who will take us on from here. This is faith in action."[37]

That is really the message of 1 Corinthians 10:13—"There hath no temptation taken you but such as is common to man: but God is faithful, who will not suffer you to be tempted above that ye are able; but will with the temptation also make a way to escape, that ye may be able to bear it." One of the most important aspects of this promise is partially obscured by the translation of the phrase "a way to escape." First, the Greek includes the definite article, not the indefinite article—it reads "*the* way," not "*a* way." Second, "the way" provided is not a means of *escape*, as if we could find a way around or away from the trials. Rather, it is the way *through* the trials—the way to emerge on the other side. What this verse says is that you, the believer, will never face a trial that

[37] Keller, p. 73.

will be more than you can bear. God always provides the means to survive anything He allows to confront you (cf. Jer. 29:11). Sometimes we complicate situations by trying to make our own way around a problem, but God says we are to trust Him and keep to *His* way *through* the difficulty. This is precisely what Israel must do to conquer the Jordan.

Encouragement for Israel

Having received from God the instructions he was to give the priests, Joshua called a meeting.

> And Joshua said unto the children of Israel, Come hither, and hear the words of the Lord your God. And Joshua said, Hereby ye shall know that the living God is among you, and that he will without fail drive out from before you the Canaanites, and the Hittites, and the Hivites, and the Perizzites, and the Girgashites, and the Amorites, and the Jebusites. Behold, the ark of the covenant of the Lord of all the earth passeth over before you into Jordan. Now therefore take you twelve men out of the tribes of Israel, out of every tribe a man. And it shall come to pass, as soon as the soles of the feet of the priests that bear the ark of the Lord, the Lord of all the earth, shall rest in the waters of Jordan, that the waters of Jordan shall be cut off from the waters that come down from above; and they shall stand upon an heap (Josh. 3:9–13).

Joshua had a message for Israel from God. It is significant that Joshua emphasized that this word was from "*your* God." He wanted to remind Israel of their special relationship with God and His special interest in them. Joshua also said the message was from "*the living* God." In contrast with the dead gods of the Canaanites, Israel's God is living. And that living God does not just exist—He is "*among you*." That is, as the *living* God, He was working on Israel's behalf and guaranteeing both present and future help. Joshua was "affirming that the God who marches with Israel is one who is able to act and to perform mighty deeds in contrast to the pagan gods that have eyes but cannot see."[38] He was not remote and hard to reach; neither was He offering help from a distant place. He would actively drive out their enemies. The God Who had begun "a good work in [them would] perform it" (Phil. 1:6).

This encouragement was important because the instructions were going to be difficult to believe. There had never been a miracle quite like the one Joshua promised. Yes, God had parted the waters of the Red Sea, but that was a long time ago (forty years) and under different circumstances. Moses had been in charge then and had already proven that he was an instrument of God by having pronounced the plagues on Egypt. Joshua was something of a novice. He had never been responsible for a miracle. The Red Sea parted when Moses held

[38] Madvig, p. 266.

up his staff and God sent a strong wind to make a path through the water. Joshua would not be using Moses' staff, nor was there any indication that God would send a wind to part the waters before Israel crossed. Besides, the Red Sea was a standing body of water, and the Jordan was a flowing river. Making a path through running water would be a different kind of miracle from making a path through standing water. God was about to perform a unique miracle.

In the crossing of Jordan, the ark of the covenant would be the focal point. Remember that it contained the Law and was covered by the mercy of God. Israel would cross this river fully mindful of God's demands, of their own inadequacy, and of their need for mercy. Joshua also says that this covenant was made by "the Lord of all the earth." This is the first time this phrase is used in Scripture, and it occurs only six other times in the Bible (Josh. 3:13; Ps. 47:7; Isa. 54:5; Mic. 4:13; Zech. 4:14; 6:5). This title is significant in that it emphasizes God's universal sovereignty. The people of Canaan and the surrounding region believed in local deities. Each city had its own patron god. One god ruled in the mountains and another in the valleys or the plains. Joshua wants Israel to remember that *Yahweh* ("the LORD," 3:9) was their LORD in Egypt. He was their LORD in Sinai. He was their LORD at Jordan. And He would be their LORD in Canaan. He would be their sovereign as they marched through the river and when they emerged on the other side.

Knowing Who God is and that He would be with them, Joshua told each tribe of Israel to select one man to represent them. He didn't tell them why; he just said he would need one man from each tribe. We will find out in the next chapter what they were to do, but for now they were simply being chosen. Then Joshua told Israel what was about to happen. The priests carrying the ark would walk into the river and "the waters of Jordan shall be cut off from the waters that come down from above; and they shall stand upon an heap."

Obedience of Israel

I imagine that by now most of the people of Israel are glad that they aren't the priests bearing the ark and that they get to follow by about a half-mile. Walking into the flooded river sounds a little scary to me, but the priests and all Israel obeyed.

> And it came to pass, when the people removed from their tents, to pass over Jordan, and the priests bearing the ark of the covenant before the people; and as they that bare the ark were come unto Jordan, and the feet of the priests that bare the ark were dipped in the brim of the water, (for Jordan overfloweth all his banks all the time of harvest,) that the waters which came down from above stood and rose up upon an heap very far from the city Adam, that is beside

> Zaretan: and those that came down toward the sea of the plain, even the salt sea, failed, and were cut off: and the people passed over right against Jericho. And the priests that bare the ark of the covenant of the Lord stood firm on dry ground in the midst of Jordan, and all the Israelites passed over on dry ground, until all the people were passed clean over Jordan (Josh. 3:14–17).

The details of this crossing are significant. First, consider *the timing*. The river was at flood stage. You would think that God could have arranged for Israel to get to Canaan at some time other than flood season. After forty years of waiting, couldn't God have timed this better? A few weeks either way and they could have avoided such a difficult crossing because the river's water level would have been much lower. Conditions for crossing couldn't have been much worse. This does, however, provide an interesting coincidence of detail. Based on the typical growing season in that part of the world and the time of year when the river would be flooded, it is likely that it would be time to harvest the barley and flax crops (Josh. 4:18; cf. Exod. 9:31). This fits perfectly with the fact that Rahab hid the two spies under the stalks of flax that she was drying on her rooftop (Josh. 2:6).

Several details involved in *the method* of Israel's crossing of the Jordan are also important. The text gives us a bare-bones account of what happened:

1. The priests carrying the ark dipped their feet "in the brim of the water."
2. The source of the river's water was "cut off."
3. The water above Adam (nearly twenty miles north of Jericho) "heaped up."
4. The waters "that come down from above" Adam to "the salt sea failed."
5. The priests "stood firm on dry ground in the midst of Jordan."
6. The people "passed over on dry ground."

The priests carrying the ark had to walk as far as they could, and then keep walking. They didn't stop at the water's edge but dipped their feet in the brim of the water. As soon as they did that, the waters that fed the Jordan from the north were "cut off" nearly twenty miles away. Can you visualize what this passage describes? If a flooded river were to be suddenly and completely dammed up at one point by a landslide or some other means, what would happen to the water downstream of the new dam? It would continue to flow toward its destination. As it continued on its way, the water level in the riverbed would rapidly recede to a trickle before disappearing altogether, but it would take at least a little time for the water to run off.

We sometimes take this passage to say that the priests "had to get their feet wet" before God cut off the water. That is true, but I believe the text actually describes the priests wading into the edge of the water all the way to the middle of the river. Their faith was not a one-step faith but a continual-walk faith. As they continued to wade into the river, they had to go by faith that the water would continue to recede and that whatever means God was using to stop the flow of the water would continue to hold.

By the time the rest of Israel approached from their half-mile distance, the water had completely run off and God had miraculously dried up the riverbed. This was not a "path" through a river. The entire southern half of the Jordan "failed." No wonder all Israel could cross quickly. They didn't have to walk single file. They had a twenty-mile-wide highway at their disposal. What an impact it must have had on the inhabitants of Canaan! The flooded Jordan was gone. That which provided their greatest defense from Israelite incursion was no obstacle at all to Israel's God.

Some commentators speculate that God used a landslide to block the river. God has at times used natural means to accomplish supernatural works. The text indicates otherwise in this case. It says the water that had fed the river had heaped up. The Hebrew word rendered *heaped up* means "congealed" or "clotted." It is the word you would use to describe what happens to gelatin after you mix it with warm water and allow it to cool in the refrigerator. It "sets up," or "congeals." The waters of the Jordan north of Adam didn't freeze or disappear. They jelled. A landslide wouldn't cause that. Further, we'll see that after Israel crossed, God let the water go and the river returned to flood stage. A natural landslide that completely blocked the flow of water long enough for twenty miles of river to run off and two million people to cross with all their goods would need supernatural intervention to be so thoroughly breached at the right moment that the river would suddenly begin to flow again at full strength. There is no satisfactory way to explain this as a natural phenomenon without distorting the clear language of the text. Joshua may be describing something beyond your experience, but as an eyewitness and participant he describes something that really happened.

The Lessons

When we consider how Israel was told to follow the ark of the covenant, we learn something of what God expects of His people—not to *become* His people but because we *are* His people. We are to sanctify ourselves, being separate and distinct from the world around us, by obeying His commands and keeping our eyes on His mercy and grace. Second, we see a demonstration of

God's almighty power as He removes the most daunting of obstacles—and He does it without fanfare or spectacle. There were no lightning flashes or rumblings from heaven as Israel crossed the Jordan. They just walked across a dry riverbed that moments before had been flooded. Third, we see that God does intervene when we're distressed, turning difficulties into blessings as we overcome obstacles by His power. Fourth, this shows us how we should act when we face a difficult or dangerous situation, calmly following God's instructions and trusting Him to do His will. Even if the circumstances threaten our lives, we don't have to be afraid. God leads wherever we go, even "through the valley of the shadow of death" (Ps. 23:4).

Finally, we get a glimpse of Christ's work of redemption. This picture will become more vivid in the next chapter, but it is introduced in this brief account. *God* took Israel across the river. The outcome of the miracle was that "all the people were passed clean over Jordan." Much could be made of the significance of the word *clean* here. It ties in well with the whole notion of sanctification—having passed through the river, Israel stood on the other side *cleansed.* As tempting as it may be to read this passage this way, that's not what the Hebrew text says. The word translated *clean* doesn't mean "spotless." It means "completely." I've already made the point that crossing the Jordan depicts our salvation. When we receive Christ Jesus as Lord and Savior, our sins are forgiven and we enter the realm of our new Father and King. But the fact that we are new creatures in Christ (2 Cor. 5:17) doesn't change the fact that we still have a sin nature with which we struggle (Rom. 7:21). We must work together with Christ to *keep* ourselves "unspotted from the world" (James 1:27). The most important part of this picture isn't the *cleansing* but the *complete* nature of salvation. Joshua didn't mean that the people wouldn't need a bath. His point is twofold: everyone got completely across, and not one was left behind or lost in the crossing. Hebrews 7:25 says, "He [Christ] is able also to save them to the uttermost that come unto God by him"—that is, each of God's children is completely saved. Further, in John 6:37–39, Jesus indicates that all of God's children will be saved—none will be left behind or lost.

> All that the Father giveth me shall come to me; and him that cometh to me I will in no wise cast out. For I came down from heaven, not to do mine own will, but the will of him that sent me. And this is the Father's will which hath sent me, that of all which he hath given me I should lose nothing, but should raise it up again at the last day (John 6:37–39).

I hope you'll be encouraged to face whatever obstacle confronts you today in confidence that Christ can and will make a way for you. Like the trainer at the fitness center, He will spot for you and assist you in performing the exercises that are too much to handle on your own. He knows this training will help strengthen your spiritual muscles—make you spiritually fit. Remember that wherever you go, He is leading you; and wherever He leads, you must follow.

> Do not look so much upon painful circumstances and difficult situations as unpleasant trials of your faith which have to be endured, but rather, thankfully regard them as golden occasions for you to prove afresh the sufficiency of Him who never fails those who fully trust Him.[39]

[39] Arthur Pink, *Gleanings in Joshua* (Chicago: Moody Press, 1964), p. 77.

10
Two Memorials

Joshua 4:1–9, 20–23

It's 9:30 on a Monday morning in mid-July. The church auditorium is filled with nearly 250 children, most of whom apparently ate a breakfast that was way too sweet. They are having a hard time settling down for the opening of vacation Bible school. Our VBS leader walks out onto the platform and starts the program. After reciting pledges to the American flag, the Christian flag, and the Bible, he leads in prayer, followed by a few songs and choruses. Then he says, "We are going to have a contest, and I need a few volunteers." Immediately, 150 hands shoot into the air. The volunteers are so eager to be chosen that they can barely keep their seats. They can't wait to participate in whatever is going to happen next. They have no idea what might be involved, but they know they want to do it.

Perhaps we become more cynical with age, but adults tend to be slower to volunteer blindly. The children at the VBS program might be a little apprehensive about what they will have to do as volunteers, but they basically trust the adults in charge not to make them do something dangerous or hurtful. Adults are also more likely to be self-conscious. Kids aren't as worried about being embarrassed as adults are. They just want to participate. Somewhere between childhood and adulthood, most of us lose our enthusiasm for volunteering for duties that are not fully disclosed.

The Monument in Gilgal

Israel's Crossing

> And it came to pass, when all the people were clean passed over Jordan, that the Lord spake unto Joshua . . . (Josh. 4:1).

Once again we see an emphasis on the complete nature of the crossing—the people were "clean passed over" Jordan (cf. 3:17 and 4:11). The Jordan can be considered a river of judgment. Its very name is a compound of the Hebrew words *jor*, meaning "spread," and *dan*, meaning "judging." Some fourteen hundred years later, John would baptize in the Jordan. His baptism was not identical with the baptism of the New Testament church (Acts 18:24–19:5)[40] but was more closely related to the Jewish practice of proselyte baptism, which symbolized a convert's rejection of his former religion and his desire to worship the God of Israel. It involved a sort of self-judgment—acknowledging one's sin guiltiness and the intention to change from living to fulfill one's own desire to living to obey God's commands. That is why John's use of the Jordan for baptism was significant. It pictured entering into judgment and emerging cleansed. Israel's crossing Jordan took them from where they had been to where they ought to be. It transported them from their former lives in the wilderness to their new lives in the land of promise. That is what the Holy Spirit's regeneration does for the child of God. In the baptism of the Holy Spirit, a person is transformed from being dead in trespasses and sins to being alive in Christ.

Collecting the Stones

In Joshua 3:12, each of the twelve tribes of Israel was told to select a man for some undisclosed purpose. This whole procedure reminds me of what Jesus Christ did when He called His apostles. In virtually all of those cases described for us He simply said, "Follow me" (Matt. 4:18–22; 9:9; John 1:43–51). That is also what the Lord Jesus says to those who are His today (Matt. 16:24;

[40] Baptism practiced by the New Testament church was similar to John's in many respects, but unlike John's it was specifically Christ-centered (Acts 19:3–5). Christian baptism is a public testimony that the person being baptized has acknowledged that he deserves to die for his sins, but that he has been made alive in and through the resurrection of Christ. It is, in essence, a believer's "pledge of allegiance" to Christ. It tells those who witness it that he has repented of his sin and trusted Christ alone to save him, that he is now identified as one of Christ's followers, and that others can expect to see evidence of the change in him as he becomes more and more like Christ.

Mark 8:34; John 10:27). We are to trust Him enough to follow Him, even though we don't know every place the path may take us or precisely what service He may want of us. In the case of the representatives of Israel in Joshua 4, I don't know whether the tribes took volunteers, voted, or appointed someone. The various tribes may have used independent methods to designate their representatives. We aren't told in Joshua 3 what these men were chosen to do. We find out in the opening verses of chapter 4.

> The Lord spake unto Joshua, saying, Take you twelve men out of the people, out of every tribe a man, and command ye them, saying, Take you hence out of the midst of Jordan, out of the place where the priests' feet stood firm, twelve stones, and ye shall carry them over with you, and leave them in the lodging place, where ye shall lodge this night. Then Joshua called the twelve men, whom he had prepared of the children of Israel, out of every tribe a man: and Joshua said unto them, Pass over before the ark of the Lord your God into the midst of Jordan, and take you up every man of you a stone upon his shoulder, according unto the number of the tribes of the children of Israel (Josh. 4:1*b*–5).

After crossing the river, Joshua received more instructions from God. Each of Israel's tribal representatives chosen in 3:12 was told to select a stone from the bed of the Jordan River and carry it to the camp on the other side. Why didn't God assign this task to the priests? Is there any significance to His using men from each tribe? I think there must be. Did you notice the emphasis placed on this one fact? Verse 2 says, "Out of every tribe a man." Verse 4 says, "Out of every tribe a man." Verse 5 makes the same point while giving a hint of why He did it this way—"according unto the number of the tribes of the children of Israel." God wanted all Israel to identify with this project. This was not to be something done for them by the priests but was something in which they were involved and in which each person had a stake.

Erecting a "Sign"

What was the purpose of the stones? They were to be erected into a monument that was to be "a sign" among them.

> That this may be a sign among you, that when your children ask their fathers in time to come, saying, What mean ye by these stones? Then ye shall answer them, That the waters of Jordan were cut off before the ark of the covenant of the Lord; when it passed over Jordan, the waters of Jordan were cut off: and these stones shall be for a memorial unto the children of Israel for ever (Josh. 4:6–7).

The word rendered *sign* is a strong word for a portent or pledge. We might say it is a word for something particularly ***sign**ificant*. One of the words used to describe Jesus' miracles is the Greek equivalent of this word. We sometimes think of Jesus' miracles simply as God's way of helping an individual in need. But each miracle had a teaching purpose—it was a *sign*.

There were three ways in which the monument to be erected in the new camp at Gilgal was to be a sign. It was to *sign*ify that Israel had crossed Jordan by God's power. The stones taken from the riverbed would provide permanent testimony to the fact that God had stopped the river to allow Israel to cross. There would have been no camp at Gilgal without God's miraculous intervention to bring them into the Promised Land. Second, the monument would *sign*ify that they had crossed the Jordan unmarked. They came through the river on dry ground, unharmed by the floodwaters of "judgment." Third, it *sign*ified God's pledge of future blessing. He had brought them this far; He would not fail to keep all of His Word.

Building a "Memorial"

As a memorial, the monument in Gilgal would remind all future generations of Israel that *judgment lay behind them*. That is the essence of the message of the gospel. Christ Jesus took upon Himself the punishment for the sins of those who believe on Him. That is what Jesus meant when He said, "He that heareth my word, and believeth on him that sent me, hath everlasting life, and shall not come into condemnation; but is passed from death unto life" (John 5:24). Judgment is behind us. Eternal life is ahead. No wonder it is called good news (gospel)!

Further, the fact that they would need to remember implies that the miracle of the crossing would never be repeated. Joshua also made it clear to the people of Israel that *they must teach their children what God had done for them.*

> And he spake unto the children of Israel, saying, When your children shall ask their fathers in time to come, saying, What mean these stones? Then ye shall let your children know, saying, Israel came over this Jordan on dry land. For the Lord your God dried up the waters of Jordan from before you, until ye were passed over, as the Lord your God did to the Red sea, which he dried up from before us, until we were gone over (Josh. 4:21–23).

A memorial is not much use if nobody knows what it means. Each generation would have to be instructed. They wouldn't have personally witnessed the crossing, and unless someone told them about it, they wouldn't know. The memorial was a reminder to future generations of God's faithfulness and Israel's faith.

Years later, when John the Baptist was preaching in this very vicinity, it is probably this monument to which he referred when he said, "And think not to say within yourselves, We have Abraham to our father: for I say unto you, that

God is able of these stones to raise up children unto Abraham" (Matt. 3:9). John's point was not that God could turn stones into people (although that would not be much different from what He did when He made Adam from the dirt). His point is that God could use the memorial of the crossing of Jordan to lead others to Himself. Being born a physical descendent of Abraham was not meritorious. One must believe in the power and mercy of God.

As a parent, have you ever answered your children's questions by saying, "Someday you'll understand," or, "I'll tell you all about it when you are older"? That is a dangerous thing to do. The question they asked may never come up again if you don't give some kind of substantive answer when they ask. Sure, they probably won't fully understand the answer. But trying to give honest answers to a child's questions, especially about spiritual matters, will encourage learning, trust, and communication.

Some are tempted to say, "That's why I send my kids to church." It is important to notice Joshua's emphasis. He didn't say, "When your children shall ask in time to come saying, 'What mean these stones?' you must *send them to the pastor*." Neither did he say they should send them to the Sunday school teacher or the teacher in the classroom. He said that the children would ask their *fathers*, and the fathers must "let your children know." *The primary responsibility to teach the truths of Scripture to the next generation does not fall upon the leaders of the church but on the leaders of the family.*

That is still true today. It is the father who is to rear his children in "the nurture and admonition of the Lord" (Eph. 6:4). Some people delegate to others total responsibility for training their children. Others go to the opposite extreme and refuse to listen to godly instruction from anyone outside the family. Still others expect the help of pastors and teachers but then undermine the process by their critical spirits. Parents and church leaders are to work together, telling of God's great power and mercy and teaching God's Word consistently so that each successive generation can hear and accept the truth.

Memorializing Unity

The one final purpose of this memorial was to serve as a symbol of the unity of God's people.

> And the children of Israel did so as Joshua commanded, and took up twelve stones out of the midst of Jordan, as the Lord spake unto Joshua, according to the number of the tribes of the children of Israel, and carried them over with them unto the place where they lodged, and laid them down there. . . . And those twelve stones, which they took out of Jordan, did Joshua pitch in Gilgal (Josh. 4:8, 20).

Representatives of all twelve tribes carried the stones out of the riverbed to the site for the memorial. Then those stones were joined into a monument by Joshua, their leader. He used twelve stones, not nine or ten, to signify the unity of the people of Israel. Even after the breach among the tribes following Solomon's death, while the kingdom was divided, when Elijah built his altar to face the challenge of the prophets of Baal, he used twelve stones (1 Kings 18:30–31). Israel was a unit, even when they didn't want to be. The text says that Joshua *pitched* the stones in Gilgal. That is the same word used for erecting the tabernacle (Num. 1:51). It means "to raise" or "to cause to stand." In literal terms, the text says simply that Joshua built the monument by stacking the stones together. Symbolically, Israel found their unity by following their God-appointed leader.

The same principle is true today. Who is the God-appointed leader of the church? Be careful. Some will identify the pastor or elders as the God-appointed leaders of the church. That's true, but only in a limited way. As I've said before, those leaders find their parallel in the tribal leaders of Israel. The Leader (singular) of the church is Jesus Christ, its Head (Eph. 1:22; 4:15; Col. 1:18). The unity of the church is accomplished by Christ (Eph. 4:1–7; Col. 3:11). Each of the stones in Joshua's monument differed from all the others, but they were joined into a single structure. Similarly, the church is to demonstrate unity in diversity. No two members are identical, but each contributes to the whole, having been built into the structure by Christ (1 Cor. 1:12–13; Eph. 2:14–22; 4:15–16).

The Monument in the River[41]

> And Joshua set up twelve stones in the midst of Jordan, in the place where the feet of the priests which bare the ark of the covenant stood: and they are there unto this day (Josh. 4:9).

[41] It should be noted that at Joshua 4:9 the NIV reads, "Joshua set up *the* twelve stones *that had been* in the middle of the Jordan at the spot where the priests who carried the Ark of the Covenant had stood. And they are there to this day" (emphasis mine). The NIV translators chose not to translate here, but to provide their own speculative emendation, adding the words "the" and "that had been" on their own authority. They assumed that the account in Joshua 4 resulted from an ancient editor's combining two conflicting accounts, one of which had the memorial built on shore and the other built in the river. Since the text clearly requires a visible monument on shore, they concluded that the Hebrew reading is in error that says Joshua built a monument in the river. I prefer to allow the Hebrew reading to stand (as do the KJV, NKJV, NASB, and others), believing that the Hebrew describes two monuments.

This monument was distinct from the other in that this one was erected by Joshua alone. He took twelve stones, representative of all of God's people, but he selected the stones and erected the monument without any involvement of the rest of Israel. He used them to build a monument in the middle of the river that had separated Israel from their destiny. I've skipped the verses in Joshua 4 that describe the priests' exit from the river because I intend to discuss them in the next chapter, but shortly after the building of this monument, the priests will leave the river, and the water that had congealed will be released to continue on its way toward the Dead Sea.

The Bible doesn't describe that event in any detail. It just says that "the waters of Jordan returned unto their place, and flowed over all his banks, as they did before" (4:18*b*). I imagine that when God let the waters of Jordan go, they sped down the valley like a flash flood. If so, the crushing force of the water swept away anything in its path. It may be that the raging waters crushed the pile of stones in the river when they crashed into the structure. It may be that the water overwhelmed the monument, leaving it unharmed and visible whenever the river was low. Either way, the essential picture is the same.

Both monuments—the one in Gilgal and the one in the river—represent Christ Jesus. The one in Jordan pictures Christ taking upon Himself the crushing force of the righteous wrath of God in judgment for our sins. The one in Gilgal pictures Christ having come from the waters of judgment to perpetually stand as the victor over sin and death, providing salvation for those who trust Him. While Christ on the other side of the grave provides eternal life, it was Christ on the cross that provided safe passage for us to the other side.

Meaning of the Monuments

There are several lessons to be learned from these two memorials, most of which I've already touched on or implied in the discussion above. First, God's instruction concerning these monuments demonstrates that *God's works are worth recording and remembering*. God has done things in your life that are worth remembering and repeating to your children and grandchildren. You've probably never experienced anything quite as spectacular as the parting of the Red Sea or the drying up of Jordan. Neither have I. But God's providential direction of my life has been just as real, if usually more subtle. If we want our children to know God, we must pass on to them His works of grace in our own lives.

Second, *God's command to remember what He has done points to our natural tendency to forget.* When events are recent and the surprise and delight of experiencing God's providence on our behalf is fresh, we're tempted to believe we could never forget what He has done. But we're wrong. As time passes, we'll be distracted by circumstances and frightened by new situations. Our memories of God's past blessings will be less vivid than our fear of current threats. We have to remember on purpose. We can't trust our memories to recall God's actions spontaneously.

Third, *we need to remember what God has done for His people in the past,* not just what He has done for us personally. We have the Bible to help us remember what God has revealed about Himself through what He has done for His people, but we must study the Bible, and Old Testament study is vital. Systematic study of the Old Testament is one of the most neglected arenas in ministry today. The early church had to confront the false teaching of a heretic named Marcion. Marcion and his followers claimed that the apostle Paul presented a new God in Jesus Christ. The God of the Old Testament had been replaced by the God of Christianity. The Hebrew Scriptures (Old Testament) were to be set aside in favor of the new teachings of Paul. Christian leaders rallied to the defense of the truth and refuted Marcion. They asserted that there is one God, presented consistently in both the Old and New Testaments. They also insisted that God's revelation of Himself through the history of the Old Testament was profitable for our instruction, which is what Paul said in 1 Corinthians 10:11. We reject the Marcionite heresy today in theory, but we may be guilty of being *practical* Marcionites if we ignore or neglect the study of the Old Testament.

Fourth, *we need to make providing for the instruction of the rising generation a priority.* That is why most churches today invest more time and money in programs for children and teens than for senior citizens. The older believers ought to be investing in the youth so that they can pass on their faith. But let me briefly express a vital *caveat*. Children's ministries must be more than babysitting and play time. A junior church program may have value if the time is used primarily for instructing children in the truths of Scripture and the character of God. Teen ministries must be more than Christian alternative entertainment. Youth activities have value only if they point teens to Christ and teach them to know God. The typical approach to children and youth ministries has mostly taught the rising generation that they are entitled to have fun and has failed abysmally to teach them to know and love God. That is at least part of the reason so many Christian parents are seeing their children grow up *at* church but never grow *into* the church. In our attempts to make our instruction age-appropriate, we've failed to really instruct.

Finally, Joshua's monument in Gilgal illustrates that *we need to demonstrate the corporate unity of God's people*. Those who are His are one in Him (Eph. 4:1–16; Phil. 2:1–2). Each individual congregation should be characterized by the unity of the believers who worship together there. This unity goes beyond the doors of the local church. The world should see a unity among believers from other congregations as well. I'm a pastor of an independent Baptist church, and independent Baptists often assume that we are truly independent. We are prone to have such a cloister mentality—"We stand on our own and need no one else"—that we not only neglect but actively deny any *continuity of the faith* or *community in the faith*. This is a grave error.

We don't have too much problem acknowledging that *faith in Christ is trans-ethnic*. Still, we sometimes act as if we wish believers of other ethnicities would worship elsewhere. We readily admit that *faith in Christ is also trans-generational*. We want to pass our faith on to our children, and we express gratitude for those of earlier generations who passed their faith on to us. We even admit that many of the believers of earlier generations would not have identified themselves as independent Baptists—although we probably assume that they would have if they had thought about it. But we really struggle with admitting that *faith in Christ is trans-denominational*. We paint with too broad a brush when we denounce churches with other labels.

Please understand that I'm not advocating an artificial ecumenical unity that is accomplished at the expense of the truth. Clearly, fidelity to the truth is paramount (Rom. 16:17–19). Not everyone who claims to be a Christian is really a child of God. But a person doesn't have to agree with me on every point to be a Christian brother or sister. Yes, there are doctrinal distinctives that are important. But there are faithful believers who are not Baptists. I am a Baptist because I hold to a particular set of doctrinal positions that have traditionally been identified as "Baptist." I also recognize that I am still learning—I don't know everything there is to know, and some things the Bible teaches still confuse me. I don't intentionally believe something I am pretty sure is wrong, but it would take a profound level of arrogance to assume that I couldn't be wrong. Given the fact that some of the things I think I know could be in error, I need to recognize the essential unity of God's people in Christ despite our differences.

Joshua raised a monument in Gilgal to the goodness and mercy of God on behalf of His people. The monument stood as a memorial for all of God's people. At that time, most of them were Israelites; but some of them were Egyptians (Exod. 12:38), a few may have been Edomites (Josh. 15:17), some who would join them would be Canaanites (Josh. 6:23), at least one would be a Hittite

(2 Sam. 11:3–17) and another a Philistine (2 Sam. 15:19–22). Remember the words of John the Baptist:

> And think not to say within yourselves, We have Abraham to our father: for I say unto you, that God is able of these stones to raise up children unto Abraham (Matt. 3:9).

11

Entering Canaan

Joshua 4:10–19, 24; 5:1–12

Years ago I was listening to a missionary give a report about his ministry in Japan. I'm ashamed to admit that I don't remember much about him or his work, but he made one statement I'll never forget. He said, "An unsaved person has every right to look at anyone who calls himself a 'Christian' and expect to find the answer to his every need." Think about that a minute. If I'm going to apply to myself the designation "Christlike one," I'd better look a lot like Christ. That's what Paul meant when he challenged the believers in Ephesus to be "followers of God" (Eph. 5:1). The Greek word translated *followers* is *mimetes*, from which we get the English words *mime* and *mimic*. In this sense, following God is not simply to come along behind Him. It is to *imitate* Him. Since you may be the best picture of God your neighbor, friend, or relative will ever see, it's important to make that image lifelike. If you and I expect to witness effectively to the world around us, they'd better be able to see in us an accurate picture of God.

Completing the Crossing

Finishing the Project

In the last chapter we considered the memorial monuments Joshua built in the Jordan River and at the camp on the other side. In the process, I skipped the half of Joshua 4 that provides a little more description of the crossing. I want to return to that passage now. The first thing emphasized in these verses is that Joshua *finished the project*.

> For the priests which bare the ark stood in the midst of Jordan, until every thing was finished that the Lord commanded Joshua to speak unto the people, according to all that Moses commanded Joshua: and the people hasted and passed over. And it came to pass, when all the people were clean passed over, that the ark of the Lord passed over, and the priests, in the presence of the people. . . . And the Lord spake unto Joshua, saying, Command the priests that bear the ark of the testimony, that they come up out of Jordan. Joshua therefore commanded the priests, saying, Come ye up out of Jordan (Josh. 4:10–11, 15–17).

The priests, who had been told to "stand still in Jordan" (3:8), had done just that. They stayed in the middle of the riverbed until they were told to leave. Despite the great honor those priests must have felt, having been called upon to lead all Israel into the Jordan, they remain nameless. The record doesn't focus on who they were. It doesn't even say much about what they did. But I'm struck by the great faith of these anonymous men. They had to walk into a place of great danger. It might not seem that valiant to us as we read about the event from the comfort of our easy chairs, but those men walked into a flooded river with nothing but the promise of God to encourage them. Then they stood in the middle of a dry riverbed, patiently trusting God to hold back the waters while their countrymen crossed around them. They stood there a little longer while the tribal representatives fetched the stones for the monument in Gilgal and while Joshua assembled a monument in the riverbed. Their steadfast obedience provides a great example for you and me to emulate. *It is difficult to convince our unsaved neighbors that our God is great and powerful if we tremble in fear when we feel threatened by circumstances.*

Joshua also saw fit to tell us that the people of Israel didn't waste any time as they crossed the river. They "hasted and passed over." All Israel obeyed the command to cross, and they did so without hesitation. They couldn't carry the ark—that job went to individuals specifically selected by God. They did what they could to make the job of the priests as easy as possible by following instructions quickly without needing constant prodding. What an encouragement that must have been to Joshua! I'm sure the Lord Jesus must get frustrated with us when we hesitate, dawdle, or make excuses for being slow to obey. We need to demonstrate this sense of urgency in our response to the instruction of the Word of God.

The element of this story that has perhaps the greatest *theological* significance is that the ark led the way into the river but didn't come out until safe passage had been provided for all who crossed. When Jesus Christ "walked into the river" for us, He didn't pull up short after the ordeal in Gethsemane. He didn't turn back after the trials before the Sanhedrin, Pilate, and Herod. He didn't ask for relief after being scourged and crowned with thorns. He went all the way to the cross. When challenged to prove His deity by coming down from the cross, He stayed, as it were, "in the midst of Jordan." He didn't come down from the cross until He had provided safe passage to the Father for all who would believe (John 1:12–13). His death at Calvary paid the penalty for all who come, and not one that the Father gives Him will be lost (John 6:37). Jesus' victory cry, "It is finished" (John 19:30), announced that He had fulfilled His obligation to His Father by providing the means of salvation for you and me.

Fulfilling Promises

In the crossing of the Jordan, we also see evidence of four fulfilled promises.

> And the children of Reuben, and the children of Gad, and half the tribe of Manasseh, passed over armed before the children of Israel, as Moses spake unto them: about forty thousand prepared for war passed over before the Lord unto battle, to the plains of Jericho. On that day the Lord magnified Joshua in the sight of all Israel; and they feared him, as they feared Moses, all the days of his life (Josh. 4:12–14).

Reuben, Gad, and half of Manasseh kept their promise to lead the way into Canaan. These men had already received their inheritance on the east side of Jordan. The enemies who had occupied that land had been defeated under Moses' leadership, and their families were settling into that territory. The men of these tribes were able to advance into Canaan unencumbered by the need to haul their property or protect their wives and children. But their brethren still had to conquer the people who lived in the land that would be theirs. Therefore, Reuben, Gad, and Manasseh didn't just lead the way. Contributing about forty thousand[42] to the military action, they "passed over *armed* before the children of Israel." They were prepared and willing to fight to defend and assist their brethren who hadn't yet received their inheritance.

Their faithfulness is a picture of the attitude and behavior that should be displayed by the mature believer today. We are to lift up the fallen (Heb. 12:12–13). We are to bear one another's burdens (Gal. 6:1–2). Those who have already tasted victory over the enemies that confront them are responsible for

[42] The total number of fighting men in Reuben was 43,700 (Num. 26:7); in Gad 40,500 (Num. 26:18); and in Manasseh 52,700 (Num. 26:34). If half of Manasseh settled east of Jordan, that would bring their total down to about 26,000. So the total available troops from the two-and-a-half tribes east of Jordan would have been about 110,000. Sending 40,000 "equipped for war" and unencumbered represented a substantial forward force. It also left some 70,000 to guard their families in the absence of the men deployed for action across Jordan.

assisting new converts and weaker brethren (Rom. 15:1). This is not to assume any spiritual superiority over our brethren. Your brother may need your help and defense today, and you may need his tomorrow. The assistance is mutual. Reuben, Gad, and half of Manasseh were leading the way, not because they were better but because they had already received part of the promise of God that others were still awaiting. It was understood that the rest of Israel would come to their aid when and if it were ever needed (see Josh. 22:11–34).

The second promise fulfilled here is God's magnification of Joshua in the eyes of the people (4:14; cf. 3:7). Apparently, Israel was so impressed by the way God had used Joshua in the crossing of Jordan that they experienced an attitude adjustment. Under Moses, Israel as a whole was characterized by complaining and murmuring (Exod. 15:24; 16:2; 17:3; Num. 11:1; 14:2; 16:41). Under Joshua, Israel was characterized by obedience and trust (Josh. 24:31; Judg. 2:7). Israel had demonstrated the same response to Moses that the disobedient or unregenerate heart has toward God. But under Joshua, Israel's response pictures the way the obedient believer responds to God. The believer who is fully surrendered to God, who is learning to obey and to enter into victorious Christian living, should find it easy to obey joyfully and without complaint. Those who find themselves constantly grumbling or complaining about the circumstances of life through which God takes them should examine their hearts (2 Cor. 13:5). Perhaps they're still on the wrong side of "Jordan," living as "carnal" Christians or even still unsaved.

After Israel crossed the river and the priests had exited the riverbed, God released the waters of Jordan, and the river returned to flood stage. This is, in a sense, a third fulfilled promise. It proves that God had kept His word in getting Israel safely across the river. The means He used left no room for doubt that this was God's doing, even to the timing of the return of the water. God must have released the water while the priests were still standing in the middle of the river, maybe even while Joshua was building the monument. It took a miracle of God's timing for the water to have traveled twenty miles downstream, arriving at the point of Israel's crossing at the very moment the "soles of the priests' feet were lifted up unto the dry land." Actually, the priests probably heard and maybe even felt the rumble of the water's approach well before they reached the shore. Imagine their relief when they reached the high-water mark just as the waters surged back to the level they had flowed only hours before!

Once Israel had entered the Promised Land, they established a camp at Gilgal. Canaan was their new dwelling place. Israel recognized that the crossing of the river was permanent. There was no going back. God had provided a way in, but not a way out. Granted, Reuben, Gad, and half of Manasseh would go back across to settle the land they inherited, but that would be much later and at a different time of year. For now, we should see that Israel realized that God's means of crossing the Jordan into the Promised Land was a one-way street. Spiritually, that points to the believer's security in Christ. We can't be un-reborn (1 Pet. 1:23–25). We can't be un-sealed (Eph. 1:13–14). We can't be dis-indwelt (Rom. 8:9–11). We can't be un-adopted (Eph. 1:5–6). The bride can't be divorced from the Bridegroom (Eph. 5:23–32). We can't be separated from the love of God (Rom. 8:35–39). *God's work in saving us cannot be undone.*

Removing the Reproach

Forty Wasted Years

Israel had wasted forty years wandering in the wilderness. This period of distrust and rebellion had brought upon Israel a great reproach. When they worshiped the golden calf and broke the law of God, they'd forsaken the covenant with God that they'd entered into at Sinai (Exod. 32–33). They also forsook their covenant at Paran (Num. 13–14). God had brought the former generation to the edge of Canaan, and they had been afraid to trust God to give them the land. They had, in effect, rejected the Promised Land. At the same time, they rejected God's leadership, clamoring for another leader to take them back to Egypt (Num. 14:4). Israel as a nation had decided they didn't want the gift God had offered them or the guidance He had provided for them. Their decision placed them in the position of facing God's judgment rather than receiving His grace. The unbelievers among them would face the eternal judgment of God while the disobedient and fearful children of God would face His chastisement (Heb. 12:6–7). Their cry, "Would God we had died in this wilderness" (Num. 14:2), God answered:

> . . . as ye have spoken in mine ears, so will I do to you: your carcasses shall fall in this wilderness; and all that were numbered of you, according to your whole number, from twenty years old and upward, which have murmured against me (Num. 14:28*b*–29).

Israel would spend forty years—one year for each day the spies had enjoyed in the land God had promised to give them—wandering in the wilderness until they got what they asked for: the death of a generation (Num. 14:33–34). Their distrust of God and disdain for His covenants earned them "the reproach of Egypt" and the scorn of the world. Moses feared that Egypt and the inhabitants of Canaan would look upon Israel and God with contempt.

> And Moses said unto the Lord, Then the Egyptians shall hear it, (for thou broughtest up this people in thy might from among them;) and they will tell it to the inhabitants of this land: for they have heard that thou Lord art among this people, that thou Lord art seen face to face, and that thy cloud standeth over them, and that thou goest before them, by day time in a pillar of a cloud, and in a pillar of fire by night. Now if thou shalt kill all this people as one man, then the nations which have heard the fame of thee will speak, saying, Because the Lord was not able to bring this people into the land which he sware unto them, therefore he hath slain them in the wilderness (Num. 14:13–16).

Moses was right. Why should the world have any respect for people who claim to be God's children but are afraid or unwilling to follow their God? *Many professing believers today want to go to heaven but don't want to* ***be*** *Christians.* If we go nowhere with God, make no progress in our Christian lives, we should expect the world to treat us with the contempt we deserve. Such an attitude should also cause one to doubt the genuineness of his faith.

Reconciliation with God

Now that the new generation has moved across the Jordan, several things are going to happen in Gilgal before the actual campaign of conquest begins. The reproach of Egypt must be removed. These events illustrate to Israel and the world around them that Israel was making a distinct break between the former life they had led and the new life they would lead. Building the monument to memorialize the crossing is one of those events. Three others include circumcising the men (5:1–9), celebrating Passover (5:10), and eating the produce of the land (5:11–12).

> And it came to pass, when all the kings of the Amorites, which were on the side of Jordan westward, and all the kings of the Canaanites, which were by the sea, heard that the Lord had dried up the waters of Jordan from before the children of Israel, until we were passed over, that their heart melted, neither was there spirit in them any more, because of the children of Israel. At that time the Lord said unto Joshua, Make thee sharp knives, and circumcise again the children of Israel the second time. And Joshua made him sharp knives, and circumcised the children of Israel at the hill of the foreskins. And this is the cause why Joshua did circumcise: All the people that came out of Egypt, that were males, even all the men of war, died in the wilderness by the way, after they came out of Egypt. Now all the people that came out were circumcised: but all the people that were born in the wilderness by the way as they came forth out of Egypt, them they had not circumcised. For the children of Israel walked forty years in the wilderness, till all the people that were men of war, which came out of Egypt, were consumed, because they obeyed not the voice of the Lord: unto whom the Lord sware that he would not show them the land, which the Lord sware unto their fathers that he would give us, a land that floweth with milk and honey. And their children, whom he raised up in their

> stead, them Joshua circumcised: for they were uncircumcised, because they had not circumcised them by the way. And it came to pass, when they had done circumcising all the people, that they abode in their places in the camp, till they were whole. And the Lord said unto Joshua, This day have I rolled away the reproach of Egypt from off you. Wherefore the name of the place is called Gilgal unto this day (Josh. 5:1–9).

The solution to the problem of the reproach of Egypt upon Israel was for Israel to be reconciled to God. This started with the *performing of the rite of circumcision*. Joshua was actually told to *make* the knives for this procedure. The word rendered *sharp* in the KJV is "flint" in the Hebrew. Precisely why Joshua was to make flint knives rather than using bronze ones that would have been more common and readily available is not made clear in the text.

From the perspective of a military tactician, this was a serious mistake for a couple of reasons. First, moving an army into enemy territory and then performing surgery that would incapacitate them for several days would make them vulnerable to enemy attack. It also sacrificed what we might call "offensive momentum." It would have made more "sense" to circumcise the men *before* crossing the river. The camp would have been more secure in the territory Israel already held. Further, the river crossing would have Israel at an emotional peak and the enemy as demoralized as possible. It would seem sensible to launch the military campaign immediately. But God has His own way of doing things. He is not bound by strategic conventions and doesn't need the advice of military commanders.

As *strategically dangerous* as this appeared to be, it was *spiritually necessary*. Circumcision was the mark of identification of Israel as God's people. Circumcising the army now marked Israel's decision to deliberately forsake forty years of rebellion during which a generation had failed to obey this simple command. "The crossing of Jordan symbolizes death and rebirth, and the renewal of circumcision constituted Israel anew as the people of God."[43] This generation of Israel was consciously choosing to participate in the covenant with God. This act also indicated Israel's submission to God. God expects those who love Him to demonstrate it by their obedience (Exod. 20:6; cf. John 14:15, 21, 23–24). This was also a prerequisite for celebrating the Passover (Exod. 12:48). In their rebellion, Israel had refused to commemorate God's bringing them out of Egypt, with the last recorded instance of the celebration of Passover being when Israel was at Sinai (Num. 9:5). It was important for the generation entering Canaan to be ceremonially prepared to celebrate that holy day.

[43] Madvig, p. 274.

Circumcising the army was also *spiritually instructive*. Have you ever hesitated to witness to a lost person or instruct a believer because you were afraid of how he might react? It is good to be conscious of the feelings of others, or we might be brutish and offensive rather than meek and winsome in the way we represent God. But we must never be more afraid of man's reaction than we are of God's displeasure (Matt. 10:28). One of the lessons taught by circumcising the army in enemy territory is that Israel knew that *the anger of God is more to be feared than the attack of men*. It also showed Israel's confidence *that the help of God is the best security if we want to succeed*. They didn't need the Jordan River to protect them. God was their protector. Actually, since the Jordan hadn't provided much protection for Canaan, how safe would Israel have been had they hidden behind Jordan rather than obeying God? Ultimately, what this illustrates is that *everything we do for God should begin with repentance and worship.*

We have a tendency to be less than patient in our service for the Lord. We want results, and we want them *now*. We treat evangelism as if our primary purpose is to *win converts*, when Jesus actually told us to *make disciples*. Disciple making takes time, requiring patient instruction in "all things whatsoever I have commanded you" (Matt. 28:19–20). The Lord Jesus Himself took three-and-a-half years to train twelve apostles. Do we really think a twenty-minute presentation of the gospel is adequate? It may be all a given individual needs in order to hear and respond to the truth, but our job isn't finished with a conversion. It's just getting started. Sometimes we've been guilty of teaching new converts to evangelize their neighbors before we even teach them to worship the God Who saved them.

The high-pressure evangelistic tactics popular among us in the 1960s and '70s made for impressive sounding statistics as we were able to report hundreds or even thousands of conversions each year. But few of those who "made decisions to accept Christ" actually stayed in the church and grew spiritually mature. I'm convinced that *where there is no changed life there has been no real conversion*. We've made a multitude of spiritual orphans—people who don't really know Christ and don't have the Holy Spirit within them but are convinced they're on their way to heaven because a church worker told them they'd be saved if they repeated the right words.

Once the men had been circumcised, Israel was ready to *celebrate Passover*. It was no accident that the Lord brought Israel into Canaan in time to be prepared by the fourteenth day of the first month (Lev. 23:5).

> And the children of Israel encamped in Gilgal, and kept the passover on the fourteenth day of the month at even in the plains of Jericho. And they did

> eat of the old corn of the land on the morrow after the passover, unleavened cakes, and parched corn in the selfsame day (Josh. 5:10–11).

Passover was to be a special holiday celebrating God's faithfulness to His people. Several events in Israel's recent history could be considered "Passover" events. Israel's enemies had just "passed over" an opportunity to attack them in their weakened condition as the army recovered from surgery. Israel itself had "passed over" the Jordan River without being soaked by its waters or soiled by the riverbed. Similarly, a generation before, Israel had "passed over" the Red Sea. But the primary significance of Passover was to commemorate Israel's being spared the tenth plague on Egypt in which the firstborn of each household died. When the Lord brought death that night (Exod. 12:12, 23, 27, 29), He passed over those houses properly marked by the blood of the lamb and spared any people who remained inside. It was this event that Israel had been told to commemorate annually.

This first Passover celebration in a generation was a historic event. The hearts and minds of all Israel were focused on the grace and mercy of God, Who spared the firstborn of Israel years before. No wonder the people were prepared to spare those in Rahab's house when they saw the scarlet cord hanging from the window. They couldn't help but make the connection between Rahab's situation and their own. We, too, mustn't miss the event's anticipation of Christ, "our Passover" (1 Cor. 5:7). *It is His blood applied to our hearts that delivers us from the just judgment of God* (Heb. 10:22).

The final event marking Israel's departure from wilderness life to their new life in the Promised Land was a change of diet.

> And the manna ceased on the morrow after they had eaten of the old corn of the land; neither had the children of Israel manna any more; but they did eat of the fruit of the land of Canaan that year (Josh. 5:12).

During forty years' wandering in the wilderness, Israel had been fed by God's miraculous provision of manna. Now that God had brought them into the land "flowing with milk and honey," the manna was no longer necessary. God was still the provider, but the means of provision had changed.

The reference to the "old corn of the land" needs a little explanation. First, the word translated *corn* doesn't refer to that ear of sweet corn that I love to eat with butter, salt and pepper, as quickly as it can be cooked after it's pulled from the stalk. The grain we call *corn* was unknown in England in 1611, when the King James Bible was translated, and it was certainly unknown in ancient Palestine. The Pilgrims were introduced to this grain in 1620 by the Native Americans who taught them to grow it. The word in the Hebrew is a generic term best rendered *grain*. It may have been barley, which was ready to harvest at the time of Passover. Or it may have been wheat or oats or rye, which would not have been ready for several weeks yet. If any of the latter, Israel was eating last year's crop, which they could have taken from storehouses found in the countryside. However, the word *corn* could be understood in an even broader sense to refer to any produce. The reference to "the fruit of the land" is certainly not limited to fruit but would include vegetables, grains, and possibly even dairy products. The point Joshua is making is that God had kept His promise. Israel could now indulge in foods they would have had only limited access to during their years in the wilderness. In a sense, they had moved from the "milk of the word" (manna) to the "strong meat" (Heb. 5:12–14), having grown up.

Applying the Lessons

There are at least three important spiritual applications to be drawn from this passage. God once again demonstrated that His power is total and universal. The God Who provided for Israel in the wilderness was able to take them through the Jordan unscathed and set them up in the land He had promised. God put Israel in situations requiring them to fear and obey Him. They had to trust God enough to be unafraid of threatening circumstances, like the rushing waters of the Jordan and the well-armed inhabitants of the land. On foot in the riverbed, they were defenseless without God's intervention. In their weakness following surgery, they were unable to defend themselves against their enemies. Finally, the leaders of Israel learned that *spiritual preparation for battle is vital in order to be victorious*. Building memorials, circumcising the army, recovering from surgery, celebrating Passover, and adjusting to a new diet all took time. But time spent preparing is time well spent.

> It is neither the first business of the church to "win the world for Christ" nor of the individual Christian to seek the salvation of his relatives and companions: rather, it is to "show forth the praises of Him who hath called us out of darkness into His marvelous light" (1 Pet. 2:9) by our entire subjection to His word. God has nowhere promised to use those who make not conscience of obeying Him in all things.[44]

Arthur Pink did *not* say that seeking the salvation of friends and family is not the business of the church. He said that we must never allow obedience in one area alone, evangelism, to take priority over personal obedience to all of God's commands. Before we are really prepared to be effective witnesses of the gos-

[44] Pink, p. 133.

pel of Christ, we must demonstrate a willingness and desire to put God first and to subject our wills to His.

When the apostle Paul challenged believers in the church at Corinth to consider that “some have not the knowledge of God,” he did *not* say, “Get busy and preach the gospel.” He said, “**Awake to righteousness, and sin not;** for some have not the knowledge of God” (1 Cor. 15:34). If we want our neighbors to know God, we must do more than *tell* them about Him. We must *show* them God through our lives.

12
The Conquest of Jericho:
Preparing for the Assault

Joshua 5:13–6:10

After graduating from a Christian liberal arts college with a degree in music education, I took a job as a schoolteacher. I'd spent four years studying education courses designed to train me to teach what I'd learned in my fields of concentration: music and Bible. So, naturally, the school that hired me assigned me to teach the sixth grade. The entire curriculum. Including history, math, science, grammar, literature, spelling, physical education, and (OK, one subject I'd actually trained for) Bible.

Teachers were to start work one week before the students showed up for the first day of school. This "in-service" week was for orienting the new teachers to the school facility and personnel, instructing all teachers on school policies and schedules (which apparently changed somewhat from year to year), and allowing time for the teachers to organize our classrooms and prepare our unit plans for the first semester and detailed lesson plans for the first week.

Most of the first two days was spent in meetings. On the afternoon of the second day I was finally given copies of the textbooks I was expected to teach that year and a curriculum guide for the material. The curriculum guide was especially helpful. It was designed to suggest which sections of each text should be covered each day in order to complete the material by the end of the year. Basically, I was told, "Just follow this curriculum guide and study the textbooks and you'll know what to do." It sounded so easy. Why did I feel so overwhelmed? I'll tell you why. I knew that on Monday morning I would be introducing myself to a classroom full of thirty-two twelve-year-olds, several of whom had reputations for being chronic disciplinary problems. I knew that they knew more about this school and even the study materials than I did. I wasn't just overwhelmed; I was terrified. My overall objective was clear. I was supposed to teach this group of students a specific body of material in the coming year—hopefully without seriously injuring anyone in the process. I needed a plan that was a lot more specific than "Follow the book."

A Closed City

As Israel celebrated Passover week, eating unleavened bread for seven days, the recently circumcised army continued to rest and recuperate. I imagine Joshua, who had been circumcised in Egypt, may have been a little restless. As soon as the Passover celebrations ended, it would be time for Israel to advance into Canaan. Since God had intentionally brought Israel to this specific place, it seems reasonable to assume that the first city He expected Israel to confront would be Jericho, the nearest significant city to their camp.

God had been very specific about Joshua's objective—to take the land (1:1–9). He had not been at all specific about how that was to be accomplished. God told Joshua to study "this book of the law" and "do . . . all that is written therein" in order to "have good success" (1:8). He didn't promise to provide specific strategies for each battle or for any particular battle. So how does a band of nomadic tribesmen take a fortified city? That question weighed heavily on Joshua's mind as he slipped out of camp to find an observation post from which he could survey the city and consider his options.

> And it came to pass, when Joshua was by Jericho, that he lifted up his eyes and looked, . . . Now Jericho was straitly shut up because of the children of Israel: none went out, and none came in (Josh. 5:13*a*; 6:1).

Joshua didn't spend Passover week relaxing in camp or sitting in his tent brooding. He took his responsibilities seriously, but he wasn't overcome by them. I suspect that Joshua had sought out a solitary place to meditate on his responsibilities as Israel's leader. I also believe he "was by Jericho" to learn what he could that might be helpful for planning a strategy for taking the city. As he looked at Jericho, Joshua saw for himself the strength of the enemy.

According to the findings of archaeological excavations done in and around Jericho in the 1930s,[45] Jericho was a beautiful city, but it was also a military

[45] I'm referring here to the work of John Garstang done from 1930 to 1936. Since then, however, other archaeologists have challenged the dating of the fortress described in these

base. It was the chief fortified city of the lower Jordan valley, strategically located to protect the region from any invaders—like Israel—who might make it across the river from the east. This was a city that absolutely must be subdued before Israel could advance. To bypass this city would leave their flanks exposed to a powerful enemy and might endanger the families of Reuben, Gad, and Manasseh that had been left on the far side of Jordan, not to mention any women and children who would remain in the new camp at Gilgal while the army went to war.

Rather than being a large city with a miles-long wall surrounding it, Jericho more closely resembled a large medieval castle. There was a central fortress that enclosed an area of about six acres and was surrounded by farms and perhaps villages. Most of the inhabitants of Jericho probably didn't live permanently within the walls of the city, but they would go there to do business or for protection when threatened by attack. It was built at the top of an ancient mound with slopes steep enough that it was difficult to approach. John Garstang describes a double wall surrounding the city. The average thickness of the inner wall was twelve feet and of the outer wall six feet. The walls were built with a gap between them varying from twelve to fifteen feet across. Apparently several businesses and residences were built between the walls, which would explain Rahab's house being "upon the wall" (Josh. 2:15). The walls' foundations were adequate to support stone structures standing as much as thirty feet high.

However, more recent discoveries have modified Garstang's description. Peter Colon says, "Surrounding the entire city was an enormous earthen embankment with huge, stone retaining walls at its base. At the top of the embank-

---

paragraphs and suggest that the city destroyed by Joshua came from a different era. Most notable is the work of Kathleen Kenyon, based on her excavations of Jericho from 1952 to 1958. While providing ample evidence of a mighty Jericho destroyed by fire circa 1440 BC, Kenyon challenged the double-wall theory of Garstang and suggested on the basis of her belief in a late date for the Exodus that by the time Joshua destroyed the city, Jericho was small and sparsely populated. While she may be correct that the two walls came from different eras, her later date for Joshua's conquest is almost certainly wrong. The few artifacts she has identified as belonging to the Jericho of Joshua's day are probably better understood to have come from the brief Moabite occupation of the site early in the period of the Judges (Judg. 3:12–30). Since the Bible indicates that Jericho was not rebuilt for several generations after the destruction described in Joshua 6, the structure Garstang described better fits the evidence and timetable of Israel's conquest of the city under Joshua. If a mighty Jericho had fallen and been rebuilt before Joshua's time, it seems strange that the city Joshua destroyed would have left the paltry evidence of its existence described by Kenyon. See John Garstang, *The Story of Jericho*, 2nd ed. (London: Marshall, Morgan and Scott, 1948) and Kathleen Kenyon, *Digging Up Jericho* (New York: Frederick A. Praeger, 1957). For a summary, see Leon Wood, *A Survey of Israel's History* (Grand Rapids: Zondervan, 1970, rev. 1986), pp. 74–78.

ment stood a colossal, 46-foot-high mud-brick wall."[46] Jericho's fortifications were impressive.

An Armed Captain

A closed fortress was not all Joshua saw from his vantage point overlooking Jericho. As he pondered his options, he was confronted by a soldier who was not just armed for battle but was ready to fight with his sword already drawn.

> When Joshua was by Jericho, that he lifted up his eyes and looked, and, behold, there stood a man over against him with his sword drawn in his hand: and Joshua went unto him, and said unto him, Art thou for us, or for our adversaries? And he said, Nay; but as captain of the host of the Lord am I now come. And Joshua fell on his face to the earth, and did worship, and said unto him, What saith my lord unto his servant? And the captain of the Lord's host said unto Joshua, Loose thy shoe from off thy foot; for the place whereon thou standest is holy. And Joshua did so (Josh. 5:13–15).

It was apparently obvious to Joshua that the man standing before him wasn't one of Joshua's troops. Perhaps he could tell by the way the man was dressed or by the type and quality of weapon he carried. It is unlikely that Joshua would know on sight every man in Israel's camp since the army numbered over six hundred thousand. But Joshua didn't ask the man to identify himself by tribe. He didn't ask him why he was out of camp and who his commanding officer was.

If he wasn't from Israel's camp, who was he? Joshua expected to find no friends or allies among the inhabitants of Canaan, so the logical conclusion would be that the man was an enemy. Joshua's reaction to being confronted by this armed man is another indication of his character. He demonstrated courage when he didn't run back to camp to get help and didn't sound a signal to call for reinforcements. He approached the man alone, assuming he represented a threat. Joshua also demonstrated discretion in that he didn't attack the man without provocation. He confronted the man directly with the question "Are you for us or for our adversaries?" The first thing Joshua needed to know about the man was where his loyalties lay.

The man's reply is classic. Imagine Joshua's initial confusion when the man answered the question "Are you for us or for our adversaries" by saying,

---

[46] Peter Colon, "Archaeology Confirms the Walls 'Fell Flat,'" *Israel My Glory*, Vol. 62, No. 1 (Bellmawr, NJ: Friends of Israel Gospel Ministry, Inc.), January/February 2004, p. 16.

"No." The man insisted that he hadn't come to this place to fight for Israel or for Israel's enemies. He had come "as captain of the host of the Lord." It had seemed pretty clear-cut to Joshua that a man armed for battle with his sword drawn must be prepared to fight either on the side of Israel or on the side of the Canaanites. This man implied that the real issue was whether Joshua was fighting for the Lord or for His enemies.

When we find ourselves engaged in conflict, we are tempted to recruit people to our side to help us. We may even pray for the Lord to help us in the situation, expecting Him to be on our side. At a basketball game between two Christian high schools, both teams are likely to be found in the locker room before the game praying for divine assistance. Which team should God help? Isn't it better to say that those involved in the game should be on God's side rather than asking God to choose a side? I think God is more concerned that the conduct and character of the players demonstrate Christlikeness than He is that one team or the other scores more points.

Who was this man on the hill beside Jericho who identified himself as "captain of the host of the Lord"? It was the Lord Himself. Joshua witnessed a *Christophany*, a preincarnate appearance of Jesus Christ. There are at least three evidences that this man was not just an angel but was, in fact, God. When the man identified himself, Joshua immediately fell down on his face. It is possible that Joshua's bowing to the ground was voluntary and that he could have been mistaken. By itself, this doesn't constitute proof of the man's deity. But it is also possible that Joshua fell to the ground intuitively because he sensed that the man was God, or even involuntarily, as did the soldiers who tried to arrest Jesus in Gethsemane (John 18:5–6). Second, Joshua worshiped the man. When Daniel fell on his face in fear before the angel Gabriel, the angel didn't let him remain on his face but set him upright (Dan. 8:16–18). In Joshua's case, his worship was actually encouraged. He was told to remove his sandals ("shoe" KJV) because he stood on holy ground. It is not that Joshua was unwittingly standing on some ancient shrine but that any place God reveals Himself is made holy. Because of Joshua's familiarity with the books of Moses, these instructions immediately confirmed to Joshua's mind that this man was the "I Am," Who spoke to Moses at the burning bush (Exod. 3:5–14). The third evidence for this man's identity as God is found in Joshua 6:2. As the conversation progresses, the man speaking to Joshua is identified as "the LORD."[47]

---

[47] This is one of those instances in which the Bible's chapter divisions get in the way. Chapter and verse divisions were not part of the inspired text. They were added later to help readers find specific passages. Generally, they are very helpful, but they occasionally interrupt the flow of the narrative and cause the reader to miss vital connections between passages.

A Plan for Conquest

A Call to Faith

Jericho was shut up tight—no one could enter or exit the city (6:1). Granted, if all the people associated with Jericho took refuge within its walls, conditions were probably quite crowded. Further, Israel had substantial numerical advantage over Jericho. But with no heavy weapons, and no experience at siege warfare, taking the city wouldn't be easy. To complicate matters, Jericho was well supplied with water. There were sufficient springs inside the walls, so the fortress of Jericho "under ordinary circumstances could easily withstand a siege of several years."[48] That would make besieging the city a bad strategy for Joshua to employ. Israel would have to find a way to breach the walls and take the city.

> And the Lord said unto Joshua, See, I have given into thine hand Jericho, and the king thereof, and the mighty men of valour. And ye shall compass the city, all ye men of war, and go round about the city once. Thus shalt thou do six days. And seven priests shall bear before the ark seven trumpets of rams' horns: and the seventh day ye shall compass the city seven times, and the priests shall blow with the trumpets. And it shall come to pass, that when they make a long blast with the ram's horn, and when ye hear the sound of the trumpet, all the people shall shout with a great shout; and the wall of the city shall fall down flat, and the people shall ascend up every man straight before him. And Joshua the son of Nun called the priests, and said unto them, Take up the ark of the covenant, and let seven priests bear seven trumpets of rams' horns before the ark of the Lord. And he said unto the people, Pass on, and compass the city, and let him that is armed pass on before the ark of the Lord. And it came to pass, when Joshua had spoken unto the people, that the seven priests bearing the seven trumpets of rams' horns passed on before the Lord, and blew with the trumpets: and the ark of the covenant of the Lord followed them. And the armed men went before the priests that blew with the trumpets, and the rereward came after the ark, the priests going on, and blowing with the trumpets. And Joshua had commanded the people, saying, Ye shall not shout, nor make any noise with your voice, neither shall any word proceed out of your mouth, until the day I bid you shout; then shall ye shout (Josh. 6:2–10).

The flow more naturally divides the chapter after 5:12, since 5:13–15 are much more closely connected to the narrative in chapter 6 than to that which precedes them.

[48] Eugene H. Merrill, *An Historical Survey of the Old Testament* (Grand Rapids: Baker Book House, 1966), p. 157.

The Lord has come to see Joshua to provide both encouragement and a plan. The Lord said He had given Jericho into Joshua's hand. Amazing! This city that seemed virtually impregnable was Joshua's for the taking. This was a great encouragement, but it was also humbling. Jericho would fall, but not because Joshua was clever. The victory would be God's gift.

A Call to Obedience

That God would give the city to Israel in no way diminished Joshua's responsibility. God expects us to obey even when He has told us His purpose and guaranteed its accomplishment. The Lord began His instructions for Joshua with the imperative "See." This word means more than simply "look." It means "*to take note of*, or *to keep steadily in mind*." We use the word in this sense when a parent gives a child a job to do and says, "*See* that you get it done before dinner." You don't want your son to watch the job get done. You want him to take note of the fact, and keep steadily in mind, that he has a responsibility to fulfill and a deadline for doing it. Yes, God had given Jericho to Joshua, but God has instructions for Joshua to follow to obtain the victory.

I'll admit that if I were Joshua my excitement at God's encouragement may have waned a bit when I heard the instructions God laid out for taking Jericho. The plan is at best unusual. As a military strategy, it seems absurd, but that is precisely the point. Israel wouldn't take Jericho by superior strategy but by a superior God. This "battle" would illustrate the truth stated by Paul, "For the weapons of our warfare are not carnal [fleshly], but mighty through God to the pulling down of strongholds" (2 Cor. 10:4).

God said the ark must lead the way as they were crossing the Jordan. But the marching order God described for taking Jericho began with the men of war in front. This was an enormous fighting force, even if ill-equipped. There were over 530,000 men in Israel's army (Num. 25:51).[49] That is about the number of troops the United States deployed in 1991 to fight the Gulf War.

Some commentators have suggested that when God brought down the walls of Jericho He brought down only the section of wall in front of the Israelite army, leaving the rest of the wall (including Rahab's house) standing to keep the inhabitants from escaping. I suppose that's possible, but I don't think it

---

[49] Arthur Cundall claims Israel's army numbered only 40,000 (*Judges and Ruth* [Downers Grove, IL: Intervarsity Press, 1968], p. 199). He has mistaken the number of soldiers contributed by the Transjordanian tribes (Josh. 4:13) as the total number mobilized by Israel, ignoring the figures provided by Moses' final census recorded in Numbers 26. The total was actually 601,700. But about 70,000 from Reuben, Gad, and half of Manasseh apparently stayed in Transjordan when the rest of Israel crossed the river, leaving approximately 530,000 in the fighting force.

was necessary. If the walls of Jericho encompassed an area of six acres, the city's circumference was only a little over 600 yards. Assuming that the army would prefer to keep a safe distance from the walls to stay out of range of archers, they may have marched around "greater Jericho" rather than marching up against the walls. If "greater Jericho" covered 360 acres, as some sources suggest, the circumference of the army's path was about 4700 yards. The 530,000 men in Israel's army could have stood three feet apart and surrounded the city with 112 rows of soldiers. When the walls came down, the inhabitants of the city had nowhere to go. This alone would have been an intimidating sight for those who protected Jericho.

Coming behind this enormous army was a tiny band of seven priests. They could easily be overlooked in the shadow of the vast multitude they followed, but their role was vital. Their white linen robes symbolized the righteousness of God. The rams' horns they carried were not the normal instruments used by the priests. Usually, they played much more sophisticated silver trumpets (Num. 10:1–10).[50] So why use rams horns on this occasion? One reason might have been the distinctive, plaintive sound of the rams' horns that might have served to terrify the Canaanites. Another reason would be the special significance of the rams' horns to Israel. The Hebrew word translated "rams horns" is *yobel*. Throughout the book of Leviticus, this word is translated "Jubilee." That is the name given to the celebration God said Israel must observe every fifty years in which they would free all slaves, cancel all debts, and revert all estates to their original owners. To Israel *Jubilee* meant *freedom*. Hearing the sound of the *yobel* would signify that God was returning to Israel the land He had promised their forefathers. He was bringing them into this land to give them their freedom in Him.

There was one other reason for the use of the rams' horns. The sound of a ram's horn was both feeble and crude compared to the sound of a silver trumpet. On a silver trumpet you can play a tune and play it loud. On a ram's horn you just blow. These simple instruments indicated that Israel's victory wouldn't come by the strength of the sound of the trumpet nor the skill with which it was played but by faithful adherence to the explicit instructions of God (cf. 1 Cor. 1:21). Churches today would do well to remember this principle. To be blessed of God is to be pleasing in His sight. A church doesn't

[50] The instruments called "trumpets" in the Bible were actually more closely related to the modern-day cornet or trombone. Modern trumpets have a cylindrical bore, meaning that the interior diameter of the tubing is the same from the mouthpiece until you get to the flared bell. Cornets and trombones have a conical bore. While there are sections of a consistent bore in those instruments (cornet's valves and trombone's slide), both are made of tubing whose interior diameter gradually increases throughout its length. Biblical trumpets were instruments with a conical bore. Martin Luther was correct in his German translation of the New Testament when he tells the church to listen for the "last trombone" (1 Cor. 15:52; 1 Thess. 4:16).

need more effective programs, more exciting music, or more special events to please God. A church needs total individual and corporate obedience to the Word of God and the faithful proclamation of the whole counsel of God.

Behind this little band of white-robed priests carrying rams' horns and in front of the rest of the people of Israel came the ark of the covenant—the symbol of the presence of God. As Israel approached Jericho, God wasn't a long way out in front. He was in their midst. Having renewed the covenant at Gilgal, Israel as a nation was the people of *Yahweh*, and *Yahweh* was the God of Israel. The presence of the ark in their midst served as a *restraint for the flesh*—reminding them to obey God because He was with them. It served as a *stimulant for the spirit*—reminding them to believe God because He was with them. It was also the *symbol of the righteous judgment of God*. They would need that reminder to be able to carry out God's command to utterly destroy the enemy.

In this unique attack on the city of Jericho, there is some question concerning who participated in the march. Madvig says, "Only 'the armed men' were involved. The women, children, and livestock remained in the camp."[51] He understands the marching order to be that the forty thousand troops ("armed guard") from the Transjordanian tribes went before the ark and the rest of the soldiers ("the rear guard") followed. He may be right.

But the word rendered *rear guard* in the NIV and NASB, and by the enigmatic "rereward" in the KJV, means simply "a gathering together." There is nothing in the word to indicate that they are a military force or are armed. Translating the word "rear *guard*" is interpretive on the basis of the military action.[52] I'm inclined to read it differently. It's not a critical point, but I think the "armed men" in the front were the entire fighting force of Israel and "those who came behind" were the rest of the multitude of Israel. If so, everyone in the camp participated in the march, and only the soldiers stormed the city. There was no nursery or "children's church" program for the youngsters back in Gilgal while the grown-ups were involved in taking the city. Everybody was to participate in this battle.

The priests weren't allowed to advance until everyone was in place. If Israel's camp at Gilgal were only a mile from Jericho, and they were to march around a circle enclosing 360 acres, the total march roundtrip was at least four miles. That is a long hike for a little tyke, and a long way for a mother to carry an infant.

---

[51] Madvig, p. 278.

[52] J. J. Lias concurs in *The Pulpit Commentary*, Vol. 7, Joseph Exell, ed. (Chicago: Wilcox and Follett Co., n.d.), p. 99. Keil dissents in *Joshua, Judges, Ruth*, p. 65, arguing on what I believe to be the insufficient ground of the silence of the text.

To complicate matters, one of the cardinal instructions God gave Joshua was that the people were to maintain *absolute silence* during the march. This would require a level of discipline rarely observed in today's churches, much less in society at large. I know people who won't come to the church I pastor on Sunday evenings because we don't have special programs for children or teens during the evening services. One of the reasons we don't have such programs is that I believe it is vital to teach our children to attend to the preaching of the Word and to worship with the adults. Must we really plan alternative activities for children and teens whenever we assemble? Do we have to assume that adults will walk in and out of the service to use the restroom or get a drink of water? Is it really asking too much for folks to give themselves to uninterrupted worship for an hour or so?

God's instructions for Israel's conquest of Jericho should also teach us a lesson in reverence as we worship. We have good reasons for rejecting the formalism of Roman Catholicism with its emphasis on empty ritualism. But we need to beware lest we reject *organization* and *reverence* in the name of informality. The seraphim hide their faces in the presence of God (Isa. 6:2). Without reverence there is no worship, and we fail to fulfill our highest purpose in meeting together. Contrary to popular opinion, *noise and excitement do not necessarily indicate the presence of God*. In Elijah's case, the Lord was *not* in the wind, the earthquake, or the fire. He was in the still small voice (1 Kings 19:11–12).

Maintaining silence on this march was an important factor in the overall plan for conquering Jericho. The Lord wanted to teach Israel and the Canaanites some important lessons about Who He is.

> The fall of Jericho sent a powerful message to the Canaanites that Israel's successes were not mere human victories of man against man, but victories by the true God of Israel over their gods. This event, following closely upon the crossing of the Jordan by miraculous means, impressed upon the people that the same God who had led their fathers out of Egypt and through the Red Sea was with Joshua just as surely as He had been with Moses.[53]

[53] Spiros Zodhiates, *The Hebrew-Greek Key Study Bible* (AMG Publishers, 1984, 1991), p. 300–301.

13
The Conquest of Jericho:
Seven Days' March

Joshua 6:7–27

When I go visiting, I'm always on guard for loose animals. I'm never happy to hear the approach of barking dogs when I get out of the car. I'll admit I'm nervous around dogs I don't know and that don't know me. Still, I've been bitten only once. Ironically, the dog that bit me I never saw coming. Most dogs try to intimidate intruders by making lots of noise, but there are others that approach without warning. They're suddenly in your face, making no more noise than a low-pitched growl deep in their throats. A dog like that is so confident of his ability to defend his territory that he feels no need to try to scare you away. Those are the dogs that *really* scare me.

Armies often use tactics similar to noisy dogs. Using intimidation as a tool, they set out to "shock and awe" the enemy. Generally, the intent is to so demoralize the opposing forces that they give up the fight and avoid unnecessary loss of life. In the case of Israel's advance on Jericho, the silent, steady approach of the massed forces of Israel had to be intimidating in both the discipline and the confidence it displayed.

The First Six Days' March

Passover week had ended and Joshua had his marching orders. As odd as his instructions seemed, it was time to start. Each day for six days, the entire host of Israel was to *march once around Jericho*, then *return to camp*.

> And he said unto the people, Pass on, and compass the city, and let him that is armed pass on before the ark of the Lord. And it came to pass, when Joshua had spoken unto the people, that the seven priests bearing the seven trumpets of rams' horns passed on before the Lord, and blew with the trumpets: and the ark of the covenant of the Lord followed them. And the armed men went before the priests that blew with the trumpets, and the rereward came after the ark, the priests going on, and blowing with the trumpets. And Joshua had commanded the people, saying, Ye shall not shout, nor make any noise with your voice, neither shall any word proceed out of your mouth, until the day I bid you shout; then shall ye shout. So the ark of the Lord compassed the city, going about it once: and they came into the camp, and lodged in the camp. And Joshua rose early in the morning, and the priests took up the ark of the Lord. And seven priests bearing seven trumpets of rams' horns before the ark of the Lord went on continually, and blew with the trumpets: and the armed men went before them; but the rereward came after the ark of the Lord, the priests going on, and blowing with the trumpets. And the second day they compassed the city once, and returned into the camp: so they did six days (Josh. 6:7–14).

A Terrifying Sight

As strange as this plan may have sounded to Israel, imagine what must have been going through the minds of the inhabitants of Jericho. Surely they had the Israelite camp at Gilgal under surveillance. They knew the atmosphere in the camp was changing as Israel arose in the morning and began to organize into ranks for a march toward Jericho. The assault the people of Jericho had long feared was about to begin. As they took refuge behind the walls of the city, readying themselves for its defense, they took comfort in the knowledge that the city was well fortified and well supplied. Even so, the group marching toward Jericho was not just a tribe. It was an entire *nation*. What a terrifying sight! The army of Israel may not have had heavy weapons, but they were a huge, well-organized fighting force of over 530,000 men. They brought with them the ark of God. The fact that they also brought along their women and children indicated to the people of Jericho that Israel was supremely confident, expecting success.

An Ominous Sound

The average citizen of Jericho may not have been immediately privy to the information that Israel was on the move. Most of the people of the city may have *heard* Israel coming before they actually saw them. The sound would have been ominous. It may be that the first hint they had of Israel's approach wasn't even easily identifiable as sound. It was more of a distant rumble, like thunder or an earth tremor—something felt more than heard. I've sat in a stadium watching a college football game and heard the sound of eighty thousand fans stomping their feet. It's an awesome sound, starting as a vibration that gradually accumulates to a bass rumble. As perhaps two million Israelites moved toward Jericho (that's twenty-five times the number of people at that football game), four million marching feet made their impact on the land.

While the people of Jericho were still trying to decide if the almost subliminal vibrations were real or imagined, the city officials sounded the cry, "To the walls! Israel is coming!" Looking out from the top of walls that were thirty feet high and stood atop a mound rising above the level of the valley, the inhabitants of Jericho could see row upon row of Israelites seeming to blanket the earth as the leading edge advanced toward them. But before they came within range of the archers who waited along the ramparts, Israel turned aside and began to move around the city. Uncertain of Israel's intent, the watchers on the walls would soon notice that while they still felt the shock of all those marching feet, the forces of Israel moved on their way without shouted commands. They marched around the city without anyone calling cadence for the marchers or hurling curses or insults at their adversaries. Like a well-trained guard dog on patrol, they continued on their way without a sound. The eerie silence of the multitude must have heightened the tension within the city.

I can guess at the mingled confusion and fear that the defenders of Jericho must have felt as they watched the silent multitude slowly circle the city. But to the consternation of the watchers, the host of Israel turned aside and headed back to Gilgal after one circuit of Jericho. Israel hadn't actually done anything but march in a circle. No weapons had been brought to bear against the city. No threats had been made. Maybe this was just some kind of massive scouting expedition. Jericho was safe. For now.

Then morning came. Israel was again on the move. The people of Jericho were again called to take up their positions in defense of the city. What would Israel do today? Once again the host advanced toward the city. Once again they turned aside. Once again they marched silently around Jericho and returned to Gilgal. What was going on? By the morning of the third day, the people of Jericho were up and watching to see if Israel would come again that day. Perhaps by then they were a little less tense, anticipating another pointless circuit of the city. They weren't disappointed. Like the first and second, the third day passed without incident. And then the fourth day. And the fifth. By the sixth day, do you think the defenders of Jericho bothered to prepare their weapons? Feeling secure inside a city that Israel had yet to find a way to attack, maybe they just stood on the walls and taunted the Israelites.

A Great Success?

What might Israel have thought of their days marching around Jericho? Had they accomplished anything? No cracks had appeared in the walls. No representative of the city had volunteered to surrender. Had there been any point at all to getting everybody out of camp on a four-mile silent march every day for six days straight? Israel's accomplishment during those six days had less to do with conquering Jericho than with honoring and glorifying God. God is honored and glorified when His people obey Him. In today's churches we tend to measure success on the basis of tangible results. We assume that the church with lots of converts and new programs must be successful, while the church where conversions are rare and programs are few must be useless or dead. During Israel's march around Jericho there were no new converts and no new programs. All they did was consistently obey God and let Him do as He saw fit. And God was pleased.

Next time you're tempted to be puffed up in pride because of your "accomplishments" or deflated in despair because of your lack of "success," ask yourself which prophet was more pleasing to God: Jonah or Jeremiah? Jonah preached one sermon and the population of Nineveh was converted. Jeremiah preached in Jerusalem for nearly fifty years with virtually no visible success and a great deal of negative reaction. But Jeremiah obeyed and honored God and is remembered as a faithful prophet while Jonah resented his assignment and is remembered for his rebellion. The leader who brings the greatest glory to Christ is not the one with the most impressive visible results. He's the leader who most faithfully obeys his commission to teach the whole counsel of God (Acts 20:27; 1 Tim. 5:17; 2 Tim. 4:1–2).

The Seventh Day's March

An Early Start

The instructions for the seventh day were different from those for the first six. This time the host of Israel was to *march seven times around Jericho*, then *enter the city.*

> And it came to pass on the seventh day, that they rose early about the dawning of the day, and compassed the city after the same manner seven times: only on that day they compassed the city seven times. And it came to pass at the seventh time, when the priests blew with the trumpets, Joshua said unto the people, Shout; for the Lord hath given you the city. And the city shall be accursed,

> even it, and all that are therein, to the Lord: only Rahab the harlot shall live, she and all that are with her in the house, because she hid the messengers that we sent. And ye, in any wise keep yourselves from the accursed thing, lest ye make yourselves accursed, when ye take of the accursed thing, and make the camp of Israel a curse, and trouble it. But all the silver, and gold, and vessels of brass and iron, are consecrated unto the Lord: they shall come into the treasury of the Lord. So the people shouted when the priests blew with the trumpets: and it came to pass, when the people heard the sound of the trumpet, and the people shouted with a great shout, that the wall fell down flat, so that the people went up into the city, every man straight before him, and they took the city (Josh. 6:15–20).

The tactics on the seventh day were essentially the same as those used on the six previous days. Line up. March to Jericho. March around Jericho. Only this time it was more difficult. On the seventh day Israel had farther to walk. If they were marching around an area of 360 acres with a circumference of 4700 yards, the largest circle likely, each circuit was nearly 2.75 miles. Seven times around that circle would be a march of just over nineteen miles. This was not an early morning stroll they could finish before breakfast. They would need to get an early start. After this march, Israel was expected to subdue the city. I have no idea whether the weather that day was hot or cold, raining or dry; but even in the most comfortable conditions this promised to be a long, tiring day.

The fact that Israel started earlier than usual on the seventh day probably got the attention of the inhabitants of Jericho. I wonder what they were thinking as Israel continued a second time around the city without returning to Gilgal? Were they bored? Amused? Apprehensive? Angry? I don't know. I suspect that it had to be unnerving to watch two million people march silently around their city hour after hour. The more times Israel circled the city, the more damage they did to the land on which they marched. If it were raining, their feet gouged a massive trench around the city that day. If it were dry, the cloud of dust they kicked up may have nearly obscured the city from their view. Neither scenario would have pleased the folks in Jericho.

A Victory Shout

God's instructions for Israel said that after seven silent circuits of Jericho Joshua would command the seven priests to blow their rams' horns. That would be the signal for the host of Israel to shout. This was not the voice of singing. Two million parched throats uttering their first sound all day were raised in a loud, raucous cry that reverberated up and down the valley. A vital lesson is found in the fact that Israel was to sound the Jubilee (*yobel*) and shout their victory cry *while the walls still stood.* God wanted Israel to trust Him enough that they were willing to celebrate victory while the opposition was intact. That is hard to do. It is a lot easier to rejoice and proclaim victory once the walls come down.

We have to be cautious to avoid misapplying this principle. The principle illustrated here applies only to the clear promises of God. There are some things God has promised us that we have a right to claim by faith. For instance, we can claim Christ's joy (John 16:24), peace (John 14:27), and eternal life (John 10:27–28) even in the face of our adversary. But Israel's shouting down the walls of Jericho does *not* support the "name it and claim it" school of theology that says God is bound to give you anything you demand of Him. God is under no obligation to give us things simply because we want them (James 4:3). God hasn't promised me a thousand people in church or weekly offerings of $25,000. The truth is I'm not at all certain that being given the responsibility of pastoring a church of a thousand with a $1.25 million annual budget would constitute a "blessing." Neither has God promised you a house at the beach or a $250,000 annual income. You can't prove that would be a "blessing" either. God has promised to take care of those who are His. We must let Him determine the nature and timing of any "blessing" He may choose to bestow, and we must acknowledge that our future glorification is "blessing" enough (Rom. 8:18).

A Collapsed Structure

When Israel shouted, the walls of Jericho "fell down flat." The Hebrew word translated *flat* means, literally, "under it." Some have suggested that the walls dropped straight into the earth as if falling down an elevator shaft. That is a possible interpretation. It wouldn't have been unprecedented for God to open up the earth to swallow the walls (Num. 16:30–32). But I'm not sure that's a necessary interpretation. Israel was marching around the city at some distance. The walls could fall "under" the city by simply tumbling outward from their foundations down the slopes of the mound on which the city was built. Garstang's excavations in the 1930s uncovered walls that had fallen outward down the mound and that showed signs of being burned at the time of their collapse. It is difficult to imagine any other cause for the walls Garstang uncovered to have fallen like they did. Citing the work of Bryant G. Wood, a recognized authority on the archeology of Jericho, Peter Colon describes the findings of modern archeologists:

> Piles of mud bricks from the collapsed wall were found in 1997, confirming the walls were not destroyed by a battering ram, but that they collapsed. . . . A layer of ash three feet thick with remnants of burnt timbers and debris was found. . . . Of particular interest to excavators was that Jericho showed no signs of having been plundered. . . . Among the destroyed buildings were found many large jars full of charred grain. Normally, ancient conquerors

> carried off grain as spoils of war. But not at Jericho. The grain also indicated the city was not under siege for long. Had it been, the food would have been gone. However, the most fascinating discovery was on the north side of the city. The wall and houses built against it were preserved. . . . Is it possible [Rahab's] house was located on the north side?[54]

How the walls fell is less important than *why* they fell. The passage points to a threefold cause for the collapse of the walls. First, the walls were brought down *by God*, Who promised they would fall. Second, the walls were brought down *by faith* when Israel shouted victory while the walls stood. Third, the walls were brought down *by obedience* in that Israel followed God's directions exactly. All three were necessary and complementary components for bringing them down. Israel could have marched and shouted for years and the walls would have stood without the promise of God to bring them down. God's bringing the walls down was contingent upon the obedient faith of Israel.

Victory over Jericho

When the walls of Jericho collapsed, every man of Israel went "straight before him, and they took the city" (Josh. 6:20*b*).

> And they utterly destroyed all that was in the city, both man and woman, young and old, and ox, and sheep, and ass, with the edge of the sword. But Joshua had said unto the two men that had spied out the country, Go into the harlot's house, and bring out thence the woman, and all that she hath, as ye sware unto her. And the young men that were spies went in, and brought out Rahab, and her father, and her mother, and her brethren, and all that she had; and they brought out all her kindred, and left them without the camp of Israel. And they burnt the city with fire, and all that was therein: only the silver, and the gold, and the vessels of brass and of iron, they put into the treasury of the house of the Lord. And Joshua saved Rahab the harlot alive, and her father's household, and all that she had; and she dwelleth in Israel even unto this day; because she hid the messengers, which Joshua sent to spy out Jericho. And Joshua adjured them at that time, saying, Cursed be the man before the Lord, that riseth up and buildeth this city Jericho: he shall lay the foundation thereof in his firstborn, and in his youngest son shall he set up the gates of it. So the

[54] Colon, p. 16. For more information see "The Walls of Jericho," by Bryant G. Wood, *Bible and Spade*, Spring 1999, pp. 35–52, available from the Associates for Biblical Research, and "Did the Israelites Conquer Jericho? A New Look at the Archaeological Evidence," also by Wood, *Biblical Archaeology Review*, March/April 1990, pp. 44–58.

> Lord was with Joshua; and his fame was noised throughout all the country (Josh. 6:21–27).

The fighting that day was brutal. Without giving an unnecessarily graphic description, Joshua records that they "utterly destroyed" every person and animal within the city. But he hadn't forgotten the promise made to Rahab. The soldiers sent to rescue Rahab and her household as soon as Israel entered the city were the only two Israelites she knew and who knew her. Their presence would go a long way toward allaying her family's fears as they fled the slaughterhouse Jericho had become. The scarlet cord hanging from the window would help all the Israelite soldiers identify the home they were to spare. Of course, being the only house on the wall still standing probably helped, since it proved sparing Rahab was God's intent. Once they got Rahab, her family, and their property out of the city, they took them to a place outside their camp at Gilgal. They were apparently quarantined there until, at some undisclosed time, the necessary rituals could be performed[55] to admit Rahab's household as "naturalized citizens" of Israel, with Rahab eventually marrying a leader in the tribe of Judah (see chap. 6).

I can't help noticing the contrasts between this event and a similar event that had occurred about five hundred years earlier. God had determined to destroy the cities of Sodom and Gomorrah for their wickedness. Because God wanted to spare Abraham's nephew, Lot, and his family, He sent two angels (appearing as men) into Sodom to warn Lot of the coming destruction. They offered to protect and remove from the city any of Lot's household who would come. For all of Lot's efforts that night, none of his married sons or daughters believed him or sought the refuge the Lord offered. Lot himself delayed and had to be forcibly removed from the city. Even then, his wife looked back and was destroyed. Lot and two daughters were the only survivors, and they left with virtually nothing (Gen. 19:1–29). Lot, who had enjoyed contact with God for years, failed to convince his family to believe. Rahab, who had known God for days, gathered her whole household. In a sense, Lot's family represents Israel, who had all the advantages of centuries of communication with God but at the crucial moment rejected their Messiah and only a remnant will be saved. Rahab's family represents the Gentile church, which had none of the advantages of Israel but believed Jesus' offer of salvation from destruction and turned to Him in simple faith.

In the process of destroying Jericho, there were a few valuables Israel was to salvage. They were to keep the metals, specifically gold, silver, brass, and iron. These were to be dedicated to the Lord and deposited in the tabernacle treasury.

---

[55] Those rituals are specified in Lev. 13:46; Num. 5:3; 31:19; and Deut. 23:3 and 14 but are not described here.

The designation of these goods as the property of God served the same function as the tithe. Giving Him the goods from the first city taken illustrated the truth that all things belong to God. It demanded faith that Jericho was just a start—God would also give Israel the rest of the land. It demonstrated that all glory for the victory was God's alone.

When the fighting was over and the metals collected and properly deposited, Israel was to burn the city and its contents (cf. Deut. 7:25–26). This may have been just one more surprising detail for Israel. As the conquest of Canaan progressed, Israel was explicitly commanded to take the goods from other cities they sacked (Josh. 8:2). Usually, the spoils of war go to the victor. But that was precisely the point. *God* was the victor, so the spoils belonged to Him. As a matter of fact, anyone keeping anything from the city for himself was condemned for the crime of stealing from God. Further, in the coming campaign Israel would leave most of the cities standing so that they wouldn't have to build cities to occupy once the land was theirs. But this city was to be completely destroyed.

I'm sure this was hard to do. During Israel's forty years in the wilderness God had miraculously preserved the clothes and shoes the people wore (Deut. 29:5). I don't know for sure if that means they'd had nothing new for decades, but I do know they had been living in tents and hadn't gone on any shopping trips to Wal-Mart or the mall. How hard would it be to burn all these nice homes full of useful goods and the shops full of new wares? It seemed so wasteful. But God said it was necessary. He wanted Israel, the inhabitants of Canaan, and all who would learn of these events to understand just how seriously He takes our sin. This destruction points to the evilness of sin and the justice of God in judging it. God has a perfect right to judge sin whenever, wherever, and however He chooses. In the case of the Canaanites, He had cursed them generations before but had extended centuries of grace. He had even given them forty years advance warning that Israel was coming to claim their birthright. Rahab and her family were the only converts while God withheld His just wrath.

While Jericho burned, Joshua pronounced a curse upon anyone who would rebuild the city. When God destroys something, it can be unwise to rebuild it. While the city was resettled rather quickly (Josh. 18:21; Judg. 3:13–14; 2 Sam. 10:5), apparently no one made any attempt at *refortifying* Jericho for about seven hundred years. During the reign of Ahab, a man named Hiel of Bethel began construction, and the curse of God was fulfilled.

> In his days did Hiel the Bethelite build Jericho: he laid the foundation thereof in Abiram his firstborn, and set up the gates thereof in his youngest son Segub, according to the word of the Lord, which he spake by Joshua the son of Nun.

Significance of the Battle

We should learn at least three lessons from the narrative describing the destruction of Jericho. T*he city ultimately fell through the quiet, faithful perseverance of Israel.* Elaborate preparation and impressive display were not necessary. We live in a culture that expects immediate gratification. We do our banking at automated teller machines. We buy our lunch at a drive-through window. We want news in sound bites, dinner in microwaveable packages (unless delivery is an option), and communication via instant messaging. We expect immediate answers to prayer and overnight spiritual maturity. But spiritual growth takes time. In Canaan, total victory for Israel was still a long way off. But their patient obedience had succeeded in subduing the first enemy they faced.

Second, we see that *when we really surrender and obey God completely, He shows Himself strong on our behalf.* The abundant resources God draws upon for our aid are so far beyond our own ability as to be incomprehensible. That is what Paul is talking about when he describes Christ as "him that is able to do exceeding abundantly above all that we ask or think, according to the power that worketh in us" (Eph. 3:20). We don't have to understand how the outcome will be accomplished through our efforts. We simply need to obey God and trust Him to know what He is doing through us.

Finally, from the fall of Jericho we learn that *all genuine victory comes from God.* The old spiritual says, "Joshua fit the battle of Jericho." But the song is wrong. Joshua led Israel to Jericho, but it was God's doing when "the walls came a-tumblin' down." No credit for this victory fell to Joshua or to Israel. True, without their obedience Jericho would still stand, but it was God Who commanded and then enabled them to obey. Similarly, Paul admonishes the believer to "work out your own salvation with fear and trembling, for it is God which worketh in you both to will and to do of his good pleasure" (Phil. 2:12*b*–13). We must work to become more like Christ as we demonstrate that we are His, but it is ultimately God working in us that gives us victory.

> There is little doubt as to who really fought the battle of Jericho. The Lord Himself was the Commander-in-chief. This episode of Jericho's fall teaches that it is not vain to trust the Lord. When He promises victory and prescribes the course to that victory, those who believe the promise and follow the course will enjoy the victory.[56]

[56] Michael P. V. Barrett, "Who Fought the Battle of Jericho?" *Biblical Viewpoint*, XXVI (Greenville, SC: Bob Jones University, 1992), p. 32.

14
Israel's Humiliation

Joshua 7:1–12

One of the characteristics of drama is that the audience is often privy to information that isn't available to the people in the story. For instance, in a series of television movies, actor Peter Falk portrays a smarter-than-he-looked homicide detective named Columbo. The story lines develop fairly predictably. In the opening scenes, a crime is committed and covered up by the perpetrator. The audience knows exactly what happened and who did it. As the story progresses, they watch as characters do things they would never have done had they known there was a killer among them. Sometimes others lose their lives because they ignorantly place themselves in danger. Eventually, the apparently dimwitted and bumbling detective sorts out the clues and proves the murderer guilty, but not without a lot of trouble that could have been avoided if only he had known what the audience knew all along.

In this section of Joshua, we see a similar narrative tool being used. In the first verse of Joshua 7, we are told something that Joshua doesn't yet know.

> But the children of Israel committed a trespass in the accursed thing: for Achan, the son of Carmi, the son of Zabdi, the son of Zerah, of the tribe of Judah, took of the accursed thing: and the anger of the Lord was kindled against the children of Israel (Josh. 7:1).

We know exactly what happened and who did it. As we read on, we realize that had Joshua known that God was angry with Israel for violating His command to keep nothing for themselves, this episode would have developed quite differently. Because Joshua was in the dark, he moved on the basis of the information at hand, and the consequences were disastrous.

Pressing the Attack

Seizing the Momentum

From the ancient and honorable trade of the blacksmith we get the expression "Strike while the iron is hot." The smith who strikes the iron when it is cool risks breaking the iron and damaging his tools. For the iron to be hammered into the desired shape, it must be hot and malleable, fresh from the furnace. Generally, this is very good advice for other areas of life. Gardeners should plant when the soil is freshly tilled. Students who have diligently studied for a test don't want to have it postponed a few days—they want to be tested when the material is fresh in their memories. Athletic teams speak of capitalizing on an opponent's mistakes by seizing the momentum and gaining advantage when the other team is disorganized or distracted. Sometimes, in their haste, they make mistakes of their own. Overconfidence can lead to reckless enthusiasm that can leave them vulnerable and shift the advantage back to their opponent.

Armies, too, like to press the attack while they have the advantage. It can be foolish to take a break after a great victory. It gives the enemy time to regroup and recover. It may also squander enthusiasm and energy that can be hard to work up for the next attack. Joshua, like any competent commander, knew this. Jericho, the fortress of the region, was now a blazing ruin. Ai, a relatively insignificant neighboring town, could be troublesome if ignored. So, while Jericho burned, without returning to camp in Gilgal, "Joshua sent men from Jericho to Ai."

> And Joshua sent men from Jericho to Ai, which is beside Bethaven, on the east side of Bethel, and spake unto them, saying, Go up and view the country. And the men went up and viewed Ai (Josh. 7:2).

Devising a Strategy

Joshua is to be commended for keeping at the task. He wasn't content to celebrate a single victory. He sent men ahead to evaluate the task, just as he had sent spies into Jericho. These men returned quickly with their report and recommendation.

> And they returned to Joshua, and said unto him, Let not all the people go up; but let about two or three thousand men go up and smite Ai; and make not all the people to labour thither; for they are but few (Josh. 7:3).

Remember that Israel had just spent much of the day marching nearly twenty miles in circles around Jericho, then spent more time and energy destroying the city, killing its inhabitants, and salvaging valuables for the tabernacle treasury. This was by far the most strenuous day's activity since the army's circumcision. Most of the men were exhausted. Only a handful would be fit enough to be physically capable of moving against Ai. Having checked out the situation in Ai, the men Joshua sent there suggested that Joshua needed to send only "two or three thousand men" to Ai. The others should be allowed to rest.

Failing at Ai

Joshua acted on the information he had, but the outcome wasn't what he expected.

> So there went up thither of the people about three thousand men: and they fled before the men of Ai. And the men of Ai smote of them about thirty and six men: for they chased them from before the gate even unto Shebarim, and smote them in the going down: wherefore the hearts of the people melted, and became as water (Josh. 7:4–5).

It is difficult, and probably inappropriate, to blame Joshua for taking the advice of his military advisors. Surely he chose men to observe Ai that he could trust to give him good advice. He deployed to Ai the maximum number of men they recommended, a unit that represented about 1½ percent of the total army of Israel. But those three thousand men were put to flight. They were humiliated and chased back to rejoin the rest of Israel's army. Thirty-six of the best men in Israel's army were killed. Thirty-six families were grieving the loss of a husband, father, brother, son. No wonder Israel was terrified and Joshua and the elders of Israel were discouraged.

> And Joshua rent his clothes, and fell to the earth upon his face before the ark of the Lord until the eventide, he and the elders of Israel, and put dust upon their heads (Josh. 7:6).

Any good commander grieves when one of his men loses his life, especially if that loss of life might have been avoidable. However, from a strictly military point of view, the appropriate reaction would be to express sympathy for the grieving while encouraging the people. For the leadership to despair would be deeply demoralizing for the nation. After all, thirty-six dead was about 1½ percent of the force that attacked Ai, and only 0.0068 percent of the total army of Israel. An army of over 530,000 is not greatly weakened by the loss of 36 men.

The depth of Joshua's despair shows that he was both a deeply devout and a truly compassionate leader. He was concerned for God's reputation, for the grief these deaths caused specific people, and for the fear that had come upon all Israel.

Praying for Guidance

Joshua's Despair

When Joshua went into mourning, he turned to God in prayer, crying "Alas, O Lord God . . . "

> And Joshua said, Alas, O Lord God, wherefore hast thou at all brought this people over Jordan, to deliver us into the hand of the Amorites, to destroy us? would to God we had been content, and dwelt on the other side Jordan! O Lord, what shall I say, when Israel turneth their backs before their enemies! For the Canaanites and all the inhabitants of the land shall hear of it, and shall environ us round, and cut off our name from the earth: and what wilt thou do unto thy great name (Josh. 7:7–9)?

To his credit, Joshua recognized a problem and desired to make it right. "This is not the murmuring of unbelief and rebellion. It was the struggle of a man of faith who was brutally honest with God and was seeking answers to his urgent questions."[57] *Something* had caused Israel to run from their enemies; he just didn't know what it was. On the other hand, Joshua seems to have lost his perspective. Yes, the rout at Ai was serious, and the loss of life was important, but it wasn't calamitous. The army wasn't significantly weakened in any tangible way. The problem was not *manpower*; it was *morale*. Joshua was so distraught that he blamed God for the defeat, asking, "Did you just bring us across Jordan so the Amorites could kill us? We'd have been better off on the other side of Jordan!"

Aren't we a lot like Joshua here? When problems come up, are we tempted to concede defeat and throw in the towel in despair? We may even make ridiculous accusations against God. It will help if we will remember that *we don't always have all the pertinent information*. Actually, we *never* have *all* the pertinent information because only God knows everything. This event in Israel's history illustrates that when we're faced with difficulties, when we've been defeated, we need to keep our perspective and seek God's leading. All is not lost. We may be "cast down," but we are "not destroyed" (2 Cor. 4:9). We may suffer for a time, but glory shall ultimately "be revealed in us" (Rom. 8:18).

[57] Madvig, p. 285.

Joshua was guilty of the sin of unbelief. In the face of defeat, he decided God wasn't trustworthy. *Unbelief isn't a weakness for which we deserve pity. It's a sin for which we deserve blame.* In Joshua's case, as in yours or mine, unbelief brings inconsistent thinking. Elijah after the great victory over the prophets of Baal on Mount Carmel (1 Kings 18:17–40), when threatened by Jezebel, ran away in fear and in despair begged God to take his life (1 Kings 19:1–4). After one day of fighting, with Jericho in ruins, Joshua wanted to withdraw from the region and quit fighting because Ai had whipped his army. It does seem that Joshua was basically concerned for God's glory, asking, "What wilt thou do unto thy great name?" His mistake was in thinking that God was helpless without Israel.

God's Rebuke

Joshua should have known the answer to his questions. He should have known why Israel had been defeated. Had he rested on his faith in God, rather than responding to his fear of circumstances, he would have remembered that God had promised to bless Israel as long as they obeyed Him and to destroy Israel if they failed to wholly follow Him. If the battle at Jericho went without a hitch and the battle at Ai was a disaster, something must have happened in the meantime to cause a shift in Israel's position before God. Instead of blaming God, Joshua should have been searching the camp for violations of God's instructions. That is precisely what God told Joshua in the next verses.

> And the Lord said unto Joshua, Get thee up; wherefore liest thou thus upon thy face? Israel hath sinned, and they have also transgressed my covenant which I commanded them: for they have even taken of the accursed thing, and have also stolen, and dissembled also, and they have put it even among their own stuff. Therefore the children of Israel could not stand before their enemies, but turned their backs before their enemies, because they were accursed: neither will I be with you any more, except ye destroy the accursed from among you (Josh. 7:10–12).

God let Joshua have his say; then He dealt with him. He told Joshua to get up off his face. Joshua shouldn't be lying on the ground when he had work to do. *He had no business praying for guidance when he had perfectly clear instructions he had failed to obey fully.* It wasn't God who had failed Israel; it was Israel who had sinned against God. This conquest of Canaan was a team effort, so they were collectively involved in the sin and suffered the general consequences of it. Israel's sin involved violation of their covenant with God—God would give them the land, but they must completely obey Him. In this first test of their obedience, they had failed. They had kept for themselves some of that which God had commanded them to offer to Him. God also said they had "stolen." The word used implies that the action was carefully planned and carried out by stealth and deceit. It also emphasizes their violation of the eighth commandment, making them lawbreakers punishable by death. Further, by acting surprised and dismayed by the defeat at Ai when there was sin in the camp, the thief or thieves had "dissembled," or played the hypocrite. They had even committed idolatry by putting that which was God's "among their own stuff."

Much later in Israel's history, God made a similar charge against the nation.

> Will a man rob God? Yet ye have robbed me. But ye say, Wherein have we robbed thee? In tithes and offerings. Ye are cursed with a curse: for ye have robbed me, even this whole nation. Bring ye all the tithes into the storehouse, that there may be meat in mine house, and prove me now herewith, saith the Lord of hosts, if I will not open you the windows of heaven, and pour you out a blessing, that there shall not be room enough to receive it. And I will rebuke the devourer for your sakes, and he shall not destroy the fruits of your ground; neither shall your vine cast her fruit before the time in the field, saith the Lord of hosts (Mal. 3:8–11).

Israel was putting "among their own stuff" that which was God's. Keeping for ourselves that which belongs to God is a serious offense. It demonstrates *the sin of unbelief* that if we give to God first He is able to make what we have left adequate to meet our needs. It demonstrates *the sin of pride* in assuming we're entitled to keep all that God has given us. It demonstrates *the sin of idolatry* by having greater confidence in material things than in the God Who made all things.

God told Joshua that it was the sins of Israel demonstrated by this act of greed that caused Israel to flee from their enemies. They were reaping what they had sown. As a result, God would not bless Israel. God has promised to show Himself strong on behalf of those whose hearts are perfect toward Him. He never promised to fight for the willful or the disobedient. God said, "Neither will I be with you any more, except ye destroy the accursed thing from among you." Israel had sinned. But Joshua had failed in his responsibility to enforce the regulations he had announced. God's blessing could not be reinstated until Joshua did his job.

Why Did the Attack on Ai Fail?

Many preachers and commentators suggest one or more of four possible reasons for the failure of Israel's attack on Ai. First, some have said that the attack was misguided because it was based on the advice of Joshua's men rather than on the counsel of God. In support of this view, we know that God gave Joshua instructions for the attack on Jericho. It is assumed that Joshua should have waited for instructions for this battle too.

Others have said the attack failed because Joshua sent only three thousand men instead of taking all the people. When attacking Jericho, everyone was to be involved. It is assumed that Joshua should have realized that the battle for Jericho was intended as a pattern for the rest of the conquest of Canaan and should have taken everybody on to Ai.

A third view suggests that the attack on Ai failed because the army didn't take the ark of God with them. The presence of the ark had been a vital part of the instructions for crossing the Jordan and for conquering Jericho, so it is reasoned that Joshua should have kept it with the army in future battles.

Some suggest that the attack failed because Joshua relied on human strength. Having evaluated Ai and found the enemy a weak one, Joshua made the mistake of assuming that a superior force of three thousand would be sufficient.

All four of these views have some merit on the basis of the events immediately preceding the move against Ai. All four are based on deduction by implication from God's instructions concerning the conquest of Jericho. They each have the same critical weakness—*there is no explicit statement from Scripture to support any of them*. Each suggestion is based on assumptions. They share the weakness of being unsupported by subsequent events. In the course of the conquest of Canaan, God doesn't give Joshua instructions for every battle. Actually, special instructions are rare. After the destruction of Ai and Bethel (see chap. 15), most of the people return to Gilgal to stay while the army engages in various campaigns throughout the region. Jericho is the *only* battle in which everyone participated. The ark stays in Gilgal until it is moved to Shiloh (Josh. 18:1). There is no evidence that it goes with the army as they subdue Canaan. It is just as likely that sending only three thousand men against Ai demonstrated greater confidence in God than in human strength. Much later, Gideon would have to demonstrate his faith by paring his army of 36,000 down to a mere 300 men (Judg. 7:1–8).

The problem with Israel's attack on Ai was not tactical, but spiritual. God had told Joshua to conquer the land by obeying "this book of the law" (Josh. 1:8). Moses had sent men ahead to scout the land, and Israel failed because they refused to listen to the faithful military advisors who believed God would give them victory. Joshua himself had been one of the advisors whom Israel disregarded. Sending men to scout Ai had solid precedent. What would be the point if he weren't going to listen to their advice? The move against Ai was based on the examples of history and experience and on all the information Joshua had. He had reason to believe the tactics recommended were appropriate.

Further, Joshua's intent was to please God by pressing the attack. He had been assigned the task of taking the land, so seizing the momentum and moving ahead was an act of obedience. Waiting for more guidance might imply lack of faith and dereliction of duty. The instructions God had given for taking Jericho were clearly unique. The Lord had met Joshua as he scouted the city and told him to use a strange method that Joshua had no reason to believe would be repeated. Besides, Joshua firmly believed that God was blessing and providing strength for the battle of Jericho, and he didn't want to squander the momentum God had given them. His evaluation of the enemy's strength and Israel's weariness, in proportion to the power of God to provide victory, was accurate. Moving against Ai at the end of such an exhilarating yet exhausting day was an act of supreme confidence in God. That is why the defeat affected him as it did—he was confused and distressed because he had trusted God and lost.

I think it is far better to just let *God* tell us why Israel failed. He said *the failure was caused by unresolved sin committed during the conquest of Jericho*. He said nothing about sin in the attack on Ai. Joshua didn't fail because he neglected to ask God for instructions concerning Ai. Joshua failed because he neglected to enforce the instructions God had given him concerning Jericho. That is why God told him to stop whining, find the perpetrator, and remove the stolen items. Without removing the curse because of Israel's disobedience in Jericho, Israel would have lost no matter what they did in Ai. Taking everyone would have increased only the potential loss of life. Taking the ark wouldn't have helped. Sitting around asking God what to do about Ai wouldn't have helped either. When Joshua tried that after the fact, he was rebuked and told to finish the job at Jericho before worrying about Ai. Because of the theft reported in 7:1, *nothing* Joshua could have done would have produced victory in Ai. On the other hand, had the goods not been stolen or had the thief been caught before marching against Ai, *anything* Joshua did would have secured a victory. The loss in Ai wasn't about Ai. It was about Jericho.

What Does This Teach Us?

The incident at Ai can help us learn how we should respond to defeat in our own lives or in the life of the church. First, we need to understand that *not every difficulty is a **defeat***. There may be any number of reasons that we face trials and tests. Those who tell you that trouble in your life is evidence of

God's displeasure have forgotten that "the trying of your faith worketh patience" in order to help you grow to maturity (James 1:3–4). Paul says we are to "glory in tribulation" because "tribulation worketh patience, and patience, experience; and experience, hope: and hope maketh not ashamed; because the love of God is shed abroad in our hearts by the Holy Ghost which is given unto us" (Rom. 5:3–5). Israel faced many difficulties in Canaan and had to fight many battles before they could claim to control the land. With the exception of a few summary statements that we'll look at later about territory they failed to capture, this is the only *defeat* recorded.

Second, we need to admit that ***real*** *defeat comes as the result of sin in some area of life*. We have not necessarily been defeated when things don't go our way. We have been *defeated* when one of the enemies of our souls (the world, the flesh, or the Devil) gains an advantage and we fall into sin. We may not be swift to realize that sin is the cause of our distress. We may blame God. We may protest our innocence. We may point to all the things we've been doing right and wonder why we would be in such straits over something as insignificant as . . . whatever comes to mind. In Israel's case, *the sin was essentially their failure to tithe—they kept for themselves something that belonged to God.* When you are faced with something that looks and feels like defeat, you need a thorough spiritual examination. Evaluate your own heart and life to be sure no personal sin is contributing to the removal of God's blessing. If sin is identified, confess it to God in sorrow for any reproach brought on His name by your actions or attitude.

Third, we must realize that *being defeated in battle does* ***not*** *mean we've lost the war*. A single defeat is certainly disruptive, but it need not destroy us. The Lord promised through Isaiah, "When the enemy shall come in like a flood, the Spirit of the Lord shall lift up a standard against him" (Isa. 59:19). Don't wallow in the despair of self-pity or self-reproach. Having confessed and forsaken your sin, get up and get on with serving God.

15
Israel's Cleansing

Joshua 7:13–26

The church had been planning their week of evangelistic meetings for weeks. A guest evangelist had been called in, public announcements made, and fliers printed and distributed. The opening services on Sunday had been great. There was a spirit of enthusiasm in the congregation, many of whom had brought unsaved neighbors, friends, and relatives to the meetings to hear the gospel. A public invitation was given, calling on people to believe that Jesus, the Son of God, had died for their sins and risen from the dead to offer eternal life to those who would repent of sin and turn to Christ. Many responded. It was clear that the Lord was working in this congregation and community.

On Monday afternoon, the host pastor dropped the guest evangelist off at a local department store after lunch so he could do a little shopping. About an hour later, the pastor pulled up to meet his guest. Just as the evangelist reached for the handle of the car door, two men rushed out of the department store and grabbed his arms. Thinking this was a mugging, the pastor hurried to his defense only to be shown security credentials. The evangelist was being held for shoplifting. He had stolen an inexpensive camera, even though he had more than enough cash in his pocket to pay for it and had a better camera at home.

This one inexplicable act of greed cost this evangelist more than a week of meetings. It cost him his credibility in the Christian community as well as at home. It cost him his reputation. It cost him his opportunity to minister for the Lord. It cost him his livelihood. It did more harm than that. It was years before the host church recovered from the shock of a man they had trusted and respected having done this. Many of those new converts were confused and disillusioned by this man's actions.

We may never know for sure what motivated this man to do this. We know that we are all susceptible to temptation. Covetousness is a dangerous thing. One seemingly insignificant sin can have devastating consequences we never imagined.

God Instructs Joshua

Fulfilling Responsibilities

In the previous chapter we saw that God allowed Joshua a brief pity party and then told him to get up. God told Joshua why Israel had been humiliated following Israel's defeat at Ai: they hadn't obeyed in Jericho. Now we'll look at what God told Joshua to do about it.

> Up, sanctify the people, and say, Sanctify yourselves against tomorrow: for thus saith the Lord God of Israel, There is an accursed thing in the midst of thee, O Israel: thou canst not stand before thine enemies, until ye take away the accursed thing from among you. In the morning therefore ye shall be brought according to your tribes: and it shall be, that the tribe which the Lord taketh shall come according to the families thereof; and the family which the Lord shall take shall come by households; and the household which the Lord shall take shall come man by man. And it shall be, that he that is taken with the accursed thing shall be burnt with fire, he and all that he hath: because he hath transgressed the covenant of the Lord, and because he hath wrought folly in Israel (Josh. 7:13–15).

The first thing Joshua had to do was get up. That alone is a challenge when you are discouraged or depressed. But God wasn't going to allow Joshua to lie around feeling sorry for himself. Rather than staying on his face in despair, he had a job to do. He was to "sanctify the people." He was to tell all of them collectively, and each of them individually, to "sanctify yourselves against tomorrow." Joshua had to organize a solemn and formal assembly of Israel. He was to announce that someone among them had stolen from God. Therefore, the nation would be unable to stand in the face of their enemies until the sinner was found and removed. Israel had to stop their mourning over the loss at Ai (and any leftover celebration of the victory at Jericho) to engage in personal evaluation of the condition of their own souls. Joshua's role in their sanctification was as an overseer, making sure they did what they were told, but the people had to obey.

Joshua had to sanctify the people, and they had to sanctify themselves. Sound a little confusing? In chapter 8, I described the differences between positional and practical sanctification (Josh. 3:5). We see the same ideas illustrated again in this passage. Sanctifying Israel was something God had done when He chose to make a covenant with them as His own people. That covenant was and is an eternal promise God has made for Israel, and it can't be undone. Our positional sanctification through salvation is similar—God has placed us in Christ forever and irrevocably (Heb. 10:14). Practical sanctification is the process by which the believer grows into a more and more perfect replica of Christ (Phil. 2:12). The whole problem in regard to Ai was that Israel, as God's people, had not obeyed.

Identifying the Culprit

Joshua told Israel they couldn't put this off. He said, "In the morning . . . ye shall be brought." The verb used here means to "come near" as before a judge or for presentation of an offering. This verb is used in Exodus 22:8 in the context of an examination before a judge in search of a thief. It is used in Exodus 29:10 in the context of a special ceremony for the sanctification of Aaron and his sons as Israel's priests in which a bullock was "brought" to the tabernacle to be slaughtered as an offering. Joshua was telling Israel that *they would have to come close to God for personal examination* to identify the person or persons who had violated God's command concerning the goods of Jericho. They'd better do some soul-searching tonight.

God gives instructions to the church similar to the ones He gave Israel in this instance. Believers are commanded to periodically assemble to celebrate the Lord's Supper. This ceremony is sometimes called "Communion" because we are "brought" before God. Paul tells us to "let a man examine himself" (1 Cor. 11:28) before participation. The purpose of that self-examination is not to determine whether a person should participate in Communion. For the believer, participation is not optional; it is commanded. We are to examine ourselves because we will be participating and we need to do so with a clear conscience. That is why Paul's command continues, "And so let him eat."

Joshua told Israel how he planned to identify the culprit without describing the actual procedure. It would be an orderly process that would identify the guilty party by gradually narrowing the field of suspects to a single individual:

1. The tribe the Lord taketh

2. The family which the Lord shall take
3. The household the Lord shall take
4. Shall come man by man (to identify) he that is taken

At each layer of the selection process, the choosing would be done by the Lord. Exactly how the selection would be done is left unstated. The usual, and probably correct, assumption is that the high priest would use the Urim and Thummim (Exod. 28:30). The Urim and Thummim are mentioned as items placed in the breastplate worn by the high priest, but their use is not described in Scripture. They may have been precious stones of the same size and shape but of different color that the high priest would use to determine the answer to a yes-or-no question, with one stone representing yes, the other no. During a divine examination, the high priest could have reached into the breastplate to withdraw a stone, trusting God to guide his hand to grasp the appropriate one.

Whatever the method, we know that in order to find the person responsible for the removal of God's blessing from Israel, the tribal leaders would take their turns standing before the high priest until God identified the guilty tribe. The family heads would follow, then the heads of households, then each individual until eventually the culprit was identified.

Of course, *we* already know who did it. We were told in Joshua 7:1 that the thief was "Achan, the son of Carmi, the son of Zabdi, the son of Zerah, of the tribe of Judah." But God didn't reveal the culprit to Joshua immediately. We must not make the mistake of thinking that the examination process was carried out so that *God* could find out who did it. God always knew who did it.

Applying the Principles

Why did Israel have to go through this rather harrowing process? First, Joshua and the magistrates *had to learn to administer justice by God's guidance.* This multilayered examination would provide them an expeditious means of doing their duty while requiring them to rely on God.

Second, this procedure *provided a motivation for everyone in Israel to engage in a careful self-evaluation.* Don't you think there were probably others in Israel besides Achan who had sinned against God in one way or another? The congregation of Israel was likely to have been neither more nor less perfect than the congregation of your church or mine. I suspect that many people confessed sins that night.

But Joshua was looking for a particular sinner, guilty of a specific sin, and the text is clear that there was only one individual in Israel who had real cause to fear the judicial search the next day. Therefore, another purpose for the process was *to allow the guilty an opportunity to confess*. We will see that he didn't until it was too late. He waited to admit his sin until he was identified.

A fourth reason to go through all this was *to avoid any confusion in Israel about who the culprit was*. Not only did the procedure identify the guilty but it also cleared the innocent. The process would narrow it down to a particular man from a particular household within a particular family in a particular tribe. The guilty man was not just some guy named Achan. It was "Achan, the son of Carmi, the son of Zabdi, the son of Zerah, of the tribe of Judah." History and gossip could never apply the stigma of guilt to an innocent man by the same name. Imagine the relief in the hearts of each tribal leader when his tribe was found not guilty! Individually, once the perpetrator was named, no one need continue to ask, "Lord, is it I?" (Matt. 26:22).

Joshua Performs His Duty

A Challenging Task

Once again we find Joshua facing what had to be an unpleasant task and deciding he had better start early.

> So Joshua rose up early in the morning, and brought Israel by their tribes; and the tribe of Judah was taken: and he brought the family of Judah; and he took the family of the Zarhites: and he brought the family of the Zarhites man by man; and Zabdi was taken: and he brought his household man by man; and Achan, the son of Carmi, the son of Zabdi, the son of Zerah, of the tribe of Judah, was taken (Josh. 7:16–18).

If the process required the tribal representatives to come in birth order of the patriarchs, the first three tribes (Reuben, Simeon, Levi) would have been cleared. Judah, the fourth-born of Jacob, came next. As Caleb, the likely representative of Judah (Num. 34:19), took his place before Joshua and the high priest, it must have felt like a formality. Surely Caleb couldn't be chosen. I can hardly imagine his mingled chagrin and outrage when the priest indicated that his tribe was responsible. And how must Joshua have felt? Caleb was the only man in Israel who had stood with him in the face of the multitude forty years before when Israel decided not to trust God to give them the land. What a humiliating blow this must have been to both of these godly leaders! But they offered no protest. They were less concerned about their own prestige than they were for the good of Israel and the glory of God.

A Critical Confrontation

The process continued until Achan was identified.

> And Joshua said unto Achan, My son, give, I pray thee, glory to the Lord God of Israel, and make confession unto him; and tell me now what thou hast done; hide it not from me (Josh. 7:19).

I'm struck by the way Joshua confronted Achan. Despite the depth of his grief over the scandalous defeat in Ai, his empathy for what must have broken the heart of his dear friend Caleb, and his anger for actions that had cost the lives of thirty-six men, Joshua dealt with Achan without railing accusations. He didn't launch into a tirade listing all the trouble this one man's greed had caused. He didn't even glower at him threateningly and say, "OK, boy; you're in a heap of trouble now." By calling him "son," Joshua confronted him meekly, almost gently, but still authoritatively. As a "son," Achan must answer to authority. As a "father," Joshua didn't enjoy what he had to do.

How can someone "give . . . glory to the Lord God" by confessing sin? In Achan's case, admitting what he had done would glorify God *by verifying God's omniscience*. God had correctly identified the guilty individual from a field of over 530,000. Second, true confession would glorify God *by demonstrating God's holiness* in hating sin. Genuine confession (saying the same thing about our sin that God says about it) must recognize the inherent evil of the sin. It must realize how the sin dishonors God by showing contempt for His authority and by opposing His purity. True confession results in the sinner's broken heart. Third, confession of sin glorifies God *by affirming God's justice* in dealing with sin.

A Superficial Confession

As the process of selection moved inexorably toward identifying one man as the culprit, Achan maintained his silence. He had nothing to say until he was cornered.

> And Achan answered Joshua, and said, Indeed I have sinned against the Lord God of Israel, and thus and thus have I done: when I saw among the spoils a goodly Babylonish garment, and two hundred shekels of silver, and a wedge of gold of fifty shekels weight, then I coveted them, and took them; and, behold, they are hid in the earth in the midst of my tent, and the silver under it (Josh. 7:20–21).

It is important to note in verse 19 that Joshua distinguished between Achan's need to confess his sin to God ("make confession unto him") and to admit his sin to Joshua ("and tell me now what thou hast done"). It seems that Achan did the latter but never the former. He told Joshua what he had done, but he never made genuine confession to God.

Consider what Achan described as the progression of his sin. He said, "I saw." But the sin wasn't in the seeing. It was in that he "coveted" what he saw. Covetousness is idolatry—considering the thing desired to have greater value than obeying God. Covetousness has been aptly defined as "when our desires exceed the present portion God has allotted us."[58] Achan's coveting the goods he saw led to his taking what he coveted, and taking them forced him to hide them.

We have to guard our eyes. David said, "I will set no wicked thing before mine eyes" (Ps. 101:3). There wasn't anything inherently wicked in a Babylonian garment, silver, or gold. We'll find later in the conquest of Canaan that the Israelites were allowed to keep these things for themselves. Estimates of the value in today's money of the goods Achan kept range from $8,000 to $25,000, a substantial boost to his family's wealth, but they were hardly worth the price. When confronted by such temptations, God expects me to "turn away mine eyes from beholding vanity" (Ps. 119:37).

It is not at all surprising that Achan hid the things he took. When we sin, we like to keep it secret too. One of the points of this whole episode is to prove the futility of hiding our sin. Hiding sin is evidence, first, that we know it is wrong. The fact that Achan hid the stuff made it impossible to argue that he had missed the orders telling him what to do with it. But *hiding our sin is also evidence that we are more concerned with what* ***people*** *think than what* ***God*** *thinks*. We aren't capable of keeping our sin from God. We can only hide it from other people. When Achan hid the goods he took, he proved that he didn't want his neighbors to know he had them, but he didn't care that God knew. Maybe he thought God wouldn't notice, which really amounts to a blasphemous denial of God's omniscience. Or maybe he thought God wouldn't care, which amounts to a blasphemous denial of God's holiness. Whatever he thought, the things he took became a burden to him that he could never enjoy. Like any other sin, those new clothes and money brought him neither the pleasure nor the security he anticipated.

[58] Pink, p. 206.

Joshua Administers Justice

Having heard Achan's "confession," Joshua sent men to Achan's tent to fetch the evidence. Then he pronounced and carried out the sentence.

> So Joshua sent messengers, and they ran unto the tent; and, behold, it was hid in his tent, and the silver under it. And they took them out of the midst of the tent, and brought them unto Joshua, and unto all the children of Israel, and laid them out before the Lord. And Joshua, and all Israel with him, took Achan the son of Zerah, and the silver, and the garment, and the wedge of gold, and his sons, and his daughters, and his oxen, and his asses, and his sheep, and his tent, and all that he had: and they brought them unto the valley of Achor. And Joshua said, Why hast thou troubled us? the Lord shall trouble thee this day. And all Israel stoned him with stones, and burned them with fire, after they had stoned them with stones. And they raised over him a great heap of stones unto this day. So the Lord turned from the fierceness of his anger. Wherefore the name of that place was called, The valley of Achor, unto this day (Josh. 7:22–26).

The messengers Joshua sent to Achan's camp found the goods Achan had admitted hiding there. Those things conclusively proved his guilt before all Israel. The sentence of death was pronounced, Achan and his family were stoned, and their bodies and property were burned.

Does that strike you as unnecessarily harsh? It is an ugly picture, to be sure. We have to keep in mind that thirty-six lives had been lost due to Achan's sin. The law clearly demanded death for a person guilty of intentionally doing something that cost another man his life. But God actually identifies Achan's primary offense as having taken for himself things that were rightfully God's (Josh. 7:15), making him guilty of idolatry and blasphemy, sins that were also punishable by death (Deut. 17:1–5).

Why would God demand the destruction of Achan's family? Does the fact that there are similar instances of such judgment in the Old Testament mean that God usually holds an entire family accountable for the father's sin? Let's consider the biblical evidence.

The first instance of a family "execution" involves Korah and his rebellion against Moses. According to Numbers 16:27–33 Korah and his followers, with all their families and livestock, were swallowed alive by the earth.

In Daniel 6 the advisors to King Darius had maneuvered the king into forbidding anyone to worship any god other than himself for thirty days. The decree pronounced that the penalty for disobedience was that the guilty would be cast to the lions. When Daniel persisted in prayer, the sentence had to be carried out despite the king's desire to do otherwise. After Daniel survived the night with the lions, Daniel 6:24 describes the king's punishment of the scheming advisors by casting them and their families into the lions' den.

An additional case involved Haman and is mentioned in Esther 9:25. When King Ahasuerus (Xerxes) of Persia discovered that Haman had plotted to kill Queen Esther and her people, he had Haman and his family destroyed.

The few other examples of family executions in Scripture are all military in nature, such as the destruction of the families and people of Sihon and Og as Israel approached the Promised Land, described in Numbers 21:35 and Deuteronomy 2:26–37.

Given this list of instances, I see no reason to conclude that family executions were the norm. There were no examples from Genesis, which covers the first two thousand years of history, and only a handful from the next two thousand years. Actually, they were extremely rare. Furthermore, if we analyze the situations, the list shrinks. I don't think we should count the execution of Haman's family or the families of the men who plotted against Daniel because their punishments were decreed by pagan kings who may or may not have acted justly. The case of Korah was extraordinary in that God personally executed the rebels and their families. Besides, in Numbers 16:14–26, the verses immediately preceding the description of their being swallowed by the ground, we read that Moses sent criers throughout the camp warning everyone to stay away from the rebels or they would be punished with them. The text indicates that the families stayed with the rebels, showing their support of the rebellion. They died for their own sins.

When we consider the circumstances in each example, we can narrow the list of God's command for judicial executions of entire families to only *one* instance: the case before us in Joshua 7. While the execution of Achan was clearly in keeping with the law, why kill the wife and children? The text is not clear. God doesn't always explain Himself. However, Deuteronomy 24:16 says, "The fathers shall not be put to death for the children, neither shall the children be put to death for the fathers: every man shall be put to death for his own sin." In the light of that verse, it is best to conclude that Achan's family died with him for the same reason Korah's family died with him: they were participants in the theft, at least in helping him hide the goods and in failing to report his theft to the proper authorities. That failure cost thirty-six men their lives and demonstrated the family's own idolatry. The biblical principle for punishing sin is summarized in Ezekiel 18:2–4.

> What mean ye, that ye use this proverb concerning the land of Israel, saying, The fathers have eaten sour grapes, and the children's teeth are set on edge? As I live saith the Lord God, ye shall not have occasion any more to use this proverb in Israel. Behold, all souls are mine; as the soul of the father, so also the soul of the son is mine: the soul that sinneth, it shall die.

You need not fear that God will punish you for your father's sins. He won't punish your children for your sins. However, we should learn a lesson from Korah and Achan. The father has great power to influence his family, and they may follow him in his own rebellion and suffer for it. Wives, sons, and daughters, be sure you place obedience to God over loyalty to a sinful father or husband. But woe be to the husband/father who forces his family into such an awful dilemma.

The dramatic execution that accomplished the total eradication from Israel of Achan and all that pertained to him was important for two reasons. It provided an important object lesson to demonstrate the holiness of God in the eyes of the whole nation. *Everyone learned the futility of trying to hide his sin from God.* The fact that God required all Israel to participate in the purification of the nation by carrying out God's sentence taught them the seriousness of the consequences of sin. *Everyone learned that God hates sin in His own people as much as He hates sin in those who are not His people.* Once again we see evidence that the distinction between Israel and the Canaanites was not racial, but ethical and spiritual. Achan and his family were treated precisely the way God had commanded the inhabitants of Jericho to be treated.

I find myself trying to read between the lines, wishing for more information. Who was this man Achan? We know his lineage, but we don't know the man. How did he manage to get a Babylonian garment, silver, and gold out of Jericho and hide them in his tent without being seen or suspected? Was the situation in Jericho as the walls came down and Israel stormed in really so chaotic that no one would notice a man salvaging goods and slipping all the way back to the camp in Gilgal? Were the commanders of Israel so inattentive that they could lose track of a man for so long? Was Joshua so remiss in his supervision of the battle that such a thing could easily happen?

Perhaps the Lord will explain it to me when I get to heaven. For now, I'm left guessing. I'll tell you what I suspect, though. We know there were at least two men who entered Jericho when the walls came down and left to take goods back to camp.

> And the young men that were spies went in, and brought out Rahab, and her father, and her mother, and her brethren, and all that she had; and they brought out all her kindred, and left them without the camp of Israel (Josh. 6:23).

Those two, or men assisting them, were probably the only ones who had what the law would call "means" and "opportunity" to commit the crime Achan committed. In the process of gathering up Rahab, her family, and "all that she had," it is at least conceivable that one of the men decided to carry along a little extra for himself. That may be why the spies remain unnamed in the narrative. I admit, it seems a little obvious—you'd think Joshua would have thought of that and checked them first. It is clear, however, that Joshua trusted these men completely. He would no more suspect them than he would Caleb. Besides, God told him how to find the man, and He didn't suggest a tent-to-tent search.

Another hint may support my supposition. Rahab and her family were taken into Israel as converts—legally Israelites by "profession of faith" rather than by birth. When Rahab eventually married, she married a man from the tribe of Judah—Achan's tribe. While it is possible that Rahab's future identification with Judah is simply a providential coincidence, it is also possible that the spies responsible for Rahab's safety were from Judah and that they took her and her family to Judah's camp. They had to take them somewhere.

If my guesswork is correct, it would also help explain the severity of the sentence against Achan and his family. Rahab and her family gladly forsook Jericho and all that it represented in order to be identified with Israel and Israel's God. At the same time, Achan decided he preferred the goods of Jericho to the promises of God, essentially forsaking Israel and Israel's God for Jericho and what it represented. Achan and his family from the tribe of Judah traded places with Rahab and her family from Jericho. Rahab and her family were rescued to participate in Israel's blessing while Achan and his family were condemned to take their place in Jericho's destruction.

Important Lessons

This is one of the saddest chapters in the book of Joshua, but we can learn several lessons from this episode in Israel's history. First, it vividly illustrates how *one man's sin can impact the lives of others*. Achan's sin was committed in secret, but its consequences touched everyone in Israel. Those closest to him paid most dearly. Achan probably thought it a little thing—keeping for himself that which would represent the tithe. I'm sure it never occurred to him that thirty-six unnamed men would lose their lives, thirty-six homes would lose a husband or father or brother. The things he expected to help his family be more comfortable or secure actually brought them death and destruction. Deliberate disobedience can have disastrous consequences.

If I'm right in my suspicions about Achan's identity as one of the spies or one of the men assisting the spies, these events also illustrate that *even the most trusted and respected among us is capable of great sin.* After forty years in the wilderness, I'm sure he saw things he wanted as soon as he entered Jericho. Did he start thinking about how nice it would be to have those things while hiding in the hills before going back to Gilgal? When he found out that the plan to take Jericho included destroying all those nice things, did he begin to imagine ways to get the goods out of the city undetected? Dabbling with temptation is a dangerous thing, and no one is immune. If a man like King David could commit the sins he committed, what makes you think you could never do such a thing? "Let him that thinketh he standeth take heed lest he fall" (1 Cor. 10:12).

We also learn something of *the danger of overconfidence.* Even a leader of Joshua's caliber was susceptible. He didn't consider the possibility that one of his people could have so flagrantly violated a direct and clear command. In a way, Joshua's confidence was born of his faith. Joshua wouldn't think of disobeying God's command to destroy Jericho and salvage the gold and silver for God, so it never occurred to him that anyone else would. It is foolish to forget humanity's tendency to sin. It affects us all. "Every man is tempted when he is drawn away of his own lust, and enticed. Then when lust hath conceived, it bringeth forth sin: and sin, when it is finished, bringeth forth death" (James 1:14–15).

God's grace and mercy often postpone judgment for sin, allowing a sinner to continue in sin for a while. We must remember that because God is holy and just, He has the perfect right to judge sin whenever and wherever He chooses.

> Present day pastors, teachers, and evangelists fail to impress on their listeners the terrible consequences of wrongdoing. They speak softly of sin as though it were nothing more than mere human weakness, winked at and easily overlooked by a loving, compassionate Christ.[59]

We must never forget the awful price the Lord Jesus paid to make our forgiveness possible. And we must *beware of complaining to God that we deserve better treatment on the ground of His justice.* You don't want *justice.* If you got justice, you'd get what Achan got. *You want and need mercy.* When you start to think that God hasn't been "merciful enough," you aren't thinking about

[59] Keller, p. 108.

mercy anymore. Mercy, by definition, is undeserved. You have no right to demand mercy. But God, in His grace, extends it every day. Instead of complaining about what you don't have, or what you'd like to have, or how you wish you'd be treated, rejoice in that He has "blessed us with all spiritual blessings" in Christ Jesus (Eph. 1:3).

16
Restored to Fellowship

Joshua 8:1–8

Have you ever experienced a time of such deep remorse for sin that you felt dirty, defiled, useless, and unforgivable? If you haven't, perhaps you've never admitted just how hideous God considers sin. In times like that, you may confess your sin to God, beg His forgiveness, and still feel mired in shame and despair. You wish you could hear the audible voice of the Lord saying, "Fear not, neither be thou dismayed"; but you hear only silence. That is one reason studying, memorizing, and meditating on the Scriptures is so important. You need the reminder from God's Word that He has *already* told you, "I am with you always" (Matt. 28:20), "I will never leave thee, nor forsake thee" (Heb. 13:5), "I will be merciful to their unrighteousness, and their sins and their iniquities will I remember no more" (Heb. 8:12), and "If we confess our sins, he is faithful and just to forgive us our sins, and to cleanse us from all unrighteousness" (1 John 1:9). Satan wants to keep you wallowing in despair. God wants to pick you up and get you going again in His service.

In the hours following Jesus' arrest in the Garden of Gethsemane, Peter repeatedly denied any relationship with Him. Peter's fear in the face of rising opposition and his confusion over the course of events led him to distance himself from the Lord. In the aftermath of his sin he experienced deep remorse. Peter's sorrow led him to repentance and restoration (Luke 22:61–62). Following Christ's resurrection, we find Peter with the other apostles (John 20:1–10), and we see that Jesus specifically said He wanted to meet with Peter (Mark 16:7). The primary point of Jesus' telling Peter three times to "feed my lambs/sheep" (John 21:15–17) seems to have been to reinforce in Peter's mind that he had been forgiven and restored to fellowship and service. That is why "when he [Christ] had spoken this, he saith unto him [Peter], Follow me" (John 21:19).

God's Encouragement

Just as Christ encouraged Peter and renewed his call to service following his restoration, the Lord encouraged Joshua and renewed his call to service once the sins of Achan had been purged from Israel.

> And the Lord said unto Joshua, Fear not, neither be thou dismayed: take all the people of war with thee, and arise, go up to Ai: see, I have given into thy hand the king of Ai, and his people, and his city, and his land (Josh. 8:1).

God forgave Israel's sin. Confession had been made—Joshua and Israel acknowledged that their defeat at Ai had been their own fault. Repentance had been demonstrated—Joshua and Israel obediently rooted out the sin and removed it. Restitution had been paid—the stolen goods, with the remainder of Achan's property, were dedicated to God and treated according to His instructions.

Restored Fellowship

All Israel was genuinely grieving over the way the nation had failed God and the reproach they had brought on His name. In the midst of their mourning this national tragedy, God spoke words of encouragement to Joshua. Genuine sorrow was important, but Israel must not be overcome with grief to the point of despair. They needed to be confident of God's forgiveness. He was still their God; they were still His people. Canaan was still God's gift to Israel; they must still fight to conquer and control the land.

It is important to note that the Lord's words to Joshua indicated that fellowship had been restored, but they also implied that honor and respect were not. Israel's relationship with God was mended, but their reputation before the Canaanites needed improvement. The small band from Ai had put them to open shame. God promised them victory over Ai, and they could go against the city in confidence; but they actually had to go. Victory over Ai wouldn't come while they licked their wounds in Gilgal.

Renewed Promise

The fact that Israel had been defeated at Ai was no excuse for quitting. Neither is the fact that you have lapses in your own faithfulness any excuse for giving up and dropping out. *God intends His promises to encourage diligence, not laziness.* After spending fifty-seven verses affirming the truth of Christ's resurrection and describing its significance in guaranteeing our ultimate victory in future glory, does Paul close by saying, "Therefore, brethren, live any way you want"? Absolutely not! He says, "Therefore, my beloved brethren, be ye steadfast, unmoveable, always abounding in the work of the Lord, forasmuch as ye know that your labour is not in vain in the Lord" (1 Cor. 15:58).

God's Instructions

The removal of the sin in Israel was a prerequisite for receiving further instructions. When the instructions were given, God expected them to be carried out.

> And thou shalt do to Ai and her king as thou didst unto Jericho and her king: only the spoil thereof, and the cattle thereof, shall ye take for a prey unto yourselves: lay thee an ambush for the city behind it (Josh. 8:2).

The Spoils of War

All Ai was given to Israel. Just as we are to make no compromise with sin, Israel was ordered to show no mercy to the inhabitants of Ai. This time the goods of the city were to be salvaged for personal use before the city was burned.

God intended the destruction of the goods at Jericho to teach Israel the principle of the tithe—the first-fruits belong to God (Exod. 23:19). Israel was to give to God that which came first as a demonstration of faith that God would provide what they needed through that which would follow. Israel was so confident in God's promise to give them the land that they kept nothing from the first great city they conquered. To wait until the harvest is in and the bills are all paid to decide how much you can "afford" to give is an act of unbelief—walking by sight rather than by faith. For that sin, Achan had paid with his life.

On the other hand, God intended the salvaging of the goods from Ai to illustrate God's reward for faithfulness. God would provide for those who trusted Him. Still, 530,000 soldiers (actually over 600,000 counting the ones still in Transjordan) and their families weren't going to get rich by dividing the goods from Ai, a city with a population of about 12,000. There is no biblical justification for claiming that if you give $100 to the work of the Lord today, He will give you back $200 next week. What the Bible actually teaches is that *if you will honor God by giving generously to His work, He will take care of you* (Phil. 4:16–19). While Israel salvaged significantly less spoils from Ai than they had burned in Jericho, the spoiling of Ai also proved the folly of Achan. If only he had waited! His covetousness had caused him to take for himself something God would have gladly given him in His own time.

The Strategy for Ai

What about the difference in *strategy* for taking this city? When coming against the mighty fortress of Jericho, the method used was audacious. It was also majestic—silently marching around the city until time to shout, in absolute confidence of the ultimate outcome. For lowly, insignificant Ai, Joshua was to prepare an ambush—a surprise attack by stealth. It is difficult to imagine a greater contrast between strategies for taking the cities of Jericho and Ai. Furthermore, God wasn't even going to provide the details for this attack. Joshua would have to work them out on his own. Just how does an army of 530,000 ("all the people of war"—v. 1) surprise and ambush an army of about 3000?

With the overwhelming superiority of the Israeli force, why bother with an ambush? If you're trying to kill a spider with a "smart-bomb," you don't need to be very stealthy. I'm convinced that part of the reason for this method for dealing with Ai was to teach Joshua and all Israel, and us by their example, a lesson in humility. Joshua's newest assignment was going to be both a troublesome strategy to devise and a humiliating one to implement.

An ambush is usually the strategy of a grossly inferior force or a coward. Such a method implied that Israel's 530,000 soldiers had to hide in the hills, sneak up on the enemy, and launch a surprise attack from behind to defeat just 3000 or so Canaanites. Having to turn tail and run from their enemy to draw them into a trap where others could attack would be an embarrassing admission of their own cowardice. An ambush would make Israel in general and Joshua in particular look utterly foolish to the other inhabitants of the land. But Joshua's prestige had been tarnished—he had proved himself to be an imperfect leader. To be restored to a place of honor and respect, Joshua had to be willing to suffer the pain of humiliation.

Woe be unto the sinner who says, "I'm willing to admit I made a mistake, but you'd better not expect me to grovel." Anyone unwilling to do a little necessary groveling when he has been wrong is suffering from a chronic case of pride that is still unresolved and will keep him from true restoration. The genuinely repentant heart of even the greatest among us gladly says, "I abhor myself, and repent in dust and ashes" (Job 42:6). Each of us must be prepared to do whatever is necessary to be right with God—even if it means "groveling." If God thought it necessary for a great man such as Joshua to stoop to ambushing Ai, and Joshua was willing to do so (he would personally lead the group that had to flee from the enemy), how much more should you and I be willing to offer abject apology and beg forgiveness when we've sinned against someone?

Having been assigned the task of preparing an ambush, Joshua worked out the details of his plan.

> So Joshua arose, and all the people of war, to go up against Ai: and Joshua chose out thirty thousand mighty men of valour, and sent them away by night. And he commanded them, saying, Behold, ye shall lie in wait against the city, even behind the city: go not very far from the city, but be ye all ready: and I, and all the people that are with me, will approach unto the city: and it shall come to pass, when they come out against us, as at the first, that we will flee before them, (for they will come out after us) till we have drawn them from the city; for they will say, They flee before us, as at the first: therefore we will flee before them. Then ye shall rise up from the ambush, and seize upon the city: for the Lord your God will deliver it into your hand. And it shall be, when ye have taken the city, that ye shall set the city on fire: according to the commandment of the Lord shall ye do. See, I have commanded you (Josh. 8:3–8).

Joshua started by sending thirty thousand soldiers into hiding behind Ai. Apparently their earlier experience had taught him something about being better prepared for confrontation with the enemy. We know the root cause of Israel's earlier defeat had been disobedience, but sometimes defeat is caused by haste, lack of discipline, or failure to adequately prepare. God does expect us to be good stewards of the resources He has provided. Besides, God had told Joshua to take all the men of war, so Joshua had to find something for everyone to do.

This deployment was going to require a certain level of self-denial on the part of the thirty thousand men sent into hiding. In order to keep from being seen, they had to take their position by night. Then they had to hold their position for at least thirty-six hours until the battle would begin. They would have to get close to a city already at a heightened state of alert. They would have to watch and wait, without being spotted, for two nights and a day. That would mean no cooking fires, no noise, and very little movement. A handful of men would find this a challenge. It would take great skill and discipline for an army of thirty thousand to carry out those orders.

Full cooperation would be necessary from every man under Joshua's command. We will see just how the troop movements were employed when we consider the actual battle in the next chapter. Some attacks are launched precipitously. This one would have to unfold gradually. Tasks would be different. As in any ambush, timing would be critical for all the aspects of the battle plan to come together successfully. Teamwork was essential. Such cooperation should characterize the work of the local church. Too often Christians spend so much time and energy bickering, fault finding, and straining gnats that they fail to plan, prepare, and discipline themselves for the work assigned by God. It is possible for a congregation to fail to accomplish God's work due to lack of cooperative effort (1 Cor. 12:12–27; Eph. 4:16).

As important as was the planning and executing of a sound strategy, it was still God Who would give Israel victory over their enemies. Good organization alone is no guarantee of success. Without being led by God, the most disciplined organization and the most careful allocation of resources may be efficient but will not be effective. *Efficiency* can be defined simply as "getting things done" while *effectiveness* is "getting the *right* things done." It is possible to be efficient without being effective. Our churches may successfully run many activities but still fail to truly minister God's grace to the saints and the gospel to the lost.

In our spiritual walk, we must rely on God for our direction and strength. We must also be actively involved. The sluggard expects God to do it all. The self-sufficient expects his own efforts to be enough. The balanced Christian knows that blessing comes from God when we diligently exercise obedience.

An Important Spiritual Lesson

Israel's corporate experience in the land of Canaan illustrates our individual experience in the Christian life. We need to deal with personal sin just as thoroughly and ruthlessly as Israel had to deal with Achan. Peter had to acknowledge the grievous nature of his sin and desire a renewal of fellowship and usefulness. You and I must do the same. In the process, we must not be too proud to accept the humiliation we brought on ourselves by our disobedience and willfulness. When we've confessed our sin for what it really is and been forgiven and restored, we need to get on with the business of serving God.

It is vital for each of us to understand the important distinction between being in a *state* of sin and committing an *act* of sin. In Revelation 12:10, Satan is called "the accuser of our brethren" who "accused them before our God night and day." The Greek words translated *accuser* and *accused* are *kategoros* and *kategoreo*, from which we get the English word *category* or *categorize*. Satan wants you to think of yourself as living in a *state* or *condition* of sin. He wants to "categorize" a sinner, labeling him with a particular sin to make him think he can't overcome it. God wants to separate the sin from the sinner, dealing with *acts* of sin.

This applies specifically to believers who fall into sin. Before we are saved, we are each sinners *categorically*. The unbeliever is a guilty lawbreaker, justly doomed to damnation, regardless of the particulars of his sin. Dealing with *acts* of sin without confronting the *state* he is in is pointless. That is, an adulterous husband can experience remorse for his infidelity, break off his illicit relationship, ask his wife's forgiveness, and remain faithful to his wife . . . and still go to hell as an unforgiven sinner. Personal reformation avails nothing without confession and repentance before God and asking forgiveness on the basis of the blood of the Lord Jesus Christ, Who died in our place and rose from the dead to give eternal life. Without becoming a new creation in Christ, trying to correct acts of sin is like taking aspirin to cure cancer. It may make us feel better, but it won't improve our condition.

However, when a person has been born again by the power of God, being saved by the grace of God through faith in the Lord Jesus, he is no longer *categorized* a sinner. He is categorically a child of God. He does not and cannot exist in a *condition* or *state* of sin. Yes, he will sin. But he no longer needs the radical re-creation involved in salvation. It is in this condition that a person is to deal with *acts* of sin. We believers "confess our sins" (plural) and God forgives "our sins" and washes us clean from the stain of unrighteousness (1 John 1:9).

Salvation in Christ remedies the *condition* of sin (Rom. 6:1–18). From the time of your rebirth forward, God addresses *acts* of sin. When you tell a lie, Satan says, "You're a liar; you'll never change"; God says, "You have lied, but I can give you victory." If you've been unfaithful to you spouse, Satan says, "You are an adulterer," while God says, "You've committed adultery." Our own means of expression often betrays the influence of this unbiblical thinking. We accept society's terminology when talking about homosexuality if we say something like, "Homosexuals can be forgiven too." We are categorizing people by the particulars of their sins. A person without Christ who commits homosexual sins is neither more nor less a lost sinner than the best man among us without Christ. It isn't homosexuality that will doom him to hell; it is the fact that he is categorically a sinner. On the other hand, a believer who commits a homosexual sin is not categorically a homosexual. He is categorically a believer who has disobeyed God and committed an act of sin that must be confessed and forsaken—just like the believer who lies or gossips or steals or swears.

You may have particular weaknesses, particular sins that you find especially tempting. If you believe you are bound by a "besetting" sin over which you will never have victory, you need to study Romans 6 and consider what it means to be "dead to sin" and to be "more than conquerors." The organization called Alcoholics Anonymous labels people who are habitual drinkers "alcoholics" and teaches them that they will always be alcoholics. Some are practicing alcoholics; others are "recovering" alcoholics. That is not the message of Scripture. It is Satan who wants men and women to think they will always be "alcoholics." God wants to set them free from the sin of drunkenness. Furthermore, AA tends to make it even harder to win an "alcoholic" to Christ. When he was drunk, he knew he needed help. When or if he manages to sober up through AA, he may be sober but still be lost.

The enemy will surely continue to attack you at your point of greatest weakness, but God wants you to remember when faced with each onslaught that He has provided the necessary power to defeat the temptations that assail you. Israel lost to Ai that first time because there was an unresolved act of sin in their midst. When it was dealt with properly, fellowship with God was restored. He had further instructions for them, and He expected them to get up and confront the very enemy that had so humiliated them. There is no excuse for a child of God to sit around convinced that "God can't use me because I'm a . . ." whatever label Satan wants you to wear. If you've confessed your sins, "He is faithful and just to forgive us our sins and to cleanse us from all unrighteousness" (1 John 1:9). Don't insult God's integrity by doubting His Word.

17
Victory at Ai

Joshua 8:9–35

Tim was finding it increasingly difficult to keep his bills paid. Creditors were calling the house at all hours wondering when they were going to get the money he owed them. It felt as though his wife was constantly on his case, wondering why the bills were piling up. Although neither Tim nor his wife had a high-paying job, both worked and brought home steady paychecks. They didn't live extravagantly. Where was all the money going, anyway? What Tim's wife didn't know was that Tim had a secret. He liked to play the lottery.

Neal Boortz, a nationally syndicated radio talk-show host based in Atlanta, has said of Georgia's state-run lottery that "the government has finally discovered a way to tax stupidity." Cartoonist Johnny Hart, creator of the B.C. comic strip, has defined the lottery as "millions of stupid people putting their money in a pot to make one stupid person rich." Tim didn't see it that way. He was tired of working so hard and dreamed of winning the jackpot. He was squandering his and his wife's hard-earned money on wishful thinking.

When Tim's wife discovered bags of lottery tickets Tim had stashed in the garage, the scene that followed wasn't pretty. She was angry and hurt. She felt robbed and betrayed. And she was right. Tim, to his credit, was deeply remorseful. He begged his wife's forgiveness and promised never to buy another lottery ticket. But his years of deception had cost him his wife's trust. She didn't believe him, and who could blame her? Again, Tim did the right thing and volunteered to go with her to their pastor for counseling. The pastor dealt with the sins involved. Tim was aware of the problems caused by his deception and theft. He hadn't thought about the fact that his behavior indicated an idolatrous coveting of material things. He wanted more, and he wanted to get it without effort. By purchasing lottery tickets, Tim demonstrated, first, that he was discontent with what God had given him, and second, that he didn't trust God to take care of him and his family through his own labors and thrift.

Tim got the message. He sought and received good financial advice that set him up on a supervised budget. For a while, he had only limited access to funds so that he could avoid the temptation to start misusing the money again. Over time, as Tim demonstrated more character and the bills got paid, Tim and his wife grew closer than they had ever been. As painful as the revelation and confrontation had been, and as rigorous as the remedy had to be, they had managed to correct the problems and removed much of the cause of strife in their lives. They spent more time together, and the time spent was more intimate. Tim's wife felt more loved than she had in a long time, and Tim began to feel successful and appreciated. He had also been set free from the constant fear of discovery.

Dealing with sin in a person's life is never fun. The process of confrontation, confession, restitution, and restoration can be emotionally grueling, but it is immensely rewarding when the people involved behave with the right spirit. Often, at the end of the process, the offender and the offended can have a closer bond of friendship and fellowship than they enjoyed before the rift occurred. In the events of Joshua 8, Israel is still recovering from the sin of Achan at Jericho. The sin has been dealt with and removed, but Israel still faces a disciplinary program designed to verify their faith in and trust of God, after which they will be expected to reconfirm their willingness to participate in the covenant God had made with Israel at Sinai. Once that is done, they will be poised for close fellowship with God and successful conquest of Canaan.

Setting the Trap

Planning the Attack

God had promised Israel He would give them victory in a rematch with Ai, but He had assigned Joshua the responsibility of planning an ambush for the battle. In Joshua 8:3–8 we have the bare outline of the battle strategy.

> So Joshua arose, and all the people of war, to go up against Ai: and Joshua chose out thirty thousand mighty men of valour, and sent them away by night.

> And he commanded them, saying, Behold, ye shall lie in wait against the city, even behind the city: go not very far from the city, but be ye all ready: and I, and all the people that are with me, will approach unto the city: and it shall come to pass, when they come out against us, as at the first, that we will flee before them, (for they will come out after us) till we have drawn them from the city; for they will say, They flee before us, as at the first: therefore we will flee before them. Then ye shall rise up from the ambush, and seize upon the city: for the Lord your God will deliver it into your hand. And it shall be, when ye have taken the city, that ye shall set the city on fire: according to the commandment of the Lord shall ye do. See, I have commanded you.

Thirty thousand men would move into hiding during the night about thirty-six hours before the battle would commence. Joshua would approach the city with more of the army with him to draw out the army of Ai. He figured Ai would expect Israel to run away again, so that is exactly what they would do. When the soldiers of Ai charged out of the city to chase the army of Israel, the soldiers in hiding behind the city would seize it and burn it.

> Joshua therefore sent them forth: and they went to lie in ambush, and abode between Bethel and Ai, on the west side of Ai: but Joshua lodged that night among the people. And Joshua rose up early in the morning, and numbered the people, and went up, he and the elders of Israel, before the people to Ai. And all the people, even the people of war that were with him, went up, and drew nigh, and came before the city, and pitched on the north side of Ai: now there was a valley between them and Ai. And he took about five thousand men, and set them to lie in ambush between Bethel and Ai, on the west side of the city. And when they had set the people, even all the host that was on the north of the city, and their liers in wait on the west of the city, Joshua went that night into the midst of the valley (Josh. 8:9–13).

Having been given their assignments, the band of thirty thousand slipped out of camp to find a secure position in which to hide through the following day and night. They found such a place between Ai and Bethel, another little town to the west of Ai. Joshua spent the night in the camp with the rest of Israel.

According to his habit when faced with a big job, Joshua was up and getting organized early the next morning (cf. 3:1; 6:12; 7:16). Even an ambush, perhaps even especially an ambush, needs an orderly preparation. First, he "numbered the people." The activity the word *numbered* (Hebrew *paqad*) brings to mind is taking a census, but the word is actually a difficult one to translate. Fifty-seven times *paqad* is rendered "visited," which falls short of conveying the word's significance. The idea of "visiting" your neighbor conjures images of sitting in the kitchen chatting over a cup of coffee or a glass of iced tea. But when God "visited" Sarah in Genesis 21:1, it was for the purpose of making Sarah capable of conceiving a child in her old age (eighty-nine years). The result of that "visit" was the birth of Isaac less than a year later. The meaning of *paqad* in such a context is "an action on the part of God which produces a beneficial result for His people."[60] In Numbers 1, Moses *paqad* the men in Israel over twenty years old. He was doing more than counting noses. Moses was organizing the men into armies by tribes. In Numbers 1 we are given head counts of the number of soldiers in each group, so we think of it merely as a census. Over 110 times, *paqad* is used in a military context where it might be better translated "mustered," "inspected," or "reviewed." It indicates a commanding officer's organization and inspection of troops before moving against the enemy. Joshua started that morning, not counting, but organizing the troops.

Positioning the Pieces

With the soldiers arranged in their ranks, Joshua marched them to a new location. They pitched camp on the north side of Ai, on the hills across the valley from the mound on which Ai was built. This made the host of Israel quite visible to the people of Ai. The enormous size of the army of Israel would have made it impossible for the inhabitants of Ai to notice that a substantial number of men were missing. If you were to see an army of over five hundred thousand soldiers marching in ranks toward your city, and setting up an orderly military encampment just across the valley, you probably would not be thinking, "You know, I thought there were over half a million of them—where are the others?" Neither would you be likely to notice that another five thousand men had been dispatched to move to the west of Ai.

This group, tiny by comparison to the army of Israel, may still have outnumbered the army of Ai. Joshua 8:25 tells us that the total population of the city was twelve thousand. If the population were divided into roughly equivalent groups of able-bodied men, women, children, and the infirm or elderly, the likely size of Ai's army would have been between three and four thousand men.[61] This band of five thousand was assigned the dual task of cutting off reinforcements that might come from Bethel to aid their neighbors and to block Ai's escape route once the trap was sprung.

Joshua, though, didn't stay with *any* of the groups of soldiers. He left the safety of the camp on the hills north of Ai and went into the valley between the camp and the city, where he spent the night alone. He had placed himself in a position of great danger. Joshua was the bait.

---

[60] Zodhiates, p. 1651.

[61] Keil and Delitzsch estimate Ai's army to have numbered no more than 3000 (p. 77).

Springing the Trap

Ai's Haste

Early the next morning, the watchers from Ai spotted Joshua alone in the valley. Seeing an unprecedented opportunity to capture Israel's great leader, they swallowed the bait "hook, line, and sinker," as the old fishing cliché goes.

> And it came to pass, when the king of Ai saw it, that they hasted and rose up early, and the men of the city went out against Israel to battle, he and all his people, at a time appointed, before the plain; but he wist not that there were liers in ambush against him behind the city. And Joshua and all Israel made as if they were beaten before them, and fled by the way of the wilderness. And all the people that were in Ai were called together to pursue after them: and they pursued after Joshua, and were drawn away from the city. And there was not a man left in Ai or Bethel, that went not out after Israel: and they left the city open, and pursued after Israel (Josh. 8:14–17).

In the United States' efforts to rid the world of terrorists, a bold but impossible goal, the president didn't send our entire military to Afghanistan. He sent some soldiers to Iraq. He kept some home. Nearly the same effort and expense has gone into beefing up homeland security as has gone for search and destroy missions and other direct military action. Even a commander of a superpower moving against a grossly inferior foe knows better than to leave his home unprotected. But not the king of Ai. In an act of supreme overconfidence, he foolishly led his men in a precipitous attack, rushing headlong out of the city at dawn, leaving it undefended. Obviously, the thirty thousand men Joshua sent to hide behind Ai had successfully established their position and remained undetected. The king of Ai had no idea they were there.

Joshua's Role

When Joshua saw Ai coming, he fled. This was apparently a prearranged signal because when Joshua turned and ran, the host of Israel camped in the hills fled also. How humiliating! The Israelite army of five hundred thousand was being chased down the Wilderness Road ("the way of the wilderness") by a band of three thousand Canaanites. When God told Joshua to prepare an ambush, he didn't spare himself. Joshua didn't appoint someone else to impersonate him, the way Saddam Hussein used to do. He didn't stay in the background while others had to run like cowards. He didn't stay with the forces in hiding so that he could lead an attack. He led the way in humiliation in order to be in a position to lead in victory.

> And the Lord said unto Joshua, Stretch out the spear that is in thy hand toward Ai; for I will give it into thine hand. And Joshua stretched out the spear that he had in his hand toward the city. And the ambush arose quickly out of their place, and they ran as soon as he had stretched out his hand: and they entered into the city, and took it, and hasted and set the city on fire (Josh. 8:18–19).

The Lord didn't make them run far before He told Joshua to signal the army that it was time to turn and attack the enemy. As Joshua turned and raised his spear toward the city, he was close enough that the thirty thousand men who had been hiding for two nights and a day could see the signal.

Ai's Destruction

The hidden troops immediately rose up, hastily looted Ai, and set it on fire.

> And when the men of Ai looked behind them, they saw, and, behold, the smoke of the city ascended up to heaven, and they had no power to flee this way or that way: and the people that fled to the wilderness turned back upon the pursuers. And when Joshua and all Israel saw that the ambush had taken the city, and that the smoke of the city ascended, then they turned again, and slew the men of Ai. And the other issued out of the city against them; so they were in the midst of Israel, some on this side, and some on that side: and they smote them, so that they let none of them remain or escape. And the king of Ai they took alive, and brought him to Joshua. And it came to pass, when Israel had made an end of slaying all the inhabitants of Ai in the field, in the wilderness wherein they chased them, and when they were all fallen on the edge of the sword, until they were consumed, that all the Israelites returned unto Ai, and smote it with the edge of the sword. And so it was, that all that fell that day, both of men and women, were twelve thousand, even all the men of Ai. For Joshua drew not his hand back, wherewith he stretched out the spear, until he had utterly destroyed all the inhabitants of Ai. Only the cattle and the spoil of that city Israel took for a prey unto themselves, according unto the word of the Lord which he commanded Joshua. And Joshua burnt Ai, and made it an heap for ever, even a desolation unto this day. And the king of Ai he hanged on a tree until eventide: and as soon as the sun was down, Joshua commanded that they should take his carcase down from the tree, and cast it at the entering of the gate of the city, and raise thereon a great heap of stones, that remaineth unto this day (Josh. 8:20–29).

When Joshua turned back to face the men of Ai, he caught them by surprise. They were so startled that they stopped their pursuit of Israel and looked back to see what Joshua was pointing at. What they saw was terrifying. There were swarms of Israelite soldiers coming out of their city, while the smoke of the burning buildings was clearly visible against the sky. As they were struck by the devastating realization that their wives and children must be dead, their property gone, and their homes destroyed, the main force of Israel's mighty army turned back from running and attacked the dumbfounded troop from Ai. It was Ai's turn to run, and there was no escape. With the bulk of Israel's army behind them, the men of Ai were running toward the soldiers who had looted and burned their city. Joshua's ambush had gone precisely according to plan. While Joshua held his spear aloft as Moses had done with his staff in a battle with the Amalekites many years before (Exod. 17:10–13), every man of Ai was killed in the jaws of Joshua's trap.

There was one exception. The king of Ai was spared from the general slaughter to face official execution. He was hanged on a tree until sunset, at which time his dead body was taken down and buried under a heap of stones at the gate of the city. Kings tend to like memorial tombs. Pharaohs had built great pyramids as memorial burial sites. This mound, though, would serve as a perpetual reminder to any future inhabitants or travelers that "Here lies a man who dared to kill thirty-six Israelite soldiers and thought he could defeat the whole Israelite army"—not the kind of memorial most kings want. This execution and burial were designed to further demoralize the Canaanites Israel would confront in the months to come.

In the last chapter, I said that one reason God ordered Joshua to use an ambush instead of a frontal attack on Ai was to teach Israel the necessary humility of confession and repentance for sin. In the events we have just reviewed, I see a second lesson from the battle that reinforces the first. The ambush carried out by Joshua and Israel's army was something of an illustration of how sin works. Sin will ambush God's people at every opportunity. Temptation will bait you into thinking you are invincible, get your attention, lead you away from safety, then turn on you to destroy you. That is what happened to Achan. It could happen to anyone in Israel or in the church.

Arthur Pink has pointed out several similarities between Joshua's actions in Joshua 8 and the work of the Lord Jesus Christ.[62] The battle with Ai can be seen as an object lesson tracing Christ's activities in providing our redemption. Three nights before the battle with Ai Joshua was communing with God, just as Christ was communing with the Father before His incarnation, being with God from the beginning (John 1:1–2; Phil 2:6). Two nights before the attack, Joshua was camping with the people, as Christ in His incarnation "was in the world" (John 1:10–11), "in the likeness of men" (Phil. 2:7). On the night before the attack, Joshua was alone in the valley of humiliation, as Christ at His trial and crucifixion "humbled himself, and became obedient unto death,

[62] Pink, pp. 209–33.

even the death of the cross" (Phil. 2:8). On the morning of the attack, Joshua seemed to be defeated, appearing to the enemy as if he were fleeing in terror. Similarly, Christ looked weak and defeated both to His friends (John 20:19) and to His enemies (Matt. 27:62–66) when He died on the cross and was buried. Finally, during the battle Joshua turned from his flight and directed the forces from an elevated place as he held his spear aloft. Christ, having returned from the grave and ascended to be with the Father, intercedes on our behalf (Heb. 7:25) and directs our warfare in this life (Eph. 1:22–2:10; Col. 1:18; 2:19).

Worshiping the Lord

Some have suggested that Joshua's building of a "great heap of stones" over the body of the king of Ai implies that Joshua offered sacrifices there. While that is possible, I think it is unlikely. Nothing in the text actually says that. The only implication of it is in the similarity of terms used to describe this memorial heap and other heaps used as altars. We do know, however, that after this battle Joshua built an altar at another place and worshiped the Lord there.

> Then Joshua built an altar unto the Lord God of Israel in mount Ebal, as Moses the servant of the Lord commanded the children of Israel, as it is written in the book of the law of Moses, an altar of whole stones, over which no man hath lift up any iron: and they offered thereon burnt offerings unto the Lord, and sacrificed peace offerings. And he wrote there upon the stones a copy of the law of Moses, which he wrote in the presence of the children of Israel. And all Israel, and their elders, and officers, and their judges, stood on this side the ark and on that side before the priests the Levites, which bare the ark of the covenant of the Lord, as well the stranger, as he that was born among them; half of them over against mount Gerizim, and half of them over against mount Ebal; as Moses the servant of the Lord had commanded before, that they should bless the people of Israel. And afterward he read all the words of the law, the blessings and cursings, according to all that is written in the book of the law. There was not a word of all that Moses commanded, which Joshua read not before all the congregation of Israel, with the women, and the little ones, and the strangers that were conversant among them (Josh. 8:30–35).

It was time to complete the process of restoration to full fellowship with God that began with the command to find the person who had taken "the accursed thing" from Jericho. Instead of launching another attack on a nearby city, or hosting a victory celebration, Joshua mustered Israel for a march to Mount Ebal, thirty to fifty miles away.[63]

There is no record that the Lord spoke to Joshua and said, "Go to Mount Ebal, offer sacrifices, and read the law." So, why did he do this, and why go so far? Remember the general instructions God had given Joshua? He said, "This book of the law shall not depart out of thy mouth, but thou shalt meditate therein day and night that thou mayest observe to do according to all that is written therein. For then thou shalt make thy way prosperous, and then thou shalt have good success" (Josh. 1:8). The "book of the law" to which God was referring may have been all the books of Moses (Genesis to Deuteronomy), or it may have specifically meant the book of Deuteronomy. It is in Deuteronomy 11:29 that we read,

> And it shall come to pass, when the Lord thy God hath brought thee in unto the land whither thou goest to possess it, that thou shalt put the blessing upon mount Gerizim, and the curse upon mount Ebal.

Then in Deuteronomy 31:11–12 we find,

> When all Israel is come to appear before the Lord thy God in the place which he shall choose, thou shalt read this law before all Israel in their hearing. Gather the people together, men, and women, and children, and thy stranger that is within thy gates, that they may hear, and that they may learn, and fear the Lord your God, and observe to do all the words of this law.

It is obvious that Joshua had taken God at His word and studied the books of Moses. By taking Israel to Mounts Ebal and Gerizim, Joshua was demonstrating confidence that God had, in fact, given them all of Canaan, even though Israel controlled only a small corner of it so far. Once there, they built an altar of raw, untooled stones. Joshua prepared the surface of some of the stones by covering them with plaster (Josh. 10:32; cf. Deut. 27:4) upon which he engraved "the law of Moses" (probably the Ten Commandments) while Israel watched. Then he offered sacrifices on the new altar. After that, Joshua arrayed Israel in two companies—one standing at the base of Mount Ebal, the other across the narrow valley at the base of Mount Gerizim.

As they stood in their places, Joshua read "all the words of the law," particularly Deuteronomy 28, the portion of Moses' books called "The Blessings and the Cursings," and possibly chapters 29 and 30 as well. The "blessings" portion of the reading pronounced promises of God upon Israel if they fully obeyed

---

[63] According to the Samaritan Pentateuch, this altar was supposed to have been built on Mount Gerizim (see Deut. 27:4–5). That citation provides the basis for claiming that the Samaritan temple found there is the true place of worship, which prompted the Samaritan woman's question to Christ in John 4:20.

Him as they came into the land. The "cursings" part was the recitation of the consequences that would befall Israel if they disobeyed God. To the reading of both the blessings and the cursings, the congregation of Israel said, "Amen." This was a public, verbal recommitment of the nation to the covenant of Sinai that the former generation of Israel had forsaken. The circumcision of the army at Gilgal and the celebration of Passover were signs of participation in this covenant. Their hearing the reading of the law and verbalizing their promise to obey were also important for those who were God's people.

It must not escape our notice that this covenant was renewed not just with the army of Israel, but with the women, children, and foreign converts—"strangers who were conversant among them." They all shared the same privileges and responsibilities under the Law that the men of Israel possessed. God's grace is not limited by ethnicity, age, or gender.

It is at this juncture in the narrative that the ark of the covenant is mentioned for the last time in the book. Sinai's covenant has been renewed by this generation. Participation in the covenant had been reestablished by circumcision at Gilgal. Fellowship within the covenant had been broken by the disobedience at Jericho. Restoration to fellowship was possible after the cleansing of the camp by dealing with Achan. Now we see that renewal in fellowship accomplished at Mount Ebal.

According to Deuteronomy 11:29, Mount Ebal was the mountain from which the cursings were read. Why build an altar on that mountain instead of on Mount Gerizim, where the blessings were read? Because the offering on the altar on Mount Ebal signified the removal of the curse of sin. In Israel's case, the offering was in regard to the sin of Achan. But the altar serves a larger purpose—to provide a picture of Christ, Who bore the curse of sin for us. As a monument to victory, it reminds us of the law. Israel had broken the law, so a sacrifice was necessary to forgive their transgression.

Engraving the law on the sides of the altar shows the effect of the law on our own hearts. It condemns us. We are all lawbreakers. Our only hope is in the effectiveness of the sacrifice of Christ on our behalf. Only Jesus Christ obeyed the law perfectly. Only He could be a satisfactory sacrifice for our sins. Yes, we are saved by *grace*, not by the *law*. But no one can be saved by grace who does not first recognize and admit that he is condemned by the law. The message of salvation starts with the law. "For all have sinned" (Rom. 3:23). "There is none righteous, no, not one" (Rom. 3:10). It does not stop there. The good news ("gospel") is that Christ Jesus paid the penalty for us.

> Christ came to free man from the law's bondage. He freed us not by changing the rules but by obeying the rules in our place and suffering the consequences

> of our disobedience. Two things were necessary for God to be just in saving sinners: the demands of the law had to be completely obeyed, and the penalty of the broken law had to be completely paid. Jesus Christ did both, and both are foundational to the gospel.[64]

If you've confessed your sin and trusted Christ alone to save you, the curse of the law has no more effect on you. You have been justified before God. Believers have an obligation to live obediently in service to our Savior. To pretend to worship Christ yet refuse to obey Him is the height of hypocrisy. God is neither impressed with nor appeased by the hypocritical worship of rebels. Nothing we do can enhance or detract from our acceptance in Christ. "To know that God loves us as He loves His Son and that God accepts us as He accepts His Son ought to put the real joy in serving Jesus."[65]

> What shall we say then to these things? If God be for us, who can be against us? He that spared not his own Son, but delivered him up for us all, how shall he not with him also freely give us all things? Who shall lay any thing to the charge of God's elect? It is God that justifieth. Who is he that condemneth? It is Christ that died, yea rather, that is risen again, who is even at the right hand of God, who also maketh intercession for us. Who shall separate us from the love of Christ? (Rom. 8:31–35*a*).

---

[64] Michael P. V. Barrett, *Complete in Him* (Greenville, SC: Ambassador-Emerald International, 2000), p. 131.

[65] Barrett, p. 143.

18
The Canaanites Respond

Joshua 9:1–13

Former Alabama Chief Justice Roy Moore created quite a ruckus when he had a 5,280-pound granite monument engraved with the Ten Commandments erected in the rotunda of the Alabama Judicial Building. Its installation sparked protests demanding its removal on the grounds of the establishment clause in the Bill of Rights. Opponents claimed it represented an unconstitutional government endorsement of Christianity. Counterprotests arose insisting that Justice Moore had a right to erect the monument, demanding that it stay. A federal judge ruled that the monument had to be removed from state-owned property, and Justice Moore refused to comply with the court order. His eight colleagues on the Alabama Supreme Court overruled him and suspended him from his seat on the bench. A series of appeals upheld the federal judge's decision, and the United States Supreme Court refused to hear the case, allowing the lower court's ruling to stand. The monument had to go.

I believe the decision of the courts was a miscarriage of justice in that the U.S. Constitution actually says that "Congress shall make no law" establishing or restricting religion. The monument in Alabama had not been erected by act of the U.S. Congress, so the establishment clause was irrelevant. The federal judiciary is, indeed, legislating from the bench, and it is their actions that are unconstitutional.

Why the outcry? The presence of the Ten Commandments at the state courthouse implies the existence of a fundamental legal code that is absolute and universal. If the U.S. legal code is based upon it (and there is no disputing that it is), then the U.S. code is actually inferior to that upon which it is based. If the commandments underlying U.S. law really came from God, then there is a court higher than ours, presided over by a Judge greater than any man, and each of us must answer to that Judge on the basis of His law. The American Christian minority shouldn't be surprised by the reaction of the unbelieving majority. While most unbelievers will never admit it, they know in their hearts that they must either stamp out God or make peace with Him.

Enemy Reactions

Satan's attacks on the believer can take many forms, but they fall into two general categories: external assault and internal subversion. The Canaanite responses to Israel's victories represent both types.

The "Roaring Lion"

The first response Joshua mentioned was the formation of an enemy alliance against Israel.

> And it came to pass, when all the kings which were on this side Jordan, in the hills, and in the valleys, and in all the coasts of the great sea over against Lebanon, the Hittite, and the Amorite, the Canaanite, the Perizzite, the Hivite, and the Jebusite, heard thereof; that they gathered themselves together, to fight with Joshua and with Israel, with one accord (Josh. 9:1–2).

Why form an alliance? Because Israel had enjoyed great success at the stronghold of Jericho and subsequently destroyed Ai. The overwhelming nature of Israel's victories, besides the sheer numbers of Israel's people, made it obvious to the Canaanites that Israel had bigger plans. Further, Israel hadn't stayed in the southeastern corner of the region. After the destruction of Ai, Israel had penetrated farther into the territory—all the way to Mount Ebal. It was beginning to look as though Israel intended to lay claim to the entire territory from the Jordan on the east, to the Mediterranean on the west, and to Phoenicia (Lebanon) to the north. The other inhabitants of the region were feeling less than secure.

What Israel did at Mount Ebal was highly significant to the indigenous peoples for at least two reasons. Offering sacrifices to the Lord (*Yahweh*) indicated that there was a new god in charge. Of course, Israel knew that there had never been any other god but the one true God, but the Canaanites didn't think that way. They thought there were many gods who exercised authority over particular people and particular geographic regions. In some ways anticipating Catholicism's idea of "patron saints," each city had its own territorial god. The people of the region would assume that the Israelite cult had somehow gained supremacy over the local cults of Jericho and Ai. Since their own cults were closely related, recognizing and honoring each other's deities, they all felt threatened. At Mount Ebal Israel also recited their legal code and inscribed it on the stones of their altar. This implied that there was a new "law of the land" that Israel would assume superseded the laws of the Canaanite peoples. Like Justice Moore's monument, its presence provoked unbelievers to action.

In short, *the sacrifices and reading of the law at Mount Ebal constituted Israel's claim to all of Canaan*. Even though only a small corner of it had as yet been subdued, Israel claimed authority over the whole. No wonder the Canaanites were worried. In the face of this threat, some of the Canaanite leaders decided the expedient course of action would be to join forces in defense against the Israelite invasion.

The "Subtle Serpent"

Not everyone in Canaan joined the alliance against Israel.

> And when the inhabitants of Gibeon heard what Joshua had done unto Jericho and to Ai, they did work wilily, and went and made as if they had been ambassadors, and took old sacks upon their asses, and wine bottles, old, and rent, and bound up; and old shoes and clouted upon their feet, and old garments upon them; and all the bread of their provision was dry and mouldy (Josh. 9:3–5).

The leaders of the Gibeonites were less optimistic about their ability to defend themselves against the Israelites, so they adopted a different approach to securing their survival. They had the same reasons for forming an alliance as did the Hittites, Amorites, Canaanites, Perizzites, Hivites, and Jebusites. They just thought it would be more prudent to form an alliance *with* Israel than to join one *against* them.

As the story develops, we see that Joshua was well prepared for the frontal assault of the enemy allied against Israel. But once again, he was not fully alert to the potential danger of a subtle alliance with those God had told him to destroy.

Enemy Identification and Strategies

The Canaanite Alliance

Who were "the Hittite, and the Amorite, the Canaanite, the Perizzite, the Hivite, and the Jebusite," the people who formed an alliance against Israel? Prior to Israel's crossing of Jordan, the people of Canaan lived in independent city-states, each with its own "king" and militia. Some of them were larger and more powerful than others, so we sometimes see one or another exercising some authority over, or at least providing some leadership for, others. These city-states were more-or-less organized into groups by ethnicity—certain people groups occupied the cities and villages in various regions.

Some of those groups are historically distinguishable from one another. The Hittites, who descended from Canaan, the grandson of Noah, were by Joshua's time a distinct people. They had roots in the region (see Gen. 10:15–19 and 23:3–20), but during the nearly six hundred years between Abraham and Joshua, the Hittites had migrated to the land known as Anatolia—modern Turkey. While they may have maintained a continual presence in Canaan, on at least two occasions in their history, the Hittites expanded their holdings from their Anatolian homeland to occupy territory as far south as Damascus.[66]

The first period of Hittite expansion occurred during the reign of Marshili I, who extended Hittite holdings into Europe to their west and Syria to their southeast. He brought the first dynasty of Babylon to an end when he sacked the city then controlled by the fifth and final successor of Hammurabi. The second, and greatest, expansion of the Hittites was during the period beginning with the reign of Shuppiluliama I and ending with the reign of his grandson Hattushili III, from the mid-fourteenth century to the mid-thirteenth century BC. Under Hattushili III, the Hittites established formal diplomatic relations with Egypt when his daughter married Ramses II. This occurred by the time Israel's history was approaching the midpoint of the period of the judges.

The Amorites are sometimes treated as being distinct from the Canaanites, and sometimes not, making it difficult to distinguish between them. While the Bible sometimes lists them separately, they occupied the same territory—the eastern Mediterranean coastal plain to Egypt's Sihor River (Josh. 13:3). Further,

[66] Hoffner, pp. 127–55.

their names mean essentially the same thing. The basic meaning of the Hebrew word *Canaan* is "to sink or to be low." In its first use in Genesis 9:18–21, it connotes a depraved moral character. However, it seems in general usage among the people called by that name to have come to designate them as "sundowners" or "westerners," the people who live where the sun sinks low. It is likely that they deliberately shifted the application of the meaning to avoid the original stigma, although they were certainly a people characterized by moral depravity. The Mesopotamian word *Amorite* was used to designate people from the west, regardless of their ethnicity. It generally referred to a people that occupied a region we know as Syria, but included all of Syria-Palestine.[67]

The Perizzites, Hivites, and Jebusites are virtually indistinguishable, although the Jebusites are the people who controlled Jerusalem (Josh. 15:63; Judg. 1:21; 2 Sam. 5:6–8).

It becomes even more difficult to distinguish among these groups when we find the Scriptures using the names almost interchangeably. For instance, in Genesis 36:2–3 we read that Esau married three *Canaanite* wives, who are then identified as being a *Hittite*, a *Hivite*, and an *Ishmaelite*. Further, in Ezekiel 16:3 God describes Jerusalem, saying, "Thy birth and thy nativity is of the land of Canaan; thy father was an Amorite, and thy mother an Hittite."

Apparently any distinctions between these peoples were subtle and not especially important, even to the Israelites. Since they all apparently descended from the same grandson of Noah—Canaan—they should all be thought of as *Canaanites*. The various names designate different lines of descent from Canaan, or different tribes of Canaanites. Although their relationships diverged centuries before the various sons of Jacob developed distinct tribal identities, their relationships with one another were at least ethnically similar to the relationships of the tribes within Israel. As we will see, Reubenites, Gadites, Ephraimites, and so on, will occasionally act independently but will all still be *Israelites*.

The greatest difference is that the Israelites represented a political and religious unit while the Canaanites generally did not. In this case, however, they have banded together against a common enemy—Israel. Exactly what they end up doing, we will see in chapter 20 (Josh. 10:1ff.).

The Gibeonite Deception

Gibeon was a city about twenty miles west of Israel's camp at Gilgal and about five miles northwest of Jerusalem. It was on the northeastern edge of the

[67] Keith N. Schoville, "Canaanites and Amorites," *Peoples of the Old Testament World*, Hoerth, Mattingly, Yamauchi, eds. (Grand Rapids: Baker Books, 1994), pp. 157–82.

territory occupied by the cities named in the coalition against Israel (see Josh. 10:3), which will be significant later. For now, the most important fact of its location is that it was only five or six miles southwest of Ai, probably the very next city Israel would encounter if they continued their expansion into Canaan in the same direction they had begun.

These people were desperate. It is far too early in history to use the cliché of seeing the "handwriting on the wall," since that event occurred during the life of Daniel in Babylon over eight hundred years later; still the Gibeonites were justifiably convinced that their destruction was imminent. In their desperation, they concocted a plan to deceive Joshua into making an alliance with them.

> And they went to Joshua unto the camp at Gilgal, and said unto him, and to the men of Israel, We be come from a far country: now therefore make ye a league with us. And the men of Israel said unto the Hivites, Peradventure ye dwell among us; and how shall we make a league with you? And they said unto Joshua, We are thy servants. And Joshua said unto them, Who are ye? and from whence come ye? And they said unto him, From a very far country thy servants are come because of the name of the Lord thy God: for we have heard the fame of him, and all that he did in Egypt, and all that he did to the two kings of the Amorites, that were beyond Jordan, to Sihon king of Heshbon, and to Og king of Bashan, which was at Ashtaroth. Wherefore our elders and all the inhabitants of our country spake to us, saying, Take victuals with you for the journey, and go to meet them, and say unto them, We are your servants: therefore now make ye a league with us. This our bread we took hot for our provision out of our houses on the day we came forth to go unto you; but now, behold, it is dry, and it is mouldy: and these bottles of wine, which we filled, were new; and, behold, they be rent: and these our garments and our shoes are become old by reason of the very long journey (Josh. 9:6–13).

The Gibeonites prepared an elaborate ruse. They selected a group to act as emissaries to travel to meet with Joshua. With beat-up wineskins, moldy bread, and worn-out clothing and shoes, they presented themselves as having traveled a long distance for the specific purpose of seeking an alliance with Joshua and Israel.

The first thing we see about this meeting is that the Gibeonites came to Gilgal. Our focus at the moment is on the Gibeonites and their strategy—I won't address Israel's failure until the next chapter. However, it's important to see at this point that Israel was right where they belonged, at the place of their consecration to God, yet they still failed. How could that happen? Arthur Pink has said, "If we are gratified with our consecration, pleased with our self-denial, puffed up with our obedience, or proud of our prayerfulness and increasing dependence upon God, we are headed for disaster."[68] That is essen-

[68] Pink, p. 243.

tially the same thing Paul told the believers in Corinth when he warned, "Let him that thinketh he standeth take heed lest he fall" (1 Cor. 10:12). How often we become susceptible to failure immediately following great success!

We have to note that, unlike their countrymen from the cities around them, the Gibeonites came for peace. This was not the proverbial "Trojan horse" (another anachronistic cliché referring to an event that wouldn't occur for a couple hundred years). The Gibeonites didn't come to make war with Israel, either openly or covertly. They came to escape destruction. Still, there is no evidence in these verses that they shared Rahab's desire to serve God. It seems, at least at this point, that they hoped to outwit God by their craftiness. The actions of the Gibeonites imply an attitude remarkably similar to that of the person who prays for "salvation" in order to escape the judgment of hell with no intention of changing allegiance and obeying Christ. Such a prayer is futile. There is nothing salvific in mouthing the words of a prayer where there is no change of heart.

We see that when the Gibeonites were interrogated by Joshua and the elders, the narrative now identifies their ethnicity, calling them "Hivites." They were inhabitants of the city of Gibeon, but they were members of the tribe of Hivites—a people group Israel had been told to destroy. Joshua didn't know that yet. This is another example of the historian giving the reader information that was not yet available to the people participating in the events.

We further see that Joshua knew the law concerning an alliance. Forty years earlier, God had warned Israel, "Take heed to thyself, lest thou make a covenant with the inhabitants of the land whither thou goest, lest it be for a snare in the midst of thee" (Exod. 34:12). Shortly before Moses' death and Joshua's inauguration, which occurred just a few weeks before this meeting with the Gibeonites, Moses had given the following clear instructions:

> But of the cities of these people, which the Lord thy God doth give thee for an inheritance, thou shalt save alive nothing that breatheth: but thou shalt utterly destroy them; namely, the Hittites, and the Amorites, the Canaanites, and the Perizzites, the **Hivites**, and the Jebusites; as the Lord thy God hath commanded thee (Deut. 20:16–17).

With these instructions, why would Joshua even consider such an alliance? Because he knew Moses' instructions concerning *distant* cities were different from his orders for those in the immediate vicinity. In the verses immediately preceding the order to destroy every living being in the Canaanite cities, Moses had told Israel they must *spare* the inhabitants of any city "very far off from thee" that accepted an offer of peace:

> When thou comest nigh unto a city to fight against it, then proclaim peace unto it. And it shall be, if it make thee answer of peace, and open unto thee, then it shall be, that all the people that is found therein shall be tributaries unto thee, and they shall serve thee. And if it will make no peace with thee, but will make war against thee, then thou shalt besiege it: and when the Lord thy God hath delivered it into thine hands, thou shalt smite every male thereof with the edge of the sword: but the women, and the little ones, and the cattle, and all that is in the city, even all the spoil thereof, shalt thou take unto thyself; and thou shalt eat the spoil of thine enemies, which the Lord thy God hath given thee. Thus shalt thou do unto all the cities which are very far off from thee, which are not of the cities of these nations (Deut. 20:10–15).

It is no accident that the Gibeonites repeatedly insisted that they were from "a far country" (Josh. 9:6), "a very far country" (9:9), and had traveled a "very long journey" (9:13) to get there. The very wording of their request for peace would remind Joshua of the command of Moses to offer peace to distant cities. Joshua wanted to do what was right. He wanted to obey God.[69]

Joshua had no reason to believe that an alliance with the Gibeonites was necessary for Israel's protection. His purpose was only to show mercy, and that is commendable. Joshua had complete confidence in Israel's eventual total conquest of the land. When he challenged the Gibeonites' request for an alliance on the ground that they might be neighbors he was duty-bound to destroy, Joshua didn't say, "Peradventure ye dwell among the Canaanites." He said, "Peradventure ye dwell among *us*" (Josh. 9:7). *Joshua and "the men of Israel" assumed that Israel already possessed all the land.* That's a remarkable statement of faith, considering the short list of cities conquered so far: Jericho, Ai, and Bethel.

Joshua exercised at least a measure of caution. He performed an inspection of the Gibeonites and their baggage. Their background "legend" was so carefully prepared that Joshua's search merely reinforced the impression that the Gibeonites were telling the truth. Everything looked as if they had come a long way.

Maybe Joshua was in too much of a hurry to do a thorough investigation. I suspect that the Gibeonites' story appealed to his pride. They implied that they had come a long way just to see him ("We be come from a far country," Josh. 9:6). They insisted that Joshua and Israel were greater than the Gibeonites ("We are thy servants," Josh. 9:8). Then they said that Joshua's fame had already reached their far country ("We have heard," Josh. 9:9–11). They let Joshua con-

[69] It is worth noting that Solomon actually voiced an invitation to Gentile nations to come in his dedicatory prayer at the temple in 1 Kings 8:41–43.

clude that the Lord had already magnified His name in the eyes of foreigners from distant lands ("because of the name of the Lord," Josh. 9:9; cf. 3:7).

Such flattery can make fools of the best of men. When a man is famous and admired, he begins to feel invincible. He may throw caution to the winds, assuming he has no need of counsel and even no need of God. He is powerful, clever, and influential. Nothing can go wrong. A celebrity who is morally upright, honest, and humble is incredibly rare, and *men of God are not immune to the seduction of fame.* Pride led to problems in the lives of Kings Hezekiah and Uzziah. After the Lord Jesus commended Peter for correctly identifying Him as the Messiah of God, saying He would give Peter the "keys of the kingdom" (Matt. 16:19), Peter thought he could tell the Lord what to do. Peter actually rebuked the Lord Jesus for announcing that He was going to Jerusalem to die, saying, "This shall not be unto thee" (Matt. 16:22), as if Peter intended to prevent the Lord from doing what He said. For this arrogance, Peter was soundly rebuffed—"But he turned, and said unto Peter, Get thee behind me, Satan: thou art an offence unto me: for thou savourest not the things that be of God, but those that be of men" (Matt. 16:23).

Perhaps it was the flattery of the Gibeonites that tipped the scales in Joshua's mind. Joshua decided he needn't bother the Lord with this. He would make a decision on his own (see Josh. 9:14). That will be the subject of chapter 19.

Applying the Principles

Israel's early successes over Jericho and Ai/Bethel had confirmed the fears of the inhabitants of the land. Most responded by forming an alliance to *oppose* Israel. One group responded by seeking an alliance *with* Israel. There are lessons to be learned from the responses of both the Canaanite coalition and the Gibeonite embassy.

Have you ever noticed that the more you try to obey the Word of God, the more intense the opposition you face? That opposition can come from different sources and for several reasons. Some *opposition may come from our chief adversary, the Devil.* Someone has said, "The Devil doesn't mind your commitments, as long as you don't try to put them into practice." However, we blame the Devil for much of the opposition we face even though he may not have been directly involved. Further, a lot of the opposition we experience comes from within our own hearts. We have no idea the strength of our own natural inclination for wickedness until we try to avoid sin and obey God.

Some *opposition comes because people see the obedient Christian as a threat.* The very fact that you obey the Lord places the disobedience of others in sharper relief, and people tend to resent that. It is amazing, and in some ways a testimony to the truth, to see the way that all types of people will band together to oppose the cause of Christ. In Jesus' day, the Pharisees and Herodians were bitter adversaries. The Pharisees advocated strict adherence to the rabbinical interpretations and applications of the Mosaic Law. The Herodians were a political party known for advocating compromise with Rome. Perhaps the only time these two groups agreed on anything was when they decided to join forces in an attempt to discredit or destroy Jesus Christ (Matt. 22:15–16; Mark 3:6; 12:13).

While overt opposition can be uncomfortable, covert subversion can be at least as dangerous. War with the Canaanite coalition represented a less significant threat to Israel's security than did a treaty with the Gibeonites. Why did God forbid Israel to make treaties with the people of the land? Because of the danger of corruption through ungodly influences. When God told Israel to "utterly destroy" the inhabitants of the land in Deuteronomy 20:16–17, He told them why in verse 18—"That they teach you not to do after all their abominations, which they have done unto their gods; so should ye sin against the Lord your God." We, too, need to be on guard against the subversive influence of worldliness. Simple exposure to the corruption of the world can lead to compromise.

Another danger in making a league with the Gibeonites was the potential violation of the principle of the "unequal yoke": the believer is not to be "unequally yoked" with an unbeliever (2 Cor. 6:14). We usually cite this verse in connection with marriage, which is perfectly appropriate. On the basis of this principle, God forbids a believer to marry an unbeliever. But there are other kinds of "yokes" besides marriage. I believe this principle also forbids political alliances with unbelievers for the purpose of achieving a common objective, or business partnerships for the purpose of making money, or any other official linking of believers with unbelievers that could lead to compromise of the principles of God's Word.

Finally, *we need to guard against internal lusts or longings that can result in compromise with sin.* For instance, what a person thinks of as earnestness or zeal may actually be impatience or presumption. On the other hand, one may rationalize his slothfulness by calling it a "holy caution." How can we tell the difference? That's the problem. You and I are no more able to distinguish between zeal and presumption, slothfulness and caution, without the help of the Lord, than Joshua was able to tell whether the Gibeonites were from Canaan or a far country without asking "counsel at the mouth of the Lord" (Josh. 9:14).

I suppose in a way it seems that Joshua had an advantage over us in that he could expect God to direct him in some audible or tangible way. However, he had been told to study "this book of the law" (Josh. 1:8) in order to know what to do. So the advantage is really ours. We have much more than the five books of Moses. We have all sixty-six books of inspired Scripture to guide us. God has provided us with His full revelation and told us it is all we need in order to know how to live.

> All scripture is given by inspiration of God, and is profitable for doctrine, for reproof, for correction, for instruction in righteousness: that the man of God may be perfect, throughly furnished unto all good works (2 Tim. 3:16–17).

For you and me to avoid compromise with sin, we need careful, constant self-examination in the light of Scripture. If we'll allow God's Word to instruct and discipline us, we'll find that God's Word is sufficient to equip us.

Commenting on the court's actions to remove the Ten Commandments from the Alabama Supreme Court, syndicated columnist Cal Thomas asked the following insightful question:

> Will an irreligious people who worship their personal golden calves of pleasure and affluence be more likely to "seek first the Kingdom of God and His righteousness" (Matthew 6:33) if they see such displays, or be lulled into a false security that God is somehow pleased or tolerant of their increasingly secular outlook of His creation?[70]

Whether we obey God does not depend on stone monuments in front of court houses. It depends on the Spirit within us enabling us to obey the Word before us. We must remember that God writes His Word in our hearts (Jer. 31:33), and we must not allow our baser nature to rebel against the Law of the Land.

[70] Cal Thomas, "Conflicting thoughts bubble up from battle over Commandments," *Athens Banner-Herald*, Friday, August 29, 2003, p. A10.

19

Honor Despite Deception

Joshua 9:14–27

Bill had been teaching in a Christian high school for several years when he became convinced that the Lord was leading him to accept an offered position as associate pastor in a church several hundred miles away. Selling his home and moving his family, he was eager to start a new phase of ministry.

After being in his new post less than a week, Bill discovered that it was not quite what it had seemed. His job description when he arrived had important differences from what had been previously discussed. There were serious problems with the church's finances, and Bill had significant problems with aspects of the ministry philosophy of the pastor. When he confronted the senior pastor who had hired him, the man admitted that he'd intentionally misled him. He justified his actions on the ground that he believed Bill was the man for the job and he knew Bill wouldn't have taken the job if he'd known the truth.

Bill was confused. He had diligently prayed for the Lord's leading and had been convinced his move had been due to the Lord's direction. He now had a dilemma. Should he honor his contract, or consider the pastor's deceptions justification for leaving? Bill decided that for whatever reason, God had allowed him to misread the situation and make a move he wouldn't have made had he known the truth. He decided to stay at least for the duration of his one-year agreement. He had made a promise. He would keep his word.

Joshua's Failure

Like the machinations of the pastor mentioned above, the Gibeonites' carefully thought out charade had successfully fooled Joshua and the elders of Israel. They were convinced they were dealing with representatives of a distant city with whom they could make peace with God's blessing (Deut. 20:10–15).

> And the men took of their victuals, and asked not counsel at the mouth of the Lord. And Joshua made peace with them, and made a league with them, to let them live: and the princes of the congregation sware unto them (Josh. 9:14–15).

Walking by Sight

Joshua and Israel's elders took the evidence of the spoiled food at face value. They were walking by sight, not by faith. They accepted falsified evidence noncritically, without any more than a superficial evaluation or verification, trusting their own judgment to discern the truth.

One of Satan's most effective traps is to present us with temptations that seem innocuous. Have you ever tried to defend your choices by saying, "I don't see anything wrong with it"? We all have. In many cases that is precisely the problem. We don't *see* what is truly wrong. Israel entered into a treaty agreement with a Canaanite tribe on the basis of what they could *see*. Joshua would never have made this alliance with the Gibeonites if they had presented themselves as they really were. In the same way, *no believer would fall prey to temptation if it were presented as it really is from God's perspective*. It is easier to pretend that we don't need God to help us discern the truth. Rather than trusting in the Lord with all our heart, we lean upon our own understanding and forfeit God's direction of our paths (Prov. 3:5–6). Sometimes the problem is that we haven't looked carefully enough. You'd think that Joshua could have taken a little more time to check the Gibeonites' story more thoroughly. But that isn't the reason God gives for Joshua's failure. God says Joshua failed because he "asked not counsel at the mouth of the Lord."

A Hasty Decision

Joshua's dilemma was that no matter what he did, he risked violating a command of God. To destroy the Gibeonites when they really were from a distant land and wanted peace with Israel would disobey God's command in Deuteronomy 20:10–15. To make peace with the Gibeonites when they were really inhabitants of the land of Canaan would disobey God's command in Deuteronomy 20:16–17.

What choices did Joshua have? He could have accused the Gibeonites of being local spies and killed them out of hand. That is probably the action we would have expected if Joshua were really a bloodthirsty, genocidal sociopath as he is sometimes portrayed. But because Joshua was actually a peaceful and merciful man, he *wanted* to spare the Gibeonites if he could. Another option, then, would have been to hold these visitors in custody, demand specific directions to their homeland, and dispatch a band of Israelite emissaries to confirm their story. If the Gibeonites had really been from a distant land, this would take some time. The conquest of Canaan could continue—the strength of the army of Israel wouldn't have been significantly diluted by the absence of a few. Another option Joshua doesn't seem to have considered is that he could have asked God for direction. He had precedent for such action in the instructions God had given him when he had to find the one in the camp who had stolen goods from Jericho. Throughout the process of bringing the people before the Lord, it was always God Who revealed the individual's guilt or innocence, ultimately identifying Achan as the thief.

Joshua and the elders of Israel decided on their own to swear a solemn oath to the Gibeonites that they would let them live. The Gibeonites could go home in peace, confident that Israel wouldn't destroy them. Because he didn't ask for wisdom as he looked, trusting his own judgment, Joshua made a treaty on insufficient grounds. Having been deceived was no excuse. Joshua should have known he needed God's counsel in this matter. Without having proved conclusively whether these men were telling the truth, he should never have forged this alliance without the unambiguous direction of the Lord.

Joshua's Honor

It wasn't long before Joshua and all Israel discovered they had been duped. The Gibeonites were neighbors with whom God had forbidden Israel to make an alliance.

> And it came to pass at the end of three days after they had made a league with them, that they heard that they were their neighbours, and that they dwelt among them (Josh. 9:16).

We aren't told how long the emissaries from Gibeon were in Israel's camp before Joshua and the tribal leaders ("princes") decided to make an alliance with them, but probably not long. How ironic that only three days after agreeing to peace with the Gibeonites Joshua found out they had lied to him! It is possible that had Joshua shown a little patience, the truth would have been revealed simply through the normal course of events, and this alliance might never have been joined, but it isn't safe to assume so. It is more likely that once the treaty had been negotiated there was no longer any need for pretense.

The point of this event is *not* that we should drag our feet making decisions, expecting dangers to reveal themselves on their own. The real lesson is that *temptations will deceive us* until it's too late, *then mock us* once we've walked blindly into Satan's trap. Satan isn't satisfied simply with leading us astray. He then gloats in revealing our folly to our own discredit or destruction. To avoid his snares, we must "ask . . . counsel at the mouth of the Lord" (Josh. 9:14).

Swearing in the Name of the Lord

The implication of the language of verse 15 is that once Joshua and Israel's elders had decided to make peace with the Gibeonites, that decision was ratified in a formal ceremony in which Israel "made peace . . . made a league . . . [and] sware unto them" that they would "let them live." When verse 16 tells us that Israel discovered the deception three days later, it indicates that they had entered into this treaty on a specific date.

This is significant because it implies the solemn nature of the oath they had sworn. Typically, such an oath would be formalized in five parts. First, there would be a verbal assertion of the truth—swearing that the participants in the oath spoke truthfully. Second, there would be a solemn acknowledgment of the presence of God—that God was witness to the promises being made. Third, there would be an invocation asking God to testify to the truth of what was said. Fourth, the oath makers would call upon God to avenge the lie if they spoke falsely. Finally, the vow would be "confirmed by seven sacrifices, seven witnesses, or seven pledges."[71]

To Israel, swearing such an oath was an act of worship. Therefore, violation of such a vow would not only make a person the target of God's just vengeance for having lied under oath but would also make him guilty of blasphemy for having called on God to testify to the truthfulness of the lie. This was serious business. Psalm 15:1–4 describes those who are righteous. One of the characteristics listed is that he "sweareth to his own hurt, and changeth not." That is,

---

[71] Zodhiates, p. 1664. The very word used, *shava* ("to swear an oath"), is related to the word *sheva* or *shiv'ah*, meaning "seven."

a righteous man keeps his word even if it proves not to be personally beneficial. From one of the books Joshua was commanded to study day and night, Leviticus 19:12 says, "And ye shall not swear by my name falsely, neither shalt thou profane the name of thy God: I am the Lord."

Keeping His Word

Joshua had a problem. Should he violate his oath, making him guilty of blasphemy and profanity for having taken God's name in vain, in order to obey the command to destroy the Gibeonites because they were neighbors? Or should he spare the Gibeonites, avoiding the sins involved in breaking his vow, and place himself in the position of having failed to fully obey God's instructions in conquering the land?

> And the children of Israel journeyed, and came unto their cities on the third day. Now their cities were Gibeon, and Chephirah, and Beeroth, and Kirjath-jearim. And the children of Israel smote them not, because the princes of the congregation had sworn unto them by the Lord God of Israel. And all the congregation murmured against the princes. But all the princes said unto all the congregation, We have sworn unto them by the Lord God of Israel: now therefore we may not touch them. This we will do to them; we will even let them live, lest wrath be upon us, because of the oath which we sware unto them (Josh. 9:17–20).

Perhaps to help put "the fear of the Lord" in the hearts of the conniving sneaks, Joshua marched the host of Israel to the gates of the cities of the Gibeonites. But when they got there, "they smote them not, because the princes of the congregation had sworn unto them by the Lord God of Israel." Joshua and the princes of Israel were more afraid of the wrath of God for having abused His name and reputation than they were of the possible consequences of honoring their oath.

The congregation of Israel was decidedly unhappy, obstinately complaining against the decision of their leaders. The text doesn't say whether they wanted revenge for being deceived or were just interested in destroying and looting the cities for their own personal benefit. But Joshua and the princes were adamant. They had sworn an oath in God's name. They could not harm the Gibeonites.

They chose wisely. It is better to demonstrate proper reverence for God's name and to take our lumps for having sworn foolishly than to try to minimize the consequences of our disobedience by committing blasphemy. We would do well to keep that in mind in our worship today. Much that is done in the name of advancing the gospel is manipulative and even deceptive, besmirching the integrity of God. *Better to be honest and forthright and unpopular than to compromise for the sake of public applause*. By deciding to honor his oath to the Gibeonites, Joshua proved he was more concerned with protecting God's reputation for fidelity and truthfulness than he was with appeasing the congregation of Israel or with saving his own skin. It is a shame that that kind of integrity is in such short supply today.

Announcing the Consequences

Israel would honor the pledge made by their leaders—they would let the Gibeonites live. But without violating the treaty, Israel could impose consequences for having been deceived.

> And the princes said unto them, Let them live; but let them be hewers of wood and drawers of water unto all the congregation; as the princes had promised them. And Joshua called for them, and he spake unto them, saying, Wherefore have ye beguiled us, saying, We are very far from you; when ye dwell among us? Now therefore ye are cursed, and there shall none of you be freed from being bondmen, and hewers of wood and drawers of water for the house of my God (Josh. 9:21–23).

Nothing in Israel's vow to the Gibeonites required they be granted equal status within Israel's socioreligious structure. The Gibeonites had not approached Israel as a sovereign nation wanting a reciprocal agreement between equals; they had come as supplicants, asking for mercy and twice calling themselves "thy servants" (Josh. 9:8–9). Therefore, it was appropriate for Joshua to inform the Gibeonites that they would be the servants of Israel.

In the wording of his declaration, Joshua said the Gibeonites were "cursed" (*'arar*). This is one of six different Hebrew words translated "cursed" in the Old Testament. Its particular application designates something or someone as hemmed in, forbidden, or dedicated to a particular purpose.

> Thus the first curses in Gene. 3:14, 17, "Thou art cursed above all cattle" and "Cursed is the ground for thy sake" mean, "You are banned from all the other animals" and "Condemned be the soil [i.e., its fertility to men is banned] on your account."[72]

In Joshua 6:18 and 7:1, this word applied to Jericho, its inhabitants, and its goods. Since the metals were to be kept for the treasury of the tabernacle, the "curse" didn't indicate that everything was to be *destroyed* but that everything was *devoted exclusively to God*. Achan's sin in taking of the "accursed" thing was not in keeping for himself things that were *vile* but in keeping things for his own use that had been devoted to God. When Joshua said the Gibeonites were "cursed," he wasn't just calling names, nor was he saying they would

---

[72] Zodhiates, p. 1601.

ultimately face damnation by God. He meant *the Gibeonites would have a specific and limited role within Israel in the service of God.*

Pledging Their Submission

To their credit, the Gibeonites took this news pretty well.

> And they answered Joshua, and said, Because it was certainly told thy servants, how that the Lord thy God commanded his servant Moses to give you all the land, and to destroy all the inhabitants of the land from before you, therefore we were sore afraid of our lives because of you, and have done this thing. And now, behold, we are in thine hand: as it seemeth good and right unto thee to do unto us, do. And so did he unto them, and delivered them out of the hand of the children of Israel, that they slew them not. And Joshua made them that day hewers of wood and drawers of water for the congregation, and for the altar of the Lord, even unto this day, in the place which he should choose (Josh. 9:24–27).

The initial intent of the Gibeonites had been to outwit God—to trick Him into having to spare them. When the host of Israel marched up to their gates and Joshua confronted them with their lies, they discovered that "God is not mocked" (Gal. 6:7). He discerns "the thoughts and intents of the heart" (Heb. 4:12). *Joshua's confrontation evoked a response of faith and willing service.* The Gibeonites responded to Joshua's pronouncement of servitude with words strongly reminiscent of Rahab's declaration of faith in Joshua 2:9–11. Like Rahab, they were convinced that God was going to give Israel all the land. Like Rahab, they believed their lives were forfeited if they did not make peace with Israel and "the Lord thy God." Granted, their statement lacks the clarity of Rahab's "for the Lord your God, he is God in heaven above, and in earth beneath" (Josh. 2:11). Still they admitted their own fear of God and willingly submitted to His authority.

In many ways, this response parallels the conversion of an unbeliever. They admitted their guilt and the fact that they deserved wrath. They professed Israel's righteousness and that their anger was justifiable. Most importantly, they begged for *mercy*, not justice. They made no excuses other than their fear. They took full responsibility for having done wrong, without trying to blame Israel or any outside influence. They didn't even try to invoke the peace treaty they had negotiated through deception. They didn't say, "You have to spare us because you promised." They said, "You're right. We lied because we were afraid. Do to us whatever you believe is appropriate. We are at your mercy." As a result, the Gibeonites weren't just spared; they were actually *blessed* in the service of worship.

Just weeks before, Israel had stood on the opposite shore of Jordan and listened to the final words of Moses. In the declaration of the renewal of God's covenant with Israel, God had made it plain that His covenant extended to all social classes within the camp.

> Ye stand this day all of you before the Lord your God; your captains of your tribes, your elders, and your officers, with all the men of Israel, your little ones, your wives, and thy stranger that is in thy camp, **from the hewer of thy wood unto the drawer of thy water:** that thou shouldest enter into covenant with the Lord thy God, and into his oath, which the Lord thy God maketh with thee this day: that he may establish thee to day for a people unto himself, and that he may be unto thee a God, as he hath said unto thee, and as he hath sworn unto thy fathers, to Abraham, to Isaac, and to Jacob. Neither with you only do I make this covenant and this oath; but with him that standeth here with us this day before the Lord our God, **and also with him that is not here with us this day** (Deut. 29:10–15).

The fact that the Gibeonites were to be "hewers of wood and drawers of water" (Josh. 9:21) did *not* make them slaves with no rights. It implies that they would be on the lowest rung of the social ladder, but the very wording acknowledges *their acceptance into the ranks of Israel as full participants in their society*. They would enjoy the same rights and privileges as the leaders of the tribes. The princes intended to honor their word, even to this extent, making them chop wood and draw water "unto all the congregation." When the Gibeonites responded with what amounts to an infantile statement of faith, Joshua modified the pronouncement, adding that their service would be both "for the congregation, and **for the altar of the Lord**" (9:27). The Gibeonites were not only to participate in Israel's society but also were inductees into God's covenant with Israel.

There would now be three general levels of those who handled Israel's worship. The *priests* who performed the sacrifices would come from the tribe of Levi, particularly the family of Aaron. *Levites* from other families had other duties in the administration of Israel's worship. Now there were added these *Gibeonites*, the wood choppers and water drawers, who as a group would come to be called the "temple servants," or *Nethinim* (see 1 Chron. 9:2).

Historical Significance of This Alliance

Fulfilling God's Curse

In the course of these events, we see God's sovereignty demonstrated in several ways. Some nine hundred years before Israel entered Canaan, God had pronounced a curse (ʻ*arar*) upon the descendants of Canaan, Noah's grandson. Among those descendants was a tribe called the Hivites (Gen. 9:25). The Gibeonites were identified as part of that tribe in Joshua 9:7. That curse meant that the Canaanites were to be devoted to God for whatever purpose He chose. It was called a "curse" because it usually indicated coming destruction, but God sometimes put those under this ban to other uses. In Jericho, nearly everything was destroyed, but Rahab and her family, as well as certain metals, were kept for service to the Lord. Now we see God continuing to fulfill His "curse" in ways perhaps unexpected but still consistent with His original pronouncement. Most of the inhabitants would be destroyed, but the Gibeonites would be singled out for service.

Avenging Israel's Crimes

We also see God's sovereignty in His working with Israel, particularly in reaping the results of the sin of Jacob's sons. Over four hundred years before Israel entered Canaan, Simeon and Levi had deceived the inhabitants of Shechem into making a false treaty with them by undergoing circumcision. Then while the men were recovering from their surgery, those two had gone through the town and slaughtered them all (Gen. 34:13–29). Significantly, Shechem is identified as "the son of Hamor the **Hivite**" (Gen. 34:2). The priests and Levites of Joshua's day could hardly protest being given the Gibeonites/Hivites as assistants on the ground of a treaty achieved by deception. If anything, the Hivites had a grievance against the Levites. That these two groups of deceivers were assigned to serve the Lord together was a remarkable evidence of God's mercy and forgiveness.

Maintaining Joshua's Vow

Despite four centuries of the Gibeonites' faithful service of drawing water and cutting wood for the tabernacle, a time came when King Saul decided to purge Israel of the Gibeonites. The Bible doesn't tell the story when it happened but recounts it later during the reign of David. For reasons undisclosed, "Saul sought to slay them in his zeal to the children of Israel and Judah" (2 Sam. 21:2). We find out about it because David asked God why Israel had been suffering a famine for three years, and God said it was because Saul "slew the Gibeonites" (21:1). When Saul violated Israel's treaty with the Gibeonites four hundred years after its ratification, God would not let the violation go unpunished. All Israel suffered for Saul's treachery.

When David asked the Gibeonites how he could repay them for Saul's treachery, their answer was both gracious and highly significant. They did not want financial reparations, nor did they want vengeance on anyone in Israel other than the one who had broken the treaty (21:3–4). They asked that seven of Saul's descendants be turned over to them for execution. Why? Because the original alliance had been confirmed with seven sacrifices, and they had trusted the word of Israel's leaders. Since Saul had willfully violated that trust and slaughtered many of the Gibeonites despite the solemn oath that bound him, the lives of seven of Saul's offspring would serve as retribution, in effect re-establishing the covenant. This was *not* a propitiation by human sacrifice but an act of *justice* by imposing the death penalty on those responsible for having blasphemed God by breaking an oath sworn in His name. Clearly, God intended for Israel to keep their promise to the Gibeonites.

Later, we see Solomon offering sacrifices in Gibeon (1 Kings 3:4; 2 Chron. 1:3ff.). It was there he had his dream in which the Lord asked him what gift he desired from God, and he asked God for wisdom to rule His people well.

About five hundred years later, the Gibeonites show up again in Ezra. In chapter 8, Ezra provides a summary list of the people who volunteered to leave their homes scattered throughout the Persian empire and return to Jerusalem to rebuild the city and reestablish their worship. The faithful who would make the trip would be but a remnant of all the people since most would choose not to return. Within the list, Ezra especially requests that Iddo and "his brethren the Nethinims" come to be "ministers for the house of our God" (Ezra 8:17). We find that among those who actually went back to Israel were "two hundred and twenty Nethinims: all of them were expressed by name" (8:20). *The Gibeonite* Nethinim *(temple servants) were included among the faithful remnant of Israel that was restored to the land following the Babylonian captivity.*

One final historical note of consequence is found in Nehemiah. A man named Melatiah the Gibeonite, along with other men from Gibeon, helped Nehemiah rebuild the walls of Jerusalem (Neh. 3:7). When it came time for Nehemiah to register those who had returned to Jerusalem with Zerubbabel, he listed ninety-five men of Gibeon (with their families), counting them among Israel's exiles who had returned home. *Israel kept their word to the Gibeonites, and at least a remnant of the Gibeonites had remained faithful to God.*

Applying the Principles

Each of us will be faced with making decisions without having any definitive way of *proving* the right choice. It may be impossible for us to tell from looking at the situation whether one choice or another will violate a command of

God. Because of our own finite nature, we never have all the information—only God is omniscient. Because of the spiritual immaturity that characterizes all of us before the coming resurrection, we can be deceived by appearances.

So what are we to do? In such situations, James tells us, "If any of you lack wisdom, let him ask of God, that giveth to all men liberally, and upbraideth not; and it shall be given him" (James 1:5). God wants us to do right, and He wants us to know what right things we should do. We must acknowledge the inadequacy of our "own understanding" (Prov. 3:5) and ask Him to lead us. He has given us an absolute promise that He will give us what we need in abundance ("liberally"). He will never rebuke or scold us for asking ("upbraideth not") because *asking for help is what we are commanded to do*. With the twin tools of Scripture and prayer, excusing our sinful choices on the basis of ignorance is never justifiable.

But what about Bill? About eight months after Bill became an assistant pastor, it was time to decide whether to agree to another year's service. The situation had improved—the pastor had apologized and promised important changes. Bill had no indication from the Lord that he should go anywhere else, so when the pastor begged him to stay another year, he agreed. The second year became increasingly intolerable. Bill found that the pastor habitually misled and manipulated the congregation and the staff. Bill was finding it difficult to assist the pastor in ministry with a clear conscience and was considering breaking his contract.

Then allegations of serious moral improprieties began to be made against the pastor. Bill was looking for a place to hide. However, it became apparent that God had providentially put Bill at that place to help the church weather the storm. The allegations against the pastor proved to be true, the pastor was disciplined and removed, and eventually the church asked Bill to stay as senior pastor. Bill went on to have several years of successful ministry at that church.

G. Campbell Morgan once said, "A false step taken by a Christian can be forgiven by God. But you must live with the consequences the rest of your life." That's true. Joshua's false step linked Israel to the Gibeonites for centuries. Joshua's mistake was that he didn't ask God for direction, trusting his senses (particularly *tasting* molding bread and *seeing* worn-out clothes) to guide him. But God was working even through the Gibeonites' deception and Joshua's negligence.

Does that mean we are doomed to live in constant fear of making a wrong choice? No! The lesson of this event goes deeper than that. It proves that even when we mess things up, if we truly seek to honor God, He can use our errors in judgment to His glory. You say you've made some huge mistakes? Who hasn't? I don't mean to trivialize this because all disobedience is serious. But our God is a great and gracious God. He wants us to make the best choices. Sometimes God, in His wisdom, may even permit us to be deceived, despite our best efforts, to accomplish something we might never have dreamed.

As in Bill's case, if choices are made based on our study of Scripture, evaluation of options, and prayer, with a genuine desire to honor God, I believe we are incapable of making serious mistakes. *We cannot derail God's program—we are secure in His care.*

20
A New Challenge

Joshua 10:1–9

I enjoy watching professional baseball. Having spent most of my life in the Southeast, I decided years ago that I'd pull for what was the only team in the South—the Atlanta Braves. Cheering for the Braves was tough in the 1980s when they were perennially awful. A commonly seen bumper sticker in the Atlanta area in those years said, "Go Falcons! And take the Braves with you!" The fans who stuck with them did so more out of sympathy than any real expectation of success. Things turned around in 1991 when the Braves went "from worst to first." They are now the only team in any professional sport to have ever won their division for fourteen straight years—and counting. A prime reason for their success has been their great pitching staff; but after the 2002 season, the owners decided it was time to let some of their high-priced pitchers go.

As the 2003 season began, Tom Glavine, who was one of the best pitchers of the 1990s and had spent his entire career with the Braves until he signed as a free agent with the Mets, had to come back to what had been his home field to pitch against his old teammates. After having been a crowd favorite for years, it was difficult for him to face being introduced to a loud chorus of boos from his former fans. They had loved him when he pitched for them, but in a Mets uniform, many of his former fans saw him as more than just an opponent—he was a traitor and an enemy. When someone switches sides, even in a contest as mundane and insignificant as baseball, his former friends and supporters are bound to be unhappy.

The Canaanite Alliance Moves Against Gibeon

In Joshua 9:1-2, before the Gibeonites are introduced, we're told that all the peoples of Canaan had decided to form an alliance to defeat Israel. They had "gathered themselves together, to fight with Joshua and with Israel" (9:2). This coalition specifically included the Hivites, a group to which the Gibeonites belonged. When word reached their former allies that the Gibeonites had successfully negotiated peace with Israel, imagine their surprise! Little wonder that neighbors to the south and west of Gibeon decided to turn their immediate wrath upon the *Gibeonites*. They postponed a move against Joshua until they had dealt with the potentially dangerous action of their countrymen.

> Now it came to pass, when Adoni-zedec king of Jerusalem had heard how Joshua had taken Ai, and had utterly destroyed it; as he had done to Jericho and her king, so he had done to Ai and her king; and how the inhabitants of Gibeon had made peace with Israel, and were among them; that they feared greatly, because Gibeon was a great city, as one of the royal cities, and because it was greater than Ai, and all the men thereof were mighty. Wherefore Adoni-zedec king of Jerusalem sent unto Hoham king of Hebron, and unto Piram king of Jarmuth, and unto Japhia king of Lachish, and unto Debir king of Eglon, saying, Come up unto me, and help me, that we may smite Gibeon: for it hath made peace with Joshua and with the children of Israel. Therefore the five kings of the Amorites, the king of Jerusalem, the king of Hebron, the king of Jarmuth, the king of Lachish, the king of Eglon, gathered themselves together, and went up, they and all their hosts, and encamped before Gibeon, and made war against it (Josh. 10:1–5).

Of all the cities mentioned, Jerusalem was closest to Gibeon, and had the most to fear from a Gibeonite/Israelite alliance. Adoni-zedek,[73] king of Jerusalem[74] and leader of the Jebusites, recruited several neighboring kings and their armies to move against Gibeon immediately.

Their rationale for taking such action tells us a little more about Israel's new allies. Gibeon was apparently a large city, stronger and wealthier than many

---

[73] *Adoni-zedek*, which means "lord of righteousness," is synonymous with *Melchizedek* ("king of righteousness). It was apparently a title for Jebusite kings, as *Pharaoh* was for Egyptian kings and *Abimelech* for Philistine kings (Keil and Delitzsch, p. 103).

[74] *Jerusalem*, meaning "the founding or possession of peace," was called *Salem* in Abraham's day (Gen. 14:18) and is the city where Abraham met Melchizedek. It is sometimes referred to by the name of its Canaanite inhabitants: *Jebus* in Judges 19:10–11; 1 Chronicles 11:4, or *Ir-Jebusi*, translated "city of the Jebusites" (KJV) in Judges 19:11, or the contracted form *Jebusi* in Joshua 18:16, 28; 15:8; and 2 Samuel 5:8 (Ibid.).

other cities in the region. Furthermore, "all the men" of the city were "mighty." This city was not a cowardly weakling that might have been expected to quiver in fear at the first threat. It was a city that was expected to provide substantial resistance to the invaders and assistance to the general cause of "homeland security." Gibeon's peace with Israel would not only strengthen Israel's already superior forces, but it would also be deeply demoralizing to other people of the region. If a city that powerful and important thought they had to sue for peace to survive, what was to become of other, weaker cities? Would this tempt other cities to try to make peace agreements with Israel? It was vital to both the defense of the region and the cohesion of the opposition that this alliance not be allowed to stand.

The southern cities' decision to move swiftly against the Gibeonites also indicates something of how much the Canaanites both hated and feared Israel and their God. Until recently, Americans thought the combination of our location, our wealthy economy, and our strong military pretty well insulated us from attack by Islamic zealots who cried out for our destruction. In recent years we've been hit a few times, the most spectacular attack coming on September 11, 2001. But even that wasn't a full-scale, armed assault. It proves that they hate us, but they are still relatively powerless to harm us. That hatred is just as violent, and in some ways even more vicious, when aimed at their own people who convert to Christianity. In most Muslim countries, conversion to Christianity is a capital offense. If there is anyone the zealots hate worse than American Christians, it's *Arabic* Christians.

This should come as no surprise. *Being identified with the one true God, and Jesus Christ His Son, makes us defectors from the world.* The Lord Jesus said, "If the world hate you, ye know that it hated me before it hated you" (John 15:18). True Christians will *always* face the enmity of the world. Any professedly Christian movement that enjoys widespread popularity should be treated with great suspicion. Genuine revival will be characterized by heartbroken confession and radical conversion. "Popular Christianity" isn't characterized by the Christianizing of the culture so much as by the secularizing of Christianity. James denounces those who profess Christ but retain their worldly associations—"Ye adulterers and adulteresses, know ye not that the friendship of the world is enmity with God? whosoever therefore will be a friend of the world is the enemy of God" (James 4:4). John says much the same thing—"Love not the world, neither the things that are in the world. If any man love the world, the love of the Father is not in him" (1 John 2:15). Becoming a Christian is more than just joining a church or reciting a formulaic prayer. *Genuine conversion involves a radical change of loyalties.* You cannot be a Christian without transferring allegiance to follow your King. You may not follow perfectly, but you've acknowledged a new Sovereign. The Gibeonites had discovered the effect their change of allegiance had on their former relationships.

The Gibeonites Call for Help

When the Gibeonites realized that their neighbors were moving against *them*, they immediately summoned Joshua to come to their aid.

> And the men of Gibeon sent unto Joshua to the camp to Gilgal, saying, Slack not thy hand from thy servants; come up to us quickly, and save us, and help us: for all the kings of the Amorites that dwell in the mountains are gathered together against us (Josh. 10:6).

At least four aspects of this cry for help deserve our attention. *The request was urgent*—"come up to us quickly." They needed help and they needed it fast. Despite the abruptness required by the immediacy of the need, *the request was expressed with humility*. They acknowledged that they were Israel's "servants." *The appeal was honest*. They called on Joshua to keep his word, saying, "slack not thy hand" or "don't withhold the aid you promised." They identified the enemy that had come against them as "all the kings of the Amorites that dwell in the mountains." If you check the location of the cities mentioned in verses 3 and 5, you'll find that not all of the cities were in the mountains. That doesn't mean the text of Joshua is inaccurate or that the Gibeonites spoke in error. It means that the mountain-dwelling Amorites (particularly the subtribe called the Jebusites) were preparing to attack Gibeon, and they'd brought along "all the kings" who were their allies.

Finally, the Gibeonites didn't waste time or drop hints. They got right to the point and *made a direct appeal to Joshua to "save us."* Significantly, they did not try to be reconciled with their former allies. They didn't send word to the neighboring kings claiming they were still loyal Canaanites and had just fooled Joshua. *Appealing to Joshua for aid was a clear indication of where their loyalties lay*. Further, they didn't trust their own strength. They knew that by themselves they were no match for those who were now their enemies, but they didn't consider their situation hopeless. They knew help was available. They never seem to have doubted Joshua's willingness to help. When they appealed to him, it was with the assumption that he would come to their support.

Perhaps most importantly, *the Gibeonites didn't question Joshua's ability to deliver them*. The choice of words is significant. The word translated *save* (*yasha*) can mean "deliver from danger," but it usually has great spiritual significance. The noun form of the word is *yeshua*, meaning "savior." Being transliterated into Greek, then into English, it comes to us as the name *Jesus*. Transliterated directly from Hebrew, we get the name *Joshua*. So within the text of Joshua 9:6 we have a hidden (in the English) play on words as the Gibeonites "sent unto *Yeshua*" to "*yasha* us." They were saying, "Savior, save!" The Gibeonite appeal anticipates Peter's words as he sank into the turbulent sea when he tried to walk to Jesus on the water, crying "Lord, save me" (Matt. 14:30).

When your strength is inadequate for the dangers you face, you can rely on your Savior. His "grace is sufficient" for you, and His "strength is made perfect" in your weakness (2 Cor. 12:9). When surrounded by all sorts of troubles (James 1:2), you can call upon God for the strength and ability to persevere ("wisdom"), "and it shall be given" you (James 1:5).

Joshua Responds to Their Call

Joshua's Honor

Joshua's response to the Gibeonite appeal was unhesitating and swift.

> So Joshua ascended from Gilgal, he, and all the people of war with him, and all the mighty men of valour. And the Lord said unto Joshua, Fear them not: for I have delivered them into thine hand; there shall not a man of them stand before thee. Joshua therefore came unto them suddenly, and went up from Gilgal all night (Josh. 10:7–9).

It would have been easy for Joshua to find reasons for not going to the aid of the Gibeonites. For personal reasons, Joshua might have thought that the Gibeonites were getting what they deserved. They had lied to Joshua and Israel, eliciting a promise of mercy under false pretense so that Joshua was honor-bound to refrain from killing them. Gibeon's destruction by their neighbors and former allies might well have looked like the just retribution of God. Maybe this was God's way of making sure the Gibeonites were destroyed after Joshua had promised them that Israel wouldn't kill them.

There was also an important practical reason for Joshua and Israel to refuse to help the Gibeonites. Civil war among the Canaanites would have been advantageous to Israel. Anytime his enemies are killing each other off, the job of the conqueror is easier. When President Ronald Reagan decided that it was time to bring the Soviet empire to its knees, he didn't mount an armed invasion.

Instead, he escalated the arms race to a level at which the Soviet economy couldn't compete and survive. As a result, the Soviet Union fell apart from within due to a domino effect of a collapsing economy, producing a starving and ill-equipped military, sparking civil wars, and ending up with various republics declaring and achieving their independence from the union. It was a brilliant strategy with historic significance.

Joshua might have simply sat back and watched the Canaanite coalition destroy itself were it not for one problem. He had sworn "to let them live" (9:15). Perhaps he would have had some justification for claiming that he had actually promised to *spare* the Gibeonites, not to *defend* them. But because Israel had "made peace with them, and made a league with them" (9:15), then had appointed them to be "hewers of wood and drawers of water for the congregation, and for the altar of the Lord" (9:27), the Gibeonites had a valid claim to Israel's protection. Joshua's pledge at least implied an alliance against a common enemy, and Joshua would keep his *implicit* word as well as his *explicit* word. Joshua's character was such that he wouldn't try to wriggle out of a bad deal by playing word games or looking for legal loopholes.

Joshua responded immediately. He didn't need to ask "counsel at the mouth of the Lord" (9:14; cf. Josh. 7:10–11) because his duty was clear. He was even acting on the basis of precedent found in the "book of the law" he had been told to study and follow (Josh. 1:8). Abraham had done something similar to rescue the inhabitants of Sodom from the Elamite king Chedorlaomer in Genesis 14:1–16. Joshua called his men to arms and set out to reach Gibeon by daybreak. Gibeon was about twenty-eight miles in a straight line from Gilgal, but taking his army from the low-lying Jordan River valley up into the mountains, the march wouldn't be along a straight line. This wasn't a walk around the block—it was a forced march of about thirty miles through rugged terrain while climbing some 3300 feet.

God's Approval

After moving his army swiftly through the night, Joshua was in position to rescue Gibeon. At that critical point, the Lord encouraged Joshua by saying, "Fear them not: for I have delivered them into thine hand; there shall not a man of them stand before thee" (10:8). If there were any lingering doubts in Joshua's mind about what he should do in regard to the Gibeonites, the Lord had just laid them to rest. Was Joshua wrong to have made the alliance without asking for God's direction? Yes, he was (Josh. 9:14). Was he right to keep his word to the Gibeonites? Yes, he was (Josh. 10:8). Was God's will accomplished even through Joshua's failure? Yes, it was. Paul tells us clearly that God "worketh all things after the counsel of his own will" (Eph. 1:11).

Doesn't that mean God *made* Joshua do something wrong? Absolutely not! While our logic may lead us to that conclusion, James emphatically declares, "Let no man say when he is tempted, I am tempted of God" (James 1:13). Layton Talbert says,

> Learn to see and accept where the Bible draws a line. Distinguish between express statements of Scripture and logical leaps—extensions that may make sense but do not enjoy the "luxury" of explicit biblical affirmation.[75]
>
> It is vital to learn to detect where reason veers off from the road of explicit biblical statement. Once you step off the edge of the cliff of clear revelation, trusting in the power of logic to levitate your position, the fact is you are still standing out in thin air with nothing under you.[76]

We must balance our theology of responsibility. Emphasizing God's sovereignty to the exclusion of man's responsibility, we may blame God for sin, violating the clear teaching of Scripture. If we emphasize man's responsibility to the exclusion of God's sovereignty, we may claim God merely reacts to what man does, constantly having to fix things and modify His plan in order to work things out. That violates Scripture by making man sovereign, essentially calling the creature greater than the Creator. Neither are we allowed to deny both by declaring that the truth is somewhere in the middle. God is absolutely sovereign. Man is personally culpable. Exactly how this works is beyond my puny abilities to fully understand or adequately explain. But the Bible repeatedly insists that *God is always in control of events*, and *man is always responsible for his own sin*. Perhaps Joseph said it best when speaking to his brothers who had sold him into slavery only to discover he had been exalted to a position in which it was possible for him to save his family from famine, telling them, "ye thought evil against me; but God meant it unto good" (Gen. 50:20).

But was there any benefit to *Israel* from this alliance? One happy consequence of it was that the conquest of Canaan would be much easier if the various cities could be dealt with individually or in small groups. If all the Canaanites had managed to form their own coalition and move their combined armies against Israel, they would have presented a formidable challenge. That was clearly their intent. But the surprise defection of the Gibeonites to Israel ignited a passionate response among their neighbors that benefited Israel unexpectedly.

It is hard to imagine Joshua having devised a strategy that more effectively divided the forces arrayed against him than did this alliance. This new coalition represented a split-off group from those allying themselves against Israel in

---

[75] Layton Talbert, *Not by Chance: Learning to Trust a Sovereign God* (Greenville, SC: BJU Press, 2001), p. 255.

[76] Talbert, p. 253.

Joshua 9:1–2. Israel will have an opportunity to deal with them independently before having to face the larger and more potent northern alliance in Joshua 11 and 12, which would have been even more powerful had the southern cities been able to join forces with them.

We may be tempted to think, "Since God is going to work everything out, it really doesn't matter what I do." That, too, would be wrong. God's promises are never intended to inspire *indolence*, but *fervency*. Paul says that the certainty of the coming resurrection and glorification of the believers should result in faithful service for the Lord.

> So when this corruptible shall have put on incorruption, and this mortal shall have put on immortality, then shall be brought to pass the saying that is written, Death is swallowed up in victory. O death, where is thy sting? O grave, where is thy victory? The sting of death is sin; and the strength of sin is the law. But thanks be to God, which giveth us the victory through our Lord Jesus Christ. **Therefore, my beloved brethren, be ye steadfast, unmoveable, always abounding in the work of the Lord, forasmuch as ye know that your labour is not in vain in the Lord** (1 Cor. 15:54–58).

Joshua did not respond to the Lord's promise of victory by assuming it gave him an excuse to quit or even to rest. He reacted with even greater zeal, falling upon the Gibeonites' attackers "suddenly." He didn't hesitate or plan a stealthy guerrilla attack. His army stormed upon the enemy and won a great victory (see Josh. 10:10–43—discussed in chapter 21).

Applying the Principles

While the Gibeonites originally approached Joshua to negotiate peace by deception, they acted courageously in their infant faith. Like Rahab, who thought she had to lie to protect the spies, the Gibeonites had no experience with God's mercy and grace. The swift, fierce opposition of their old friends and allies, and the Gibeonites' steadfast dependence upon Israel and Israel's God to deliver and protect them, proves that their change of loyalties was genuine, despite the timid and dishonest beginning to the relationship.

New converts often face their greatest opposition immediately. They may be forsaken or even attacked by their old friends and family. New converts may be the most vulnerable among us. A husband and wife I know both came to Christ as adults. Over the course of several months, as they studied the Bible and became more active in the local church, they demonstrated tremendous growth in the Lord. At one point, they revealed that the wife had grown up in a home involved in the occult. She had participated in satanic rituals since she was a little girl, particularly under the instruction of her mother and sisters. They asked for urgent prayer. They weren't tempted to revert to occult practices because the power of God had gloriously broken the spiritual bonds and set them free in Christ. The problem was the ferocity of the reaction of her mother and sisters when she told them she had trusted Christ. They would call her at all hours of the night just to scream at her. She would get up in the morning or come home after work to find threatening messages scrawled on the windows or doors or dead animals on the porch. They wanted prayer, not so much for their personal safety, but for the protection of their children and the salvation of her mother and sisters.[77]

Lacking experience or depth of training in the Word of God, new converts are not well prepared to face the strong opposition without assistance. Mature believers must stand prepared to help. "We then that are strong ought to bear the infirmities of the weak" (Rom. 15:1). Mature believers must offer themselves sacrificially for the good of others.

> And let us not be weary in well doing: for in due season we shall reap, if we faint not. As we have therefore opportunity, let us do good unto all men, especially unto them who are of the household of faith (Gal. 6:9–10).

New converts need extra help, not disdain or criticism. The sudden alliance of temptation and sin will attack the weakest ones. Mature believers and novices face a common enemy. We also serve the same master. We aren't in this battle alone. We need each other's support.

> Brethren, if a man be overtaken in a fault, ye which are spiritual, restore such an one in the spirit of meekness; considering thyself, lest thou also be tempted. Bear ye one another's burdens, and so fulfill the law of Christ (Gal. 6:1–2).

[77] Many years after their conversion they were still faithful to their church and active in various ministries. Their children were fine. And her mother and one sister had been saved!

21
Victory in the Mountains

Joshua 10:9–43

On Sunday, June 27, 1976, armed gunmen from the Popular Front for the Liberation of Palestine hijacked Air France flight 139, diverting it first to Libya and then to Entebbe, Uganda, which was under the dictatorship of Idi Amin. The terrorists separated the Jewish and Israeli passengers from the others, holding Jews in the airport terminal as hostages, announcing their intent to kill them all if the hijackers' Palestinian cohorts being held in Israeli prisons were not released immediately.

Israel did not do what the terrorists expected. They did not negotiate. They did not arrange a "prisoner exchange." They did exactly what they should have done and dispatched a team of crack commandos, led by a young officer named Jonathan Netanyahu, to rescue the hostages. On July 4, 1976, as we Americans were celebrating the Bicentennial of our Declaration of Independence, those Israeli special forces stormed the airport at Entebbe, freeing virtually all of the captives.

> The heroic rescue symbolized the State of Israel's unique role as the sovereign protector of Jews everywhere, and inspired a generation to believe that the Jewish people were intent on defending themselves, regardless of the consequences.[78]

---

[78] Michael Freund, "Remember Entebbe?" *Jerusalem Post*, July 9, 2003. (Jonathan Netanyahu was the older brother of Benjamin, who went on to serve as Israel's prime minister from 1996-99. Jonathan was the only Israeli casualty of the Entebbe raid.)

In some ways the world is remarkably unchanged since the days of Joshua. The Amorite kings threatened a group Israel had sworn to protect. Their miscalculation of Joshua's resolve would cost them dearly.

Joshua's Attack

When Israel moved against Jericho, they had approached deliberately, almost in slow motion. Their stately, silent circling of the city for seven days, awaiting the moment to sound the rams' horns and shout, evoked a sense of drama and awe. When they conquered Ai, they had to employ a carefully planned and choreographed ambush. But in dealing with the armies of the southern mountain cities (called Amorites by the Gibeonites), Joshua launched a precipitous, headlong attack.

> Joshua therefore came unto them suddenly, and went up from Gilgal all night (Josh. 10:9).

The fact that Israel's army "went up from Gilgal all night" implies that they arrived at daybreak. Since this was an emergency response to the Gibeonites' call for help, there had been no opportunity to prepare. When word came of the crisis in Gibeon, the army had to get organized quickly—packing provisions, gathering weapons, preparing to march. We have no idea how they had spent the previous day, but it was almost certainly not in their beds. They wouldn't have been well rested for an all-night march. Then, after a high-speed march of nearly thirty miles, climbing nearly three thousand feet into the mountains, they arrived at Gibeon at dawn. It would have been nice to have had the luxury of a day or two to rest and reconnoiter, but the danger to the Gibeonites made haste imperative.

So they fell upon the coalition forces arrayed against Gibeon. The enemy apparently had no idea Israel would come to the aid of the Gibeonites. Further, they probably assumed they had plenty of time to punish Gibeon before Israel could arrive and get organized for one of their typically complicated battle strategies. When the forces of Israel came charging out of the hills at dawn, the coalition forces were caught completely by surprise. Apparently in almost total disarray, the enemy fled.

God's Aid

The Amorite forces led by Adoni-zedek hoped to escape by fleeing through the mountains and heading to the lowlands. Had they badly underestimated the threat posed by an army of over 530,000? Sheer numbers alone gave Israel an overwhelming advantage. The Amorites may have assumed that their familiarity with the terrain, their expectation that their territorial gods would protect them, and their passion to defend their own cities more than compensated for Israel's superior numbers. Maybe they never intended to face Israel without the unified support of the northern cities. Regardless, they apparently miscalculated on at least three fronts. They didn't anticipate Israel's unbiased treatment of "strangers" that would lead them to the defense of Gibeon. They didn't understand Israel's dedication to total victory over the Canaanites (including the Amorites). They didn't comprehend the power of the one true God Who fought for Israel.

> And the Lord discomfited them before Israel, and slew them with a great slaughter at Gibeon, and chased them along the way that goeth up to Beth-horon, and smote them to Azekah, and unto Makkedah. And it came to pass, as they fled from before Israel, and were in the going down to Beth-horon, that the Lord cast down great stones from heaven upon them unto Azekah, and they died: they were more which died with hailstones than they whom the children of Israel slew with the sword (Josh. 10:10–11).

Swift Success

When Israel swept out of the hills, many of the Amorite forces died right there at Gibeon. The text says there was a "great slaughter" there, but most of the enemy armies escaped along the road leading up to Bethhoron. This place has been described as being nearest to Gibeon, only four hours distant on the northwest, on a lofty promontory between two valleys, one on the north, the other on the south, and was separated from Lower Bethhoron, which lies further west, by a long steep pass, from which the ascent to Upper Bethhoron is very steep and rocky, though the rock has been cut away in many places now, and a path made by means of steps. This pass between the two places leads downwards from Gibeon towards the western plain and was called sometimes the ascent, or going up to Bethhoron, and sometimes the descent, or going down from it (v. 11).[79]

[79] Keil and Delitzsch, p. 105.

Israel's army had made a rapid, all-night march to get to Gibeon and now had to chase the enemy several more hours farther into the mountains ("along the way that goeth up to Beth-horon"). As they passed through that region and were heading back down the steep, rocky slope toward the valley below and the plain beyond ("in the going down to Beth-horon"), God's activity on behalf of Israel became obvious.

Supernatural Storm

God had been involved all along because it was He Who had "discomfited" ("confounded, routed") the enemy at Gibeon. Now He sent a shower of enormous hailstones onto the fleeing enemy, which demonstrated direct divine intervention in three ways. The *unusual size* of the hailstones had been seen before only in the plague of hail on the Egyptians (Exod. 9:18–34). The *unusual effect* of the hail was sufficient to cause massive death and destruction on a scale at least as great as that same Egyptian plague. The *unusual discrimination* of the hail, crushing the Amorites but striking none of the Israelites who pursued and engaged them, was unprecedented. Granted, the plague on Egypt had spared Israel in Goshen (Exod. 9:26), but in this case the army of Israel doesn't seem to have enjoyed the protection of a geographically remote location. In Egypt, the hailstones had killed "all that was in the field, both man and beast" (Exod. 9:25). The hail that fell at Bethhoron killed only the Amorites in the battlefield. It is possible that the hail fell as the Amorites fled down the slope from Bethhoron before Israel started to descend. But even so, the hail hit the moving target of the Amorites and missed the pursuing army of Israel. The hail didn't fall on a particular *location* but on a particular *people* identified by their political/religious affiliation.

Joshua, the commander of Israel's army, faithfully records that the hailstones killed more of the Amorite forces than he and his forces killed in battle. God had made it clear to Joshua, and Joshua makes it clear to us, that this battle wasn't won by military skill but by the intervention of God. The hailstorm had a threefold effect. *It increased Joshua's faith* as he once again saw God act in fulfillment of His promise. *It increased Gibeon's faith* as they witnessed Israel and God coming to their defense. And *it increased the enemies' fear* as any hope of victory over Israel disintegrated when they were confronted by the overwhelming power of God.

Stalled Sun

The evidence of God's help emboldened Joshua to make a remarkable, even audacious, request.

> Then spake Joshua to the Lord in the day when the Lord delivered up the Amorites before the children of Israel, and he said in the sight of Israel, Sun, stand thou still upon Gibeon; and thou, Moon, in the valley of Ajalon. And the sun stood still, and the moon stayed, until the people had avenged themselves upon their enemies. Is not this written in the book of Jasher? So the sun stood still in the midst of heaven, and hasted not to go down about a whole day. And there was no day like that before it or after it, that the Lord hearkened unto the voice of a man: for the Lord fought for Israel. And Joshua returned, and all Israel with him, unto the camp to Gilgal (Josh. 10:12–15).

The word *then* that introduces verse 12 doesn't necessarily mean "after these things," but may mean "at that time." It is impossible to know whether Joshua asked for more time as the enemy fled the scene at Gibeon and the hailstorm struck them during the extended day or whether he asked for more time for mopping up after the storm. The text could be understood to say either. Neither is there any reason to assume that the request was made toward the end of a full day's fighting, as some have thought the reference to both the sun and moon implies. The statement that "the sun stood still **in the midst** of heaven" actually makes it more likely that the request was made around midday. As Joshua chased the Amorites westward from Gibeon and toward or through Bethhoron, the sun would appear to stand over Gibeon only around noon or before (v. 12). If it were evening, Joshua would be moving toward the setting sun, and it would have looked as though the sun were over the valley of Ajalon or even over the plains to the west.[80]

While we may marvel at Joshua's boldness, still more marvelous was God's response. He did as Joshua asked and either stopped the sun's movement ("the sun stood still") or slowed its progress across the sky ("the sun . . . hasted not to go down"). It may be that this added about twelve hours of daylight for

[80] Perhaps you've heard about a report claiming that a group of scientists were tracking the movement of the stars and planets, calculating backward in time to determine their respective locations in hopes of establishing the age of the universe, only to find a glitch in their calculations. They were coming up one day short. One of the group remembered a Sunday school lesson about the sun standing still, and *voila*, the solution was found. One account also claims that the calculations were still off by less than an hour before one of the scientists remembered a story about a time when God turned back the clock for King Hezekiah. When these missing minutes were added to the equation, the scientists' mathematical formulae finally were resolved. This story has circulated on the Internet for years, but I've been unable to find any corroborating authority to verify its truthfulness. Several details lead me to doubt it: the scientists are always unnamed, their fields of study are unidentified, the name of their research facility or group is never mentioned, no published reports are cited for authenticity, and so on. Further, the story assumes the text of Joshua adds precisely twenty-four hours when that is far from clear from Joshua's account. I mention this report here not to add authority to the body of the chapter, much less to the account of Joshua, but to indicate that I have heard the story and have deliberately chosen to ignore it. I believe it is a hoax—another urban legend—and should be treated as spurious.

the pursuit of the enemy since the "day" was usually considered to be from dawn to dark. Since Joshua says the phenomenon lasted for "about a whole day," it may be that the word *whole* indicates a full twenty-four-hour period. Again, the text is ambiguous. What is clear is that this was a miracle of God. It was no optical illusion. The specific means God used is not revealed. Did the earth stop spinning for several hours? Did its rotation on its axis slow to a crawl? Was the motion of the entire universe suspended? We don't know. We do know the result of the deadly hailstorm and the lengthened day was that "none moved his tongue against any of the children of Israel."

Some people today doubt the biblical record. There are those who point out that according to the laws of physics, bringing the earth to a sudden standstill would destroy everything on the earth and probably the earth itself. These scoffers fail to recognize that the God Who created the universe and the laws by which it operates, and Who could stop the earth's movement in the heavens, could also maintain the earth and all that is in it. Remember that it is only by Him that "all things consist [hold together]" (Col. 1:17). Joshua did not invent a metaphorical legend. He recorded a historical event.

Sufficient Stamina

Whatever time it was when Joshua made his request, I'll confess that if I'm in Joshua's army, I'm probably *not* praying for a longer day. The army of Israel had had no sleep in at least the last thirty hours. What's more, they'd been constantly on the move, quick-marching into the mountains for nearly thirty miles through the night, immediately engaging the enemy in armed combat, then chasing them miles farther into the mountains, still fighting as they had opportunity. Now their commander wants the sun to stay in the sky so they can keep fighting! Doesn't he know or care that there's a limit to any man's endurance?

The fact that Joshua made this request publicly, "in the sight of all Israel," indicates an almost reckless faith in God. *Implicit in Joshua's request for more time to fight is also the request for the stamina to endure to the end of the battle.* Joshua wasn't satisfied with decimating[81] the enemy. It was his responsibility to annihilate them. Where would Joshua get the notion that God might honor either request? From the "book of the law" that was to be his guide (see Josh. 1:8).

> As thy days, so shall thy strength be. There is none like unto the God of Jeshurun, who rideth upon the heaven in thy help, and in his excellency on the sky (Deut. 33:25*b*–26).

---

[81] *Decimate* is commonly used as if it meant "to totally destroy." Its original meaning was "to kill one in ten," or "to take and destroy one tenth." It has come to mean "to kill many of" or "to destroy much of." To totally destroy is to *annihilate.*

Joshua had the promise of God that He controlled the sky and was available to exercise His help "upon the heaven." Further, asking for a longer day wouldn't deplete their energy if God were supplying the strength "as thy days."

The Lord has promised you and me, as believers in Christ Jesus, the same stamina to endure to the end—"Being confident of this very thing, that he which hath begun a good work in you will perform it until the day of Jesus Christ" (Phil. 1:6). That's why Paul could say with confidence,

> The Spirit itself beareth witness with our spirit, that we are the children of God: and if children, then heirs; heirs of God, and joint-heirs with Christ; if so be that we suffer with him, that we may be also glorified together. For I reckon that the sufferings of this present time are not worthy to be compared with the glory which shall be revealed in us (Rom. 8:16–18).

Our confidence isn't in *who* we are but in *Whose* we are. No obstacle we face can "separate us from the love of God which is in Christ Jesus our Lord" (Rom. 8:39). *The day may be long, but the victory is sure!*

The reference to "the book of Jasher" (v. 13) bears mentioning. The book of Jasher (or "book of the righteous") is not a part of the canon of Scripture. Since this is the only actual quotation in the Scripture from that book, and it is written as an excerpt from a song, it is generally assumed that Jasher was a collection of songs or poems in praise of the mighty acts of heroes of the theocracy. Support for such an assumption is found in a reference to the same book in 2 Samuel 1:18, which mentions teaching the children of Judah the use of the bow. Jasher may have been an independent work, or it may have been the same as "the book of the wars of the Lord" mentioned in Numbers 21:14, which refers to the work of God delivering Israel from the Egyptians at the Red Sea and the Amorites at Arnon. Joshua's reason for mentioning the poetic reference to this battle in the book of Jasher was not to lend authenticity to his account by cross references to another book but "to set forth before other generations the powerful impression which was made upon the congregation by these mighty acts of the Lord."[82] It is important to point out the inclusion of verse 15 as part of this quotation from an extrabiblical source; otherwise, the account gets confused. Joshua 10:43 says, "And Joshua returned, and all Israel with him, unto the camp to Gilgal." That statement is quoted verbatim in Joshua 10:15 as the concluding stanza of the song about this battle attributed to the book of Jasher. Joshua and Israel did not return to Gilgal until after the battle described in verses 16–42 was concluded.

---

[82] Keil and Delitzsch, p. 107.

Kings' Arrest

As Joshua surveyed the battlefield on the slopes below Bethhoron, he saw that many of the Amorites lay crushed under the hailstones. But there were many more still fleeing.

> But these five kings fled, and hid themselves in a cave at Makkedah. And it was told Joshua, saying, The five kings are found hid in a cave at Makkedah. And Joshua said, Roll great stones upon the mouth of the cave, and set men by it for to keep them: and stay ye not, but pursue after your enemies, and smite the hindmost of them; suffer them not to enter into their cities: for the Lord your God hath delivered them into your hand. And it came to pass, when Joshua and the children of Israel had made an end of slaying them with a very great slaughter, till they were consumed, that the rest which remained of them entered into fenced cities. And all the people returned to the camp to Joshua at Makkedah in peace: none moved his tongue against any of the children of Israel. Then said Joshua, Open the mouth of the cave, and bring out those five kings unto me out of the cave. And they did so, and brought forth those five kings unto him out of the cave, the king of Jerusalem, the king of Hebron, the king of Jarmuth, the king of Lachish, and the king of Eglon. And it came to pass, when they brought out those kings unto Joshua, that Joshua called for all the men of Israel, and said unto the captains of the men of war which went with him, Come near, put your feet upon the necks of these kings. And they came near, and put their feet upon the necks of them. And Joshua said unto them, Fear not, nor be dismayed, be strong and of good courage: for thus shall the Lord do to all your enemies against whom ye fight. And afterward Joshua smote them, and slew them, and hanged them on five trees: and they were hanging upon the trees until the evening. And it came to pass at the time of the going down of the sun, that Joshua commanded, and they took them down off the trees, and cast them into the cave wherein they had been hid, and laid great stones in the cave's mouth, which remain until this very day (Josh. 10:16–27).

The kings of the fleeing armies of the Amorites took refuge together in a cave near Makkedah. This may have been a prearranged meeting in a bunker prepared as an emergency shelter. As a hiding place, it proved to be less than effective. Finding them there, Joshua had the cave sealed and guarded, apparently staying there himself to be sure these kings didn't escape (see v. 21). He then sent the bulk of the army in pursuit of the routed Amorites, continuing the battle until the victory was secured and the enemy destroyed. A few of the enemy managed to survive, making it to the protection of their walled cities, but the coalition army was essentially annihilated—"Israel had made an end of slaying them with a very great slaughter, till they were consumed" (v. 20).

When the army of Israel returned to Joshua at Makkedah, the sealed cave was opened and the kings of the Amorites were released to face judgment. When they emerged from the cave, they prostrated themselves. Then Joshua did something that may strike you as unusual or even cruel and barbaric. He called for the commanders of Israel's army to step forward and place their feet on the necks of the kings (v. 24). Compared to the atrocities the Amorites perpetrated upon their victims (i.e., Judg. 1:7), this was tame. It was actually symbolic of total subjugation of the enemy. It was also symbolic of the fulfillment of a promise of God.

> **Every place whereon the soles of your feet shall tread** shall be yours: from the wilderness and Lebanon, from the river, the river Euphrates, even unto the uttermost sea shall your coast be. There shall no man be able to stand before you: for the Lord your God shall lay the fear of you and the dread of you upon all the land that ye shall tread upon, as he hath said unto you (Deut. 11:24–25).

Placing the soles of their feet on the necks of the kings of the Amorites pictured Israel's complete domination by the power and authority of God. The fact that Joshua 10:25 adds, "Thus shall the Lord do to all your enemies against whom ye fight," echoing the message of Deuteronomy 11:25, indicates that this is precisely the picture Joshua had in mind. It was an object lesson to Israel to trust God completely, and a lesson for the Canaanites that they were not capable of keeping Israel from possessing that which God gave them.

Once the image was clear to "all the men of Israel" (v. 24), Joshua personally executed the kings. He had the bodies hanged on trees for the rest of the day, then taken down and cast into their cave/bunker, marking it by sealing it with stones.

The battle, particularly the dispatching of the kings, pictures the conquest of sin in our lives. The real victor is Christ, seen figuratively in Joshua. Paul encourages the believer to "reckon ye also yourselves to be dead indeed unto sin, but alive unto God through Jesus Christ our Lord" (Rom. 6:11). But at the same time, sin is not totally eradicated. That's why Paul immediately followed his statement that we are "dead indeed unto sin" by commanding,

> Let not sin therefore reign in your mortal body, that ye should obey it in the lusts thereof. Neither yield ye your members as instruments of unrighteousness unto sin: but yield yourselves unto God, as those that are alive from the dead, and your members as instruments of righteousness unto God (Rom. 6:12–13).

Satan's defeat doesn't end the sin principle until THE END. The battle continues, and we must remain engaged in the war against our own lusts (James 1:14) and the wiles of Satan (Eph. 6:11–13). But we do so confident of ultimate victory (1 Cor. 15:51–58).

Joshua's Achievement

Joshua's victory over the five kings of the Amorites actually launched a broader campaign.

> And that day Joshua took Makkedah, and smote it with the edge of the sword, and the king thereof he utterly destroyed, them, and all the souls that were therein; he let none remain: and he did to the king of Makkedah as he did unto the king of Jericho. Then Joshua passed from Makkedah, and all Israel with him, unto Libnah, and fought against Libnah: and the Lord delivered it also, and the king thereof, into the hand of Israel; and he smote it with the edge of the sword, and all the souls that were therein; he let none remain in it; but did unto the king thereof as he did unto the king of Jericho. And Joshua passed from Libnah, and all Israel with him, unto Lachish, and encamped against it, and fought against it: and the Lord delivered Lachish into the hand of Israel, which took it on the second day, and smote it with the edge of the sword, and all the souls that were therein, according to all that he had done to Libnah. Then Horam king of Gezer came up to help Lachish; and Joshua smote him and his people, until he had left him none remaining. And from Lachish Joshua passed unto Eglon, and all Israel with him; and they encamped against it, and fought against it: and they took it on that day, and smote it with the edge of the sword, and all the souls that were therein he utterly destroyed that day, according to all that he had done to Lachish. And Joshua went up from Eglon, and all Israel with him, unto Hebron; and they fought against it: and they took it, and smote it with the edge of the sword, and the king thereof, and all the cities thereof, and all the souls that were therein; he left none remaining, according to all that he had done to Eglon; but destroyed it utterly, and all the souls that were therein. And Joshua returned, and all Israel with him, to Debir; and fought against it: and he took it, and the king thereof, and all the cities thereof; and they smote them with the edge of the sword, and utterly destroyed all the souls that were therein; he left none remaining: as he had done to Hebron, so he did to Debir, and to the king thereof; as he had done also to Libnah, and to her king. So Joshua smote all the country of the hills, and of the south, and of the vale, and of the springs, and all their kings: he left none remaining, but utterly destroyed all that breathed, as the Lord God of Israel commanded. And Joshua smote them from Kadesh-barnea even unto Gaza, and all the country of Goshen, even unto Gibeon. And all these

> kings and their land did Joshua take at one time, because the Lord God of Israel fought for Israel. And Joshua returned, and all Israel with him, unto the camp to Gilgal (Josh. 10:28–43).

Some have suggested that these verses describe in more detail the movements and victories of Israel's army while pursuing those who had attacked Gibeon. However, the region encompassed by the cities named and territories claimed included virtually everything to the south and west of Jericho, all the way to Egypt. That's a lot more land than the fleeing Amorites would have covered in their haste to get to the protection of their walled cities. Joshua is probably describing an extension of the battle concluded with the execution of the kings at Makkedah.

Very little detail is provided for a military campaign of historic proportion for both its success and its speed. In verses 31–32 there is an interesting tidbit of information, though. It says simply that "the Lord delivered Lachish into the hand of Israel, which took it on the second day." I find myself a little disappointed that a victory of such historic significance would be summarized in so few words. Lachish was a strong and very well fortified city that would later become a thorn in the side of military leaders of worldwide significance. In 2 Kings 18:13 and 19:7–8, we find that the great Assyrian conqueror Sennacherib was stopped at Lachish. Later yet, when Nebuchadnezzar of Babylon was expanding his kingdom, he, too, *failed* at Lachish (Jer. 34:7). Joshua took the city in just two days! Again, we see evidence of Joshua's humility in that he doesn't make a big deal of this victory. Most leaders would have at least described how the battle was won, and probably wanted a monument erected besides.

What had started out as a rescue mission for the Gibeonites had turned into an enormously important series of victories for Israel. They were obeying God's command, and He was keeping His promise to give them the land. The entire campaign is summarized in the words, "And all these kings and their land did Joshua take at one time, because the Lord God of Israel fought for Israel" (Josh. 10:42). Finally, it was time for Israel to "return . . . unto the camp to Gilgal" (10:15, 43).

Israel now controlled about one-third of Palestine. They had taken the territory apparently with *no further casualties*, since "all Israel" returned to Gilgal with Joshua. No wonder Joshua's fame was spreading throughout Canaan just as God had promised. Joshua's own account makes it clear that he intended for God's name to be glorified. Joshua was just a man doing what God told him to do. *The victories were less a testimony to Joshua's ability as a leader or a warrior than they were to the sovereignty of God.*

Satan's Arousal

All is not over. Rest in Gilgal is really just a respite. As Joshua 11 opens, we'll see that Satan has been aroused. The northern coalition of Canaan prepares to attack. Israel cannot relax their guard. Constant vigilance will be necessary. Sometimes our greatest challenges come on the heels of our greatest victories. "Be sober, be vigilant; because your adversary the devil, as a roaring lion, walketh about, seeking whom he may devour" (1 Pet. 5:8). But you need not fear "because greater is he that is in you, than he that is in the world" (1 John 4:4).

22
The Great Campaign

Joshua 11–12

Before my seminary days, I spent several years as a music teacher in a Christian school. One of the biggest events on our annual calendar, as far as my teaching responsibilities were concerned, was the spring statewide music festival. Much of what we did in my music classes was intended to prepare the students for competition and evaluation at that festival.

Our school had about two hundred fifty students, so we were too large to be classed with some of the smaller schools. But some of the schools against whom we competed were five times our size. In categories where students performed individually, the size of the school was less important than it was for group competition; so our choral groups got a lot of my attention. A "choral group" was defined as having twelve to twenty-four singers. Fewer than twelve and it was an "ensemble." More than twenty-four and it was a "choir." We didn't have enough students to field a choir. Unfortunately, most of the larger schools fielded both choirs and choral groups. Their choral groups were formed by handpicking the best singers from their choirs. Ours was formed by recruiting anybody willing to sing. To be competitive in the field with the larger schools' choral groups took a lot of work.

Over the years, we generally managed to hold our own, scoring higher than some of the large schools. One year we managed to really impress the judges. When the scores were announced, we went from stunned incredulity to ecstatic euphoria in seconds. We had won the state competition! We were on our way to the national festival!

As we celebrated on the bus ride home, it hit me. The national festival? That's where the state champions from all over the country met to compete. If I had thought winning the state would be tough, what would competing at nationals be like? Winning the state was so unexpected, I hadn't looked beyond the state competition. From playing in baseball leagues and basketball tournaments, I knew in principle that the more you win the stiffer the competition becomes. I was learning that this was a universal axiom, applying to any endeavor.[83]

Joshua and Israel were about to learn that victory over the southern coalition had been cause for rejoicing but was not an excuse for relaxing. Tougher challenges lay ahead.

Mobilizing the Northern Coalition

In the opening verses of Joshua 9 we saw that the various peoples of Canaan were organizing an alliance against Israel. When Gibeon made peace with Israel, their neighbors in southern Canaan moved against them, only to be destroyed. It didn't take long for word to reach the ears of the kings in the north that their southern allies had been defeated.

> And it came to pass, when Jabin king of Hazor had heard those things, that he sent to Jobab king of Madon, and to the king of Shimron, and to the king of Achshaph, and to the kings that were on the north of the mountains, and of the plains south of Chinneroth, and in the valley, and in the borders of Dor on the west, and to the Canaanite on the east and on the west, and to the Amorite, and the Hittite, and the Perizzite, and the Jebusite in the mountains, and to the Hivite under Hermon in the land of Mizpeh. And they went out, they and all their hosts with them, much people, even as the sand that is upon the sea shore in multitude, with horses and chariots very many. And when all these kings were met together, they came and pitched together at the waters of Merom, to fight against Israel (Josh. 11:1–5).

[83] For those who care about the rest of the story, in seven years of competition our choral groups placed in the top three in the state six times. We actually won the state twice, with the event I've recounted being the first. The analogy with Joshua and Israel breaks down at the point of moving up to a higher level of competition. Joshua went on to total victory. We never did well in the nationals. The first time, I was completely unprepared for the level of competition we faced. We scored much higher the second time but were still competing "over our heads" with some of the groups there. But the experience was worth the effort.

This northern coalition was a much more formidable foe for Israel than the southern coalition had been. The southern group had comprised five kings and their cities, led by Adoni-zedek of Jerusalem. The northern group was a larger alliance led by Jabin of Hazor, who had been "the head of all those kingdoms" (11:10). Jabin called the kings and their armies to gather at Merom, where they would organize and launch an attack against Israel.

Up to this time, Israel had been the aggressor, with the Canaanites merely trying to defend their cities. This was the first attack prepared against Israel, intending to put Israel on the defensive. It is also likely that the massed forces led by these kings would have outnumbered the army of Israel. Their infantry was so vast that Joshua described it as "much people, even as the sand that is upon the sea shore in multitude" (11:4). The benefit of having an overwhelming numerical advantage was gone.

This was also the first group of Canaanites Israel faced that included a *cavalry with war chariots*. Israel would be on foot, fighting what amounted to an armored division. The tactical advantage alone that a cavalry with chariots would have in the field was enormous. They represented a large force ("with horses and chariots very many," v. 4) with far greater speed, maneuverability, and fire power than any band of foot soldiers possessed. These advantages would give the cavalry a huge psychological edge over the infantry, whose confidence would certainly waver in the face of such a force. It would be a daunting prospect to Israel to be standing on the ground with a sword in hand knowing they had to fight a mounted and armored cavalry.

Responding to the Northern Coalition

Encouraging Faith

As is typical when His children have evident cause to fear, God brings comfort and encouragement.

> And the Lord said unto Joshua, Be not afraid because of them: for to morrow about this time will I deliver them up all slain before Israel: thou shalt hough their horses, and burn their chariots with fire (Josh. 11:6).

A recurring theme in Joshua is stated in verse 6—"Be not afraid because of them." Sitting in a comfortable chair at my desk, I'm tempted to wonder why Joshua and Israel might have been afraid. God had given them repeated victories and intervened miraculously on their behalf. Why worry about a bunch of blustering Canaanites? But as we've already seen in this book, and have experienced in our own lives, we can be quite vulnerable immediately after a great victory. Coming on the heels of their conquest of the five kings of the south, Israel discovered the northern kings were planning an attack. These kings weren't just blustering; they had *teeth*. Based on the circumstances alone, Israel had a lot to fear.

There was much more to this situation than the circumstances indicated—*God was fighting for Israel*. God promised success against this alliance, but Israel had to attack. This sounds easier than it may have been. Hazor was located about ten miles north of the Sea of Galilee. It had dominated the region for decades and was by far the largest and most powerful city Israel would confront. "The waters of Merom," where the armies were gathered, were about eight miles west-northwest of Hazor. Joshua 10 ends with Israel having returned to their base camp at Gilgal, three or four miles north of the northern end of the Dead Sea. Joshua 11 doesn't specifically say that Israel was still there, but it doesn't indicate that they had left either. If Israel were still at Gilgal when they got word of the northern coalition's plans to attack, they had to travel over eighty miles north to get there.

God told Joshua that "tomorrow about this time" He would "deliver them up all slain." Does that mean that Joshua had to march his army there in one night? They had traveled about thirty miles through the night to rescue the Gibeonites, but I doubt that they ran the equivalent of three marathons in the space of a single day to get to Merom. It would have been possible, because *anything is possible with God*. But the text doesn't demand it. I suspect that Joshua is again summarizing. The kings of the north had organized the attack, and Joshua had taken Israel to meet them. Having seen the host under Jabin's command spread out "as the sand that is upon the sea shore," Joshua was worried. The Lord encouraged him to "be not afraid," promising to "deliver them up all slain" (11:6) on the following day.

Besides telling Joshua to attack the enemy with confidence, He also told him that Israel must burn the chariots and "hough" the horses. To "hough" (pronounced "hoe"), or "hamstring," a horse is to cut the tendon at the joint in its hind leg. This makes the horse permanently lame and virtually useless. Some in Israel may have thought this incredibly wasteful. If they were going to defeat the armies of Canaan, why not *confiscate* their horses and chariots instead of *destroying* them? Israel on foot was frightening enough to their enemies. Imagine the terror they could inspire if they had a cavalry! But that's precisely the problem. God did not want the Canaanites to fear Israel's *army* (or cavalry). He wanted them to fear *Him*. Joshua's destruction of the horses and chariots demonstrated disdain for the methods of the world. He didn't need advanced weaponry to be victorious and secure. He needed the Lord.

Exercising Obedience

Joshua did exactly what the Lord told him to do. He attacked the armies of the northern coalition.

> So Joshua came, and all the people of war with him, against them by the waters of Merom suddenly; and they fell upon them. And the Lord delivered them into the hand of Israel, who smote them, and chased them unto great Zidon, and unto Misrephoth-maim, and unto the valley of Mizpeh eastward; and they smote them, until they left them none remaining. And Joshua did unto them as the Lord bade him: he houghed their horses, and burnt their chariots with fire. And Joshua at that time turned back, and took Hazor, and smote the king thereof with the sword: for Hazor beforetime was the head of all those kingdoms. And they smote all the souls that were therein with the edge of the sword, utterly destroying them; there was not any left to breathe: and he burnt Hazor with fire. And all the cities of those kings, and all the kings of them, did Joshua take, and smote them with the edge of the sword, and he utterly destroyed them, as Moses the servant of the Lord commanded. But as for the cities that stood still in their strength, Israel burned none of them, save Hazor only; that did Joshua burn. And all the spoil of these cities, and the cattle, the children of Israel took for a prey unto themselves; but every man they smote with the edge of the sword, until they had destroyed them, neither left they any to breathe (Josh. 11:7–14).

As Joshua obeyed, God acted. While Jabin and company were preparing to attack Israel, they didn't expect Israel to attack them. Caught by surprise, the enemy fled in three directions. Some headed northward up a valley to Merom's west, some headed north up a different valley to Merom's east, and others ran toward a valley to the east-northeast. But Joshua didn't let them escape. He pursued and annihilated the enemy army. He caught and destroyed the enemy cavalry. Then, while sacking the cities that had sent the army against Israel, Joshua executed all of their inhabitants. As gruesome as this seems, keep in mind what I said at the outset of our study: God's judgment is just; God's patience is great; and God's authority is absolute (see chap. 1).

Joshua burned the city of Hazor, in part as punishment for taking leadership against Israel and in part to provide a warning to other cities that might be tempted to lead a future attack. Israel was permitted to "spoil," or salvage the goods from, the other cities in the region. Israel had been living in tents for a generation. They saved most of the cities so they wouldn't have to rebuild an infrastructure from scratch. Once the Canaanites were destroyed, the buildings would remain for Israel's use.

Summarizing the Conquest of Canaan

The verses that follow the description of the destruction of the armies and cities of the north provide a summation of Israel's conquest of Canaan.

> As the Lord commanded Moses his servant, so did Moses command Joshua, and so did Joshua; he left nothing undone of all that the Lord commanded Moses. So Joshua took all that land, the hills, and all the south country, and all the land of Goshen, and the valley, and the plain, and the mountain of Israel, and the valley of the same; even from the mount Halak, that goeth up to Seir, even unto Baal-gad in the valley of Lebanon under mount Hermon: and all their kings he took, and smote them, and slew them. Joshua made war a long time with all those kings. There was not a city that made peace with the children of Israel, save the Hivites the inhabitants of Gibeon: all other they took in battle. For it was of the Lord to harden their hearts, that they should come against Israel in battle, that he might destroy them utterly, and that they might have no favour, but that he might destroy them, as the Lord commanded Moses. And at that time came Joshua, and cut off the Anakims from the mountains, from Hebron, from Debir, from Anab, and from all the mountains of Judah, and from all the mountains of Israel: Joshua destroyed them utterly with their cities. There was none of the Anakims left in the land of the children of Israel: only in Gaza, in Gath, and in Ashdod, there remained. So Joshua took the whole land, according to all that the Lord said unto Moses; and Joshua gave it for an inheritance unto Israel according to their divisions by their tribes. And the land rested from war (Josh. 11:15–23).

There are five important facts to note in this summary. *We have a record of Joshua's complete obedience*—"He left nothing undone of all that the Lord commanded Moses." Few have enjoyed such a commendation. Jesus, the One Whom Joshua foreshadows in many ways, told the Father in His prayer on the evening before His crucifixion, "I have finished the work which thou gavest me to do" (John 17:4). Joshua, like Jesus, was an obedient servant.

We are given geographic boundaries that mark off the extent of the territory conquered by Joshua (11:16–17; cf., 12:1–24). While the exact locations of some of the landmarks have not been firmly established today, the land Joshua captured may have been twice as extensive as the total territory ever held by Israel after Joshua. Granted, as we continue through the book, we will see evidence of the incomplete nature of the conquest, but Joshua did much more than give Israel a toehold in the land. He laid claim to all of it and subdued the inhabitants of it (11:23). It was individual and tribal failure within Israel that led to future defeats within the land.

We see that this war wasn't finished overnight. Joshua 11:18 says, "Joshua made war a long time with all those kings." This campaign took a minimum of five years and perhaps as long as seven years. In a conflict lasting that long, there must have been times when Joshua and Israel were tempted to settle down and be content with what they had taken so far without pressing on to total victory, but they didn't quit. They kept fighting until the land was subdued.

That *Joshua specifically mentioned the defeat of the Anakim* in this context is significant. Apparently, Caleb's exploits recorded in Joshua 14 occurred during this time, summarized here under Joshua's name because the passage records the success of the army under his ultimate command. The presence of the giant Anakim had been the primary cause of fear that kept Israel from attempting to take the land forty years earlier (Num. 13:28). This generation, under Joshua's command, proved that the size of the enemy is not important. The same lesson would have to be learned again much later, when Israel trembled in fear at the challenge of Goliath, who was a descendent of these very Anakim who survived in Gath. At that time, Israel would be rescued by an inconspicuous shepherd who became their "champion" and defeated the giant.

This section ends *by recording the eventual ending of hostilities*. The statement "And the land rested from war" (11:23) draws the first section of Joshua to a close. The writer of Hebrews tells us that this rest foreshadowed the final rest that will come (Heb. 4:8–11) when evil is eradicated and Christ reigns forever as King of kings and Lord of lords (Rev. 11:15; 19:16).

Listing the Defeated Kings

Joshua 12 provides two lists of defeated kings. First, the kings defeated under Moses' leadership are listed.

> Now these are the kings of the land, which the children of Israel smote, and possessed their land on the other side Jordan toward the rising of the sun, from the river Arnon unto mount Hermon, and all the plain on the east: Sihon king of the Amorites, who dwelt in Heshbon, and ruled from Aroer, which is upon the bank of the river Arnon, and from the middle of the river, and from half Gilead, even unto the river Jabbok, which is the border of the children of Ammon; and from the plain to the sea of Chinneroth on the east, and unto the sea of the plain, even the salt sea on the east, the way to Beth-jeshimoth; and from the south, under Ashdoth-pisgah: and the coast

> of Og king of Bashan, which was of the remnant of the giants, that dwelt at Ashtaroth and at Edrei, and reigned in mount Hermon, and in Salcah, and in all Bashan, unto the border of the Geshurites and the Maachathites, and half Gilead, the border of Sihon king of Heshbon. Them did Moses the servant of the Lord and the children of Israel smite: and Moses the servant of the Lord gave it for a possession unto the Reubenites, and the Gadites, and the half tribe of Manasseh (Josh. 12:1–6).

These are the kings of Transjordan—the territory east of the Jordan River that would be inherited by Reuben, Gad, and half of Manasseh.

Following this list is a roster of the kings conquered by Joshua.

> And these are the kings of the country which Joshua and the children of Israel smote on this side Jordan on the west, from Baal-gad in the valley of Lebanon even unto the mount Halak, that goeth up to Seir; which Joshua gave unto the tribes of Israel for a possession according to their divisions; in the mountains, and in the valleys, and in the plains, and in the springs, and in the wilderness, and in the south country; the Hittites, the Amorites, and the Canaanites, the Perizzites, the Hivites, and the Jebusites: the king of Jericho, one; the king of Ai, which is beside Beth-el, one; the king of Jerusalem, one; the king of Hebron, one; the king of Jarmuth, one; the king of Lachish, one; the king of Eglon, one; the king of Gezer, one; the king of Debir, one; the king of Geder, one; the king of Hormah, one; the king of Arad, one; the king of Libnah, one; the king of Adullam, one; the king of Makkedah, one; the king of Beth-el, one; the king of Tappuah, one; the king of Hepher, one; the king of Aphek, one; the king of Lasharon, one; the king of Madon, one; the king of Hazor, one; the king of Shimron-meron, one; the king of Achshaph, one; the king of Taanach, one; the king of Megiddo, one; the king of Kedesh, one; the king of Jokneam of Carmel, one; the king of Dor in the coast of Dor, one; the king of the nations of Gilgal, one; the king of Tirzah, one: all the kings thirty and one (Josh. 12:7–24).

In the accounts of the battles, only the kings heading the southern and northern coalitions had been mentioned. Since the record says Joshua conquered "the whole land" (11:23), this list is provided to help complete the picture. Note that "the king of the nations of Gilgal" mentioned in verse 23 is not to be confused with the Gilgal of Israel's encampment near Jericho. This is another Gilgal and "was probably located about forty-two miles north of Jerusalem, just south of Carmel."[84] These are the kings from the territory west of the Jordan, and their land would be distributed among the other tribes of Israel. That disbursement is described in Joshua 13–19.

[84] Zodhiates, p. 312.

Applying the Principles

It is easy to relax after a victory, isn't it? You want to sit back and savor it a while. You figure that having expended all the effort necessary to be victorious, you're entitled to a little break. We are willing to confront little challenges occasionally, but we don't like having to deal with big challenges repeatedly. The Christian life is something like being constantly in school. You work hard writing a research paper or preparing for a big test, then as soon as the paper is turned in or the test is taken, you have to start preparing for the next one. Actually, the Christian life is more like being at war. As soon as one battle is over, you have to analyze what happened, identify strengths and weaknesses, find ways to incorporate the lessons learned in that battle into your training program, and begin preparation for future conflicts, always staying alert for the possibility of unexpected enemy attack.

There are at least three important lessons for the believer to learn from the account of Joshua's great campaign. We are reminded that *entering Canaan is a picture not of life in heaven but of life in Christ.* Conquering Canaan, then, is a picture of the appropriation of our inheritance in Him. We must always be ready to accept new challenges from God. We must never be satisfied with our present level of spirituality. Becoming a new creation in Christ was the start (2 Cor. 5:17). "Putting on" the new nature requires time and effort (Col. 3:10–14).

A second lesson for us today is that *the battles that confront us must actually be fought and won*. The Christian life is not a video game that you can play in your spare time, fighting make-believe battles on a screen with no real effort and only imaginary consequences. The spiritual enemies of our soul may not be visible, but they are real (Eph. 6:12). Enemy attacks are ultimately attacks against God. As God's representatives, we are assured that our strength and security come from Christ. We don't have to be afraid that Satan might destroy us. Since the worst he can do is "kill the body" (Matt. 10:28), we are guaranteed victory. To be absent from the body is to be present with the Lord (2 Cor. 5:8), which is far better than having to continue this earth-bound struggle (Phil. 1:23–24). Satan is mighty, but Christ is *almighty.* Some battles in our spiritual lives are won quickly and decisively. Others are not. We are engaged in an ongoing conflict. We must not become complacent and give up the fight, for we know that our labor is not in vain in the Lord (1 Cor. 15:58).

To be victorious, we have to obey. What Joshua and Israel went through to possess Canaan, and what you and I go through to "work out [our] own salvation" (Phil. 2:12) is in some ways analogous to teaching a child to ride a bicycle. When my children were first learning to ride their bikes, I held the bike upright and guided it from the back, but they had to learn to pedal and steer. It was a team effort. The analogy breaks down, though, because after a while they became confident and experienced enough that they no longer needed me. They could take off on their own without any help. That never happens for us spiritually (Ps. 32:8). Driving a car to a prescribed destination may actually be a better analogy. The first few driving lessons were pretty harrowing, but both my son and daughter now drive with skill (usually) and confidence. But the analogy isn't in learning to drive but in the doing of it. No matter how skilled the driver, the car will go nowhere by the exercise of the driver's will alone. It must be powered by a fuel source. The fuel that provides the power to run the engine that propels the car represents God. The route and destination for the trip represent the Word of God. Even with a full tank of gas and running engine, and a carefully prepared map showing the destination, the car won't get there without a driver. The fuel is needed for power, the map for direction, and the driver for operation. The victorious Christian is actively steering, braking, accelerating, and shifting gears in his life, but he is powered by God and guided by God's Word.

Is there ever any rest? Yes, there is. The believer is promised "rest from war" (Josh. 11:23) in Hebrews 4:9–11:

> There remaineth therefore a rest to the people of God. For he that is entered into his rest, he also hath ceased from his own works, as God did from his. Let us labour therefore to enter into that rest, lest any man fall after the same example of unbelief.

God gives us present "rest" from frustration, discouragement, and fear. To enjoy that rest, we must have absolute confidence in Christ alone to give us "rest" in victory. We must also "labour . . . to enter into that rest." That is, we must diligently make entering that rest our goal.

The word translated *labour* in Hebrews 4:11 is rendered *study* in 2 Timothy 2:15—"Study to shew thyself approved unto God, a workman that needeth not to be ashamed, rightly dividing the word of truth." Paul is not admonishing Timothy to "learn by reading," what we usually mean by "study," but to "give diligent effort toward" being approved by God. It is the same idea expressed by the writer of Hebrews. As believers, we are all "approved unto God" because we are "accepted in the beloved [Christ Jesus]" (Eph. 1:6), but we must also work at being approved. As believers, we all have "rest" because of Christ's finished work on the cross, but we must also work at entering that rest.

Joshua entered into rest in Canaan because "he left nothing undone of all that the Lord commanded Moses" (Josh. 11:15). Likewise, you and I must leave nothing undone of all that Christ commands us to do. Still, we don't work toward the *possibility* of rest but because of the sure and certain *promise* of it. God promises us ultimate rest from sin and the curse in eternity. The rest Joshua gave Israel was temporary and incomplete. The rest we have in Christ is permanent and perfect.

We don't achieve "rest" by deciding it no longer matters what we look like. Our "rest" comes when the enemies of our soul (the world, the flesh, and the Devil) are so thoroughly conquered and subdued in our lives that we can consistently look like Christ. That is a rest we achieve only in part in this life but can anticipate in fullness when "this corruptible shall have put on incorruption" (1 Cor. 15:54). In the meantime, we "labour therefore to enter into that rest" (Heb. 4:11).

23

Dividing the Promised Land

Joshua 13:1–14:5

For several years, my wife taught the first grade in a Christian day school. Christmas parties were one of the highlights of the year for the students. Although it's probably for the wrong reasons, children tend to love Christmas. Counting down the days in eager anticipation, they await the revelation of the gifts they expect to receive. Usually, my wife had each student bring an inexpensive gift, already wrapped, for the student gift exchange. Boys brought gifts boys would be likely to appreciate, and girls brought gifts appropriate for girls. On the day of the party, the gifts would be numbered, and the children would draw numbers to see which gift they would receive. All the children were excited, expecting to find some great treasure under the wrapping paper.

Typically, some would still be pleased after they opened their gifts, but many would be disappointed. Often, a lot of trading went on after the gifts were unwrapped, as children spotted something they liked better than the gift they received and made deals to swap for what they wanted. But those with the most coveted gifts were rarely willing to make an even trade for a less appealing gift opened by someone else.

Even in something as commonplace and innocuous as the children's exchange of inexpensive gifts, we see evidence of our fallen human nature. *We tend to want more than we get, so we are often disappointed.* Some gifts are considered more appealing than others, and so are "more coveted." Covetousness isn't learned; it's natural. *Contentment* must be learned and is *super*-natural. In this section of Joshua we read of the distribution of gifts far more valuable than trinkets in a gift exchange for six-year-olds. Land will be disbursed by drawing, and trading will be forbidden. Whatever you get, you keep. The potential for conflict is enormous.

Rest from War

Joshua's Age

The campaign for the conquest of Canaan was essentially over. It had been nearly fifty years since Israel had left Egypt under Moses' leadership. Joshua had assisted Moses for forty years in the wilderness and had led Israel for at least seven more. He was nearly ninety years old, and he was tired.

> Now Joshua was old and stricken in years; and the Lord said unto him, Thou art old and stricken in years, and there remaineth yet very much land to be possessed. This is the land that yet remaineth: all the borders of the Philistines, and all Geshuri, from Sihor, which is before Egypt, even unto the borders of Ekron northward, which is counted to the Canaanite: five lords of the Philistines; the Gazathites, and the Ashdothites, the Eshkalonites, the Gittites, and the Ekronites; also the Avites: from the south, all the land of the Canaanites, and Mearah that is beside the Sidonians unto Aphek, to the borders of the Amorites: and the land of the Giblites, and all Lebanon, toward the sunrising, from Baal-gad under mount Hermon unto the entering into Hamath. All the inhabitants of the hill country from Lebanon unto Misrephoth-maim, and all the Sidonians, them will I drive out from before the children of Israel: only divide thou it by lot unto the Israelites for an inheritance, as I have commanded thee (Josh. 13:1–6).

Joshua wasn't just old; he was "stricken in years." The years had taken a toll. He had done his job, but the task wasn't completely finished. There was still "very much land to be possessed." Even though Israel controlled more territory than they ever would again,[85] God had *given* them more than they had *possessed.*

More to Do

This should have impressed Israel with the goodness and bounty of God. Even with all their successes, God wanted them to have more. It is no wonder that

[85] That is up to the present. When the Lord returns to set up His kingdom, they will certainly possess more than Joshua conquered. It's possible that there may come a time before the Lord's return in which Israel may control more land than Joshua did, but that's far from certain.

Paul described God as "him that is able to do exceeding abundantly above all that we ask or think" (Eph. 3:20). The fact that there was still much to be possessed should also warn Israel against making alliances with their neighbors. The prohibition against compromise with the wicked world around them still stood. The very presence of surviving Canaanites within the land Israel controlled represented a serious threat to their long-term stability. This fact should encourage Israel to remain fit and prepared for war. Israel controlled Canaan, but the Canaanite enemies that remained were still dangerous. Israel must not become complacent and let down their guard.

That is essentially the warning Paul sounds for believers today:

> Brethren, I count not myself to have apprehended: but this one thing I do, forgetting those things which are behind, and reaching forth unto those things which are before, I press toward the mark for the prize of the high calling of God in Christ Jesus (Phil. 3:13–14).

We must not become spiritually complacent, satisfied with our present attainments or "apprehensions." Paul is not speaking here of working toward an exalted position in Christ ("the high calling") because *every* believer already possesses that exalted position by virtue of being in Christ (1 Cor. 1:30–31; Gal. 3:26–28; Eph. 1:3). Actually, the "high calling" Paul refers to is the "upward call" or "heavenly call" of God. Paul says that *rather than living on the memories of past victories, we must stay engaged in the conflict, participating in the ongoing conquest of the enemy until we are called to heaven by God.* The battle continues. We fight the enemy until the Lord calls us home.

Inheritance vs. Possession

Besides acknowledging unpossessed territory, Joshua had to divide the land among the tribes. There are three aspects of this task that are worth noting. First, the job of dividing the land was given to the man of greatest age and widest experience in all Israel. This wasn't the sole reason Joshua was appointed this task, but it was significant. It indicates that *youth should respect age and experience*, and it shows that *the elderly need to maintain spiritual vitality.* Wisdom is not automatically acquired with age—I've known some old fools—but years of serving the Lord should produce a level of wisdom and discernment that a novice hasn't attained. It is certainly appropriate for churches to sponsor programs designed to minister to the needs of senior saints. But in making the elderly the *target of* ministry, we may fail to recognize that elderly believers should be one of the church's greatest *resources for* ministry. Senior ministries should do much more than provide entertainment and fellowship for older believers. Those ministries ought to provide means and encouragement to tap into the combined wisdom and experience of older believers in order to minister to others. We may retire from employment, but we must not retire from serving the Lord.

Second, the Lord makes a subtle but important distinction between an *inheritance* (11:23; 13:6, 7) and a *possession* (13:1). The land of Canaan was an *inheritance* in that it was in its entirety a bequest from God to Israel. Particular sections of the land were to be defined as the inheritance of particular tribes. Actual *possession* of the inheritance would be incremental. Israel would *possess* their inheritance only by *dispossessing* its current inhabitants.

Third, we see the faith involved in dividing land not yet fully possessed. After describing "the land that yet remaineth" (13:2), the Lord said to Joshua, "Divide thou it by lot unto the Israelites for an inheritance" (13:6). Joshua was distributing land *promised* but not yet *possessed*. God was identifying the boundaries to be claimed by each tribe, expecting them to go on to full possession as time progressed and their numbers increased. Joshua was acting as executor of God's will (as in "last will and testament"). The various tribes should consider each bequest their own property, but *they must still actually take possession of that which had been given.*

This again pictures our sanctification in Christ. As a believer, you are made a new creation (2 Cor. 5:17; Gal. 6:15), given new life (John 3:7–8; Titus 3:5; 1 Pet. 1:23), and assured victory (Rom. 6:6, 14) as the gift of God in Christ. But you must be transformed (Rom. 12:1–2), walk in newness of life (Rom. 6:4), and work for victory (1 Cor. 15:57–58) as you "work out your own salvation in fear and trembling" (Phil. 2:12), walking "worthy of the vocation wherewith ye are called" (Eph. 4:1). God has given us salvation in Christ; we must take what God has given. We must dispossess and conquer sin. We must work to strengthen our areas of weakness. We must learn to correct our faults. We must "put on the new man" and "put away" sin (Eph. 4:24–25; cf. Col. 3:8–16). *The righteousness of Christ that is ours by imputation must become ours by experience* (Rom. 3:20–26; cf. Matt. 5:20ff.).

Dividing the Land

I don't intend to belabor the details of the geographic boundaries established in the distribution of the land. Some of the place names and landmarks have survived, making it possible to get a pretty good idea of the boundaries of each tribe's territory, but any map showing occupied territory can only approximate the property lines. The specifics would certainly have been important to Israel, but they provide little practical value for our study.

> Now therefore divide this land for an inheritance unto the nine tribes, and the half tribe of Manasseh, with whom the Reubenites and the Gadites have received their inheritance, which Moses gave them, beyond Jordan eastward, even as Moses the servant of the Lord gave them; from Aroer, that is upon the bank of the river Arnon, and the city that is in the midst of the river, and all the plain of Medeba unto Dibon; and all the cities of Sihon king of the Amorites, which reigned in Heshbon, unto the border of the children of Ammon; and Gilead, and the border of the Geshurites and Maachathites, and all mount Hermon, and all Bashan unto Salcah; all the kingdom of Og in Bashan, which reigned in Ashtaroth and in Edrei, who remained of the remnant of the giants: for these did Moses smite, and cast them out. Nevertheless the children of Israel expelled not the Geshurites, nor the Maachathites: but the Geshurites and the Maachathites dwell among the Israelites until this day. Only unto the tribe of Levi he gave none inheritance; the sacrifices of the Lord God of Israel made by fire are their inheritance, as he said unto them. And Moses gave unto the tribe of the children of Reuben inheritance according to their families. And their coast was from Aroer, that is on the bank of the river Arnon, and the city that is in the midst of the river, and all the plain by Medeba; Heshbon, and all her cities that are in the plain; Dibon, and Bamoth-baal, and Beth-baal-meon, and Jahaza, and Kedemoth, and Mephaath, and Kirjathaim, and Sibmah, and Zareth-shahar in the mount of the valley, and Beth-peor, and Ashdoth-pisgah, and Beth-jeshimoth, and all the cities of the plain, and all the kingdom of Sihon king of the Amorites, which reigned in Heshbon, whom Moses smote with the princes of Midian, Evi, and Rekem, and Zur, and Hur, and Reba, which were dukes of Sihon, dwelling in the country. Balaam also the son of Beor, the soothsayer, did the children of Israel slay with the sword among them that were slain by them. And the border of the children of Reuben was Jordan, and the border thereof. This was the inheritance of the children of Reuben after their families, the cities and the villages thereof. And Moses gave inheritance unto the tribe of Gad, even unto the children of Gad according to their families. And their coast was Jazer, and all the cities of Gilead, and half the land of the children of Ammon, unto Aroer that is before Rabbah; and from Heshbon unto Ramath-mizpeh, and Betonim; and from Mahanaim unto the border of Debir; and in the valley, Beth-aram, and Beth-nimrah, and Succoth, and Zaphon, the rest of the kingdom of Sihon king of Heshbon, Jordan and his border, even unto the edge of the sea of Chinnereth on the other side Jordan eastward. This is the inheritance of the children of Gad after their families, the cities, and their villages. And Moses gave inheritance unto the half tribe of Manasseh: and this was the possession of the half tribe of the children of Manasseh by their families. And their coast was from Mahanaim, all Bashan, all the kingdom of Og king of Bashan, and all the towns of Jair, which are in Bashan, threescore cities: and half Gilead, and Ashtaroth, and Edrei, cities of the kingdom of Og in Bashan, were pertaining

> unto the children of Machir the son of Manasseh, even to the one half of the children of Machir by their families. These are the countries which Moses did distribute for inheritance in the plains of Moab, on the other side Jordan, by Jericho, eastward. But unto the tribe of Levi Moses gave not any inheritance: the Lord God of Israel was their inheritance, as he said unto them.
>
> And these are the countries which the children of Israel inherited in the land of Canaan, which Eleazar the priest, and Joshua the son of Nun, and the heads of the fathers of the tribes of the children of Israel, distributed for inheritance to them. By lot was their inheritance, as the Lord commanded by the hand of Moses, for the nine tribes, and for the half tribe. For Moses had given the inheritance of two tribes and an half tribe on the other side Jordan: but unto the Levites he gave none inheritance among them. For the children of Joseph were two tribes, Manasseh and Ephraim: therefore they gave no part unto the Levites in the land, save cities to dwell in, with their suburbs for their cattle and for their substance. As the Lord commanded Moses, so the children of Israel did, and they divided the land (Josh. 13:7–14:5).

The verses above are actually the first portion of the description of what may well have been the largest land distribution and settlement in history. The passage describes the division of the land east of the Jordan River among the tribes of Reuben, Gad and half of Manasseh; and it introduces the description of the land allotted to the other tribes, which will be discussed later. From this point on, the conflicts would be local battles fought by individual tribes to take possession of the territory they were given.

Assigned by Casting Lots

This account is especially remarkable in that the land distribution was accomplished with no evidence of disputing or arguing over property rights, preferences, or procedures. If you wanted to live in the mountains but were assigned land in the plains, that was too bad. You were expected to adjust your desires to what the Lord had evidently allotted you. The child at the Christmas party who gets the soap bubbles and can't trade for the toy car has to learn to be content with soap bubbles. But children aren't the only ones who struggle with this. I've known adults at church to dispute over seats in the pews or spaces in the parking lot.

I shudder to think of the potential for discord in the distribution of *land*. Being a dinner host responsible for arranging seating assignments is stressful enough. Shouldering the responsibility to assign permanent places to live would be truly terrifying. It borders on the miraculous to read in this text of so many people willingly setting aside personal ambitions and submitting to the will of the Lord in assigning them to particular territories. What a testimony to the mature faith of Israel!

How was the land distribution accomplished? They did it "by lot" (14:2). I don't know whether the boundaries were defined for the various territories, then the tribal leaders drew lots to determine which territory was theirs, or if the reverse was done, with one section being announced and a drawing held to see which tribe would get it. It doesn't matter. What is important is that Israel didn't think of this as determining their inheritance on the basis of random chance. *Casting lots* was not equivalent to a modern casino game. It *was an act of supreme confidence in the Lord to assign them the portion of His choosing.*

The use of lots to determine territorial inheritance was the method God told Israel to use so that the assignments could be seen as divine appointments, not human inventions. This procedure accomplished several things. It relieved Joshua of personal responsibility and liability if anyone dared to challenge the results as unfair. It indicated that God was protecting the interests of the minority, in that smaller tribes weren't displaced by larger tribes. It eliminated any potential for political intrigue—lobbying would be useless. Finally, it taught Israel the uniqueness of their governmental polity. They were a theocracy, answerable directly to God. Joshua and the tribal officers answered to God. They didn't exercise kingly or princely authority of their own.

Assigned Permanently

Important for Israel's future is the fact that the land assignments were perpetual. Once land was distributed, families were forbidden to sell the land they were given to anyone else (Lev. 25:23–28). Land could be leased temporarily, but Israel's law made no provision for absolute sale of land. Every fifty years there was to be a "Jubilee," one provision of which required all land leases to expire and property to revert to its original owner. The amount someone paid to lease a property would depend in part on how many years they would have use of it before the next Jubilee. I don't know whether this increased or diminished the potential for disputes. On one hand, it would seem that people would be more likely to protest results they knew would be nonnegotiable and nontransferable. On the other hand, the fact that the assignments were nonnegotiable and nontransferable eliminated any seeking of personal advantage by under-the-table trading or backroom deal making. Again, the absence of any record of disputation testifies to Israel's confidence in the Lord and willingness to submit to His authority.

The perpetual nature of each inheritance shows us that Israel's economy was certainly neither *communistic* nor *socialistic*, which forms discourage or forbid private ownership of property and private enterprise. The provision for limited leasing of the property actually encouraged private enterprise. If someone owned more land than he could put to profitable use, he could earn some money from it by leasing it to someone who could use it. At the same time, someone with the means to lease and use additional property could enjoy the profits from the investment of his resources.

However, it is also clear that Israel's economy wasn't purely *capitalistic* either. The perpetual assignment of land served to curb greed. No one would ever be able to accumulate massive land holdings and control productivity and markets. In a purely capitalistic economy people are not only permitted but even encouraged to accumulate as much wealth as possible. The only real restraint on greed is found in the character of the capitalist, and we've seen repeatedly in our own country the harm that can be caused by unbridled greed in the unscrupulous. Israel could and should practice private enterprise, but always with the proviso that one's accumulation of wealth must never harm his neighbors or the nation. One could enjoy the fruit of his labor, but it was always to be within the bounds of compassion and generosity.

The most important aspect of the perpetuity of the land assignments is that it demonstrated that *God was the ultimate owner of all the land.* He was parceling it out as He saw fit. The tribes and families of Israel would be the landholders, occupying and acting as stewards of God's property. As long as they obeyed Him, they would be permitted to stay. If they forsook the Lord, they would be expelled from His land (Deut. 8:11–20).

Supervised by Tribal Leaders

Although the details of the actual procedure for casting lots for the land aren't described, we do know that the tribal leaders were to oversee the process. Those who would be the actual recipients of the land as representatives of their tribes were supervising the assigning and distributing of the parcels. They would be able to verify the propriety of the proceedings. It would be impossible for any tribe to exercise undue influence, and the presence of all the tribal leaders protected them all from accusations of manipulation of the results. They would also be present to serve as a deliberating body to hear and decide special cases. We'll see in chapter 24 (Josh. 14:6–17:7) that two such cases were presented and decided.

In the description of the land distribution, Joshua makes it clear that when the tribes were assigned portions, the tribe of Levi did not get a particular territory. "The Lord God of Israel was their inheritance" (Josh. 13:33; cf. Num. 18:20; Deut. 10:9; 18:1–2). Levi was responsible for the spiritual oversight of Israel. They were supported by Israel's tithes and offerings—"The sacrifices of the Lord God of Israel made by fire are their inheritance" (Josh. 13:14). Instead of being given a particular region, Levi was allotted scattered cities. That way they could permeate Israel as God's representatives. While there would be a particular place for Israel to meet to offer sacrifices, the scattering of Levi throughout the land was intended to show that God was not restricted to a single location. He was the God of all Israel and could be found anywhere. Similarly, God is not to be relegated to one part of our lives or one day of the week. Christianity isn't something we go to church to *do*; it's what we *are*. We must not divide our lives into the sacred and the secular, thinking that God controls our worship but not our business or social lives. God's presence and control is to permeate all our being, all our lives, all the time.

Could there be any greater testimony to the humility and character of Joshua than the fact that he pretty much disappears from view in the land distribution program? You could argue that without his leadership, Israel would have no land to inherit. American politics has become so corrupt that we pretty much expect elected officials to use their positions for personal gain. The truly altruistic individual, who gives of himself without expectation of personal benefit, is rare indeed. Joshua's role in the conquest of Canaan had given him access to an almost unprecedented opportunity to exercise his power and influence for his own enrichment. Joshua was not corrupted in the face of temptation and opportunity far exceeding temptations that have brought low countless other men.

Nuggets Worth Noting

One noteworthy fact that emerges from the land distribution is the disproportionate space devoted to describing the territories allotted to the various tribes and the order in which the information is presented. A great deal of attention is given to the Transjordanian tribes, and they are handled first. Part of the reason for this may be that Joshua wanted to emphasize their kinship with the rest of Israel and defuse any undercurrent of feeling that the Transjordanian region wasn't really part of the Promised Land. In the distribution of land among the nine and a half tribes west of Jordan, Judah is treated first and most thoroughly, followed by the tribes of Joseph (Ephraim and the other half of Manasseh), then Benjamin. As a prophetic anticipation of their future significance, this demonstrates the sovereignty of God. Judah would ultimately be most important, as the tribe from whom David, Solomon, and eventually Christ Jesus would come. Ephraim was Joshua's tribe and with Manasseh would dominate the period of the judges. But the transition from the period of judges to the monarchy would include the reign of the first king of Israel, Saul, a Benjamite.

Buried within the description of the division of the land, Joshua provides two important footnotes. In verse 22, we read of the execution of Balaam (cf.

Num. 22:5), the man hired by the king of Moab to curse Israel only to find that every time he tried to do so he pronounced a blessing. That verse illustrates that "no man can serve two masters" (Matt. 6:24) and that "God is not mocked; whatsoever a man soweth, that shall he also reap" (Gal. 6:7). More important to our study is verse 13, where we read that "the children of Israel expelled not" some of the people of the territory God had given them. Other than the accounts involving stolen goods from Ai (Josh. 7), and the account of Joshua's failure to ask God's counsel when evaluating the Gibeonites' request for a peace treaty (Josh. 9), this is the first record of Israel's failure to obey the Lord completely. This verse lays the groundwork for understanding much of Israel's history for the four centuries that would follow.

Applying the Principles

Why did God inspire Joshua to include this record of the land distribution? Besides the historic significance and applications I've already mentioned, I can think of at least two additional reasons.

First, the description provides authenticating details for the fulfillment of God's promises to Israel. It would have been sufficient to say simply, "the land rested from war and Israel divided the land among themselves and settled it." But we've been given at least sketchy details of the procedure used in assigning territories and the specific descriptions of the territories assigned. This provides information that future generations of Israelites would need if they ever doubted either the ability of God to keep His promises or the divine nature of the allotment of land. *Israel not only conquered the land because God fought for them*, but individual *tribes and families settled the specific land that God gave them*. They had to obey God. *But actual possession was all of grace.* The land was God's gift to Israel.

Second, this record provides another illustration of the spiritual theme of Joshua: spiritual growth requires effort and attention. We must surrender to God's will, in total submission to Him, as Israel did in the casting of lots for the land. We must be consecrated to God, fully dedicated to His service, as Israel would be expected to obey the Lord, Who made them stewards of the land. We must also appropriate that which the Lord has given us, claiming as our own what God has provided. For the "works of the flesh" (Gal. 5:19–21) to be defeated in our lives, and the "fruit of the Spirit" (Gal. 5:22–23) to be displayed, God must be operating within us. Such is grace. We also have a measure of responsibility in this. Will full and perfect appropriation be possible in this life? No, because we are still doing battle with the flesh (Rom. 7:18). We have "the firstfruits of the Spirit," but we await "the redemption of the body" (Rom. 8:23). If we are alive in the Spirit, we must "walk in the Spirit" (Gal. 5:25).

If you as a believer in Christ cannot honestly claim to consistently exhibit all the fruit of the Spirit and none of the works of the flesh—*and none of us can make that claim*—then you still have more territory to possess. God has given it to you, but you must appropriate it.

24
Two Special Cases

Joshua 14:6–17:13

Any lawyer who handles estate settlements will tell you that things can get ugly when it comes time to disburse the property of the deceased. My brother is an attorney, and early in his career he did some estate work. It didn't take long for him to decide to specialize in another legal field. Even with estates of relatively little value, disputes over who gets what often (always?) arise. Claims to particular keepsakes, whether they have great intrinsic worth or merely sentimental value, can lead to permanent conflict in families, often with the lawyer and/or executor caught in the middle. If you want to be sure a particular heir will inherit a particular item, you need to put it in writing in your will. It's a rare family indeed that can settle property allotments merely on the basis of claims that "Mom promised me her diamond earrings," or "Dad promised me his hunting rifle."

As Joshua proceeded with the distribution of the land of Canaan, acting as executor of God's "will" in assigning portions of Israel's inheritance, he was presented with two special claims. One man claimed that a particular territory was supposed to go to him, and a group of sisters claimed they were supposed to get a share of the inheritance because their father had died without a son. What should Joshua do? His job was made easier by the fact that God, in His wise providence, had addressed both claims in writing.

Claim of Caleb to Hebron and Its Environs

When Israel first came to the edge of Canaan under Moses' leadership, Caleb had been one of the men sent to check out the land and its people. Because of Caleb's faithfulness to God, Moses promised that he would receive the territory through which he traveled (Num. 14:23–24; Deut. 1:36). In Joshua 14:7, Caleb says he was forty years old when the promise was made. In 14:10, Caleb says he is now eighty-five years old. Forty-five years have passed since Moses first promised him the city of Hebron and the surrounding territory. While the Transjordan region was being divided among Reuben, Gad, and Manasseh (Josh. 13:1–14:5), Caleb had held his peace. When it came time to begin distribution of the land to the west of the Jordan River, Caleb reminded the tribal leaders of Moses' promise and exercised his claim.

> Then the children of Judah came unto Joshua in Gilgal: and Caleb the son of Jephunneh the Kenezite said unto him, Thou knowest the thing that the Lord said unto Moses the man of God concerning me and thee in Kadesh-barnea. Forty years old was I when Moses the servant of the Lord sent me from Kadesh-barnea to espy out the land; and I brought him word again as it was in mine heart. Nevertheless my brethren that went up with me made the heart of the people melt: but I wholly followed the Lord my God. And Moses sware on that day, saying, Surely the land whereon thy feet have trodden shall be thine inheritance, and thy children's for ever, because thou hast wholly followed the Lord my God. And now, behold, the Lord hath kept me alive, as he said, these forty and five years, even since the Lord spake this word unto Moses, while the children of Israel wandered in the wilderness: and now, lo, I am this day fourscore and five years old. As yet I am as strong this day as I was in the day that Moses sent me: as my strength was then, even so is my strength now, for war, both to go out, and to come in. Now therefore give me this mountain, whereof the Lord spake in that day; for thou heardest in that day how the Anakims were there, and that the cities were great and fenced: if so be the Lord will be with me, then I shall be able to drive them out, as the Lord said. And Joshua blessed him, and gave unto Caleb the son of Jephunneh Hebron for an inheritance. Hebron therefore became the inheritance of Caleb the son of Jephunneh the Kenezite unto this day, because that he wholly followed the Lord God of Israel. And the name of Hebron before was Kirjath-arba; which Arba was a great man among the Anakims. And the land had rest from war (Josh. 14:6–15).

Making His Request

There are four facts worth noting in Caleb's presentation of his claim to Hebron and its environs. *Caleb stated his case publicly* before witnesses. The assembled leaders of Israel were present. Caleb, as the eldest statesman in Israel apart from Joshua, was probably the representative of his tribe, Judah. It may be that the reference to the "children of Judah" coming before Joshua means that he brought other tribal leaders with him, but it is also possible that it means that the "children of Judah" came in the person of Caleb as their representative. Either way, there were others present who could testify that Caleb was not cutting some private deal. Caleb wasn't "pulling strings" to get a special favor from his old buddy and fellow spy Joshua. He was exercising a claim to what he had been rightfully promised, and that promise was a matter of public record in the books of Moses.

Caleb made his claim at the appropriate time before the general distribution of the land began. It is not that Caleb was afraid that the lot might go against him—if God were controlling the distribution by lot, He could certainly allot Caleb the land He had promised. Caleb was saving Joshua some time by pointing out that casting lots in his case was unnecessary. God's will had already been made clear on this matter (Num. 14:24), so there was no need to seek further direction by the casting of lots. Actually, going through the process of casting lots to determine Judah's inheritance would have implied uncertainty about a matter God had already addressed. Caleb knew firsthand the events involving Balaam, as the king of Moab asked him repeatedly to curse Israel despite God's instructions (Num. 22–24). He also knew how God had responded to Joshua's begging for instructions in the matter of Achan's sin by telling him to get up and do what he had been told and quit asking God for instructions He had already given (Josh. 7). Caleb knew something we sometimes forget: *God doesn't want us to keep questioning Him about things He has already made clear.*

Caleb gave God the credit for keeping him physically strong enough to take the land God had promised him (Josh. 14:10–11). Caleb had obeyed the Lord, following Him faithfully (14:8). He was merely asking permission to take possession of the inheritance he'd been promised. God expected Caleb to conquer Hebron, so He had kept Caleb strong enough to do the job. This principle is found throughout Scripture—God equips a man for the work He assigns him.

Finally, note that Hebron was a great walled city inhabited by powerful giants (Num. 13:22, 33; Josh. 14:12). It was the mountain stronghold of the Anakim, the very people Caleb's generation were so afraid of that they decided not to try to take the land. Because Caleb was one of the oldest men in Israel, we might have expected him to ask for an easier assignment or at least to leave the actual conquest to others. But *Caleb didn't ask for a soft, easy place to retire.* He knew that taking Hebron would be one of the greatest challenges any of the tribes would face, but he was undeterred. Caleb firmly believed that the God Who promised him the territory would enable him to take it.

Possessing His Inheritance

The verses that follow provide a description of the boundaries of the territory given to Judah, ending by recording that Caleb successfully "drove thence the three sons of Anak."

> This then was the lot of the tribe of the children of Judah by their families; even to the border of Edom the wilderness of Zin southward was the uttermost part of the south coast. And their south border was from the shore of the salt sea, from the bay that looketh southward: and it went out to the south side to Maaleh-acrabbim, and passed along to Zin, and ascended up on the south side unto Kadesh-barnea, and passed along to Hezron, and went up to Adar, and fetched a compass to Karkaa: from thence it passed toward Azmon, and went out unto the river of Egypt; and the goings out of that coast were at the sea: this shall be your south coast. And the east border was the salt sea, even unto the end of Jordan. And their border in the north quarter was from the bay of the sea at the uttermost part of Jordan: and the border went up to Beth-hogla, and passed along by the north of Beth-arabah; and the border went up to the stone of Bohan the son of Reuben: and the border went up toward Debir from the valley of Achor, and so northward, looking toward Gilgal, that is before the going up to Adummim, which is on the south side of the river: and the border passed toward the waters of En-shemesh, and the goings out thereof were at En-rogel: and the border went up by the valley of the son of Hinnom unto the south side of the Jebusite; the same is Jerusalem: and the border went up to the top of the mountain that lieth before the valley of Hinnom westward, which is at the end of the valley of the giants northward: and the border was drawn from the top of the hill unto the fountain of the water of Nephtoah, and went out to the cities of mount Ephron; and the border was drawn to Baalah, which is Kirjath-jearim: and the border compassed from Baalah westward unto mount Seir, and passed along unto the side of mount Jearim, which is Chesalon, on the north side, and went down to Beth-shemesh, and passed on to Timnah: and the border went out unto the side of Ekron northward: and the border was drawn to Shicron, and passed along to mount Baalah, and went out unto Jabneel; and the goings out of the border were at the sea. And the west border was to the great sea, and the coast thereof. This is the coast of the children of Judah round about according to their families. And unto Caleb the son of Jephunneh he gave a part among the children of Judah, according to the commandment of the Lord to Joshua, even the city of Arba the father of Anak, which city is Hebron. And Caleb drove thence the three sons of Anak, Sheshai, and Ahiman, and Talmai, the children of Anak (Josh. 15:1–14).

What must have been a tremendous battle is summarized without fanfare in the simple declaration of Caleb's victory. The point is to minimize Caleb's efforts and magnify God's faithfulness. God promised victory, and He delivered. Christians would enjoy greater victory today if they would approach the "giants" in their lives with the confidence of Caleb. What God has promised, He can provide. His strength is demonstrated in our weakness (2 Cor. 12:9). In Christ, we have the strength to do anything God commands us to do (Phil. 4:13).

As the narrative continues, we find that Caleb bequeathed the southern region of the Negev Desert to his daughter, Achsah, and he gave Achsah to Othniel as a reward for service.

> And he went up thence to the inhabitants of Debir: and the name of Debir before was Kirjath-sepher. And Caleb said, He that smiteth Kirjath-sepher, and taketh it, to him will I give Achsah my daughter to wife. And Othniel the son of Kenaz, the brother of Caleb, took it: and he gave him Achsah his daughter to wife. And it came to pass, as she came unto him, that she moved him to ask of her father a field: and she lighted off her ass; and Caleb said unto her, What wouldest thou? Who answered, Give me a blessing; for thou hast given me a south land; give me also springs of water. And he gave her the upper springs, and the nether springs (Josh. 15:15–19).

The fact that Caleb's daughter is singled out for an inheritance might imply that he had no sons, but 1 Chronicles 4:15 lists three sons of Caleb: Iru, Elah, and Naam. None of them are mentioned here even though due to Caleb's age it is unlikely that they were born later. This account is included because it provides background on Othniel, who would rise to leadership in the tribe of Judah, eventually serving as a judge over Israel (Judg. 3:7–11).

Caleb's relationship to Othniel isn't clear. The text calls Othniel "the son of Kenaz, the brother of Caleb" (15:17). The wording could mean that Caleb had a brother[86] named Kenaz who was the father of Othniel, making Othniel Caleb's nephew and Achsah's first cousin (see 1 Chron. 4:13–15). However, Caleb has been identified as "the son of Jephunneh the Kenezite" (14:6). As a descendent of a forebear named Kenaz, Caleb himself could be called a "son of Kenaz." So it is possible that Othniel is a "son of" the same Kenaz from whom Caleb descended, making Othniel Caleb's "brother" several generations removed. If so, Caleb and Othniel would be cousins of some unknown degree—related by common descent from a man named Kenaz, but more distantly than uncle to nephew. There is no way to determine from the text which reading is preferable.

But why was Achsah given to Othniel? Was she merely bait to tempt some valiant young man to help in the conquest of Kirjath-sepher, and Othniel was the winner? I doubt it. While we don't know exactly how Caleb and Othniel were

---

[86] The Hebrew *'ah*, translated "brother" can also mean "relative" or simply "ally," making it impossible to determine the precise relationships being described.

related, Caleb certainly knew the man and probably had reason to believe he was interested in Achsah and she in him. Caleb was probably just offering to waive the typical "bride price" in exchange for service, and making a public announcement to that effect, fully expecting Othniel to fulfill the request. This resembles the offer Laban made Jacob—Jacob could marry Laban's daughter in exchange for seven years of labor (Gen. 29:15–30). But Caleb was a man of much greater integrity than Laban. Caleb knew what character it would take for Othniel to win his bride. True, he would have to be a *mighty* man to make the attempt. But more importantly, he would have to be a *faithful* man who believed the promises of God and a *godly* man whose obedience God could bless. Othniel could succeed only with the help of God. And succeed he did. The record simply says, "Othniel . . . took it."

At Othniel's request, Achsah asked her father for water rights in the land surrounding Kirjath-sepher, and he gave her the springs she wanted. Exactly why this is included isn't clear. It may simply be to demonstrate that Caleb loved his daughter and provided for her generously. Or it may provide historical information to support Othniel's claims to the land, helping explain his rise to prominence and influence.

Following this account, the text simply lists the cities included in the inheritance of Judah, ending with a statement that for all her victories, Judah failed to subdue the city of Jerusalem. It remained in the control of the Jebusites until David conquered the city nearly four hundred years later (2 Sam. 5:6–7).

> This is the inheritance of the tribe of the children of Judah according to their families. And the uttermost cities of the tribe of the children of Judah toward the coast of Edom southward were Kabzeel, and Eder, and Jagur, and Kinah, and Dimonah, and Adadah, and Kedesh, and Hazor, and Ithnan, Ziph, and Telem, and Bealoth, and Hazor, Hadattah, and Kerioth, and Hezron, which is Hazor, Amam, and Shema, and Moladah, and Hazar-gaddah, and Heshmon, and Beth-palet, and Hazar-shual, and Beer-sheba, and Bizjothjah, Baalah, and Iim, and Azem, and Eltolad, and Chesil, and Hormah, and Ziklag, and Madmannah, and Sansannah, and Lebaoth, and Shilhim, and Ain, and Rimmon: all the cities are twenty and nine, with their villages: and in the valley, Eshtaol, and Zoreah, and Ashnah, and Zanoah, and En-gannim, Tappuah, and Enam, Jarmuth, and Adullam, Socoh, and Azekah, and Sharaim, and Adithaim, and Gederah, and Gederothaim; fourteen cities with their villages: Zenan, and Hadashah, and Migdal-gad, and Dilean, and Mizpeh, and Joktheel, Lachish, and Bozkath, and Eglon, and Cabbon, and Lahmam, and Kithlish, and Gederoth, Beth-dagon, and Naamah, and Makkedah; sixteen cities with their villages: Libnah, and Ether, and Ashan, And Jiphtah, and Ashnah, and Nezib, and Keilah, and Achzib, and Mareshah; nine cities with their villages: Ekron, with her towns and her villages: from Ekron even unto the sea, all that lay near Ashdod, with their villages: Ashdod with her towns and her villages, Gaza

> with her towns and her villages, unto the river of Egypt, and the great sea, and the border thereof: and in the mountains, Shamir, and Jattir, and Socoh, and Dannah, and Kirjath-sannah, which is Debir, and Anab, and Eshtemoh, and Anim, and Goshen, and Holon, and Giloh; eleven cities with their villages: Arab, and Dumah, and Eshean, and Janum, and Beth-tappuah, and Aphekah, and Humtah, and Kirjath-arba, which is Hebron, and Zior; nine cities with their villages: Maon, Carmel, and Ziph, and Juttah, and Jezreel, and Jokdeam, and Zanoah, Cain, Gibeah, and Timnah; ten cities with their villages: Halhul, Beth-zur, and Gedor, and Maarath, and Beth-anoth, and Eltekon; six cities with their villages: Kirjath-baal, which is Kirjath-jearim, and Rabbah; two cities with their villages: in the wilderness, Beth-arabah, Middin, and Secacah, and Nibshan, and the city of Salt, and En-gedi; six cities with their villages. As for the Jebusites the inhabitants of Jerusalem, the children of Judah could not drive them out: but the Jebusites dwell with the children of Judah at Jerusalem unto this day (Josh. 15:20–63).

The first of the special cases that had to be decided during the land distribution had been pretty straightforward and simple. Caleb had been promised a specific region, and Joshua needed to be sure he received what had been promised.

Claim of the Daughters of Zelophehad

The narrative continues with an admittedly dull but historically important description of the territories allotted the tribes descended from Joseph. Joshua 16 describes the land assigned to Ephraim, and 17:1–13 describes that given to Manasseh.

> And the lot of the children of Joseph fell from Jordan by Jericho, unto the water of Jericho on the east, to the wilderness that goeth up from Jericho throughout mount Beth-el, and goeth out from Beth-el to Luz, and passeth along unto the borders of Archi to Ataroth, and goeth down westward to the coast of Japhleti, unto the coast of Beth-horon the nether, and to Gezer: and the goings out thereof are at the sea. So the children of Joseph, Manasseh and Ephraim, took their inheritance. And the border of the children of Ephraim according to their families was thus: even the border of their inheritance on the east side was Ataroth-addar, unto Beth-horon the upper; and the border went out toward the sea to Michmethah on the north side; and the border went about eastward unto Taanath-shiloh, and passed by it on the east to Janohah; and it went down from Janohah to Ataroth, and to Naarath, and came to Jericho, and went out at Jordan. The border went out from Tappuah westward unto the river Kanah; and the goings out thereof were at the sea. This

> is the inheritance of the tribe of the children of Ephraim by their families. And the separate cities for the children of Ephraim were among the inheritance of the children of Manasseh, all the cities with their villages. And they drave not out the Canaanites that dwelt in Gezer: but the Canaanites dwell among the Ephraimites unto this day, and serve under tribute.
>
> There was also a lot for the tribe of Manasseh; for he was the firstborn of Joseph; to wit, for Machir the firstborn of Manasseh, the father of Gilead: because he was a man of war, therefore he had Gilead and Bashan. There was also a lot for the rest of the children of Manasseh by their families; for the children of Abiezer, and for the children of Helek, and for the children of Asriel, and for the children of Shechem, and for the children of Hepher, and for the children of Shemida: these were the male children of Manasseh the son of Joseph by their families. But Zelophehad, the son of Hepher, the son of Gilead, the son of Machir, the son of Manasseh, had no sons, but daughters: and these are the names of his daughters, Mahlah, and Noah, Hoglah, Milcah, and Tirzah. And they came near before Eleazar the priest, and before Joshua the son of Nun, and before the princes, saying, The Lord commanded Moses to give us an inheritance among our brethren. Therefore according to the commandment of the Lord he gave them an inheritance among the brethren of their father. And there fell ten portions to Manasseh, beside the land of Gilead and Bashan, which were on the other side Jordan; because the daughters of Manasseh had an inheritance among his sons: and the rest of Manasseh's sons had the land of Gilead. And the coast of Manasseh was from Asher to Michmethah, that lieth before Shechem; and the border went along on the right hand unto the inhabitants of En-tappuah. Now Manasseh had the land of Tappuah: but Tappuah on the border of Manasseh belonged to the children of Ephraim; and the coast descended unto the river Kanah, southward of the river: these cities of Ephraim are among the cities of Manasseh: the coast of Manasseh also was on the north side of the river, and the outgoings of it were at the sea: southward it was Ephraim's, and northward it was Manasseh's, and the sea is his border; and they met together in Asher on the north, and in Issachar on the east. And Manasseh had in Issachar and in Asher Beth-shean and her towns, and Ibleam and her towns, and the inhabitants of Dor and her towns, and the inhabitants of En-dor and her towns, and the inhabitants of Taanach and her towns, and the inhabitants of Megiddo and her towns, even three countries. Yet the children of Manasseh could not drive out the inhabitants of those cities; but the Canaanites would dwell in that land. Yet it came to pass, when the children of Israel were waxen strong, that they put the Canaanites to tribute; but did not utterly drive them out (Josh. 16:1–17:13).

It is worth noting that while Ephraim dominated the Canaanites, they failed to drive them out of Gezer, keeping them under tribute (16:10). Also, Manasseh failed initially to even subdue the Canaanites in several cities. We aren't told how long it took for them to become strong enough to "put the Canaanites to tribute" (14:12–13), but it seems to have taken a while.

The Basis of Their Claim

In the middle of all of this, Joshua was presented with another special request (17:3–4). Zelophehad, a descendent of Manasseh, had five daughters but no sons. Typically, an estate would be distributed to firstborn sons. Since the land distribution was described as a disbursement of an inheritance, the daughters of Zelophehad filed a claim requesting that their father's estate be assigned to them. Like Caleb, they made their claim publicly, in the presence of Eleazar the high priest, Joshua, and the leaders of the other tribes ("the princes").[87] Also like Caleb, they had biblical authority for their claim.

> Then came the daughters of Zelophehad, the son of Hepher, the son of Gilead, the son of Machir, the son of Manasseh, of the families of Manasseh the son of Joseph: and these are the names of his daughters; Mahlah, Noah, and Hoglah, and Milcah, and Tirzah. And they stood before Moses, and before Eleazar the priest, and before the princes and all the congregation, by the door of the tabernacle of the congregation, saying, Our father died in the wilderness, and he was not in the company of them that gathered themselves together against the Lord in the company of Korah; but died in his own sin, and had no sons. Why should the name of our father be done away from among his family, because he hath no son? Give unto us therefore a possession among the brethren of our father. And Moses brought their cause before the Lord. And the Lord spake unto Moses, saying, The daughters of Zelophehad speak right: thou shalt surely give them a possession of an inheritance among their father's brethren; and thou shalt cause the inheritance of their father to pass unto them (Num. 27:1–7).

This claim had originally been presented to Moses just weeks before Moses' death and Israel's entrance into Canaan. But seven years of combat had intervened, and the daughters of Zelophehad reminded the leaders of the promise that had been made to them. The basis of their case rested on three facts: 1) Their father had no sons. 2) Their father had died in the wilderness, and the daughters would receive nothing if his portion were not allotted to them. 3) Their father had not participated in the rebellion of Korah but had "died in his own sin," that is, for his own unbelief in the promise like all others of his generation (except Joshua and Caleb). Moses didn't render his decision hastily or lightly but took the matter before the Lord for guidance. The Lord's instruction was clear: the daughters of Zelophehad were right, and they should receive their father's inheritance (Num. 27:7).

---

[87] It is worth noting that in the four places that Eleazar and Joshua are both mentioned (14:1; 17:4; 19:51; 21:1), Eleazar is always mentioned first. Apparently, his role as high priest was seen as a higher station than Joshua's role as military commander.

The Importance of the Ruling

As important as this decision was for these women, the ruling was even more important to Israel's law. In giving Moses his instructions, the Lord decreed that this was a legal precedent regarding the bequest of an estate.

> And thou shalt speak unto the children of Israel, saying, If a man die, and have no son, then ye shall cause his inheritance to pass unto his daughter. And if he have no daughter, then ye shall give his inheritance unto his brethren. And if he have no brethren, then ye shall give his inheritance unto his father's brethren. And if his father have no brethren, then ye shall give his inheritance unto his kinsman that is next to him of his family, and he shall possess it: and it shall be unto the children of Israel a statute of judgment, as the Lord commanded Moses (Num. 27:8–11).

Passing Zelophehad's as-yet-unclaimed estate on to his daughters in the absence of a son wasn't an *exception* to the rule. It was the *law*. A later passage added a stipulation to the inheritance law, with particular application to the clause allowing daughters to inherit.

> So shall not the inheritance of the children of Israel remove from tribe to tribe: for every one of the children of Israel shall keep himself to the inheritance of the tribe of his fathers. And every daughter, that possesseth an inheritance in any tribe of the children of Israel, shall be wife unto one of the family of the tribe of her father, that the children of Israel may enjoy every man the inheritance of his fathers. Neither shall the inheritance remove from one tribe to another tribe; but every one of the tribes of the children of Israel shall keep himself to his own inheritance. Even as the Lord commanded Moses, so did the daughters of Zelophehad: For Mahlah, Tirzah, and Hoglah, and Milcah, and Noah, the daughters of Zelophehad, were married unto their father's brothers' sons: and they were married into the families of the sons of Manasseh the son of Joseph, and their inheritance remained in the tribe of the family of their father (Num. 36:7–12).

For the land assignments to be perpetual, the land had to stay within the tribe. That is not a problem when a son inherits. If he were to marry a girl from another tribe, she would take on his tribal identity and their children would remain in the father's tribe. But if a *daughter* who inherited were to marry a man from another tribe, their children would identify with their *father's* tribe, and the land she had brought to the marriage would pass from her tribe to the tribe of her husband. Therefore, the law required that *if a daughter were to inherit, she would have to marry within her own tribe.* The Bible actually names all five daughters of Zelophehad in each context in which they are discussed so that we know that the five women who filed the claim did, in fact, conform to all the legal requirements.

This provides an interesting and important glimpse into the workings of the society of Israel, but its greatest significance may be to help establish the legitimacy of Jesus Christ's claim to be the rightful heir to the throne of David. Skeptics have often pointed out discrepancies in the genealogies of Jesus provided in Matthew 1:1–16 and in Luke 3:23–38. The genealogies are the same from Abraham to David, but Matthew traces Jesus' lineage through David's son Solomon while Luke traces it through Nathan, another of David's sons.

Since I believe absolutely in the inerrancy of Scripture, I assume that neither Matthew nor Luke is mistaken. But how can the divergent genealogies be harmonized? Several suggestions have been made. For instance, Matthew might present the *legal* line while Luke presents the *actual* line. Or there may have been a levirate marriage at one or more points in the line of descent, in which a widow married the brother of her husband and raised a son in her first husband's name. However, I think the more likely solution is found in the form of presentation of the two lists. Matthew lists from father to son while Luke lists from son to father. It is this suggestion that is relevant to the law of inheritance established in Numbers and invoked in Joshua.

As he moves forward in time, Matthew connects the names in his list using the word *gennao*, meaning "begat" or "fathered." This is a specific and unambiguous word that indicates that the name that follows descended directly from the preceding name. It is possible to use the word and skip generations, as in a grandfather "begetting" a grandson without mentioning the intervening generation, but it always indicated direct descent. Therefore, the genealogy of Jesus presented by Matthew clearly ties Joseph, Jesus' "adopted father," to the line of David by descent through Solomon.

But by moving backward through time, Luke uses a different construction and a different word, *huios*, meaning "son." This word is less mechanical in that it doesn't necessarily require direct descent but is more relational, indicating one's standing within a family. The word indicates legal status and could be used to indicate an adopted son, as Jesus' relationship with Joseph might have been. It could also be used for a daughter's husband, since there doesn't seem to have been any specific designation for a "son-in-law." In the same way that the husbands of Zelophehad's daughters could exercise all the legal rights of "sons" of Zelophehad, Joseph could have been begotten by Jacob (Matt. 1:16) and also be the "son" of Heli if Mary were Heli's daughter.

Since Mary and Joseph both had to go to Bethlehem to register (Luke 2:1–5), and they were not yet married, we assume that they were both descended from David. It is possible, then, that Luke provides *Mary's* genealogy and Matthew provides *Joseph's*. If this analysis is correct, then Matthew's genealogy proves Jesus' right to the throne by *adoption*, and Luke's proves Jesus' right to the throne by *birth*, and the importance of the legal foundation for inheritance that was established by the claim of Zelophehad's daughters becomes evident.

Possession vs. Coexistence

In the allotment of land to Judah, Ephraim, and Manasseh described in the passages we've been considering, we've seen that most of the Canaanite inhabitants of the territory were destroyed but some were conquered and put under tribute (Josh. 15:63; 16:9–10; 17:12). Allowing the Canaanites to remain in the land demonstrated disobedience because God had commanded Israel to destroy them and to possess their cities and lands. The tribes worked hard, fought long, and made a lot of progress toward full obedience. But they got tired, became complacent, and eventually decided that they'd gone far enough.

We even see evidence of selfishness and greed. Apparently, these tribes began to doubt the wisdom of destroying such a potentially valuable labor resource. Deciding it would be "wasteful" to destroy the enemies, they made them "serve under tribute" (16:10). They rationalized their disobedience on the ground of potential economic gain.

Sound familiar? President Bill Clinton ran his entire reelection campaign in 1996 on the slogan "It's the economy, stupid." Defending his manifest wickedness and manifold character flaws as irrelevant, he succeeded in convincing a plurality of Americans, including a host of professing Christians, that *economic advantage* was more important than *righteousness*. We would do well to remember that *every time a person compromises biblical principles for financial gain, he is guilty of the same disobedience as the tribes of Israel who tolerated the Canaanite presence in exchange for tribute money.*

Besides, the formula doesn't work. Disobedience will not ultimately prove to be advantageous. Israel never seems to have realized that they would have acquired more land had they obeyed. It is tempting for Christians today to think we have succeeded because we've come a long way for Christ. We can identify things that have changed in our lives: good things we now do and bad things we no longer do. But we must not become complacent in our spiritual attainments. The battle isn't over until "this corruptible shall have put on incorruption" and "death is swallowed up in victory" (1 Cor. 15:54). There are always more things that should change or that need to be strengthened.

> Brethren, I count not myself to have apprehended: but this one thing I do, forgetting those things which are behind, and reaching forth unto those things which are before, I press toward the mark for the prize of the high calling of God in Christ Jesus (Phil. 3:13–14).

25
Final Issues in Taking Possession

Joshua 17:14–19:51

Did you grow up with siblings near your own age? I'm the oldest of six children, with my only brother being two years younger than I. Since he was almost six and I was just short of my eighth birthday when the first of our four sisters was born, many of my childhood memories include just the two of us. One of the things I remember our parents trying to teach us was how to share. Some disputes were easier to solve than others.

For instance, when dinner was over and Mom brought in dessert, you might be surprised to know that sometimes my brother and I argued over who got which serving. I didn't see what the fuss was all about. I was older and bigger, so it seemed perfectly reasonable that I should get the bigger piece. I was mystified that this didn't seem fair to my brother. Eventually, our parents hit on a solution: one of us would cut the pieces and the other would get first choice. This method guaranteed that the one cutting did everything in his power to make the slices even. Occasionally Mom even let us use a ruler. Cutting equal sized servings was easy if we were having Jell-o—we didn't argue much over Jell-o, anyway. It wasn't too difficult if it were cake. Apple pie was a problem. The filling tended to ooze out the sides making it really hard to tell which piece was bigger—and Mom wouldn't let us use a scale.

While this method eliminated most of the arguing over dessert, it didn't solve the real problem. The very fact that we thought we had to be so careful in the division lest the other gain an advantage merely illustrated the depth of our infantile selfishness. But such displays of self-interest aren't limited to children fighting over who is allotted the larger piece of cake. Sometimes adults complain about their "lot" in life.

Dissatisfaction of Ephraim and Manasseh

In Joshua 16:1–17:13, we saw a description of the territory allotted to Ephraim and Manasseh, the two tribes of Joseph. In 17:14 we discover that they weren't satisfied with what they'd been given.

> And the children of Joseph spake unto Joshua, saying, Why hast thou given me but one lot and one portion to inherit, seeing I am a great people, forasmuch as the Lord hath blessed me hitherto? And Joshua answered them, If thou be a great people, then get thee up to the wood country, and cut down for thyself there in the land of the Perizzites and of the giants, if mount Ephraim be too narrow for thee. And the children of Joseph said, The hill is not enough for us: and all the Canaanites that dwell in the land of the valley have chariots of iron, both they who are of Beth-shean and her towns, and they who are of the valley of Jezreel. And Joshua spake unto the house of Joseph, even to Ephraim and to Manasseh, saying, Thou art a great people, and hast great power: thou shalt not have one lot only: but the mountain shall be thine; for it is a wood, and thou shalt cut it down: and the outgoings of it shall be thine: for thou shalt drive out the Canaanites, though they have iron chariots, and though they be strong (Josh. 17:14–18).

Their Request

Ephraim and Manasseh complained that they should have inherited more than "one lot and one portion" on the ground that they were a "great," or "numerous," people. The most up-to-date census figures for the tribes of Israel are found in Numbers 26. About seven years before this complaint was made, the population of adult men in Ephraim was 32,500 (26:37) and the adult men in Manasseh numbered 52,700 (26:34).

That may sound like a lot, until you realize that Manasseh ranked as only the sixth largest tribe, and the only tribe in Israel *smaller* than Ephraim was Simeon with 22,200 (26:14). The populations of the tribes, ranked from largest to smallest, were as follows:

1. Judah	76,500	Num. 26:22
2. Dan	64,400	Num. 26:43
3. Issachar	64,300	Num. 26:25

4. Zebulun	60,500	Num. 26:27
5. Asher	53,400	Num. 26:47
6. Manasseh	52,700	Num. 26:34
7. Benjamin	45,600	Num. 26:41
8. Naphtali	45,400	Num. 26:50
9. Reuben	43,730	Num. 26:7
10. Gad	40,500	Num. 26:18
11. Ephraim	32,500	Num. 26:37
12. Simeon	22,200	Num. 26:14

Furthermore, the only tribe to receive as much territory as Ephraim and Manasseh was Judah (and Simeon's allotment ends up being carved from Judah's). It seems that the complaint of Ephraim and Manasseh was based more on their opinion than on reality. When the patriarch Jacob gave his blessing to the sons of Joseph, he exalted Ephraim over his older brother Manasseh, saying that they would both "be great" but that Manasseh's "younger brother shall be greater than he" (Gen. 48:19). Their protest concerning their land allotment was couched in language of practicality—we are so numerous that we need more space than we've been given. But I suspect their real motive was otherwise. Being next-to-last on the population roster hardly qualifies as an excuse for needing extra land because they were so numerous. Examining their request in light of the real numbers, and considering the way Joshua responded to them, I believe three character flaws are revealed.

There is at least a hint of *pride* in their claim to more land on the basis of their greatness (Josh. 17:14). Prior to Moses, the great hero of Israel was Joseph, who had been instrumental in saving the family of their forefathers by providing for them in Egypt. Joseph's greatness was acknowledged by God in assigning to him two tribes, named after his sons. It may be that their desire for more land was based on their assumption of preeminence as descendents of Joseph. Besides, Joshua himself was an Ephraimite. Shouldn't the tribe of Israel's leader get some special consideration?

Their claim also implies *covetousness*. They seem to be asking for more than their share, despite the fact that they were already getting individual portions as the double tribe of Joseph. None of the other tribal forefathers got extra territory.

Joshua's diplomatic response to the claim of Ephraim and Manasseh was to tell them that if they were such a great people they should have no trouble taking additional territory. The wood country that he tells them they could have in addition to that already assigned was the land bordering the estate they had been given. That land was still unconquered and unallotted. It is important to see that Joshua didn't give them additional *conquered* territory that might have been allotted to another tribe. He gave them permission to expand their borders by conquest, which is precisely what God expected all Israel to do until they had possession of all the land He had given them.

Ephraim and Manasseh's response to Joshua reveals the third character flaw: *fear*. They were afraid of the Canaanites who lived there because they had iron chariots (actually made of wood with some iron plating and points). They wanted more *conquered* land. Taking new land would be too hard. Their protest had been filed on the claim that they needed more land because they were so *numerous*. Now they say they can't take the additional land by force because they are too *weak*.

Joshua's Reply

With subtle irony, Joshua replied to them in words that reflected the inconsistency of their argument, saying, "You are a *great* people, and are very *strong*." He added that they could have more than their original allotment. They would take the mountain that they thought was insufficient and then drive out the Canaanites in the valley even though they had iron chariots and were very strong. *Joshua's words were both a rebuke and an encouragement*: a rebuke in that they claimed the right to more land because they were so great but then feared to take extra land because they were too weak; an encouragement in that he assured them that they would successfully conquer the border lands. He didn't say it would be easy. He just said to do it.

How often we find ourselves making similar complaints to God! "He got something I didn't get; it's not fair! God never did that for me!" or "The enemy is too strong for me. I'm just too weak. Why didn't God make me stronger?" Give it a rest. The essence of covetousness is being dissatisfied with what God has given you. There is a fine line between complacency and contentment. Joshua's answer to Ephraim and Manasseh illustrates the necessary balance. Be content with what you've been given, and trust God to give you the ability to acquire and hold what you need. That attitude encourages continual effort and discourages dissatisfaction with the outcome. *We must always be content with what God is doing in our lives* (Phil. 4:11–12), but *we must never stop striving to expand our spiritual holdings* (Phil. 4:13; cf. 2:14).

Moving the Tabernacle to Shiloh

Having sent Ephraim and Manasseh to occupy their territory, Joshua's next recorded act was moving the tabernacle from its place in Gilgal, where it had stood since Israel crossed Jordan about seven years before, to Shiloh.

> And the whole congregation of the children of Israel assembled together at Shiloh, and set up the tabernacle of the congregation there. And the land was subdued before them (Josh. 18:1).

Shiloh was located within the territory recently assigned to Ephraim. The statement that "the land was subdued before them" indicates that Ephraim had successfully begun settlement of their territory by the time this move was made. Opinions differ on whether this move was sanctioned by God or Joshua moved the tabernacle to his tribal inheritance on his own initiative.

Disregarding God's Instructions?

Some writers accuse Joshua of moving the tabernacle, the focal point of Israel's worship, as *an act of expedience without God's blessing.* That is a possible interpretation. Four reasons are given to support this view. First, God had appointed Gilgal as the place for the tabernacle when Israel entered Canaan, and there is nothing in the text that indicates that God authorized moving it. Second, Gilgal was especially significant to Israel's identification with God because they renewed the covenant and became participants in it by performing the rite of circumcision there. Third, centuries later the prophets Elijah and Elisha seem to have made Gilgal their headquarters (2 Kings 2:1; 4:38), and the ancient site of Gilgal may have been the place where John the Baptist taught and baptized (Matt. 3:1–6). Finally, because the passage immediately preceding this verse describes the whining of Ephraim and Manasseh and the passage following it describes the failure of seven tribes to have "received their inheritance," some suggest that the placement of this verse in the context of Joshua implies its connection to failure.

Permitted but Not Authorized by God?

Other writers concede that Joshua may have moved the tabernacle out of expediency but that the move was at least blessed by God, if not necessarily authorized. These point out that Gilgal had been a good place to leave the tabernacle during the conquest because it was easily protected in the southeast corner of Canaan, but now that the land had been subdued it had become a difficult location. Shiloh was centrally located and would give easier access to all of the tribes once the land was settled. The fact that Joshua was the leader and Shiloh was in the territory allotted to his tribe made moving the tabernacle there practical. Further, the fact that the tabernacle stayed in Shiloh for several generations spanning 350 years or more, including the time of great spiritual revival under Samuel, implies that God was not displeased with the move. Even if moving the tabernacle had not been specifically directed by God, He seems to have blessed Israel through their worship at the new location.

Obedient to an Unrecorded Command?

It is also quite possible that *Joshua moved the tabernacle in obedience to a command of God that is simply not recorded.* Joshua had learned over the years to seek God's direction before making potentially momentous decisions, and moving the tabernacle would certainly qualify as important. Since its construction, the only time the tabernacle had been moved was when the visible representation of God in the column of fire and smoke moved. While there is no biblical evidence that God still manifested Himself visibly over the tabernacle once Israel crossed Jordan, it seems unlikely that God would have blessed the relocation of the tabernacle if it were done without His approval. The strongest support for this view comes from the mouth of God through the prophet Jeremiah, nearly 1000 years after this move was made.

> But go ye now unto **my place** which was **in Shiloh, where I set my name at the first,** and see what I did to it for the wickedness of my people Israel (Jer. 7:12).

God calls Shiloh "my place" and says it was the place "where I set my name at the first." I prefer to give Joshua the benefit of the doubt—and this verse leaves little room for doubt. I have no idea why he didn't record God's instruction to move the tabernacle to Shiloh, but if he had done it on his own initiative it seems likely that God would have called Shiloh the place where *Joshua* set His name, not the place "where **I** set my name." Actually, transferring the tabernacle from Gilgal to Shiloh symbolized Israel's complete domination of Canaan. In Gilgal, the sanctuary had been at the edge of the land. But in Shiloh it was in the heart of it.

Seven Tribes Still Unsettled

Some time must have passed since the end of Joshua 17, but how much time had elapsed between assigning the land to Ephraim and Manasseh and this move to Shiloh isn't indicated. It was long enough for Ephraim to have taken control of the region. But it must not have been too much time because we now see that seven other tribes "had not yet received their inheritance" (18:2). It had been long enough that Joshua expresses some frustration over the fact that those tribes had been "slack to go to possess the land" (18:3).

> And there remained among the children of Israel seven tribes, which had not yet received their inheritance. And Joshua said unto the children of Israel, How long are ye slack to go to possess the land, which the Lord God of your fathers hath given you? Give out from among you three men for each tribe: and I will send them, and they shall rise, and go through the land, and describe it according to the inheritance of them; and they shall come again to me. And they shall divide it into seven parts: Judah shall abide in their coast on the south, and the house of Joseph shall abide in their coasts on the north. Ye shall therefore describe the land into seven parts, and bring the description hither to me, that I may cast lots for you here before the Lord our God. But the Levites have no part among you; for the priesthood of the Lord is their inheritance: and Gad, and Reuben, and half the tribe of Manasseh, have received their inheritance beyond Jordan on the east, which Moses the servant of the Lord gave them. And the men arose, and went away: and Joshua charged them that went to describe the land, saying, Go and walk through the land, and describe it, and come again to me, that I may here cast lots for you before the Lord in Shiloh. And the men went and passed through the land, and described it by cities into seven parts in a book, and came again to Joshua to the host at Shiloh. And Joshua cast lots for them in Shiloh before the Lord: and there Joshua divided the land unto the children of Israel according to their divisions (Josh. 18:2–10).

Overcoming Complacency

Seven tribes were still camped in Gilgal. There is no evidence that they had asked for their portion or that they had made any move to stake a claim. They didn't seem very concerned about the situation. The implication is that *they were satisfied with less than total victory*, willing to stay together in the security of Gilgal rather than striking out on their own to possess the land. This is the opposite attitude of that expressed by Ephraim and Manasseh, and just as wrong. While those two tribes were not satisfied with *all* they had been given, these seven were perfectly content to take *nothing* they had been given. Joshua had rebuked the former for their greed, and he rebuked the latter for their indifference and indolence.

Perhaps in part because of the complaints of Ephraim and Manasseh, Joshua announced a new method for dividing the rest of the land. Each of the remaining tribes was to select three representatives to report to Joshua. Joshua would then send them throughout the land to "describe it" (18:4); that is, they were to survey the land and draw maps showing topography and boundaries. They were to divide it into seven plots (18:6), suitable for disbursement, and bring the written descriptions of the territories to Joshua, who would cast lots to determine which tribe got which parcel (18:7). The tribe of Levi was to get none of these properties. They would be taken care of later (Josh. 21).

Getting Busy

The tribes did as they were told, and their representatives surveyed the land. They brought a written record "in a book" (18:9) in which the remaining land of Canaan had been divided into seven specific territories. And Joshua cast lots "in Shiloh before the Lord" (18:10) to determine the inheritance of each tribe.

> And the lot of the tribe of the children of Benjamin came up according to their families: and the coast of their lot came forth between the children of Judah and the children of Joseph. And their border on the north side was from Jordan; and the border went up to the side of Jericho on the north side, and went up through the mountains westward; and the goings out thereof were at the wilderness of Beth-aven. And the border went over from thence toward Luz, to the side of Luz, which is Beth-el, southward; and the border descended to Ataroth-adar, near the hill that lieth on the south side of the nether Beth-horon. And the border was drawn thence, and compassed the corner of the sea southward, from the hill that lieth before Beth-horon southward; and the goings out thereof were at Kirjath-baal, which is Kirjath-jearim, a city of the children of Judah: this was the west quarter. And the south quarter was from the end of Kirjath-jearim, and the border went out on the west, and went out to the well of waters of Nephtoah: and the border came down to the end of the mountain that lieth before the valley of the son of Hinnom, and which is in the valley of the giants on the north, and descended to the valley of Hinnom, to the side of Jebusi on the south, and descended to En-rogel, and was drawn from the north, and went forth to En-shemesh, and went forth toward Geliloth, which is over against the going up of Adummim, and descended to the stone of Bohan the son of Reuben, and passed along toward the side over against Arabah northward, and went down unto Arabah: and the border passed along to the side of Beth-hoglah northward: and the outgoings of the border were at the north bay of the salt sea at the south end of Jordan: this was the south coast. And Jordan was the border of it on the east side. This was the inheritance of the children of Benjamin, by the coasts thereof round about, according to their families. Now the cities of the tribe of the children of Benjamin according to their families were Jericho, and Beth-hoglah, and the valley of Keziz, and Beth-arabah, and Zemaraim, and Beth-el, and Avim, and Parah, and Ophrah, and Chephar-haammonai, and Ophni, and Gaba; twelve cities with their villages: Gibeon, and Ramah, and Beeroth, and Mizpeh, and Chephirah, and Mozah, and Rekem, and Irpeel, and Taralah, and Zelah, Eleph, and Jebusi, which is Jerusalem, Gibeath, and Kirjath; fourteen cities with their

villages. This is the inheritance of the children of Benjamin according to their families.

And the second lot came forth to Simeon, even for the tribe of the children of Simeon according to their families: and their inheritance was within the inheritance of the children of Judah. And they had in their inheritance Beer-sheba, and Sheba, and Moladah, and Hazar-shual, and Balah, and Azem, and Eltolad, and Bethul, and Hormah, and Ziklag, and Beth-marcaboth, and Hazar-susah, and Beth-lebaoth, and Sharuhen; thirteen cities and their villages: Ain, Remmon, and Ether, and Ashan; four cities and their villages: and all the villages that were round about these cities to Baalath-beer, Ramath of the south. This is the inheritance of the tribe of the children of Simeon according to their families. Out of the portion of the children of Judah was the inheritance of the children of Simeon: for the part of the children of Judah was too much for them: therefore the children of Simeon had their inheritance within the inheritance of them. And the third lot came up for the children of Zebulun according to their families: and the border of their inheritance was unto Sarid: and their border went up toward the sea, and Maralah, and reached to Dabbasheth, and reached to the river that is before Jokneam; and turned from Sarid eastward toward the sunrising unto the border of Chisloth-tabor, and then goeth out to Daberath, and goeth up to Japhia, and from thence passeth on along on the east to Gittah-hepher, to Ittah-kazin, and goeth out to Remmon-methoar to Neah; and the border compasseth it on the north side to Hannathon: and the outgoings thereof are in the valley of Jiphthah-el: and Kattath, and Nahallal, and Shimron, and Idalah, and Beth-lehem: twelve cities with their villages. This is the inheritance of the children of Zebulun according to their families, these cities with their villages. And the fourth lot came out to Issachar, for the children of Issachar according to their families. And their border was toward Jezreel, and Chesulloth, and Shunem, and Haphraim, and Shihon, and Anaharath, and Rabbith, and Kishion, and Abez, and Remeth, and En-gannim, and En-haddah, and Beth-pazzez; and the coast reacheth to Tabor, and Shahazimah, and Beth-shemesh; and the outgoings of their border were at Jordan: sixteen cities with their villages. This is the inheritance of the tribe of the children of Issachar according to their families, the cities and their villages. And the fifth lot came out for the tribe of the children of Asher according to their families. And their border was Helkath, and Hali, and Beten, and Achshaph, and Alammelech, and Amad, and Misheal; and reacheth to Carmel westward, and to Shihor-libnath; and turneth toward the sunrising to Beth-dagon, and reacheth to Zebulun, and to the valley of Jiphthah-el toward the north side of Beth-emek, and Neiel, and goeth out to Cabul on the left hand, and Hebron, and Rehob, and Hammon, and Kanah, even unto great Zidon; and then the coast turneth to Ramah, and to the strong city Tyre; and the coast turneth to Hosah; and the outgoings thereof are at the sea from the coast to Achzib: Ummah also, and Aphek, and Rehob: twenty and two cities with their villages. This is the inheritance of the tribe of the children of Asher according to their families, these cities with their villages. The sixth lot came out to the children of Naphtali, even for the children of Naphtali according to

> their families. And their coast was from Heleph, from Allon to Zaanannim, and Adami, Nekeb, and Jabneel, unto Lakum; and the outgoings thereof were at Jordan: and then the coast turneth westward to Aznoth-tabor, and goeth out from thence to Hukkok, and reacheth to Zebulun on the south side, and reacheth to Asher on the west side, and to Judah upon Jordan toward the sunrising. And the fenced cities are Ziddim, Zer, and Hammath, Rakkath, and Chinnereth, and Adamah, and Ramah, and Hazor, and Kedesh, and Edrei, and En-hazor, and Iron, and Migdal-el, Horem, and Beth-anath, and Beth-shemesh; nineteen cities with their villages. This is the inheritance of the tribe of the children of Naphtali according to their families, the cities and their villages. And the seventh lot came out for the tribe of the children of Dan according to their families. And the coast of their inheritance was Zorah, and Eshtaol, and Ir-shemesh, and Shaalabbin, and Ajalon, and Jethlah, and Elon, and Thimnathah, and Ekron, and Eltekeh, and Gibbethon, and Baalath, and Jehud, and Bene-berak, and Gath-rimmon, and Me-jarkon, and Rakkon, with the border before Japho. And the coast of the children of Dan went out too little for them: therefore the children of Dan went up to fight against Leshem, and took it, and smote it with the edge of the sword, and possessed it, and dwelt therein, and called Leshem, Dan, after the name of Dan their father. This is the inheritance of the tribe of the children of Dan according to their families, these cities with their villages (Josh. 18:2–19:48).

There are a couple of statements within this passage worth noting. In Joshua 19:9 note that *Judah's inheritance was more than they needed*, so Simeon's territory was carved out of that which had originally been allotted to Judah. This is interesting for two reasons. Judah was the largest of all the tribes, nearly as large as Manasseh and Ephraim combined, and they had received about the same amount of territory given to Ephraim, yet Judah was willing to give up part of their inheritance for the sake of Simeon, the smallest of the tribes. What a contrast to the spirit of Ephraim and Manasseh! It may be that Judah was naturally inclined to generosity—after all, they were the ones who took in Rahab—but having witnessed Joshua's response to Ephraim and Manasseh's request for additional land may have encouraged them to selflessness.

That Simeon would be living within the borders of Judah will become historically important. Eventually, Simeon will lose its tribal identity and be absorbed into the other tribes. Jacob's deathbed prophecies said of Simeon and Levi, "I will divide them in Jacob, and scatter them in Israel" (Gen. 49:7). The prophecy will be fulfilled for Levi in Joshua 21, as cities within each tribe's territory will be allotted to them. The prophecy will be fulfilled for Simeon in a different way, but it will still be literally fulfilled. That assimilation seems to have been complete by the time of Ahab because Beersheba, here assigned to Simeon, is identified as belonging to Judah in 1 Kings 19:3.

Another footnote in this land distribution passage comes from Joshua 19:47. In this case, the territory assigned to the tribe of Dan proved to be too little for them.[88] So what did they do? They did what Joshua had told the other tribes to do: they went out and conquered more land that had been unassigned, traveling to the far northern edge of Palestine to do so. However, their attitude and actions in the taking of additional territory were less than honorable, as the account of Dan's conquest of Leshem (Laish), recorded in Judges 18, reveals.

A Portion for Joshua

All the tribes have been sent to settle their land, and the text has sketched their taking of the parcels. All that remains for Joshua to do is to assign Levi cities within the tribal territories, which we'll consider in the next chapter. At this point, we finally see Joshua given a home.

> When they had made an end of dividing the land for inheritance by their coasts, the children of Israel gave an inheritance to Joshua the son of Nun among them: according to the word of the Lord they gave him the city which he asked, even Timnath-serah in mount Ephraim: and he built the city, and dwelt therein. These are the inheritances, which Eleazar the priest, and Joshua the son of Nun, and the heads of the fathers of the tribes of the children of Israel, divided for an inheritance by lot in Shiloh before the Lord, at the door of the tabernacle of the congregation. So they made an end of dividing the country (Josh. 19:49–51).

Joshua was given territory in Mount Ephraim, among the people from his own tribe. *Ephraim* means "where I shall be doubly fruitful" (Gen. 41:52). Expanding on that idea, Joshua called his estate *Timnath-serah*, which means "my abundant portion." Even in the naming of his property, Joshua wanted Israel to know that he was *blessed* of God and *satisfied* with what he had been given. Unlike the seven tribes who had needed encouragement to move out of Gilgal, Joshua wasn't satisfied with mediocrity. Unlike his brethren in Ephraim and Manasseh who had been afraid they couldn't defeat the Canaanites, Joshua was unafraid to conquer his own territory. And he must have successfully taken it because "he built the city, and dwelt therein" (19:50).

---

[88] The Hebrew of this passage has been taken by some to mean simply that Dan extended their borders far from their original allotment. However, the reading in the KJV is probably accurate since the original allotment was quite small. Further support for the reading is found in the LXX. See Lias, p. 284.

Even in this event, we see the humility of this great man of God. Other than the Levites, whose cities couldn't be assigned until the tribes began settling their territories, *Joshua was the last in Israel to claim his inheritance*. If anyone in the nation had a right to first choice, it was Joshua. The distribution of land would have been an opportunity for personal enrichment almost without historical parallel, but Joshua steadfastly resisted any temptation to abuse his power. He never used his fame or position to enrich himself and never sought preferential treatment on the basis of his personal exploits.

Many a lesser man would have at least tried to manipulate the results of the lots cast by the high priest. Some would even have tried to overthrow the results and make their own decisions. Israel's later history is replete with examples of kings who usurped the office of the priesthood or defied the messages of prophecy. Even David, the greatest of Israel's kings, would temporarily succumb to the seduction of power. But Joshua, never glorying in his own success, remained humble. He was never so impressed with who he was that he forgot *Whose* he was. The lesson for our own lives is self-evident.

Applying the Principles

There are many situations to which the lessons of this passage apply. Many people are like Ephraim and Manasseh—discontented with their "lot" in life. The list of things for which we can envy others is virtually endless. We all know people who have nicer homes, drive fancier cars, make more money, enjoy better health, have greater opportunity for travel, have more friends, or enjoy greater respect than we do. The problem is not so much in the differences in our situations but in how we respond to those differences. Do we complain that we didn't get enough? Do we complain that the work is too hard? Or do we do our best and trust the Lord?

Others are like the seven unsettled tribes, who would rather stay in Gilgal than venture out into new territory. Our "comfort zones" are called that for a reason. Moving beyond the familiar can be frightening, but that is part of the definition of growth. Most of us still have spiritual territory to be surveyed and possessed, and spiritual battles to be fought and won.

Finally, Joshua provides an example for people in almost any setting. He uses his command authority for the benefit of the nation in general and Israelites in particular rather than for his own benefit. Abuse of power occurs whenever someone in authority is driven by self-interest. It manifests itself in many forms, including emotional manipulation, financial tyranny, intimidation, seduction, or simple dishonesty. It can be found in the home, the school, the workplace, and the church. Contrary to the opinions of the self-esteem gurus of our day, there is no excuse for a Christian who seeks his own good above the good of others. Our problem is not that we don't like ourselves. We love ourselves entirely too much. Paul warns "every man that is among you, not to think of himself more highly than he ought to think" (Rom. 12:3). Elaborating on that theme in his letter to the church at Philippi, Paul points to an example of selflessness even greater than Joshua—Jesus Christ, Who set aside the glories of heaven to become a man and go to the cross to die for you and for me.

> Let nothing be done through strife or vainglory; but in lowliness of mind let each esteem other better than themselves. Look not every man on his own things, but every man also on the things of others. Let this mind be in you, which was also in Christ Jesus: who, being in the form of God, thought it not robbery to be equal with God: but made himself of no reputation, and took upon him the form of a servant, and was made in the likeness of men: and being found in fashion as a man, he humbled himself, and became obedient unto death, even the death of the cross (Phil. 2:3–8).

26
The Cities of Refuge

Joshua 20:1–9

War teaches many lessons. We've learned a lot from the US-led war to remove Saddam Hussein from leadership in Iraq. One of the more unexpected lessons of that war, at least for most of the American public, is just how difficult rebuilding a political system can be. I'm convinced that many folks expected the military to sweep through Iraq, remove the Baathist regime, and say to the Iraqis, "There you go—you have your country back. We expect you to have a new government up and running in a few days."

It hasn't worked that way. The immediate response of the Iraqis to the collapse of Saddam's command structure was not organized establishment of a new system of civil law. The immediate response was celebration in the streets that quickly turned to looting. It required a strong military presence to prevent disintegration into anarchy. Aside from the need to repair the physical damage to buildings, roads, bridges and such, it has taken years just to get a new government organized. *Removing* a regime has proven to be much easier than *replacing* one.

For Joshua and Israel, the task of establishing a nation in a newly conquered territory must have been gargantuan. In some ways, the *conquest* was the easy part. *Distribution* and *settlement* had their issues but had gone pretty smoothly. From that point on, *administration* would be a constant challenge, but ancient Israel had an enormous advantage over modern Iraq. They had the Law of God recorded by Moses to guide them in their civil and religious lives. They also had a God-appointed leader and a unified commitment to follow God's Word.

The first item of administrative business, after the parceling out of the land, was the establishment of a framework for enforcing civil law. Different crimes had different prescribed punishments. A common guideline, called the law of retribution (*lex talionis*), set limits for those punishments. It was generally stated as "An eye for an eye; a tooth for a tooth" (Matt. 5:38). That is not to say that an injury that resulted in the loss of an eye *required* taking an eye from the one who caused the injury. Rather, *it set the limit* for the loss of an eye to the taking of an eye. You couldn't take the life of someone who blinded you in one eye, and you couldn't take a limb from someone who knocked out your tooth. The Law of Moses also had many particular penalties for specific crimes. Those penalties included payment of money as fines or compensation or being sold into slavery until the criminal had worked off the value of his debt. A criminal might also be sent into exile or even executed by stoning, depending on the nature of the crime.

There were several offenses for which a criminal could receive the death penalty. These included murder, rape, and adultery, but they also included defiling the Sabbath and persistently disobeying one's parents. And there are people today who consider a spanking abusive. Israel didn't have professional executioners whose job was taking the lives of those guilty of capital crimes. Instead, in some cases an interesting provision of the law required the most immediate surviving victim of the crime to be the executioner. This was generally the person who brought the charges against the one who committed the crime. In the case of rape, the girl or her father (or husband) would "cast the first stone." In the case of adultery, the spouses of the ones involved were the primary executioners. In the case of a stubbornly rebellious child, the parents were responsible for carrying out the sentence. In murder cases, the victim's next of kin was the executioner.[89] The person who was to act as the executioner was called "the avenger of blood." Keep that in mind as you read God's instructions to Joshua.

> The Lord also spake unto Joshua, saying, Speak to the children of Israel, saying, Appoint out for you cities of refuge, whereof I spake unto you by the hand of Moses: that the slayer that killeth any person unawares and unwittingly may flee thither: and they shall be your refuge from the avenger of blood. And when he that doth flee unto one of those cities shall stand at the entering of the gate of the city, and shall declare his cause in the ears of the elders of that city, they shall take him into the city unto them, and give him a place, that he may dwell among them. And if the avenger of blood pursue after him, then they shall not deliver the slayer up into his hand; because he smote his neighbour unwittingly, and hated him not beforetime. And he shall dwell in that city, until he stand before the congregation for judgment, and until the

[89] In other cases, such as Sabbath violation, tribal representatives and/or priests carried out the sentence.

> death of the high priest that shall be in those days: then shall the slayer return, and come unto his own city, and unto his own house, unto the city from whence he fled. And they appointed Kedesh in Galilee in mount Naphtali, and Shechem in mount Ephraim, and Kirjath-arba, which is Hebron, in the mountain of Judah. And on the other side Jordan by Jericho eastward, they assigned Bezer in the wilderness upon the plain out of the tribe of Reuben, and Ramoth in Gilead out of the tribe of Gad, and Golan in Bashan out of the tribe of Manasseh. These were the cities appointed for all the children of Israel, and for the stranger that sojourneth among them, that whosoever killeth any person at unawares might flee thither, and not die by the hand of the avenger of blood, until he stood before the congregation (Josh. 20:1–9).

Administering Justice

The enforcement of Israel's legal code was carried out on the basis of two underlying principles: 1) The guilty are not to be cleared, and 2) the innocent are not to be punished.

A Means for Protecting the Innocent

The cities of refuge were established in order to handle the most difficult and important legal cases—murder/manslaughter. As God had communicated through Moses (see Num. 35:6ff.), Joshua was to designate particular cities as centers for hearing those cases. These cities would provide a haven for the fugitive perpetrator until his case could be heard. Israel's conquest and occupation of Canaan had now progressed to the point that the Lord told Joshua it was time to organize the network of cities for refuge.

These cities would be an important part of Israel's law enforcement. A person guilty of taking the life of another "unawares" or "unwittingly" (Josh. 20:3) was to hurry to any of these cities and report to officials there. Joshua wasn't giving instructions on how to investigate a murder to find the killer. He assumes that the person reporting to the city of refuge had in fact caused someone's death. Obviously, if he were not responsible for the other person's death, there would be no point in turning himself in, and the stipulations of the city of refuge would not apply.

The cities had no central courthouse. A place at the gate of the city was designated for public hearings and administration of justice as well as conducting other business important to the city. The fugitive was to report to that place at the gate of the city and tell the city elders his version of what had happened.

He was promised their protection until his case was heard and properly investigated. It is understood that the avenger of blood would also appear before the appropriate officials to offer his own version of the events.

An important provision in this procedure was that each case required thorough investigation and an independent trial. Since the fugitive had confessed to having taken a life, the investigation focused on the *motive* to determine whether the crime was "manslaughter" or "murder." To convict a person of murder required the testimony of two or more witnesses. As this text indicates, these witnesses were not necessarily eye-witnesses to the crime. They were *character* witnesses to the attitude of the perpetrator toward the victim. They were to testify to whether the perpetrator "hated him . . . beforetime" (Josh. 20:5)—what American jurisprudence calls "malice aforethought." A fugitive found guilty of having taken the life of a man he hated was presumed to be guilty of intentional murder. This connection between hatred and murder wasn't *introduced* in the New Testament (1 John 3:15). It was *foundational* to the very definition of murder in the Old Testament law.

A Means for Punishing the Guilty

The penalty for murder was death. God established the death penalty for murder on the basis of man's being created in God's image—"Whoso sheddeth man's blood, by man shall his blood be shed: *for in the image of God made he man*" (Gen. 9:6). Murder is a crime ultimately directed against God. God has declared that anyone who maliciously kills another person has attempted to smite God Himself. For that, the killer must die. That basic provision of the law was commanded of Noah when he and his family exited the ark. Even following the Fall of man and the destruction of the Flood, man was still God's image-bearer. After the Flood man was given orders to protect human life by executing the murderer. Genesis 9:5 makes it clear that animals were not exempt—an animal that killed a man was to be destroyed.

The fact that this legal mandate predates the Mosaic Law and is independent of it is important. *Capital punishment for murder wasn't limited to the Israelite culture—it is binding on all humanity.* This wasn't a Jewish regulation on the same level as being forbidden to eat pork. It is a universal mandate. People today who say that executing a murderer *is* murder have completely missed the point. Executing a criminal is not the same thing as murder. *Murder* assumes both the innocence of the victim and the selfish motive of the killer. That is why taking a life in self-defense isn't a crime—the "victim" isn't innocent. It is also why taking a life accidentally isn't "murder"—the killer didn't act selfishly. By contrast, *executing a murderer presumes the guilt of the "victim" and the justifiable motive of the executioner.*

Such an execution is justifiable on three grounds. First, taking the life of a murderer is acting in *corporate self-defense*—society defending itself collectively from a person who poses a real threat to individual lives. Second, taking the life of a murderer is acting as the *designated agent of God's justice*—a responsibility specifically delegated by God to mankind (Gen. 9:6; Rom. 13:3–4). Finally, taking the life of a murderer is acting in *defense of the image of God*—showing the value of God's image in man by defending it to the death. When we refuse to execute the murderer, we disobey the direct command of God and we actually deny and devalue the sanctity of human life.

The sacrificial system of Israel included various offerings that could be made as atonement for ("to cover over") one's sins.[90] That is, when sins were confessed and appropriate reparations made, the offering of the sacrifice would reestablish fellowship within the civil/religious community and was symbolic of reestablished fellowship with God. But there was no atoning sacrifice prescribed for the murderer. The penalty for the crime was to be carried out without being mitigated by repentance or sorrow expressed by the guilty. Please understand that I didn't say that a murderer can't be forgiven by God. The distinction isn't between those sins that could be forgiven and those that couldn't. It is between those sins that could be resolved so that the sinner could be restored to fellowship in the community and a sin that permitted no restoration to fellowship. The sacrifices of the Old Testament *never* accomplished the *forgiveness* of sin (Heb. 10:4). They merely covered sins until the death of Christ could remove them (Rom. 3:25). Forgiveness has *always* been on the basis of faith (Eph. 2:8–9; cf. Rom. 4:3; Gal. 3:6; James 2:23).

Murder trials could be held in any of six cities that Israel designated (Josh. 20:7–8). The purpose of a trial was to be sure that a murderer wasn't allowed to live. The purpose of the cities of refuge was to be sure that a person who took a life unintentionally would be spared. An underlying legal principle was that the accused was considered innocent until proven guilty—as in our own system of justice (unless, I suppose, we are talking about the IRS). By the time God's law was delivered to Moses, there had been other cultures that had developed legal codes; the best known of those is the Code of Hammurabi. But one of the provisions unique to the Mosaic Law is the command to examine the motive. According to the Law of Moses, the burden of proof lay on the accuser. That is, the person who charged another with murder had to present

[90] This topic deserves much more attention than I can give it here. It is important to understand that the Old Testament "atonement" was a temporary covering of sins, needing regular sacrifices according to God's instructions. The blood of the animals did not remove sin; it covered them until Christ came to fulfill the sacrificial system with His own incorruptible blood, removing "the sins that are past" (Rom. 3:25) that had been covered by the obedient faith of the Old Testament saints (Heb. 10:11–14).

credible evidence of malicious intent from independent witnesses. Accusers did not have to prove premeditation, only enmity. They did not have to prove intent to kill, only intent to harm (Num. 35:15–25). It was assumed that if you "in enmity smite him with his hand, that he die" (Num. 35:21), you were guilty of murder. If there were no evidence of enmity of any kind (jealousy, anger, greed, hatred), then the death would be considered accidental and the claim of the avenger of blood was denied.

Glorifying God

By providing a haven for those guilty of unintentional manslaughter, the cities of refuge served as an illustration of God's character. We see *God's accessibility*. In accordance to God's instructions, they were scattered throughout the land in order to be readily accessible to everyone (Deut. 19:2–3; Num. 35:13–14). There were three of them on either side of the Jordan River. The cities were to offer shelter to those of Hebrew descent ("all the children of Israel") and the Gentiles among them ("the stranger that sojourneth among them") without discrimination. Israel was to establish and maintain a well-marked road to each city to help the fugitive find his way as he fled (Deut. 19:3). The fugitive was to be allowed to enter the city and enjoy its protection on the basis of his own testimony at the gate, pending the outcome of the formal investigation and trial.

We also see *man's accountability*. Even in the case of unintentional manslaughter there was a measure of responsibility for the carelessness that caused the loss of life. You might be cutting wood with your friend and have the head of your axe fly off and hit your friend in the head, killing him. You wouldn't be guilty of murder—he was a friend, not a man you hated. You're still responsible for failing to properly maintain your axe to avoid such an accident. You wouldn't be executed for murder, but your freedom would be restricted. You would have to leave your home and family (tribe) to live in the city of refuge. The text doesn't actually say so, but it is generally assumed that your immediate family could join you there. However, since the duration of your stay in the city could be brief or could be decades, what would your family do with any property they were leaving behind? How would they support themselves in the city of refuge? It might have been possible for your family to join you, but there would be issues to resolve. Once you were admitted to the city as a refugee, you forfeited the city's protection if you ever left—the avenger of blood could take your life.

We see *God's grace*. The refugee could leave the city only on pain of death, but his sentence ended at the death of the high priest. Have you ever wondered why God tied the length of a sentence to the life of the high priest? I think part of the answer is in seeing that his death was such a national tragedy that all lesser considerations were to be put aside. The death of the high priest was a call to national mourning. His death also signaled the release of all refugees, which is a cause for celebration. Our Great High Priest is Jesus Christ. His death on the cross was cause for mourning, but it also signaled the release of prisoners—sinners like you and me. In ancient Israel the death of the high priest *set aside* the claim of the avenger of blood. Christ's death for your forgiveness ought to make you glad to honor requests for forgiveness from those who wrong you. In a sense, the death of the high priest prefigures the propitiating death of Christ, our great High Priest (Heb. 9:23-28). While the high priest's death "satisfied" the claim of the avenger of blood in the immediate temporal realm, the death of Christ satisfies the wrath of God eternally and permanently releases the believer from the consequences of his sin. This is not because God decides to ignore sin but because *his debt has been paid*. That is great news! Since your debt has been paid, you don't have to be afraid that God will change His mind and make you pay the debt again. That is exactly what Paul meant when he said,

> Who shall lay anything to the charge of God's elect? It is God that justifieth. Who is he that condemneth? It is Christ that died, yea rather, that is risen again, who is even at the right hand of God, who also maketh intercession for us (Rom. 8:33–34).

I've found that if I spend some time each day just thinking about this truth it is much easier to cope with difficulties or disappointments.

Picturing Salvation

Israel often placed special significance to names of people and places. The names of the cities of refuge are an example of this. The six cities were Kadesh, Shechem, Hebron, Bezer, Ramoth, and Golan. *Kadesh* means "holy" or "set apart," signifying the special function of the cities that were set apart by God for this service to His people. *Shechem* means "shoulder," implying strength, safety, or security. Even in our language today, we speak of finding comfort in a "shoulder to cry on." *Hebron* means "fellowship," signifying the gracious provision of fellowship with God given to the undeserving sinner. *Bezer* means "a fortified place," calling to mind the protection offered by the city.

Nahum uses this word to describe God—"The Lord is good, a strong hold (*bezer*) in the day of trouble, and he knoweth them that trust in him" (Nah. 1:7; see also Ps. 41:2). *Ramoth* means "height" or "exaltation," pointing toward the exalted status of Christ and our exaltation with Him by His grace (Rom. 8:17). Finally, *Golan* means "exultation" or "joy," symbolizing the joy found in the forgiveness of sins when we abandon ourselves to Christ for our salvation.

In the existence and purpose of the cities of refuge we see several parallels to our salvation in Christ. The *cities were appointed* by God just as Christ was appointed to be our Savior (Heb. 3:1–2; 1 John 4:10). The *cities provided shelter* or refuge from the avenger just as Christ provides protection for the believer from the just wrath of God (Isa. 53:5–6; Rom. 5:8–9). The *cities were each located on a high place*, so they were readily visible from a distance and easy to find. Christ has been highly exalted to draw men to Himself (Phil. 2:9; John 12:34). The *ways to the cities were limited but plainly marked* just as the only way to salvation is clearly marked in Christ (John 14:4–6; Acts 4:12). *Access to the cities was easy*, just as one's salvation is "easy" in that it cannot be earned by works (Acts 16:31; Eph. 2:8–9). *Protection in the cities was available to all* without discrimination, just as Christ is available to all who will come to Him (John 6:37; Rom. 10:13; Rev. 22:17). *The death of the high priest provided full and final pardon* for the crime of manslaughter, and as we've already seen, the death of Christ our High Priest was necessary for our full and final pardon (John 1:29; Heb. 10:12, 26).

Another important parallel between the cities of refuge and salvation is that once the fugitive found refuge within one of the cities, he found security by staying within that city. In Christ, our Refuge, we are secure as we abide in Him (John 10:28–29; Rom 8:33–39). The one guilty of manslaughter in ancient Israel had only three choices. One option would be to make excuses: "It was an accident; you shouldn't be so upset." "I'll go later when it is more convenient." "It is too much trouble to relocate, or too demanding, or takes too much commitment; I'll just take my chances." "If I really try to be good, do nice things for the avenger of blood, maybe the good I do will outweigh the bad and he'll forget about my offense." Another option would be to recognize the need to flee but assume that any city would do as long as one sincerely wanted protection.

Either of those two choices might sound good and seem reasonable, but both would be disastrous because neither provided real protection from the avenger of blood. The only option that would truly save the life of the manslayer was to actually go to the nearest city of refuge for shelter on God's terms, not his own, and take up permanent residence there.

If we learn nothing else from the cities of refuge, it is vital that we see that *sorrow for sin or recognizing the peril of death is not enough to save a sinner.* Simply acknowledging God's gracious provision of refuge in Christ will not save you from the wrath of God. The only way for you to be saved is for you to flee to Christ, casting yourself upon His mercy in gratitude for the sanctuary He alone can provide. The primary lesson of the cities of refuge is this: *To be saved, you must leave everything and come to Christ* (Luke 14:26; John 10:27; 12:26).

27
Demobilization

Joshua 21–22

Joshua's tasks as Israel's commander are nearly finished. Once again the Israelites must make a transition. Under Pharaoh, the people had been slaves. Under Moses they became a coalition of closely related nomadic tribes of herdsmen, fighting occasional battles especially toward the end of Moses' leadership. Under Joshua they've been an army of foot soldiers, becoming better equipped and more experienced as they progressed in the conquest of Canaan.

Now Israel would become a settled society. They would cultivate their own crops, tend their own flocks and herds, and conduct their own trade. They would live in houses instead of tents, and in cities and villages instead of military camps. Able-bodied men would still be part of a reservist militia, but Israel wouldn't maintain a standing army. With the demobilization of the national army, Israel was in many ways reverting to being simply a confederation of independent tribes. There was one dominant factor they had in common that would be vital to keep them unified—their worship of the one true God.

The Levitical Cities

Joshua had overseen the distribution of the land of Canaan among the tribes of Israel, but the needs of one group still had to be addressed. Before Joshua could be confident that he had fulfilled all the work the Lord had given him, he had to provide an inheritance for the tribe of Levi.

> Then came near the heads of the fathers of the Levites unto Eleazar the priest, and unto Joshua the son of Nun, and unto the heads of the fathers of the tribes of the children of Israel; and they spake unto them at Shiloh in the land of Canaan, saying, The Lord commanded by the hand of Moses to give us cities to dwell in, with the suburbs thereof for our cattle. And the children of Israel gave unto the Levites out of their inheritance, at the commandment of the Lord, these cities and their suburbs. And the lot came out for the families of the Kohathites: and the children of Aaron the priest, which were of the Levites, had by lot out of the tribe of Judah, and out of the tribe of Simeon, and out of the tribe of Benjamin, thirteen cities. And the rest of the children of Kohath had by lot out of the families of the tribe of Ephraim, and out of the tribe of Dan, and out of the half tribe of Manasseh, ten cities. And the children of Gershon had by lot out of the families of the tribe of Issachar, and out of the tribe of Asher, and out of the tribe of Naphtali, and out of the half tribe of Manasseh in Bashan, thirteen cities. The children of Merari by their families had out of the tribe of Reuben, and out of the tribe of Gad, and out of the tribe of Zebulun, twelve cities. And the children of Israel gave by lot unto the Levites these cities with their suburbs, as the Lord commanded by the hand of Moses. And they gave out of the tribe of the children of Judah, and out of the tribe of the children of Simeon, these cities which are here mentioned by name, which the children of Aaron, being of the families of the Kohathites, who were of the children of Levi, had: for theirs was the first lot. And they gave them the city of Arba the father of Anak, which city is Hebron, in the hill country of Judah, with the suburbs thereof round about it. But the fields of the city, and the villages thereof, gave they to Caleb the son of Jephunneh for his possession. Thus they gave to the children of Aaron the priest Hebron with her suburbs, to be a city of refuge for the slayer; and Libnah with her suburbs, and Jattir with her suburbs, and Eshtemoa with her suburbs, and Holon with her suburbs, and Debir with her suburbs, and Ain with her suburbs, and Juttah with her suburbs, and Beth-shemesh with her suburbs; nine cities out of those two tribes. And out of the tribe of Benjamin, Gibeon with her suburbs, Geba with her suburbs, Anathoth with her suburbs, and Almon with her suburbs; four cities. All the cities of the children of Aaron, the priests, were thirteen cities with their suburbs. And the families of the children of Kohath, the Levites which remained of the children of Kohath, even they had the cities of their lot out of the tribe of Ephraim. For they gave them Shechem with her suburbs in mount Ephraim, to be a city of refuge for the slayer; and Gezer with her suburbs, and Kibzaim with her suburbs, and Beth-horon with her suburbs; four cities. And out of the tribe of Dan, Eltekeh with her suburbs, Gibbethon with her suburbs, Aijalon with her suburbs, Gath-rimmon with her suburbs; four cities. And out of the half tribe of Manasseh, Tanach with her suburbs, and Gathrimmon with her suburbs; two cities. All the cities were ten with their suburbs for the families of the children of Kohath that remained. And

> unto the children of Gershon, of the families of the Levites, out of the other half tribe of Manasseh they gave Golan in Bashan with her suburbs, to be a city of refuge for the slayer; and Beesh-terah with her suburbs; two cities. And out of the tribe of Issachar, Kishon with her suburbs, Dabareh with her suburbs, Jarmuth with her suburbs, En-gannim with her suburbs; four cities. And out of the tribe of Asher, Mishal with her suburbs, Abdon with her suburbs, Helkath with her suburbs, and Rehob with her suburbs; four cities. And out of the tribe of Naphtali, Kedesh in Galilee with her suburbs, to be a city of refuge for the slayer; and Hammoth-dor with her suburbs, and Kartan with her suburbs; three cities. All the cities of the Gershonites according to their families were thirteen cities with their suburbs. And unto the families of the children of Merari, the rest of the Levites, out of the tribe of Zebulun, Jokneam with her suburbs, and Kartah with her suburbs, Dimnah with her suburbs, Nahalal with her suburbs; four cities. And out of the tribe of Reuben, Bezer with her suburbs, and Jahazah with her suburbs, Kedemoth with her suburbs, and Mephaath with her suburbs; four cities. And out of the tribe of Gad, Ramoth in Gilead with her suburbs, to be a city of refuge for the slayer; and Mahanaim with her suburbs, Heshbon with her suburbs, Jazer with her suburbs; four cities in all. So all the cities for the children of Merari by their families, which were remaining of the families of the Levites, were by their lot twelve cities. All the cities of the Levites within the possession of the children of Israel were forty and eight cities with their suburbs. These cities were every one with their suburbs round about them: thus were all these cities (Josh. 21:1–42).

Their Provision

Representatives of the tribe of Levi came to Joshua and Eleazar the high priest to ask them to appoint cities for their tribe. They claimed the right to these cities on the basis of the promise of God through Moses in Numbers 35:2–5. The rest of the tribes understood that they were obligated to provide these cities because of the direct command of God. It was important to God that Israel provide for Levi. It was also important that Levi not be gathered in a single location but scattered among their countrymen.

The dispersion of Levi throughout Israel had actually been prophesied by Jacob. On his deathbed he made pronouncements concerning his sons. In those prophetic statements, he addressed Simeon and Levi together, saying, "Simeon and Levi are brethren; instruments of cruelty are in their habitations. . . . I will divide them in Jacob and scatter them in Israel" (Gen. 49:5, 7).

Jacob's description of Simeon and Levi as cruel and murderous is generally understood to be a reference to their deception and murder of the men of Shechem in response to the rape of their sister Dinah (Gen. 34). That may or may not have been all he meant. I'm inclined to think there was more to this than merely reminding them of their ruthlessness in avenging their sister's honor. Jacob also warned his other sons against participating in "their secret," spoke of their murder of "a man" (singular), and mentioned the destruction caused by their "self-will" (Gen. 49:6).

Jacob may have been accusing Simeon and Levi of being the instigators of the plot to murder their brother Joseph (Gen. 37:18–20). There are subtle indications in the later confrontation between the exalted Joseph and his brothers in Egypt that Joseph was aware of the discussion among his brothers while he was in the pit awaiting the outcome of their plotting. Reuben had planned to rescue him but was unavailable at the critical moment. Judah negotiated his sale rather than his murder, effectively saving his life—even if for a profit. If Reuben, the firstborn of Jacob, and Judah, the fourth born, were not arguing for his murder, who was? Simeon and Levi were second born and third born. Years later, after his exaltation, a time came when Joseph sent the brothers home to prove themselves by fetching Benjamin. Whom did he keep in prison as hostage? Simeon (Gen. 42:24). And Jacob was at first willing to sacrifice Simeon rather than risk Benjamin on a following expedition (Gen. 42:36), leaving Simeon in prison in Egypt until they were once again desperate for provisions. These hints imply that Simeon may have been the instigator of the murderous plot. Jacob's linking of Levi with him implies Levi's complicity.

It is interesting that the shared prophecy of Simeon and Levi should be fulfilled so differently for each tribe. The tribe of Simeon is given its own territory but is later subsumed into the other tribes, particularly Judah, losing its tribal identity—precisely what the prophecy of Jacob seemed to indicate would happen. But the tribe of Levi is given an exalted status and appointed as religious servant-leaders of all Israel.[91] Why the difference? Levi's status in Israel changed in Exodus 32. When Moses returned from Mount Sinai with the tablets of the law, he found Israel debauched and worshiping a golden calf. "Then Moses stood in the gate of the camp, and said, Who is on the Lord's side? let him come unto me. And all the sons of Levi gathered themselves together unto him" (Exod. 32:26). In Israel's shame and idolatry, only Levi stood with Moses. In Numbers 3:6–13 God commissioned Levi to stand in the place of the firstborn of Israel, especially consecrated to God.

Their Purpose

Joshua's designation of the levitical cities was further confirmation that Levi was a special tribe. They were set apart—sanctified—to serve God and Israel.

[91] If nothing else, this should teach us to approach unfulfilled prophecies with a healthy dose of humility. We can rarely anticipate precisely how prophecy will be fulfilled until after the fact.

While they would be permitted to keep flocks as their own property and for their own maintenance, Israel was to provide for them. The principle that those in "full-time ministry" are to be supported by those they serve was not new in Paul's epistles (Phil. 4:15–17; 1 Tim. 5:17–18). It has always been a part of God's program.

The cities of the Levites would also provide a vital link, or more accurately a network of interlocking parts, that would produce the cohesion necessary for Israel to think and act as a unit rather than as cooperating, or potentially competing, tribal groups. A total of forty-eight cities were designated. Most tribes contributed four cities, but only three came from Naphtali. The additional city came from the combined territories of Judah and Simeon, who contributed a total of nine (all of which were originally allotted to Judah.)[92] The result was that Israel was guaranteed that the Levites would be present throughout their territories on both sides of the Jordan River. While this should have produced a people unified in their worship, Israel's subsequent history demonstrates otherwise. Ancient Israel was just as prone to confusion of priorities and corruption of worship as is the church today.

Honoring Promises

The assignment of the Levitical cities was the last step in Joshua's establishing of Israel in the land Canaan. In the verses that follow, we have Joshua's record of the promises that had been honored over the course of the years of military activity.

> And the Lord gave unto Israel all the land which he sware to give unto their fathers; and they possessed it, and dwelt therein. And the Lord gave them rest round about, according to all that he sware unto their fathers: and there stood not a man of all their enemies before them; the Lord delivered all their enemies into their hand. There failed not ought of any good thing which the Lord had spoken unto the house of Israel; all came to pass.
>
> Then Joshua called the Reubenites, and the Gadites, and the half tribe of Manasseh, and said unto them, Ye have kept all that Moses the servant of the

---

[92] The cities were not very evenly distributed throughout the land. They tended to be clustered along the frontier borders and in other "endangered areas." A further evidence of God's long-term providence is seen in the assigning of cities from Judah, Simeon, and Benjamin to the descendants of Aaron. The high priest would always come from this family, and their cities were all within a few miles of Jerusalem. Despite the fact that Jerusalem was still in Jebusite hands, God knew He would locate His temple there.

> Lord commanded you, and have obeyed my voice in all that I commanded you: Ye have not left your brethren these many days unto this day, but have kept the charge of the commandment of the Lord your God. And now the Lord your God hath given rest unto your brethren, as he promised them: therefore now return ye, and get you unto your tents, and unto the land of your possession, which Moses the servant of the Lord gave you on the other side Jordan. But take diligent heed to do the commandment and the law, which Moses the servant of the Lord charged you, to love the Lord your God, and to walk in all his ways, and to keep his commandments, and to cleave unto him, and to serve him with all your heart and with all your soul. So Joshua blessed them, and sent them away: and they went unto their tents. Now to the one half of the tribe of Manasseh Moses had given possession in Bashan: but unto the other half thereof gave Joshua among their brethren on this side Jordan westward. And when Joshua sent them away also unto their tents, then he blessed them, and he spake unto them, saying, Return with much riches unto your tents, and with very much cattle, with silver, and with gold, and with brass, and with iron, and with very much raiment: divide the spoil of your enemies with your brethren. And the children of Reuben and the children of Gad and the half tribe of Manasseh returned, and departed from the children of Israel out of Shiloh, which is in the land of Canaan, to go unto the country of Gilead, to the land of their possession, whereof they were possessed, according to the word of the Lord by the hand of Moses (Josh. 21:43–22:9).

The Promises of God

God had promised to give them the land, and He has done so. God had promised to drive their enemies out of the land, and He has done so. We know from subsequent history, as well as the text of Joshua itself, that pockets of resistance remained. Israel would have to stay alert and prepared in order to protect its territory, but open hostilities had ceased. They would still face challenges of obedience and faith, but the land was theirs. God had kept His word. "God had not promised the immediate and total destruction of the Canaanites, but only their gradual extermination (Exod. 23:30; Deut. 7:22)."[93]

I'm sure you can see the parallel to your Christian walk. Your salvation is secured by God, and you're brought into possession of eternal life by His grace alone. But your growth in obedience, your emulation of Christ, requires your active participation as the image of Christ is formed in you. God has kept His word by giving you the victory. You appropriate that victory by faithful obedience.

The Promise of Reuben, Gad, and Half of Manasseh

The second honored promise addressed by Joshua is the one made by the tribes who would receive their inheritance on the east side of the Jordan

[93] Keil and Delitzsch, p. 216.

River. They had promised to fight for their brothers (Josh. 1:12–15) before settling their land, and they had done so for seven long years. They served faithfully throughout the conquest. They had even waited patiently through the lengthy process of surveying the land and appointing the boundaries of the territory as it was divided among the other tribes. They were still prepared for battle while Joshua established the cities of refuge and selected the cities for the Levites. They didn't stand down and go home until Joshua gave the order.

Have you ever struggled and toiled and prayed for a long time, trying to wait patiently for the provision of God? Have you in the meantime seen others receiving the provision of God for which you've prayed while you still wait for God to move on your behalf? Are you tempted to be resentful of God's blessings for others and His delay in your regard? Take heart. Persevere in praying for others and serving your God. "Your labour is not in vain in the Lord" (1 Cor. 15:58). Remember and emulate the faithful patience of Reuben, Gad, and Manasseh. Keep your word to God. He never fails to keep His word to His children.

The Promise of Joshua

Joshua's words to these three tribes also indicate the fulfillment of a third promise that Joshua doesn't mention directly. Throughout our study, we've seen the personal humility of Joshua demonstrated by the way he acted and the way he recorded the events that occurred during his leadership. We see that again in the fact that this chapter doesn't specifically mention *Joshua's keeping his own promise*. He simply keeps his word. He dismisses Reuben, Gad, and Manasseh exactly as he had promised. They had done their duty. Joshua discharged them with his and all Israel's gratitude. They would remain a part of the reservist militia, but he released them from their immediate military responsibilities. And he didn't send them home empty-handed. They took animals, silver, gold, brass, iron, and clothing to share with their families. In the course of the conquest, the goods from the cities of the Canaanites had been divided among Israel, and these three tribes received their share.[94]

It is obvious that God gave His full approval to the settling of Reuben, Gad, and half of Manasseh on the east side of Jordan. Commentators often treat this as their having settled for less than God's "perfect will," but the text of Scripture doesn't support this. The fact that Israel's territory eventually shrank to include only the land between the Mediterranean and the western bank of

---

[94] It is possible that the command to "divide the spoil . . . with your brethren" was a reminder to "share the booty with those who had remained in Transjordan to guard the women, children, and elderly and to care for the livestock" (Madvig, p. 356).

the Jordan doesn't change the fact that God considered the mountains of Gilead the eastern boundary of Israel, not the Jordan River.

Before allowing Reuben, Gad, and Manasseh to go home, Joshua charged them with their spiritual obligations to God. He commanded them to *love the Lord*, to *walk in His ways*, to *keep* (safeguard as precious) *His commandments*, to *cling to Him*, and to *serve Him*. This fivefold challenge is the responsibility and aspiration of every believer today. These tribesmen didn't have to obey Joshua's command in order to *become* Israelites. They were to obey because they *were* Israelites. In the same way, we don't become Christians by doing; we *do* because of what we *are*.

The Memorial Altar

Reuben, Gad, and Manasseh headed back to see their families after at least seven years of separation. They took with them their share of the spoils of war. But Joshua records something they did before they were reunited with their families.

> And when they came unto the borders of Jordan, that are in the land of Canaan, the children of Reuben and the children of Gad and the half tribe of Manasseh built there an altar by Jordan, a great altar to see to (Josh. 22:10).

This act has been interpreted a couple of ways. Most commentators seem to agree with C. I. Scofield's[95] characterization of this as an act of religious apostasy, calling what they built a "schismatic" altar—an altar of division. In light of how the situation is eventually resolved, it seems to me that we shouldn't characterize it so negatively. Actually, the word rendered *altar* would have been better translated "monument" or "memorial." To the Jewish mind, the word *altar* implies a place of sacrifice. But as the narrative explains, that clearly wasn't the intended purpose of the structure.

An Immediate Problem

Regardless of their intent, the erection of this monument provoked an immediate reaction from the rest of Israel.

[95] Dr. C. I. Scofield makes little comment on this passage. His *Scofield Reference Bible* (Oxford, 1909, 1917) contains outline headings throughout the Bible, and his title for Joshua 22 reads, "The Schismatic altar of Reuben and Gad." He also provides marginal cross references to God's warning against building altars to other gods in Deuteronomy 13 and the apostasy that brought civil war in Judges 20, even though that event involved spiritual problems in a different tribe (Benjamin) at a different location (Gibeah).

> And the children of Israel heard say, Behold, the children of Reuben and the children of Gad and the half tribe of Manasseh have built an altar over against the land of Canaan, in the borders of Jordan, at the passage of the children of Israel. And when the children of Israel heard of it, the whole congregation of the children of Israel gathered themselves together at Shiloh, to go up to war against them (Josh. 22:11–12).

The other tribes of Israel were alarmed. They were afraid that Reuben, Gad, and Manasseh had an ulterior motive in moving to the east of Jordan—to set up a competing center of worship. God had told Israel that when they came into the land they should establish a memorial of God's blessing at Mount Ebal (Deut. 27:1–10), which they had done immediately after defeating Ai and Bethel (Josh. 8:30–35). The western tribes assumed that the new monument was intended as a substitute for the memorial altar on Mount Ebal, and they even feared that it might be intended as a substitute for the altar of sacrifice in the tabernacle at Shiloh.

A council meeting of the elders of Israel was called to Shiloh. The text actually indicates that the militia was called up and assembled in preparation to invade the eastern territory and engage the assumed apostates in armed combat. This was serious business. I find myself wondering if Christians today are so alert to the actions and attitudes of brethren that represent vulnerability to spiritual danger. Perhaps the general condition of Christianity in the world today would be more biblical if more of us were alert to the danger of compromise, however well-intentioned.

A Conciliatory Confrontation

It is vital to note that for all their readiness for war, they didn't actually launch an attack. They found safety in a multitude of counselors (cf. Prov. 11:14; 15:22; 24:6). The wise decision of the council was that Israel should be prepared to do battle if necessary, but they must first confront the eastern tribes. So they commissioned Phinehas, the son of Eleazar the high priest, to lead a delegation to meet with the leaders of Reuben, Gad, and Manasseh. When they arrived in Gilead on the east of the Jordan, they got right to the point:

> And the children of Israel sent unto the children of Reuben, and to the children of Gad, and to the half tribe of Manasseh, into the land of Gilead, Phinehas the son of Eleazar the priest, and with him ten princes, of each chief house a prince throughout all the tribes of Israel; and each one was an head of the house of their fathers among the thousands of Israel. And they came unto the children of Reuben, and to the children of Gad, and to the half tribe of Manasseh, unto the land of Gilead, and they spake with them, saying, Thus saith the whole congregation of the Lord, What trespass is this that ye have committed against the God of Israel, to turn away this day from following

> the Lord, in that ye have builded you an altar, that ye might rebel this day against the Lord? Is the iniquity of Peor too little for us, from which we are not cleansed until this day, although there was a plague in the congregation of the Lord, but that ye must turn away this day from following the Lord? and it will be, seeing ye rebel to day against the Lord, that to morrow he will be wroth with the whole congregation of Israel. Notwithstanding, if the land of your possession be unclean, then pass ye over unto the land of the possession of the Lord, wherein the Lord's tabernacle dwelleth, and take possession among us: but rebel not against the Lord, nor rebel against us, in building you an altar beside the altar of the Lord our God. Did not Achan the son of Zerah commit a trespass in the accursed thing, and wrath fell on all the congregation of Israel? and that man perished not alone in his iniquity (Josh. 23:13–20).

In his confrontation of Reuben, Gad, and Manasseh, Phinehas demonstrates the principle of Ephesians 4:15—"speaking the truth in love." It has been well said that *truth alone makes one too harsh, but love alone makes one too tolerant.* Phinehas told the tribal leaders that all Israel was deeply concerned, but he gave them an opportunity to explain themselves. Israel was not afraid that these tribes would forsake the Lord for other gods but that they would rebel against God by offering sacrifices on unapproved altars. Later, the great sin of Jeroboam was not idolatry but setting up rival altars with the intent of worshiping God (1 Kings 12:26–30). The principle at stake is our submission to God's right to tell us how He wants to be worshiped.

Phinehas's reference to the sin of Peor is significant. Peor was the place where Balaam tried to curse Israel (Num. 23:28), and it was the place where Israel got involved in idolatry and in sexual immorality with Moabite women (Num. 25:1–3). Phinehas had been the hero of that event, executing a flagrant sinner and stopping the plague God had sent sweeping through the camp (Num. 25:7–9) that claimed a total of 24,000 lives. Now Peor was one of the cities assigned to Reuben (Josh. 13:20) to which these tribes were returning.[96] Phinehas knew better than many that the danger of corruption was real.

But Phinehas didn't just make threats; he offered a solution. He suggested that if they thought that the Jordan was too great an obstacle to their participation in the worship of God in Shiloh, or if the temptations of their territory were too great, perhaps it would be best for them to "take possession among us" (22:19).

Think for a minute about how remarkable an offer that was. I am one of six children. The six of us have so far produced a total of twenty grandchildren with ages ranging from newborn to twenty-one years. Sometime during the

[96] Peor was also the place from which Moses delivered his farewell address to Israel (Deut. 3:29), where Moses died, and near where he was buried (Deut. 34:6).

Christmas holiday each year we all try to get together at our parents' home for a few days. We have a great time, but you can imagine how crowded and chaotic such a gathering can be. As happy as my parents are to have everybody come, I suspect that they are at least as glad when everybody *leaves*. The upheaval in the household caused by a *brief* visit is tolerable, even enjoyable. But if we were to move in *permanently* the consequences would be serious!

For the tribes of Reuben, Gad, and half of Manasseh to "take possession" among the other tribes would be more than just an inconvenience. There would be serious consequences. The entire western territory would have to be resurveyed and reallocated. There would be crowding of borders for all of the tribes. They would have to move the eastern tribes from the land that 70,000 of their men with all of their wives and children had inhabited for over seven years. The very making of such an offer demonstrated Israel's profound love for their brethren. They were ready to have their lives disrupted and their inheritance divided for the sake of their countrymen. Some of us may not find it too difficult to be so generous toward a friend or relative who has been a great blessing to us, but few among us would be so gracious to someone we believed to be seriously in the wrong, which is precisely what Israel thought of this situation.

A Temperate Reply

The reply of the leaders of the eastern tribes to the charge of infidelity was remarkably temperate. There is no indignant protest of outraged innocence. Instead, we sense their genuine chagrin that they had been so badly misunderstood.

> Then the children of Reuben and the children of Gad and the half tribe of Manasseh answered, and said unto the heads of the thousands of Israel, the Lord God of gods, the Lord God of gods, he knoweth, and Israel he shall know; if it be in rebellion, or if in transgression against the Lord, (save us not this day,) that we have built us an altar to turn from following the Lord, or if to offer thereon burnt offering or meat offering, or if to offer peace offerings thereon, let the Lord himself require it; and if we have not rather done it for fear of this thing, saying, In time to come your children might speak unto our children, saying, What have ye to do with the Lord God of Israel? For the Lord hath made Jordan a border between us and you, ye children of Reuben and children of Gad; ye have no part in the Lord: so shall your children make our children cease from fearing the Lord. Therefore we said, Let us now prepare to build us an altar, not for burnt offering, nor for sacrifice: but that it may be a witness between us, and you, and our generations after us, that we might do the service of the Lord before him with our burnt offerings, and with our sacrifices, and with our peace offerings; that your children may not say to our children in time to come, Ye have no part in the Lord. Therefore said we,

> that it shall be, when they should so say to us or to our generations in time to come, that we may say again, Behold the pattern of the altar of the Lord, which our fathers made, not for burnt offerings, nor for sacrifices; but it is a witness between us and you. God forbid that we should rebel against the Lord, and turn this day from following the Lord, to build an altar for burnt offerings, for meat offerings, or for sacrifices, beside the altar of the Lord our God that is before his tabernacle (Josh. 22:21–29).

Their defense begins with an appeal to God as their witness. Stating their appeal twice for emphasis, they include three distinct names for God in their statement: *El*, representing God in His power; *Elohim*, representing God in His triune nature; and *Yahweh* ("Jehovah"), representing God in His eternal nature as the Covenant God of Israel. This appeal represents a strong statement of these leaders' *faith in God* and their *fear of God*, which were important if they were to prove their faithfulness to Him.

They then explained the reason they built the monument. It was emphatically *not* intended as an act of rebellion (22:22) or for the offering of sacrifices (22:23). They built it because they were afraid that future generations of the western tribes might refuse to allow the children of the eastern tribes to worship with them on the ground of the boundary represented by the Jordan River. They wanted a monument on their side of the river as a replica of the monument on the west—the one in Gilgal, not the one on Mount Ebal—to illustrate and prove their essential unity.

Some commentators depart from the text of Joshua at this point and refer to 1 Chronicles 5:25–26. That passage records the future idolatry of the eastern tribes that resulted in their judgment by being overrun and deported by the Assyrians. The conclusion often drawn is that this altar led directly to that apostasy and that Reuben, Gad, and Manasseh would have been better off to have accepted Phinehas's offer and moved to the west of Jordan. But there is nothing in the narrative, either in Joshua or 1 Chronicles, to support such a conclusion. The truth is that the western tribes of Israel also became idolatrous and were judged by being overrun and deported by the Assyrians. It happened a little later because Samaria, the capital of the ten northern tribes on both sides of the river, withstood the Assyrian conquerors a little longer.

A Peaceful Resolution

What the text actually indicates is that *Phinehas was perfectly satisfied* with the eastern tribes' explanation of their actions.

> And when Phinehas the priest, and the princes of the congregation and heads of the thousands of Israel which were with him, heard the words that the children of Reuben and the children of Gad and the children of Manasseh

> spake, it pleased them. And Phinehas the son of Eleazar the priest said unto the children of Reuben, and to the children of Gad, and to the children of Manasseh, This day we perceive that the Lord is among us, because ye have not committed this trespass against the Lord: now ye have delivered the children of Israel out of the hand of the Lord. And Phinehas the son of Eleazar the priest, and the princes, returned from the children of Reuben, and from the children of Gad, out of the land of Gilead, unto the land of Canaan, to the children of Israel, and brought them word again. And the thing pleased the children of Israel; and the children of Israel blessed God, and did not intend to go up against them in battle, to destroy the land wherein the children of Reuben and Gad dwelt. And the children of Reuben and the children of Gad called the altar Ed: for it shall be a witness between us that the Lord is God (Josh. 22:30–34).

Phinehas said he was pleased with their answer. He praised the Lord for the fact that they were innocent of the charges of infidelity and apostasy. He even delivered the good news to the tribal leaders in Shiloh, who were ready to go to war, "And the thing pleased the children of Israel" (22:33). The KJV says the Transjordanian tribes named the altar *Ed*—italicized because it does not appear in the Hebrew text (Josh. 22:34). The word means "witness." The NIV reading of this verse is helpful—"And the Reubenites and the Gadites gave the altar this name: A Witness Between Us That the Lord Is God."[97] If the godly contemporaries of Reuben, Gad, and Manasseh were satisfied that this memorial did not represent "schism" in their midst, we should accept their evaluation. The commentator who concludes that Phinehas[98] and the rest of Israel got it wrong is guilty of twin errors: reading into the text what is not there and ignoring the plain meaning of what is in the text.

Applying the Principles

The primary lesson of this event is not that we should avoid doing anything that someone else might find questionable. While we should avoid intentionally provocative actions, anything we do can be misinterpreted by others. Neither is the primary lesson that we should be alert to the spiritual dangers

[97] For no apparent reason, there is no reference to the half of Manasseh in verse 34, even though they have been included among the Transjordanian tribes every other time they are mentioned. The LXX includes them but may reflect a scribal emendation rather than a different text tradition.

[98] It is worth noting that when Eleazar the high priest died, his son Phinehas took his place and served Israel well as high priest for twenty-four years (Josh. 24:33).

faced by our brethren. While we are not to tolerate sin in our midst, neither are we to jump to conclusions or rush to judgment.

This narrative illustrates how we should handle potential disagreements among us. When the eastern tribes did something the western tribes thought was sacrilege, the western tribes did *not* launch a campaign of public denouncement or immediately engage in battle. They investigated by sending a representative who was empowered to offer a solution that would be very costly to those who believed they were in the right. They went to a great deal of trouble to *avert* open hostility and to *reclaim* those they thought were wayward. When they heard the explanation, they rejoiced in the fact that they had been wrong. Churches that practice such loving confrontation in disciplinary situations demonstrate real godliness. When individual believers practice such humility in conflict, they may find great joy in restored relationships instead of the turmoil of severed ones. Phinehas was a true "peacemaker" (Matt. 5:19). He did not avoid confrontation, but he had a heart willing to be peaceable if possible.

28
Farewell at Shiloh

Joshua 23

Few would dispute that Roger Clemens is one of the greatest pitchers in the history of professional baseball. Having spent the last few years of his career pitching for the New York Yankees, he announced his retirement after the conclusion of the 2003 season.[99] On Wednesday, October 22, 2003, in what was to be his last Major League start, he pitched in game four of the World Series against the Florida Marlins. In an impromptu interview following the game, a reporter asked Roger why he had been so successful throughout his career. His reply was an interesting commentary on various attitudes of the players involved in his chosen profession. Roger explained that he didn't think he was personally remarkable; he just worked hard. He said that some pitchers are afraid to work, unwilling to keep trying to improve. Others are happy to make lots of money, relax, and enjoy being in the big leagues. Not many guys are willing to put the effort into seeing how good they can become and what kind of impact they can have on the game.

He was talking about baseball, but Roger might as well have been describing the people of God. Some are afraid to really get involved in doing the work of the Lord. Others are content to be saved, caring nothing for truly serving God. Few indeed are willing to apply themselves diligently to making an impact for God.

As Joshua sensed the approach of the end of his life, he wanted to challenge the people of Israel to apply themselves. For a top athlete to perform at his

---

[99] Clemens's "retirement" lasted just over six weeks, ending when he announced he was signing a contract to play at least one more year, this time for the Houston Astros.

best he has to keep training, doing the same things he had to do to get to the top. For Israel to enjoy the blessing of God in Canaan, they had to continue to obey the Lord who brought them out of Egypt into the Promised Land.

Calling the Council

The army of Israel had been demobilized, the tribes had settled their lands, the levitical cities had been established, and civil war had been averted. The nation of Israel was taking root.

It was time for Joshua to call the leadership of Israel to gather for a council meeting.

> And it came to pass a long time after that the Lord had given rest unto Israel from all their enemies round about, that Joshua waxed old and stricken in age. And Joshua called for all Israel, and for their elders, and for their heads, and for their judges, and for their officers, and said unto them, I am old and stricken in age (Josh. 23:1–2).

The Audience

Exodus 18:13–26 recounts how, in the early days after Israel left Egypt, Moses would spend all day listening to grievances of the people and settling disputes. People would stand in line from dawn till dusk for an opportunity to present their cases before him. It was hard on the people, and harder on Moses.

After watching him for a while, Moses' father-in-law made an important suggestion. If Moses would appoint people to assist him, it would greatly ease the burden on everyone. He recommended establishing rulers over thousands, hundreds, fifties, and tens. When the plan was implemented, Israel had a five-tier judicial system in which each group of ten households had a "ruler" to whom they could take their cases ("ruler of tens"). Any cases he couldn't satisfactorily handle would be passed up to someone responsible for five such groups of ten households ("ruler of fifties"). Any issues that second-tier official couldn't resolve were referred to someone responsible for two groups of fifty households. If this "ruler of hundreds" couldn't resolve a matter, it could be handed on to someone responsible for ten such groups, a "ruler of thousands." This fourth tier in the judicial system probably comprised the body of leaders that was the forerunner of the Sanhedrin (Exod. 24:1–16). But appealing a case to Moses was the fifth and final step. Since the overwhelming majority of cases would be resolved in the lower "courts," this helped free up Moses' time.

Surely by the time Israel had settled Canaan those tiers of authority had resolved themselves into an established system with specific titles for officials at each level. If so, it seems likely that the list of officers Joshua called to this meeting corresponds with the judicial hierarchy described in Exodus. The text lists four distinct positions of authority, probably in order from highest to lowest ranking officials: elders, heads, judges, and officers. Since Exodus 24:1 refers to a group of seventy "elders" who accompanied Moses, Aaron, Nadab, and Abihu to a special meeting with the Lord, the "elders" Joshua called to this meeting were probably the successors of Moses' seventy men, or "rulers of thousands." Those called "heads" probably coincided with the "rulers of hundreds," those called "judges" with "rulers of fifties," and those called "officers" with "rulers of tens." The audience that Joshua called together to hear his address was a sort of judicial parliament of Israel.

The Time

The time of this meeting isn't clearly stated, but it had been "a long time" since Israel's war of conquest had ended. Ten chapters earlier, in Joshua 13:1, we are told that Joshua was "old and stricken in years." That was following forty years in Egypt, forty more in the wilderness, and seven years of combat in Canaan. But much more time has passed. Joshua was about 87 years old when the army disbanded and Reuben, Gad, and Manasseh headed home (Josh. 22). He would live another twenty-three years, dying at the age of 110 (Josh. 24:29). It's difficult to say for sure, but allowing for a little time between this address and his valedictory address in Joshua 24, and a little time after that before he died, it has probably been at least sixteen or seventeen years since the close of the previous chapter.

The Purpose

Joshua's purpose for gathering this assembly was his concern for the safety of Israel. The statement "that the Lord had given rest unto Israel from all their enemies round about" describes the end of overt military action in Canaan. In general, the enemy had been subdued. But as we'll see from Joshua's concerns, vigilance was still necessary.

Once again we see that the crossing of Jordan into Canaan symbolized not one's death and entrance into heaven but one's entrance into victorious Christian living. God parted the Jordan, but Israel had to take the land. God fought with and for Israel, but Israel had to participate with God to conquer their enemies. Even at this time, with the land at rest, there were still enemies to withstand.

That is precisely the point of Hebrews 4:3–11*a*.

> For we which have believed do enter into rest, as he said, As I have sworn in my wrath, if they shall enter into my rest: although the works were finished from the foundation of the world. For he spake in a certain place of the seventh day on this wise, And God did rest the seventh day from all his works. And in this place again, If they shall enter into my rest. Seeing therefore it remaineth that some must enter therein, and they to whom it was first preached entered not in because of unbelief: again, he limiteth a certain day, saying in David, To day, after so long a time; as it is said, To day if ye will hear his voice, harden not your hearts. For if Jesus had given them rest, then would he not afterward have spoken of another day. There remaineth therefore a rest to the people of God. For he that is entered into his rest, he also hath ceased from his own works, as God did from his. Let us labour therefore to enter into that rest.

Verses 8 and 9 are a little confusing in the KJV quoted here. In the Greek New Testament the names "Jesus" and "Joshua" are identical. In passages that use only the given name without a title (i.e., "Lord Jesus" or "Jesus Christ") the only way to determine whether the writer is speaking of Jesus or Joshua is by context. Other English versions (NKJV, NASB, NIV, etc.) correctly render the name "Joshua" in Hebrews 4:8. The writer of Hebrews is discussing Israel's history in relation to the idea of entering into rest. His point is that Joshua did not establish *absolute* rest in Canaan but provided a *foretaste* of the rest that would be ours in "another day," in which our rest would become complete in Christ—in the resurrection.

The rest Israel had in Canaan under Joshua was not the ultimate rest God intended for them, any more than the rest we have in our salvation is the ultimate rest God has for believers today. The rest that we entered into when we trusted Christ (salvation), and which grows in our daily struggle to obey in the face of temptation (sanctification), will be completed when we go to be with the Lord (glorification).

A General Appeal to Faithfulness

Joshua's message to the assembled leaders of Israel was basically an appeal to remain faithful to God. Perhaps because of his advancing age, being uncertain how much longer he would be there to lead Israel, Joshua wanted to encourage continued obedience.

> And ye have seen all that the Lord your God hath done unto all these nations because of you; for the Lord your God is he that hath fought for you. Behold, I have divided unto you by lot these nations that remain, to be an inheritance for your tribes, from Jordan, with all the nations that I have cut off, even unto the great sea westward. And the Lord your God, he shall expel them from before you, and drive them from out of your sight; and ye shall possess their land, as the Lord your God hath promised unto you (Josh. 23:3–5).

Rely on God

The first of four charges issued by Joshua was that Israel must continue to rely upon God. Seven times in Joshua 23:3–12, and four in verses 3–5 alone, Joshua referred to God by two names as "the *Lord* your *God*." The first name, "Lord," renders the Hebrew word *YHWH* ("Yahweh" or "Jehovah"). This is the name by which God revealed Himself to Moses in Exodus 6:2–7, indicating that He was the One Who kept His covenant with Abraham. The name derives from the Hebrew verb of *being* and is closely related to God's calling Himself "I AM." The name signifies not only that God is the eternally self-existent One but actually *emphasizes the fact that He is real, present, and operating immediately in this world.*

This name came to be considered too sacred to speak aloud, for fear of taking God's name in vain.[100] Since Hebrew is written without vowels, the original pronunciation of the name is uncertain. Most modern translations render the name *Yahweh*, but the more traditional spelling is *Jehovah*, based on the vowel pointing, marks within the text to aid readers in pronunciation. These marks were added by the Masoretes sometime between the ninth and twelfth centuries AD. It is possible, and perhaps likely, that, in deference to the ancient Jewish tradition against speaking the name aloud, the Masoretes intentionally marked the pronunciation of this name incorrectly. Some Hebraists have suggested that they inserted the vowels from *Adonai*, another of God's names, between the consonants *YHWH*, blending two of God's names into a sort of pseudonym for God—*Jehovah*. Such circumlocution would be consistent with many other traditional Hebrew practices. With few exceptions, when you read the word *Lord* (all capitals) in the King James, it indicates that the word in the original Hebrew is *Yahweh*/*Jehovah*.

In the expression *the Lord your God*, Joshua also uses the name *Elohim*. This is the plural form of *Eloah*, or simply *El*, a common word meaning "the great or supreme one," used by many people groups for the gods they worshiped. The

---

[100] This tradition may explain why Matthew's Gospel almost always speaks of "the kingdom of heaven" in contexts that the other evangelists call "the kingdom of God." Since Matthew's emphasis was on presenting Christ as the promised King, and his audience was predominantly Jewish, we would expect him to be especially careful of Jewish sensibilities.

plural form can be used in connection with pagan worship to designate "gods" and is used with a plural verb. When used in reference to the one true God, the plural *Elohim* is used with a singular verb. Use of the plural form certainly does not teach the triune nature of God, but it does open the door for understanding the doctrine. Since this name emphasizes God's exalted sovereignty, it is associated with His creative power and infinite wisdom. It is used nearly thirty times in the first chapter of Genesis alone.

By using the two names *Yahweh* and *Elohim* together, Joshua reminded Israel of God's grace in making covenants with Israel and His power to keep those covenants. Joshua repeatedly asserts that it was "the Lord your God" Who fought on Israel's behalf and defeated the nations of the Canaanites. Wanting the leaders of Israel to be completely dependent upon God, he asserts that "the Lord your God" would keep His promises to continue to expel Israel's enemies and give Israel possession of the land. For the nation to enjoy continued success and rest in the land, the leaders must continue to rely wholly upon God.

Be Courageous

The second charge Joshua issued to Israel's leaders was that they must be courageous.

> Be ye therefore very courageous to keep and to do all that is written in the book of the law of Moses, that ye turn not aside therefrom to the right hand or to the left; that ye come not among these nations, these that remain among you; neither make mention of the name of their gods, nor cause to swear by them, neither serve them, nor bow yourselves unto them (Josh. 23:6–7).

Sometimes we think of courage as "the absence of fear," particularly in the face of danger. Honestly, to be in a dangerous situation without fear may simply indicate *stupidity*. It is generally better to think of courage as "behaving bravely in spite of your fear"—doing what has to be done even though you are scared to death. Even that definition misses the point Joshua wants to make. He actually explained what he meant. Israel's courage would be demonstrated by their obedience. Joshua has defined courage as "strength of character and conviction demonstrated by faithful obedience of the Word of God."

What is so courageous about doing what you're told? When enemies oppose the right, and friends encourage the wrong, and even your own flesh entices you to disobey, remaining true to God's Word may be the most courageous thing you will ever do. It can take tremendous courage to steadfastly trust God when temptations assail you or circumstances look bleak. Israel must demonstrate the steadfast courage to refrain from any form of worship ascribed to other gods: invoking their names, swearing by them, serving them, or bowing to them.

Cleave to God

Joshua's third charge reminded his audience that they must cleave unto God.

> But cleave unto the Lord your God, as ye have done unto this day. For the Lord hath driven out from before you great nations and strong: but as for you, no man hath been able to stand before you unto this day. One man of you shall chase a thousand: for the Lord your God, he it is that fighteth for you, as he hath promised you (Josh. 23:8–10).

The idea expressed by the words *cleave unto* is a little difficult to express clearly and concisely. It is the same word used to describe the intimate and unbreakable relationship of a husband and wife (Gen. 2:24). Various translations have tried different ways of rendering the word. The NASB translates it "cling to." That's basically accurate, but "clinging to" someone or something may imply desperately grasping for support in weakness, and that's not the idea this word is intended to communicate. The word has also been translated "hold fast" (NKJV, NIV), which is better. It means "to adhere," or "to be firmly attached to," and it includes the idea of willing, practical obedience. It involves a *single-minded dedication of heart and life*. This is what Paul meant when he told the believers in Thessalonica to "prove all things; **hold fast** that which is good" (1 Thess. 5:21) and when he told Timothy to "**hold fast** the form of sound words" (2 Tim. 1:13).

Love God

Finally, Joshua reminded the assembled leadership that they must love God.

> Take good heed therefore unto yourselves, that ye love the Lord your God. Else if ye do in any wise go back, and cleave unto the remnant of these nations, even these that remain among you, and shall make marriages with them, and go in unto them, and they to you (Josh. 23:11–12).

In the verse that follows the command to love God, Joshua contrasts a proper love for God with its opposite—disregarding God and preferring the company and lifestyle of the people of the land. To "love the Lord your God" has both positive and negative aspects. Positively, it is to give God the supreme place in your heart. Negatively, it involves closing your heart to anything and everything that is unworthy of God.

The Rationale for Faithfulness

Now that Israel has moved into Canaan, successfully subdued the people, and settled the land, why is continuing to love God so important? They had done their part, and God had done His. Why couldn't they just go on their way, now that they have what they wanted from God? Joshua's charge sounds a clear warning against just such perverse and rebellious thinking. He gives four reasons Israel should remain faithful to God.

The Enemy's Appeal

Joshua's first argument for faithfulness is a warning to beware the snare of the enemy. In verses 6 and 7 he says that Israel must "do all that is written in the book of the law" without turning "aside . . . to the right hand or to the left." Why? "That ye come not among these nations," particularly that Israel never "mention . . . the name of their gods," or "swear by them," or "serve them," or "bow . . . unto them." The false gods of the land had a strong sensual appeal to pleasure and prosperity. To avoid the deception of false religion, Israel must be steadfast in their dedication to serve the Lord their God.

Susceptibility

Joshua also warns Israel to beware human nature. He says, "Take good heed therefore unto yourselves [or *your souls*]" (v. 11). Joshua knew that their own propensity to sin could lead them to compromise with "the remnant of these nations" and "make marriages with them" (v. 12). In the story of Rahab (Josh. 2; 6:25; cf. Matt. 1:5) we saw that the prohibition against marriage to a non-Israelite was not based on ethnicity but faith. The people of the land, almost without exception, were idolaters. As Israel's subsequent history shows, intermarriage with people from other nations was a problem only when they brought their false gods with them.

Today's popular spirit of "toleration" that forbids criticism of anything anyone believes or does is the very attitude that God consistently condemns in His people. In Israel, this command was to drive both their personal lives and their national polity. Today, we need to remember that the church is not Israel. *Believers today are commissioned to preach the gospel (Matt. 28:18–20), not purge the culture.* While we oppose evil at every opportunity, it is foolish to expect forcing heathen people to act like Christians to be the solution. Yes, we seem to be losing many of the cultural battles, but I don't think the advance of evil occurs because we haven't done enough politically. To have a positive impact on our culture, we must "take heed unto ourselves," maintaining our own love for God. Believers individually and the church collectively must remain pure of faith, single-heartedly devoted to love God above all else. We are to be "to the praise of his glory" (Eph. 1:12, 14). We know that the Great Commission is to take the gospel to the world. But we sometimes forget that the *greatest commandment* is to "love the Lord thy God with all thy heart, and with all thy soul, and with all thy mind" (Matt. 22:37–38).

Joshua warns that if Israel fails to faithfully "love the Lord your God" they would not live at peace in the land.

> Know for a certainty that the Lord your God will no more drive out any of these nations from before you; but they shall be snares and traps unto you, and scourges in your sides, and thorns in your eyes, until ye perish from off this good land which the Lord your God hath given you (Josh. 23:13).

Compromise with the world through intermarriage with the idolaters wouldn't bring the comfort and prosperity they desired and expected. It would result in all sorts of complications that would make life difficult, burdensome, even unbearable. *The only deterrent to the temptations of the world is to be occupied with God's Word.*

God's Faithfulness

As a third reason for Israel to remain faithful to God, Joshua tells them to remember the faithfulness of God.

> And, behold, this day I am going the way of all the earth: and ye know in all your hearts and in all your souls, that not one thing hath failed of all the good things which the Lord your God spake concerning you; all are come to pass unto you, and not one thing hath failed thereof (Josh. 23:14).

To "go the way of all the earth" is an interesting euphemism for death, emphasizing the inevitability of death for all humanity and the temporary nature of our residence on this earth. But Joshua wanted Israel to remember that God had done for Israel everything He had promised. To drive home the point, Joshua twice says "all" the good things God had spoken concerning Israel He had done and "not one thing" had failed.

God's Discipline

Finally, Joshua warns that just as surely as God kept His promises to bring Israel into the land and subdue their enemies before them, He would also keep

His promise to punish Israel if they forsook Him. Israel must be faithful to God, or they would face the discipline of God.

> Therefore it shall come to pass, that as all good things are come upon you, which the Lord your God promised you; so shall the Lord bring upon you all evil things, until he have destroyed you from off this good land which the Lord your God hath given you. When ye have transgressed the covenant of the Lord your God, which he commanded you, and have gone and served other gods, and bowed yourselves to them; then shall the anger of the Lord be kindled against you, and ye shall perish quickly from off the good land which he hath given unto you (Josh. 23:15–16).

When God's people disobey Him, they face His chastening. Hebrews 12:6 says, "For whom the Lord loveth he chasteneth, and scourgeth every son whom he receiveth." The discipline of God is rooted in a love so strong that He must chasten those who are His to correct them and draw them back to His side.

God's chastening takes many forms, but its uniform goal is to get our attention and bring about repentance and a restoration to fellowship with the Lord (1 Cor. 5:1–5; 2 Tim. 3:16–17). Because Christ died for us, taking upon Himself the wrath of God, we have peace *with* God (Rom. 5:1, 9). But we can experience the peace *of* God only as we live in obedient submission to our Lord, enjoying sweet fellowship that transcends the circumstances of life as we anticipate eternity (Phil. 4:6–8; Col. 3:12–17).

Applying the Principles

In his book *Joshua: Man of Fearless Faith*, Phillip Keller summarizes Joshua's message to the leaders of Israel as a series of seven prohibitions:

1. Do not turn away from God's Word!
2. Do not accommodate yourself to the world's ways!
3. Do not give your allegiance to false gods!
4. Do not set your will to serve idols!
5. Do not become subject to their deception!
6. Do not adopt the lifestyle of the pagan people!
7. Do not marry or form alliances among them![101]

[101] Keller, pp. 164–65.

These commands are timeless, just as valid in their application today as they were to Israel 3500 years ago. The quotations below provide a sample of passages in which each of these commands is repeated in the New Testament for believers today.

1. "If a man love me, he will keep my words" (John 14:23).
2. "Be not conformed to this world" (Rom. 12:2).
3. "There shall be false teachers among you . . . And many shall follow their pernicious ways" (2 Pet. 2:1–2).
4. "What agreement hath the temple of God with idols?" (2 Cor. 6:16).
5. "Let no man deceive you with vain words" (Eph. 5:6).
6. "Have no fellowship with the unfruitful works of darkness, but rather reprove them" (Eph. 5:11).
7. "Be ye not unequally yoked together with unbelievers" (2 Cor. 6:14).

Did you notice that Joshua didn't leave room for an appeal to one's "right" to be "happy"? He did *not* say, "If you find something in the culture of Canaan that you enjoy, I suppose you can have it at least in moderation. Even if God has forbidden it, it's really OK if it makes you happy." God is not nearly so concerned with making us *happy* as He is with making us *holy*.

How quickly and easily we forget the blessings of the Lord! When "counting your blessings," what do you list? We tend to think of God's blessings in terms of material wealth, physical health, or popular acclaim, so we put pay raises, good reports from the doctor, or acquiring status symbols near the top of the list. When we do that, we have fallen prey to the kind of thinking Joshua was warning Israel to avoid. In one of the most sublime passages of the New Testament, Paul describes the blessings that are ours in Christ in Ephesians 1:3–14. The things we tend to pray for are conspicuously absent from Paul's prayers (i.e., Eph. 3:14–21; Col. 1:9–18). When our love for God wanes, we need to remember His grace in our salvation and His promise of our glorification, for "the sufferings of this present time are not worthy to be compared with the glory which shall be revealed in us" (Rom. 8:18).

29

Joshua's Valedictory Address: The Introduction

Joshua 24:1–13

High school and college graduations often feature three speakers, each of whom has his own assigned task. The keynote address is usually a guest speaker invited to address the graduates, delivering a charge to encourage future success. The other two speakers are usually selected from among the graduates. One of them will deliver a speech that welcomes the students and guests to the ceremony. It is a speech of salutation or greeting, hence the name "salutatory address." Generally the longer and more important speech comes later. In it, the speaker says farewell. He may reminisce with fellow graduates about their years in school together. He will outline goals for the future and say good-bye to faculty, family, and friends. This kind of speech is called a "valedictory address" because it delivers a "valediction," or "farewell."

In many schools in the United States it is still customary for the honor of delivering the valedictory address to go to the student with the highest grade-point average, which is why that student is often referred to as the class "valedictorian." The student with the second highest average will probably deliver the salutatory address and be called the class "salutatorian." Since the best students aren't always the best speakers, some schools have broken with tradition, choosing to have the speeches made by better public speakers.

Joshua wasn't graduating; he was retiring, and retirement speeches usually offer valedictions, even if not always called valedictory addresses. Joshua's last speech is no exception. He reflects on Israel's past, outlines goals for the future, and says farewell. In this chapter, we'll examine the introductory portion of the address, Joshua's reminiscences.

The Setting of the Address

Some commentaries treat Joshua 23 and 24 as a single address. That's probably because in chapter 23 Joshua spoke as one who was facing imminent death, but his death isn't recorded until the end of chapter 24. Also, the audience identified seems to be the same in both instances.

> And Joshua gathered all the tribes of Israel to Shechem, and called for the elders of Israel, and for their heads, and for their judges, and for their officers; and they presented themselves before God (Josh. 24:1).

Joshua called for all the leadership of Israel to assemble once again. The wording of this verse is very similar to 23:2 and may indicate that only the leaders of Israel were present. But as the chapter progresses, we'll find several references to "all the people," so I'm inclined to think this meeting was a general assembly of the nation. It is likely that this meeting occurred a few years after the meeting in Joshua 23. If Joshua's death occurred shortly after this meeting's conclusion (24:29), about thirty years have passed since Israel crossed Jordan into Canaan.

In Joshua 23, it is generally assumed that Joshua assembled the leaders of Israel at Shiloh, the place where the tabernacle was set up as the center of Israel's worship. This meeting, however, was held at Shechem, which will serve as a sort of governmental center during Israel's first years in Canaan. Shechem held special spiritual significance to Israel as a historic site. The first time God promised Abram that He would give him the land of Canaan (Gen. 12:6–7) was when Abram first arrived at Shechem. Two generations later, when Jacob returned to Canaan with his family after twenty years in Mesopotamia working for his father-in-law, Laban, it was at Shechem that Jacob purged his family of the idols they had brought back with them (Gen. 35:2–5). Standing at the base of Mount Ebal, Shechem was the place where Joshua had built an altar and expressed his gratitude to God for giving Israel the land. At that time, it signified Israel's repentance and cleansing from the sin of Achan, God's fidelity to His promise of victory over Ai, and Israel's wholehearted dedication to the Lord. Shechem was a place long associated with character traits such as diligence, perseverance, and fidelity. Little wonder that Joshua chose this location to deliver what is essentially a pastor's closing message to his congregation.

The Source of the Message

Another distinction between Joshua's address in this chapter and that from the previous chapter is that in this case Joshua specifically attributes the message to God.

> And Joshua said unto all the people, Thus saith the Lord God of Israel (Josh. 24:2*a*).

Joshua hadn't called everyone together just to hear his own reminiscences and observations. They were assembled to hear a message from the Lord. The role of the pastor is to proclaim the Word of the Lord. Perhaps because it seems to please the audience, sermons today are often more closely related to the moralizing fables of Aesop than to the proclamation of the Word of the Lord. That is not what God intends preaching to be. Peter warns, "If any man speak, let him speak as the oracles of God" (1 Pet. 4:11*a*). Pastors are charged to "preach the word" (2 Tim. 4:2*a*). While Paul was talking to Timothy about his pastoral leadership of the church at Ephesus, he may well have had today's church in mind when he issued this charge:

> Preach the word; be instant in season, out of season; reprove, rebuke, exhort with all longsuffering and doctrine. For the time will come when they will not endure sound doctrine; but after their own lusts shall they heap to themselves teachers, having itching ears; and they shall turn away their ears from the truth, and shall be turned unto fables (2 Tim. 4:2–4).

Joshua's closing message to Israel was as "the oracles of God." And when God speaks, His people had better listen.

A Survey of Their History

Before getting into the meat of his message, which we'll consider in the next chapter, Joshua launched a recitation of significant events in Israel's history, starting with what may have been a rather embarrassing fact.

> Your fathers dwelt on the other side of the flood in old time, even Terah, the father of Abraham, and the father of Nachor: and they served other gods. And I took your father Abraham from the other side of the flood, and led

> him throughout all the land of Canaan, and multiplied his seed, and gave him Isaac. And I gave unto Isaac Jacob and Esau: and I gave unto Esau mount Seir, to possess it; but Jacob and his children went down into Egypt (Josh. 24:2*b*–4).

Israel's Heritage

How tactless! Joshua reminded Israel that their heritage was *idolatrous*. Their forefathers had lived beyond Jordan ("on the other side of the flood") and had worshiped idols, just like the Canaanites. He mentions only two sons of Terah, Abraham and Nachor (Nahor). The omission of the third son, Haran (Gen. 11:27), doesn't mean that Haran wasn't an idolater but that Haran wasn't one of Israel's forebears. Abraham was the father of Isaac. Nahor was the grandfather of Isaac's wife, Rebekah (Gen. 22:20–23), and the great-grandfather of Jacob's wives Rachel and Leah (Gen. 29:10, 16). The point the Lord is making is that Israel didn't become God's chosen nation because of their *forefathers'* goodness but because of *God's*.

Israel's Call

If Israel's forefathers were idolaters no better than the Canaanites, what happened? God, in His grace, called Abraham to believe and obey Him. Actually, the text says that God "took" (Heb. *laqach*) Abraham from that environment and brought him to the place He wanted him. The word *laqach* appears for the first time in Genesis 2:15, which says that "God **took** the man and put him into the garden of Eden." A few verses later, we read that God "**took** one of his ribs" (Gen. 2:21) from which He made Eve. Then in Genesis 3:6 we find that Eve "**took** of the fruit" of the Tree of Knowledge of Good and Evil. Later, we find that a great man of God named Enoch "was not, for God **took** him" (Gen. 5:24). I think we have a pretty good idea of what that word communicates.

The use of this word stresses God's sovereignty in His efficacious call. Abraham wasn't the last righteous man in Ur of the Chaldees who woke up one morning and decided he couldn't take the wickedness any more so he was getting out of town. No, Abraham was perfectly content as an idolater in Ur until God, in His grace, "took" him. We also see the juxtaposition of man's responsibility to respond to God's call by believing and following. God says that He "led" Abraham. That indicates that Abraham was a willing follower. He didn't leave his homeland and idolatry under duress. God called him and made him willing, and Abraham followed gladly to the place God intended to give him.[102] The rest of Joshua 24:3–4 also juxtaposes God's sovereignty with

[102] This is perfectly consistent with the teaching of the Lord Jesus. He said, "No man can come unto me, except it were given unto him of my Father" (John 6:65; cf. 6:44). That's God's enabling. He also said, "All that the Father giveth me shall come to me" (John 6:37*a*). That's the

man's responsibility. God "gave him Isaac," but Abraham had to participate. Isaac wasn't delivered by a stork or found in a cabbage patch. And neither were Jacob and Esau in Isaac's case.

God's grace didn't stop with Abraham. By His grace He also "gave unto Isaac Jacob and Esau." To Esau, God gave Mount Seir. The fact that Joshua mentions this would serve to remind Israel of their relationship to the Edomites to the south.[103] Jacob and his family had gone to Egypt and were now returning to claim the land given to their forefathers. But the land of Edom was the same kind of God-given inheritance for the Edomites that Canaan was for Israel. Joshua's point was that Israel was not entitled to that land and must leave Edom alone.

Israel's Redemption

Joshua didn't mention Israel's *slavery* in Egypt, but it is implied in the next significant historical event—their *deliverance* from Egypt by God's use of Moses and Aaron.

> I sent Moses also and Aaron, and I plagued Egypt, according to that which I did among them: and afterward I brought you out. And I brought your fathers out of Egypt: and ye came unto the sea; and the Egyptians pursued after your fathers with chariots and horsemen unto the Red sea. And when they cried unto the Lord, he put darkness between you and the Egyptians, and brought the sea upon them, and covered them; and your eyes have seen what I have done in Egypt (Josh. 24:5–7*a*).

God's plagues on Egypt displayed His power on Israel's behalf. It was God Who brought them out. And He didn't leave them defenseless against an avenging army. He led them across the Red Sea and destroyed the army of Egypt that pursued them. While God had *converted* Abraham from the idolatry of Ur, He *rescued* Israel from slavery in idolatrous Egypt (cf. Exod. 12:12 and Num. 33:4).

Israel's Preservation

Joshua then summarized forty years in Sinai by saying simply,

> And ye dwelt in the wilderness a long season (Josh. 24:7*b*).

---

effectual call. But that verse concludes saying, "And him that cometh to me I will in no wise cast out" (John 6:37*b*). That's man's response in faith.

[103] In Numbers 20:14 Moses requested passage through Edom for "thy brother Israel." When Edom refused them passage and assembled an army against them, Moses withdrew and went around rather than engage in armed conflict with the closest relatives Israel had in the region. See also the footnote about Caleb in chapter 6, p. 56.

That statement, spare as it is, reminded the audience, some of whom had entered the wilderness as youngsters and others who had been born there, that they endured that period only by the gracious provision of God. The nation of Israel wasn't preserved in the wilderness by their ingenuity and industry. God provided water and meat when necessary and food in the form of manna for an entire generation. He guarded and protected them in His mercy, despite enemy opposition and their own manifold failures.

Israel's Inheritance

Then Joshua summarized more recent history, events through which virtually all the leadership of Israel had lived, even though they had occurred two to three decades in the past.

> And I brought you into the land of the Amorites, which dwelt on the other side Jordan; and they fought with you: and I gave them into your hand, that ye might possess their land; and I destroyed them from before you. Then Balak the son of Zippor, king of Moab, arose and warred against Israel, and sent and called Balaam the son of Beor to curse you: but I would not hearken unto Balaam; therefore he blessed you still: so I delivered you out of his hand. And ye went over Jordan, and came unto Jericho: and the men of Jericho fought against you, the Amorites, and the Perizzites, and the Canaanites, and the Hittites, and the Girgashites, the Hivites, and the Jebusites; and I delivered them into your hand. And I sent the hornet before you, which drave them out from before you, even the two kings of the Amorites; but not with thy sword, nor with thy bow (Josh. 24:8–12).

The land of Canaan, which Israel had been enjoying for over twenty years, had become their inheritance through the fidelity of God to His promises. God gave them victory over the Amorites so that Israel could possess their land on the far side (east) of Jordan.

God delivered Israel from the Moabites. When the king of Moab had hired Balaam to curse Israel in an attempt to gain a spiritual advantage over them, God had turned the tables and used Balaam to pronounce blessings on Israel instead.

Once Israel crossed Jordan, God presented them with Jericho and all the land of Canaan, enabling Israel to defeat all the people who confronted them. We read here for the first time that God even employed hornets to drive out two kings of the Amorites.[104] He had promised to do this in Exodus 23:28 and

[104] "John Garstang (*Joshua-Judges* [London: Constable and Co., 1931], pp. 258–60) explains the 'hornet' as a reference to the Pharaoh of Egypt whose many campaigns into Canaan left the population seriously weakened when Israel invaded the land. In an alternative view, the hornet is the terror that the Lord sent to demoralize and immobilize the enemy (cf.

Deuteronomy 7:20, but Joshua's accounts of the battles had omitted this detail until now. The Lord and Joshua wanted Israel to remember that many of their battles were won not by military strength ("sword" and "bow") but by the hand of God.

Israel's Dependence

What has been the point of Joshua's tracing Israel's history to introduce his last words to the nation? We could outline this historical survey as follows:

1. Israel's heritage was idolatrous.
2. Israel's call was by God's grace.
3. Israel's redemption was by God's power.
4. Israel's preservation was by God's provision.
5. Israel's inheritance was by God's faithfulness.

This historical recitation concludes with a summary application:

> And I have given you a land for which ye did not labour, and cities which ye built not, and ye dwell in them; of the vineyards and oliveyards which ye planted not do ye eat (Josh. 24:13).

Israel hadn't worked hard enough to earn the land of Canaan. They hadn't built the cities in which they were living, and they hadn't planted the olive yards and vineyards whose produce they had been enjoying for years. God had blessed them by giving Israel possession of a functioning economy without having to build it from scratch. Israel didn't possess the land of Canaan because they deserved it. God had given all of this to them.

It was vital for Israel to grasp this, or they might be tempted to think that the manna in the wilderness was a gift from God but the food in Canaan was earned by their own efforts. They had entered the land by *God's grace*. They had been protected and secure in the land by *God's grace*. And they had been provided for in the land by *God's grace*.

All of Israel's history demonstrated two truths: *God hates sin*, and *God calls out and delivers His people*. It was God Who had brought them to this point, and only He could take them on from here. All of this served to drive home the fact of *Israel's dependence upon God*.

2:9–11, 24; 5:1)" (Madvig, p. 367). It seems much better to simply assume that God's employ of hornets was just one of the many details not recorded earlier in the summation of the conquest provided in this book. If it meant something figurative rather than genuine hornets, it is difficult to imagine what Joshua's audience thought he meant.

Applying the Principles

The same is true for us today. We know that *God's promises will be fulfilled.* We know that *God's people will be victorious.* The apostle Paul asserts his confidence by saying, "I can do all things through Christ which strengtheneth me" (Phil. 4:13). He also says, "There hath no temptation taken you but such as is common to man: but God is faithful, who will not suffer you to be tempted above that ye are able; but will with the temptation also make a way to escape, that ye may be able to bear it" (1 Cor. 10:13). The twofold basis for Paul's certainty is his confidence in Christ, Who enables, and in God, Who is faithful.

But there are two aspects to the promises of God: an unconditional aspect that involves God's program for His people, and a conditional aspect that involves participation through personal faith demonstrated by obedience. In Israel's case, God promised Abraham's offspring, particularly the family of Jacob, perpetual possession of Canaan unconditionally (Gen. 13:14–17; 15:18–21; 17:8; cf. Rom. 9:10–16). Yet He told the Israelites in particular that they must obey the Lord to remain in the land (Deut. 6:1–25). Confusion over these two aspects caused some consternation in Jesus' day. John the Baptist said to the Pharisees and Sadducees,

> And think not to say within yourselves, We have Abraham to our father: for I say unto you, that God is able of these stones to raise up children unto Abraham. And now also the ax is laid unto the root of the trees: therefore every tree which bringeth not forth good fruit is hewn down, and cast into the fire (Matt. 3:9–10; cf. Luke 3:8–9).

The Lord Jesus dealt with the same issue later. He was confronted by people claiming to be secure on the basis of their descent from Abraham, and He responded by distinguishing between *physical* descent from Abraham and *spiritual* descent from Abraham. Being physically descended from Abraham was worthless unless one also followed Abraham's example of faithful obedience to the voice of the Lord.

> They answered him, We be Abraham's seed, and were never in bondage to any man: how sayest thou, Ye shall be made free? Jesus answered them, Verily, verily, I say unto you, Whosoever committeth sin is the servant of sin. And the servant abideth not in the house for ever: but the Son abideth ever. If the Son therefore shall make you free, ye shall be free indeed. I know that ye are Abraham's seed; but ye seek to kill me, because my word hath no place in you. I speak that which I have seen with my Father: and ye do that which ye

> have seen with your father. They answered and said unto him, Abraham is our father. Jesus saith unto them, If ye were Abraham's children, ye would do the works of Abraham. But now ye seek to kill me, a man that hath told you the truth, which I have heard of God: this did not Abraham. Ye do the deeds of your father. Then said they to him, We be not born of fornication; we have one Father, even God. Jesus said unto them, If God were your Father, ye would love me: for I proceeded forth and came from God; neither came I of myself, but he sent me. Why do ye not understand my speech? even because ye cannot hear my word. Ye are of your father the devil, and the lusts of your father ye will do. He was a murderer from the beginning, and abode not in the truth, because there is no truth in him. When he speaketh a lie, he speaketh of his own: for he is a liar, and the father of it. And because I tell you the truth, ye believe me not. Which of you convinceth me of sin? And if I say the truth, why do ye not believe me? He that is of God heareth God's words: ye therefore hear them not, because ye are not of God (John 8:33–47).

We find the same dual aspects in God's promises for us today. *The redemption that is ours in Christ is unconditional.* We were chosen in Him from the foundation of the world, and our selection as His children by adoption was predetermined before the beginning of time on the basis of His good pleasure (Eph. 1:4–6). All of those He foreordained, without exception, are called, justified, and glorified (Rom. 8:30). And our position in Christ is absolute and irrevocable because no one and no thing can separate those who are His from Him (Rom. 8:31–39; John 10:27–29).

Still, *individual participation in God's redemptive program requires personal response in repentant faith.* We must believe on the Lord Jesus Christ to be saved (Acts 16:31). We must confess that Christ is Lord and call upon Him to be saved (Rom. 10:9–13). In the early church in Jerusalem, we read that the number of disciples multiplied as people were "obedient to the faith" (Acts 6:7). Yes, even our faith is a part of God's work within us, so we have no reason to boast. But we must still walk in the good works that God has foreordained.

> For by grace are ye saved through faith; and that not of yourselves: it is the gift of God: not of works, lest any man should boast. For we are his workmanship, created in Christ Jesus unto good works, which God hath before ordained that we should walk in them (Eph. 2:8–10).

30

Joshua's Valedictory Address:

The Exhortation

Joshua 24:14–23

In the introductory section of his final address to the nation, Joshua's brief summary of Israel's history demonstrated that they owed everything to God—not just their presence in Canaan, but their very existence as a people.

As you look at Joshua's charge to Israel, notice the similarity to Paul's appeal in Romans 12. In Romans 11, Paul speaks of Israel as the people of God, whom "God hath not cast away" (11:2) despite their repeated failures. He makes the point that God doesn't change His mind—that He doesn't renege on His promises—saying, "For the gifts and calling of God are without repentance" (11:29). He concludes that the Jew and Gentile alike are completely dependent upon God: "For of him, and through him, and to him, are all things: to whom be glory forever. Amen" (11:36). On the basis of this discussion ("therefore"), Paul then makes his appeal to each believer to dedicate himself to personal holiness, obeying out of gratitude for God's abundant grace.

> I beseech you therefore, brethren, by the mercies of God, that ye present your bodies a living sacrifice, holy, acceptable unto God, which is your reasonable service. And be not conformed to this world: but be ye transformed by the renewing of your mind, that ye may prove what is that good, and acceptable, and perfect, will of God (Rom. 12:1–2).

The principle that was true for Israel in Joshua's day is true for the child of God today. God had dealt with Israel with patience and mercy, bringing them from idolatry to new life in the Promised Land despite the fact that they didn't deserve it. Still today, God patiently and mercifully deals with man, who consistently comes short of glorifying Him (Rom. 3:10–23). God also, in His grace, changes unregenerate men, making them new creations and eventually glorifying all who are His (Rom. 8:29–30). On this basis, "therefore," God appeals to His people for unreserved devotion and sacrificial living for His glory.

The Charge

Devotion to God

The purpose of Joshua's historical survey was to provide the basis for the charge he was about to issue. Having told Israel *why* they owe God their allegiance, he now tells them *what* God expects of them in the future.

> Now therefore fear the Lord, and serve him in sincerity and in truth: and put away the gods which your fathers served on the other side of the flood, and in Egypt; and serve ye the Lord. And if it seem evil unto you to serve the Lord, choose you this day whom ye will serve; whether the gods which your fathers served that were on the other side of the flood, or the gods of the Amorites, in whose land ye dwell: but as for me and my house, we will serve the Lord (Josh. 24:14–15).

The most fundamental need of Israel's future was for individual, personal devotion to God and rejection of idolatry. Israel needed to have indelibly etched into their personal and national consciousness that the false gods of Canaan had been unable to withstand the one true God and had been powerless to protect the idolaters who served them. It would be utter folly for Israel to forsake their God and pursue the gods of the land (cf. Deut. 4:9–10).

That's why Joshua's charge begins by telling Israel to "fear the Lord" (cf. Ps. 111:10; Prov. 1:7; 9:10). Most folks like to define *the fear of the Lord* as "that awe and reverence that a man of sense feels in the presence of God."[105] I believe, however, that it goes much deeper than that. The Scriptures continually remind us that we are constantly in the presence of God. He made us, and He is perfectly holy and can tolerate no evil. What's more, He has absolute authority and limitless power to enforce His will. It becomes truly frightening when we realize that this is the God Who knows and stands in judgment of our every thought, every word, and every act. It is He about Whom the writer of Hebrews says, "Neither is there any creature that is not manifest in his sight: but all things are naked and opened unto the eyes of him with whom

[105] T. Alton Bryant, ed., *The New Compact Bible Dictionary* (Grand Rapids: Zondervan Publishing House, 1967), p. 173.

we have to do" (Heb. 4:13). Living in the constant realization of these truths should produce in us something closer to *terror* than simple "awe and reverence." That is why after Paul tells us that "we must all appear before the judgment seat of Christ" (2 Cor. 5:10*a*), he says, "Knowing therefore **the terror of the Lord**, we persuade men" (5:11*a*).

Rejection of Idols

If you truly "fear the Lord," it follows that you will serve the Lord "in sincerity and in truth." The word translated *sincerity* is sometimes rendered *perfect* (Gen. 17:1) or *integrity* (Gen. 20:5) or *undefiled* (Ps. 119:1). It signifies a quality of being whole, entire, complete, or unadulterated. The word translated *truth* carries the basic meaning of firmness or stability. To serve the Lord in "truth" would be to serve Him constantly with unshakable confidence. The idea is that our service to the Lord is not to be occasional or halfhearted. *We are to serve Him and Him alone all the time, in every facet of life, and with our entire being.* If our service for the Lord is compartmentalized by day of the week or kind of activity, if we think of it as a performance of duty fulfilled reluctantly, or if we obey out of a desire for personal enrichment or comfort, we aren't serving in either "sincerity" or in "truth."

The reverse is also true. God's people must not only be single-mindedly dedicated to the Lord but must just as thoroughly and enthusiastically reject all false gods. Joshua refers especially to three different pantheons to which Israel had been exposed: the gods of Abraham's family and forebears beyond Euphrates, the gods of Egypt, and the gods of Canaan.

As Joshua had just reminded them, the Lord God had taken Abraham out of Chaldean and Mesopotamian idolatry to establish a people He had chosen as His own, and He did it before Israel even existed. God delivered Israel out of idolatrous Egypt, demonstrating His supremacy over all the Egyptian gods, and He did it without any participation on Israel's part. Finally, God had destroyed the idolatrous Canaanites, proving that He is also superior to the Amorite gods, and He allowed Israel to participate with Him in this victory.

With the faithfulness of God and the impotence of these pantheons in mind, Joshua charged Israel to make up their minds. In what may be the most powerful and memorable challenge in Scripture to personal commitment to serve the Lord, Joshua urged the nation he had led for so long to "choose you this day whom ye will serve." Like any good leader, he didn't ask anything of his people that he was unwilling to do himself. He set the example for them, saying, "As for me and my house, we will serve the Lord." He had been willing to stand alone at the start of his career and was still willing to do so at the end of his life. But for Israel's sake, he encouraged them to stand with him.

Personal Choice with National Significance

The choice Joshua called for was applicable in two spheres. First, it applied nationally. Israel was making a collective decision to identify either with the Lord God, Who had brought them into Canaan, or with some other deities. Individual Israelites were also being called upon to make a personal commitment to serve the Lord and reject false gods. As a group, they made the right choice.

> And the people answered and said, God forbid that we should forsake the Lord, to serve other gods; for the Lord our God, he it is that brought us up and our fathers out of the land of Egypt, from the house of bondage, and which did those great signs in our sight, and preserved us in all the way wherein we went, and among all the people through whom we passed: and the Lord drave out from before us all the people, even the Amorites which dwelt in the land: therefore will we also serve the Lord; for he is our God (Josh. 24:16–18).

Frankly, it would have been amazing for them to have responded any other way. They told Joshua that they got the message of the history lesson. The Lord God was the One Who had delivered them from Egypt and into Canaan. It was He Who had given them victory over the people of the land. How could they possibly choose to serve the corrupt and impotent gods that had been defeated by their God? So they vowed never to forsake the Lord to serve other gods—they would serve Him alone.

The Warning

Knowing the fickleness of the human heart, Joshua responded to Israel's declaration of fidelity to God with a warning that was actually an emphatic denial of what they said they would do.

> And Joshua said unto the people, Ye cannot serve the Lord: for he is an holy God; he is a jealous God; he will not forgive your transgressions nor your sins. If ye forsake the Lord, and serve strange gods, then he will turn and do you hurt, and consume you, after that he hath done you good (Josh. 24:19–20).

Just when Israel responded the way Joshua wanted, he said, "Forget it. You can't do it." In one sense, Joshua was absolutely correct—Israel was incapable of offering to God any service that might enhance His status or make Him more complete. Since God is separate from and superior to mankind ("holy"), it is not as if He needs anything we can provide.

But the warning aspect of Joshua's statement is that God is "jealous"—He tolerates no rivals. If Israel forsook the Lord for other gods, He would "turn" and "do you hurt and consume you." This verse shouldn't be construed to teach that God changes His mind. In Malachi 3:6 God assures us, "For I am the Lord, I change not." The very fact that God never changes guarantees that if the nation of Israel changes from devotion to rebellion they will move from the place of God's blessing to the place of His judgment. God didn't destroy the Canaanites because of their ethnicity but because of their idolatry. If Israel gave lip service to the Lord, but pursued Canaanite gods, He would not forgive their presumption and would have to treat them the same way He treated the Canaanites.

Joshua's primary message to Israel was that *God will not tolerate divided loyalty*. That is precisely what it means to be "jealous." And it is a message that is often missing in modern evangelism. I wonder how long it's been since an evangelist met those responding to an "altar call" by saying, "You can't serve the Lord because if you forsake Him and continue serving prosperity or popularity, following your own selfish pursuits, God will destroy you like all the others who reject Christ." No, it's far more likely that he'll convince those who respond to his invitation that everything is fine now. They have nothing more to fear because they have "made a decision for Christ." Then the evangelist will record the number of responses and send a quarterly report to his supporters listing the numbers as evidence of the success of his ministry. His assumption that every person who walks down the aisle is converted often has little or no foundation. His rationale that at least some are probably truly saved doesn't justify the false security he has given to many who came.

Genuine conversion involves a dual response to the gospel: a negative reaction toward one's own sin and a positive reaction to the grace of God. A person who is truly born again, or regenerated, will recognize that his sin is not just harmful but that it constitutes treason against the sovereign Creator God and its penalty is death. Fearing the just wrath of God, he repents, turning from his sin to Christ. Repentance involves not only rejection of his sin but accepting the Lord Jesus Christ as his only hope for rescue. It is impossible to have your sins forgiven without also having a change of loyalty. The new Christian won't immediately understand all the implications of his new allegiance. For that matter, the mature Christian still struggles with submission. But no one who consciously *rejects* Christ's authority has truly come to Him. The genuinely repentant sinner relinquishes control of his own life in deference to the Lord Jesus Christ. "Evangelism" that encourages people to say, "I believe," or to "ask Jesus into your heart," without telling them that true believers turn from their sin to follow Christ is not proclaiming *the Evangel*.

After Joshua told Israel that lip service wasn't good enough, Israel responded by restating their dedication to serve God.

> And the people said unto Joshua, Nay; but we will serve the Lord (Josh. 24:21).

When they insisted that they were serious about this, that they really intended to serve the Lord wholeheartedly, Joshua still doesn't celebrate their decision. Instead, he issues another warning.

> And Joshua said unto the people, Ye are witnesses against yourselves that ye have chosen you the Lord, to serve him. And they said, We are witnesses. Now therefore put away, said he, the strange gods which are among you, and incline your heart unto the Lord God of Israel. And the people said unto Joshua, The Lord our God will we serve, and his voice will we obey (Josh. 24:22–24).

By saying, "Ye are witnesses against yourselves that ye have chosen you the Lord, to serve Him," Joshua told Israel that they would have to testify before the Judge that this was their decision. Essentially Joshua was saying, "You'd better be sure about this. God will hold you accountable for your promises. If you take this oath of fidelity to the Lord, there will be no turning back." The Lord Jesus said something similar when He told one volunteer, "No man, having put his hand to the plough, and looking back, is fit for the kingdom of God" (Luke 9:62; cf. 9:57ff.; John 10:27–28; 12:26).

By their response to Joshua's challenge, "We are witnesses," Israel indicated that they were willing to go on record for this decision. This wasn't just an emotional response to a popular leader's last plea. It was a purposeful choice to identify with and obey God alone, and they were willing to be held accountable for it.

Joshua again commanded that Israel remove from them any "strange gods." Don't go home thinking, "I'll take care of that eventually." Do it now. Turn your hearts from that which has captivated them to Him Who shall be "the captain of [your] salvation" (Heb. 2:10). In reply, Israel again vowed to serve God faithfully and exclusively.

The Record

Once Israel understood the solemn nature of their pledge to follow God, Joshua made an official record of the event.

> So Joshua made a covenant with the people that day, and set them a statute and an ordinance in Shechem. And Joshua wrote these words in the book of the law of God, and took a great stone, and set it up there under an oak, that was by the sanctuary of the Lord. And Joshua said unto all the people, Behold, this stone shall be a witness unto us; for it hath heard all the words of the Lord which he spake unto us: it shall be therefore a witness unto you, lest ye deny your God. So Joshua let the people depart, every man unto his inheritance (Josh. 24:25–28).

Recording "these words in the book of the law of God" constituted making this pledge a part of Israel's covenant with the Lord. Since these words are actually recorded in the book we've been studying, this statement gives evidence that in Joshua's own generation Israel considered Joshua's book a part of the canon of sacred Scripture. The set of books that they called "the law of God" was a growing library, and Joshua was acknowledged to be much more than a military or political leader. He was a prophet who delivered God's message and wrote God's Word.[106]

The people of Israel had bound themselves by an oath that the Lord would be their God and they would be His people. Joshua set up a stone marker as a historical monument to memorialize this event. It would be vital for this generation to remember the solemnity and the historical significance of this day. It would also be important for future generations to remember their heritage and their destiny.

The erection of a historical marker was not unique. Even in the book of Joshua, we've seen this done at Gilgal, on Mount Ebal, and on the eastern bank of Jordan. A similar historical monument had been built by Jacob at Mizpeh (Gen. 31:49) as evidence of his confidence in God's protection from Laban's threats when Jacob returned home after a twenty-year absence. Jacob built another monument at Bethel (Gen. 35:1–7) when he renewed his pledge to serve the Lord in response to God's having kept His promise to bless and protect him. Later, Moses built a monument to commemorate God's having blessed Israel by giving them their first military success after leaving Egypt when they defeated the Amalekites (Exod. 17:14–15). About three hundred years after Joshua's death yet another would be built by Samuel at Ebenezer (1 Sam. 7:12) to commemorate God's giving Israel victory over the Philistines. Samuel's monument is the one referred to in the second stanza of the hymn "Come, Thou Fount" by Robert Robinson.

---

[106] For discussion of the process of assimilating new books into the library of Scripture as they were being written, see "Canonization and Apocrypha," *From the Mind of God to the Mind of Man*, pp. 31–64.

> Here I raise mine **Ebenezer**; Hither by Thy help I'm come;
> And I hope, by Thy good pleasure, Safely to arrive at home.
> Jesus sought me when a stranger, Wandering from the fold of God;
> He, to rescue me from danger, Interposed His precious blood.

It's a great concept—building simple monuments to mark significant events in our spiritual growth. Our memories are faulty things. Mine gets progressively less reliable every year. A written record of how God has led and blessed in our lives can be very important to our own confidence and comfort when we face difficulties or death. It can also be of inestimable value to our children and grandchildren. If we don't pass our spiritual heritage on to them, no one else is likely to.[107] There are times in all of our lives when we should proclaim, "Here I raise my Ebenezer; hither by Thy help I'm come."

Having concluded this landmark meeting, successfully encouraging Israel to recommit themselves to serving the Lord, Joshua sent them home, "every man to his own inheritance." What a testimony to the success of Joshua's calling! He had been charged with the task of bringing Israel across Jordan, conquering the inhabitants of the land, and distributing the land to the people of Israel. As a nation, they had just renewed their covenant with God, but as individuals, every man lived on his own parcel of land. Each one had received his inheritance. When Joshua went to his grave, he could say with confidence that he had finished what God had given him to do.

Postscript

The closing verses of Joshua were probably added by the writer of Judges as a transition to connect the books as the continuing record of redemptive history. Joshua 24:29–31 is repeated almost verbatim, with a little rearranging, in Judges 2:6–9. These verses provide an important postscript to the narrative of Joshua and set the stage for the continuing record to be found in Judges.

> And it came to pass after these things, that Joshua the son of Nun, the servant of the Lord, died, being an hundred and ten years old. And they buried him in the border of his inheritance in Timnath-serah, which is in mount Ephraim, on the north side of the hill of Gaash. And Israel served the Lord all the days of Joshua, and all the days of the elders that overlived Joshua, and which had known all the works of the Lord, that he had done for Israel. And the bones

[107] In what is essentially a synopsis of five chapters of Puritan John Flavel's *The Mystery of Providence*, Layton Talbert has provided a brief but valuable appeal to believers to "personalize providence." See Appendix C of *Not by Chance*, pp. 243–45.

> of Joseph, which the children of Israel brought up out of Egypt, buried they in Shechem, in a parcel of ground which Jacob bought of the sons of Hamor the father of Shechem for an hundred pieces of silver: and it became the inheritance of the children of Joseph. And Eleazar the son of Aaron died; and they buried him in a hill that pertained to Phinehas his son, which was given him in mount Ephraim (Josh. 24:29–33).

Three Funerals

Here at the end of the book we have simple statements attesting to Israel's burial of three great leaders. First, Joshua, whose name means "Jehovah is Salvation," was buried in Timnath-serah ("my abundant portion") in Mount Ephraim ("where I shall be doubly fruitful"). His name and the name of his burial site testify to the goodness of God and the contentment of His servant Joshua. Significantly, this is the first time the title "servant of the Lord" is applied to Joshua, a title shared by Moses.

The second funeral involved the keeping of a promise that Joseph had exacted from his sons before his death over five hundred years earlier. The bones (actually the mummified remains—see Gen. 50:26) of the great patriarch that had been brought from Egypt were buried in Shechem, near the memorial stone erected by Joshua. Joseph's confidence in God's promise to bring his family back to the land He had given to Abraham was rewarded, and his burial at this place was a great testimony to the faithfulness of God.

The third funeral marked the passing of a great spiritual leader—Eleazar the high priest, son of Aaron. His death also marked the end of the generation. Like Joshua, he was buried in Mount Ephraim ("the hills of Ephraim") in a hill that belonged to his son Phinehas, famous for having defused the volatile situation in Joshua 22 that could have led to civil war.

Joshua's Legacy

The most significant statement of this section is found in verse 31. Joshua's leadership had been more than simply *efficient*—accomplishing the task appointed. It had also been *effective*—accomplishing what is important. As a people, Israel kept her vow to remain faithful to God as long as Joshua lived and throughout the lives of those associates of Joshua who outlived him. Many a leader has inspired sufficient loyalty in one of his associates that he will emulate him when under his supervision. Some leaders inspire a protégé to do the same after their death. Few indeed have had such a profound effect that *all* the men who worked with them carried on their legacy for the rest of their lives. Such was the impact of this man Joshua.

Israel's Future

Included in this testimonial is a hint of what is to come. The fact that Israel followed God faithfully throughout the lives of Joshua and the elders he led implies that a time was coming when Israel would forsake the way of the Lord. Joshua begins with the words, "Now after the death of Moses," then proceeds to announce Joshua as the new leader of Israel. While Judges begins the same way with the words, "Now after the death of Joshua," no new leader is appointed. A change looms ominously on the horizon. We see hints of the fickle nature of man while emphasizing the unwavering faithfulness of God.

Peter's message to the believer today is the same as Joshua's message to Israel:

> But as he which hath called you is holy, so be ye holy in all manner of conversation; because it is written, Be ye holy; for I am holy. And if ye call on the Father, who without respect of persons judgeth according to every man's work, pass the time of your sojourning here in fear (1 Pet. 1:15–17).

While it is our responsibility to "work out [our] own salvation with fear and trembling," we must never forget that "it is God which worketh in you both to will and to do of his good pleasure" (Phil. 2:12*b*–13).

The spiritual significance of Joshua is to remind us that ***too many people find it is easier to pray for forgiveness than to fight temptation***. With Christ as our Captain, let us resist the enemies from without and the traitor within, remembering the words of Paul:

> But thou, O man of God, flee these things; and follow after righteousness, godliness, faith, love, patience, meekness. Fight the good fight of faith, lay hold on eternal life, whereunto thou art also called, and hast professed a good profession before many witnesses. I give thee charge in the sight of God, who quickeneth all things, and before Christ Jesus, who before Pontius Pilate witnessed a good confession; that thou keep this commandment without spot, unrebukeable, until the appearing of our Lord Jesus Christ (1 Tim. 6:11–14).

Have you chosen whom you will serve? "As for me, and my house, we will serve the Lord."

Selected Bibliography

Barrett, Michael P. V. *Complete in Him*. Greenville, SC: Ambassador-Emerald, 2000.

———. "Who Fought the Battle of Jericho?" *Biblical Viewpoint* 26 1992, 24–32.

Bernard, Hantz. "The Autograph Though Dead Yet Speaketh," *God's Word in Our Hands*. Edited by J. B. Williams. Greenville, SC: Ambassador-Emerald, 2003, 279–333.

Bryant, Alton T., ed. *The New Compact Bible Dictionary*. Grand Rapids: Zondervan Publishing House, 1967.

Calvin, John. *Institutes of the Christian Religion*. Translated by Henry Beveridge. AGES Software *Comprehensive John Calvin Collection*, Version 2.0, 1996, 1997.

Colon, Peter. "Archeology Confirms the Walls 'Fell Flat,'" *Israel My Glory*. January/February 2004.

Cundall, Arthur. *Judges and Ruth*. Downers Grove, IL: Intervarsity Press, 1968.

Driver, S. R., and J. C. Miles. *The Babylonian Laws*. Oxford: Clarendon, 1956.

Epp, Theodore. *Joshua: Victorious by Faith*. Lincoln, NE: Back to the Bible Publishers, 1968.

Freund, Michael. *Jerusalem Post*, July 9, 2003.

Garstang, John. *Joshua-Judges*. London: Constable and Co., 1931.

———. *The Story of Jericho*, 2nd ed. London: Marshall, Morgan and Scott, 1948.

Henry, Matthew. *Commentary on the Whole Bible*, Vol. 2. Peabody, MA: Hendrickson Publishers, 1991 reprint.

Hoffner, Henry A. Jr. "Hittites," *Peoples of the Old Testament World*. Edited by Hoerth, Mattingly, Yamauchi. Grand Rapids: Baker Books, 1994.

C. F. Keil and F. Delitzsch, *Joshua, Judges, Ruth*. Grand Rapids: Wm. B. Eerdmans, 1968 reprint.

Keller, W. Phillip. *Joshua: Man of Fearless Faith*. Waco, TX: Word Publishing, 1983.

Kenyon, Kathleen. *Digging Up Jericho*. New York: Frederick A. Praeger, 1957.

Lias, J. J. *The Pulpit Commentary*. Edited by Joseph Exell, Vol. 7. Chicago: Wilcox and Follett Co., n.d.

Madvig, Donald H. "Joshua," *Expositor's Bible Commentary*, Vol. 3. Grand Rapids: Zondervan, 1992.

Merrill, Eugene H. *An Historical Survey of the Old Testament*. Grand Rapids: Baker Book House, 1966.

Neal, Marshall. "Accomplishing God's Will Through Means," *Biblical Viewpoint*. November 1992.

Pink, Arthur. *Gleanings in Joshua*. Chicago: Moody Press, 1964.

Schoville, Keith N. "Canaanites and Amorites," *Peoples of the Old Testament World*. Edited by Hoerth, Mattingly, Yamauchi. Grand Rapids: Baker Books, 1994.

Scofield, C. I. *Scofield Reference Bible*. Oxford, 1909, 1917.

Talbert, Layton. *Not by Chance: Learning to Trust a Sovereign God*. Greenville, SC: Bob Jones University Press, 2001.

Thomas, Cal. "Conflicting thoughts bubble up from battle over Commandments," *Athens Banner-Herald*, August 29, 2003, p. A10.

Williams, J. B., ed. *From the Mind of God to the Mind of Man: A Layman's Guide to How We Got Our Bible*. Greenville, SC: Ambassador-Emerald, 1999.

Wood, Bryant G. "Did the Israelites Conquer Jericho? A New Look at the Archaeological Evidence," *Biblical Archaeology Review*, March/April 1990.

Wood, Bryant G. "The Walls of Jericho," *Bible and Spade*. Spring 1999.

Wood, Leon. *A Survey of Israel's History*. Grand Rapids: Zondervan, 1970, revised 1986.

Zodhiates, Spiros. *The Hebrew-Greek Key Study Bible*. AMG Publishers, 1984, 1991.